HEALTH CARE IN CANADA

A DESCRIPTION AND ANALYSIS OF CANADIAN HEALTH SERVICES

RALPH W. SUTHERLAND, M.D.
M. JANE FULTON, Ph.D.

THE HEALTH GROUP, OTTAWA, CANADA

Canadian Cataloguing in Publication Data

Sutherland, Ralph W.
Health care in Canada

Includes bibliographical references and an index.
ISBN 0-9693537-0-7

1. Medical care — Canada. 2. Public Health — Canada
I. Fulton, M. Jane. II. Title

RA449.S88 1988 362.1′0971 C88-090352-X

$28.95 CDN

Published by The Health Group
445 Piccadilly Avenue
Ottawa, Canada K1Y 0H5

Second Printing 1990
Third Printing 1992

Printed by M.O.M. Printing, Ottawa

Distributed by The Canadian Public Health Association
400-1565 Carling Avenue
Ottawa, Canada K1Z 8R1

ACKNOWLEDGEMENTS

The creation and production of books can sometimes be an arduous task. Our task was made lighter by the co-operation and collaboration of many friends. The introduction of ideas and concepts can also be a challenging task. However, both the reviewers of the book and the leaders in the Canadian health care industry have found reason to believe in this book and to continue to recommend it to students in the health sciences and to practitioners in the field. We would like to acknowledge the support of the industry in this third printing.

We would like to acknowledge the central secretariat of the Faculty of Administration at the University of Ottawa for their dedication and expertise in preparing the manuscript. Susan Greenfield, our editor, transformed the manuscript into a reader-friendly book. Our colleagues and graduate students participated in the evolution of the themes in the book by evaluating their usefulness in the field. John Last provided encouragement and enthusiasm.

Our thanks also go to Health and Welfare Canada, Statistics Canada and the Institute for Research on Public Policy for permission to use selected tables and figures.

Mostly we want to thank the journalists, professors, health science students, administrators and Board members who have written or called us to say that the book increased their knowledge and understanding of Canada's health care system. And we would especially like to thank the Canadian Public Health Association for being our agents and advocates.

DEDICATIONS

Ralph Sutherland

This book is dedicated to my Mother and Father, who would have been delighted with, and reasonably impressed by, this book; to Ross, Jane, James and Robert, who continue to impress and surprise me and to be important to me; and to Buddy, who loved life so much and died so young.

Jane Fulton

I would like to dedicate this book to my daughters — Lila, Sarah, Amy and Jean — whose summer holiday in 1988 was encumbered by galleys, dictionaries and government documents; and to my parents Margaret and Blair Fulton who took us fishing on the Tlell River when the book was done.

TABLE OF CONTENTS

Part B

Canadian Health Services By Type

LIST OF TABLES

LIST OF FIGURES

PREAMBLE to Part A

Health services affect our health, wealth and happiness and all Canadians use them. They are characterized by glamor and drudgery, by humor and tragedy, by individualism and bureaucracy, by technological miracles, by personal compassion and by professional paternalism. They constitute a huge, complex and diverse industry whose parts do not have common objectives. They frequently dominate newspaper headlines and political agenda.

This subject is the stuff of authors. Bookstores and domestic bookshelves should be and are burdened with books on the evils of nursing homes, the hazards of pollution, the inadequacy of mental health services, the ethics of euthanasia, how to dissolve gallstones by changing diet and a variety of other clinical, fictional, historical, radical, unreasonable and specialized topics. But what does one read if one wants an overview of the total package of health services?

Lee Soderstrom in 1978 gave us his perception of such an overview in his book, *The Canadian Health System*, but much has happened since 1978. Other authors have looked at parts of the system, but these perspectives are too narrow to be considered an overview. This book attempts to provide the background, the general information and the social context within which Canadians seek and require health care. It describes and comments on our Canadian mosaic of health services policy, planning, organization, financing, delivery, cost and quality.

Because health and health services are of importance to everyone, this book has been written with a broad audience in mind. It is aimed at students interested in a career in health, at health workers who would like to know a bit more about their place of work, and at users of health services who wish to know more about how things work or who is responsible. This diverse audience obviously requires straightforward language combined with relatively refined concepts.

To acknowledge the dynamism of the system and its parts there is much discussion of interaction or lack of it, of harmony and disharmony, of cooperation and competition. Central to all discussions, or only momentarily in the background, is the fact that all the activities, departments, power and providers exist, or should exist, to serve either a single consumer or a group of consumers.

No effort has been made to say something about everything; the health world is too large and complex for that. An effort has been made to support concepts and principles with Canadian examples, examples which may too commonly come from Ontario.

The Scope of the Topic

Our health is affected by everything, and therefore most things that affect health are not health services. Since this book concentrates only on health services and the people who use them it must largely ignore most of those things that determine our health.

But what should be put in and what should be left out. Writing a book demands the establishment of boundaries. For instance, which of the following needs and situations should fall under the health services umbrella and therefore be discussed?

- a young adult breaks a leg;
- an elderly person living alone is having difficulty;
- workers are being damaged by the noise levels in a factory;
- there is a high level of alcoholism, obesity and illicit drug use in a community;
- the fish in a river are polluted with mercury from a pulp plant;
- an unacceptable number of deaths and injuries are occurring on a dangerous piece of highway;
- there is a high incidence of depression and low self esteem among the young unemployed;
- a severely mentally retarded child in a family with three other small children is seriously interfering with the family ability to care for the three normal children;
- there is a high rate of emotional burnout in nurses working in an intensive care unit.

Most readers might consider all of these problems to be 'health problems' and suggest that the services needed to respond should, therefore, be health services. Without much difficulty most of the activities of the worlds of labor, justice, transportation, urban planning, recreation, education, social services and pretty well everything else become 'health' services.

To provide a boundary for what could obviously be an unmanageable topic, 'health services' will be defined as those services that we normally consider to be within the field of health. There will be no attempt to resolve the question of why protection of the public from a person with tuberculosis is a responsibility of doctors, nurses and laboratory technologists (health services) when protection from drunken drivers rests with the police (legal services), protection from health hazards in the workplace rests with the department of labor, and protection from the health hazards associated with unemployment rests with no-one. Chapter 2, which examines factors affecting our health, will stray into all corners of society, but when describing health services the text will deal almost exclusively with those activities that are performed by recognized health care workers in settings accepted as part of the health system.

Our emphasis on describing current health care in Canada will not prevent comment on improvements that might be desirable in the future. This text frequently rejects today's arrangements and argues in support of expanded definitions of health and new ways of promoting and restoring health.

Whether or not to use the word 'system' is a constant dilemma. We regularly speak of the Canadian health system, but does such a system really exist? In a political sense there are only provincial health systems; in a systems theory sense there are not even provincial health systems. To the systems theorist a 'system' is a set of integrated resources and activities operating within a prescribed plan to accomplish a prescribed set of objectives within a prescribed period of time, and all parts of the system must contribute in a planned and positive way to the overall objectives. Within our patchwork of health services there are components with quite different and competing objectives, and there is often very little coordination or integration. Despite these problems with the term, 'the Canadian health system', it will probably occasionally be used. Old habits die hard.

The term, 'health care industry' will be used rarely although the word 'industry' is just as defensible as 'system'. If the industrial model is preferred, it is best not to try to conceptualize or describe health care as one industry. It is, instead, many industries having little relation to one another. There are supply industries, information technology industries, construction industries, care delivery industries and so on.

Throughout this text it would also probably make more sense to call 'health services', 'sickness services', and the health system is probably more accurately called the illness or sickness system, but to reduce confusion the conventional terms will be used. Terminological wars will be reserved for less global battlefields.

This book is arranged in two parts.

Part I looks at how healthy we are, or how sick we are, and at the factors that make us sick or healthy. It reviews the factors which affect the way we design and deliver health services and it presents an overview of the health services network in Canada up to 1988.

Part II describes the planning, programs and workers of the major components of the health care network, for example, regional agencies, hospitals, community health services, mental health services, and long term care. It describes where people will go, and what they will find available, if they become ill or injured.

Besides descriptive material there will be regular attention to problems and to the future. Personal interpretation and opinion are offered without apology throughout the book.

The sequence of material will not always seem sensible. Some information or comments will seem to be in the wrong place. Unfortunately it was difficult always to know where material should go because everything has a relationship to so many other things. When you wish to read about any particular subject it will pay to look in the index as well as the Table of Contents.

To Health Care Providers and Administrators in Training

Since this text will be of particular interest to students in health sciences or in health administration, it is appropriate here to address a few words to them specifically.

As you who seek to be leaders within the health services network read this book we hope you will keep a few of the challenges of the future in mind. Your work world is in ferment. What was taken for granted two years ago and under review a year ago is probably in a state of change now. You must, therefore, be comfortable with a significant degree of confusion and uncertainty. If you are to be happy in a health care environment you must be aware of the past but not dominated by it, be able to vigorously pursue a solution that may be outdated before it is in place, be prepared for failure and willing to see it while also noting your successes, and be continuously sensitive to many pressures and voices without feeling that everyone ought to get exactly what they want. Accept change only if it is sensible and/or publicly demanded. Evaluate new proposals but don't limit your evaluation to the new ideas; much of our health care organization and many of our health care activities have never been evaluated, though they should be. Old soldiers may inevitably fade away but inappropriate bureaucracies or habits have a tendency to survive just as well as appropriate ones.

Health services will, at times, seem too complex and too dominated by massive players for an individual provider, administrator or planner to have any effect. Your effect will, of course, usually be small but it will be real and will be important to some users or some community. Your philosophies, decisions and opinions do matter.

Some of you will unfortunately believe, either now or in the future, that opinion is synonymous with thought and you will therefore willingly provide opinions with little thought or supporting evidence. Others of you will worship facts, see little else, and expect the facts to speak for themselves. Others, hopefully most of you, will be prepared to propose and defend an opinion within the limitations of information available, with the necessary qualifications of the opinion, and with an understanding of the extent to which the opinion is based on your values and prejudices as well as on the hard evidence available.

The cross that administrators must bear is that they cannot duck the task of decision making; they must choose between programs and, indirectly, they must discriminate for or against certain people. In a similar way health care providers cannot duck the question of who should receive certain services that are in limited supply. Philosophers, newspaper reporters, social scientists and academics can expound endlessly on the need for better and better tools and rationale, and on how big and dynamic and complex our problems are, but administrators and caregivers are the ones responsible for making decisions. An administrator who is too mesmerized by the need to understand the problem perfectly may forget to choose a solution.

To avoid having opinions is to leave to others one of the greatest opportunities and pleasures (and headaches) of being an administrator. To have firm and fixed opinions without a defensible rationale assumes omnipotence. Try for the compromise — the zone of courage but not suicide.

The world of administration may demand significant adaptations from you. One of the transformations often demanded is from being writers of descriptive, footnoted and regurgitated essays to being organized, thoughtful risk takers who will do a respectable job of making decisions in situations of uncertainty.

You will often be expected to show leadership. This leadership will be nurtured by many factors including your ability to think issues through, the availability of good information and the existence in you of rather inherent personal characteristics such as honesty, sympathy, courage, and flexibility. The personal characteristics come from you. The thought will be demanded of you. Some of the information made available to you in this text and elsewhere will not always be as important as you think.

Whatever your personal approach to health care, remember the words of John Stuart Mill who said: "Men are men before they are lawyers or physicians or manufacturers; and if you make them capable and sensible men *they will make themselves* capable and sensible lawyers or physicians or manufacturers". The italics are ours; if you succeed in the health care world the credit is yours but if you fail do not blame it on someone else.

What this Book is Not

Little attention will be paid to the details or processes of planning, administration or problem solving. This is not a 'how to' text.

There will seldom be reference to the theories of the policial scientist, the sociologist, the epidemiologist, the gerontologist, the demographer or any of the other scholarly groups who regularly study (with increasing intensity) increasingly minor aspects of one or more type of health service, user or provider. The theories are not what this book is about; they are already the playground of many.

Summary

This book will try to describe the real world of Canadian health services and comment on it. It will try to look at the big picture, to produce the perspectives that one should have before proceeding to an examination of smaller components of the health services network.

Chapter 1

THE HEALTH OF CANADIANS

WHAT IS HEALTH

Protection and improvement of the health of Canadians are the most basic objectives of Canadian health services. To discuss protection or improvement of health status we need to know something about the extent to which Canadians are currently healthy or unhealthy, and why. To decide whether, or to what extent, we are healthy or unhealthy, we must have some understanding of what we mean by health.

If an elderly person has a terminal illness but is looking forward to tomorrow and is content and relaxed today, to what extent is that person unhealthy or healthy? If a star teenage athlete in excellent physical health commits suicide, was he or she healthy? If a severely physically disabled person is optimistic, has a job, accepts responsibility well and is anxious to contribute to the quality of life of his or her friends, to what extent is that person healthy or unhealthy?

Throughout this text health will be considered to be first of all a reasonably optimistic and contented state of mind. This definition is preferred because state of mind is usually the major determinant of quality of life, and an acceptable quality of life is what makes life worth living. The greatest threats to the health of Canadians are, therefore, not those things which end our lives or interfere with our physical perfection (although these are important) but those things which ruin the quality of life. To concentrate on preserving life can be discouraging because in the end everyone must die; concentrating on preserving the quality of life is, however, very apt to be rewarding because quality of life can almost always be improved.

None of this is meant to suggest that the preservation of life and of physical health is unimportant. Poor physical health can seriously damage the quality of life, and certainly death makes discussion of the quality of life of that person irrelevant, but both physical health and the preservation of life are merely means to an end. That 'end' is a life of good quality, and quality of life is, first of all, a perception in the mind of the concerned individual.

If the protection and improvement of state of mind, or quality of life, are the primary objectives of health services, then these services will be delivered with enthusiasm and purpose even if a life is near its end (although the nature of the services may significantly change at that time). Because quality of life is subjective health workers cannot protect or improve it until they know what things are important to each patient. Services can then be offered in ways that are compatible with, and in support of, the priorities of the patient.

Our preferred definition of health has been given. Others have defined it differently. In 1941 Henry Sigerist defined health as "a joyful attitude toward life and a cheerful acceptance of the responsibility that life puts upon the individual". This is still a superb definition. The World Health Organization

(WHO), in a widely used definition, stated that health was "a state of optimal physical, mental and social well being, and not merely the absence of disease and infirmity". More recently the WHO European Region has offered a better definition. Health is described as a resource for everyday living, and as the extent to which an individual or group is able to realize aspirations and satisfy needs while also changing, or coping with, the environment. Others have defined health as physical and mental well-being, as freedom from disease, pain or defect, as normal physical and mental functioning, or as a perception of the world and of oneself in it. Health care professionals tend to think of it as the absence of physical abnormalities. This book makes the proposition that the state of mind of the individual is 'the' important determinant of the level of his or her health.

Throughout the literature the word 'health' is routinely used as if it were synonymous with 'physical health'. If one wishes to speak of mental health or psychosocial health or intellectual health or emotional health one must say so; when speaking of physical health one can quite safely use the word health alone. In contrast to the literature, this text makes an alternative proposal. Throughout the book 'health' is used as a global term. When the subject is only 'physical health' or 'mental health', the appropriate adjective will be added to the global term.

The extent to which health is taken to mean 'physical health' in most of the literature is sometimes graphically illustrated. For example, a pediatrics professor presented a paper at a conference in Ottawa in 1987 titled *Psychiatric Disorders among Children With or Without Chronic Health Problems.* To the speaker, 'chronic health problems' meant chronic *physical* health problems. Physically well children were regularly referred to as the 'healthy' group whether or not they were emotionally intact, and the physically disabled were similarly routinely referred to as unhealthy,regardless of their emotional stability. It was a sad perspective to find, and a strange perspective to bring to a Conference titled *Promoting the Mental Health of Children and Youth.* Evidence of similar bias is shown in a 1984 text titled *Pediatric Risk Factors for Major Chronic Disease*, a text which deals almost exclusively with physical chronic diseases. Physicians in particular are prone to forget that a major chronic disease is often mental or emotional.

The term physical health, when used in this text, will refer to the extent to which our major body systems (musculo-skeletal, respiratory, cardio-vascular, neurological, gastro-intestinal, etc.), are physiologically intact. Physical disorders represent measurable pathology in our systems, organs or tissues, pathology which may arise from chemical, biological, hormonal, structural or other causes. Some physical conditions produce symptoms indicating mental or emotional ill health, for example, brain function may be disturbed by tumor, infection, injury or genetics. The underlying disorder is, however, known to be physical and these patients may be considered to be primarily physically ill. Classification is at times difficult, especially as an increasing number of emotional and mental disorders are confirmed as having their origins in a disturbance of physiology.

Mental health and emotional health can be used synonymously but there is also, at times, a degree of difference. Mental health carries a more psychiatric connotation. Mental ill health, therefore, tends to be associated with institutional care and inability to function in society. Emotional ill health, on the other hand, may be seen as the depression or anxiety or panic that happens to 'normal' people. It can be perceived to be 'normal' and not 'psychiatric', even though mental health workers and programs may be involved in counselling or support. Some chronic mental disorders such as schizophrenia or manic-depressive states may be the product of a systemic and physical factor but for the moment they continue to be classified as mental rather than physical disorders. Emotional disorders are predominantly a reaction to some situation, for example, bereavement, unemployment, failure, loss of independence, lack of socialization or continuing insecurity.

Intellectual health is not a commonly used term. Presumably it is used to refer to the extent to which a person is able to use his or her inherent intellectual abilities.

Social health is a collective term applying to populations rather than individuals. Social pathology exists when too many members of a population have undesirable characteristics such as fear or anxiety. Social health, as well as individual health, is threatened by such things as unemployment, war or the threat of war, starvation or natural disaster.

The concept of spiritual health or ill health is not a focus of this book. Economic health is self explanatory. Psychosocial health is presumed to mean social plus emotional health.

The Blurred Margin Between Sickness and Health

Not only do we have trouble with the word health, the definitions of disease and illness are also unclear. Because health services are created to respond to ill health or injury, our network of health services will change as our concept of ill health changes. Not everyone considers all of the following situations to represent ill health, and not everyone wishes the health system to respond to all of these situations. Nevertheless each of the following seven types of situations can be seen as disease or illness.

1) Situations in which subjective symptoms/complaints are consistent with objective observations, for example, sore throat due to tonsillitis, sore foot due to a broken bone, itchiness with a rash.
2) Situations characterized by an asymptomatic biomedical (physical) abnormality, for example, high blood pressure, asymptomatic cancer.
3) Situations with no physical abnormalities but with symptoms which are consistent with history, lifestyle or environment, for example, chronic cough in a smoker, insomnia in a situation of stress.
4) Situations with no physical abnormalities but with observable behavior patterns or described thought patterns that are outside of the normal.

5) Situations in which concerns or complaints cannot be explained after subjective and objective investigation, for example, headache, itchiness, insomnia, suspicion, sore throat, sore back.
6) Situations in which the patient sees nothing wrong and the biomedical exam indicates no abnormality but in which society sees the patient as sufficiently deviant to be considered abnormal or unacceptable, for example, homosexuality, compulsive behavior.
7) Situations in which the patient or the patient's agent wishes action but others may consider action to be unnecessary, for example, cosmetic surgery, abortion, sterilization, mild inter-personal conflict.

There is no clear line between health and ill health, normal and abnormal, the point where no external support or care is needed and the point where it is justified. When is a laceration large enough to deserve medical attention, when does unusual behavior become 'deviant' and socially unacceptable, when has anxiety or pain exceeded the levels that ought to be tolerated without attention? There is ample room for the great debates that surround the use of emergency rooms, the abuse of medicare and the overservicing or underservicing of patients.

What is called disease or illness obviously changes with the perceptions of the victims, caregivers, observers or policy makers involved. There can be disagreement as to whether or not disease or sickness exists. Sometimes disease is perceived to be the biomedically demonstrable condition whereas illness is considered to be what the patient experiences. Judy Lamarsh, when dying with cancer, said "I'm dying but I'm not sick".

If these definitions are accepted it is possible to predict that some 'healthy' persons with asymptomatic disease will, when told they have a disease, immediately become 'ill'.

The Indicators of Health Status

When deciding whether or not a particular individual is 'healthy' what indicators should be used? Would blood pressure, cardiac reserve, respiratory function and vision be measured or would degree of self confidence, level of job satisfaction, ability to cope with stress and ability to love be on the list? Emphasis on the first set of indicators would require a health bio-technocrat to do the appropriate tests. Emphasis on the second set of indicators requires the tools and uncertainties of the social scientist. The first set of indicators suggests a primary interest in physical health and the preservation of life; the second set of indicators suggests a primary interest in the quality of life. Both sets of indicators can be used.

Indicators of health status can be found in data describing populations (aggregated or collective data) or individuals. To assure oneself of a balanced view of health status, one must choose indicators of mental, physical, psychosocial and possibly spiritual and economic health. These indicators should represent behavioural, psychological, social and physical (physiological) functioning, and may include measures of attitude and perception. In the examination of health status, especially in the areas of attitude, perception and behavior, it is necessary to look for and measure positive attributes (optimism, emotional stability, contentment) as well as negative attributes (depression, emotional instability, insecurity). Psychosocial wellbeing is, even more than with physical health, the presence of positive characteristics and not just the absence of negative or pathological characteristics.

The determination of health status is more difficult when health is understood to include a great deal more than physical health. Deciding on the degree of happiness, optimism or enthusiasm that is present or desirable is more difficult than measuring the function of kidneys or the pituitary gland and deciding whether they are normal. Unreasonable expectations and asbestos fibres are both threats to health but the former are more difficult to measure and prevent.

Selection of Standards

What is 'good' health or 'bad' health or 'average' health? When is a person 'normal'? Our psyche is not expected to survive in the face of endless negative strokes or emotional deprivation but it should be able to tolerate the normal stresses of work and world. Legs are not expected to be speedier than the fastest bullet but healthy legs on healthy people should be able to climb a few flights of stairs. Therefore, the first general rule when describing health status is that standards tend to be set to be consistent with the frailties and typical performance of a human being of the appropriate age and sex. Good, normal or acceptable health tend to be defined in terms of what healthy peers do or can do.

Nowhere is this perception more confirmed than in our discussion of disability. The fact that none of us can see through the back of our heads, (we all need rear view mirrors on our cars), or that none of us can run 100 km in an hour is not seen as a disability, but to have 20/200 eyesight or to be unable to lift a cup of tea is a disability.

Reports on Health Status

The 1978-79 Canada Health Survey (CHS) conducted by Statistics Canada involved 40,000 individuals and cost $6 million. It consisted of questionnaires and personal health examinations and was designed to answer three questions:

1) Who is exposed to the risk of future illness?
2) What is the current health status of the population?
3) What is the impact of illness?

The findings said a great deal about the health status of Canadians.

— almost one half said they had no health problems and, therefore, over half reported that they had at least one health problem
— one half of those with a health problem considered it too minor or too controlled to need attention
— almost one half reported using some form of medication (pills or ointments, for example), in the average two day period. One quarter of those taking medications reported no associated health problems

- low income families experienced greater levels of emotional disorders, heart disease and chronic respiratory disease than high income families. Generally the young, male and less educated Canadians were most likely to endanger future health through current lifestyle
- 200,000 persons have definitely dangerous blood pressure (BP) elevation
- 2.6 million persons have BP elevation which probably should be lowered
- 3 million individuals have excessive blood cholesterol levels
- one quarter of women over 65 take three or more kinds of drugs
- only about one third of Canadians get enough exercise
- the prevalence of various categories of health problems is quite different when one looks at population survey data as opposed to health services data. Limb and joint diseases, and skin conditions, are much more prominent in the client generated data
- acute respiratory infections and injuries (trauma) are the major causes of disability days, (which average 15.7 per year per person)
- high BP, skin conditions and mental disorders are the conditions most commonly associated with the use of drugs
- the general prevalence of disease and disability showed little overall change in the 27 years between the Canada Sickness Survey of 1951-52 and the 1978-79 Canada Health Survey, but the physical health of children markedly increased
- many population groups are relatively unhappy, for example, women, teenagers, the elderly, the widowed, divorced and separated, low income and those in poor health.

Mortality information should not be ignored but it tells us very little about healthfulness. When we measure disability or morbidity we are concerning ourselves with quality of life more than with survival. Russ Wilkins and Owen Adams in their book, *Healthfulness of Life*, used Canada Health Survey data to examine Canadian mortality, institutionalization and noninstitutionalized disability in 1978 (See Figure 1.1). In Canada, 214,000 persons, just under 1% of the total population, were found to be residents of institutions providing long term health, and health related care. These persons were severely physically, intellectually or emotionally handicapped. Another 2.1% were severely incapacitated although not in an institution and 7.1% had intermediate restriction of one or more major activities. Another 2% were temporarily disabled by episodic illness or by an accident.

Wilkins and Adams studied 'health expectancy' rather than life expectancy. They studied not how long we live but how much of that life is characterized by several levels of disability. They used a health expectancy index to show the volume of disability free life, with the difference between health expectancy and life expectancy being the period of expected disabled life. Their data reflects physical more than emotional disability but the concept is excellent.

Although men had a shorter life expectancy they could anticipate only 0.8 years of long term institutionalization versus 1.5 years for women. Non-

FIGURE 1.1
Health Expectancy by Region, by Sex, Canada, 1978

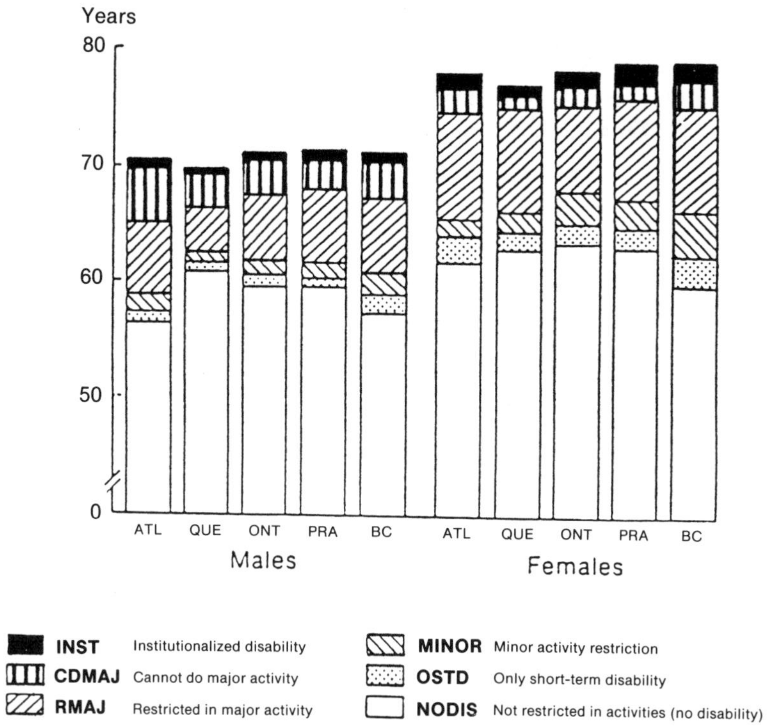

Source: Wilkins and Adams, *The Healthfulness of Life,* the Institute for Research on Public Policy, 1983.

institutional years of restricted activity were 10.8 for men and 14.0 for women, with the number of noninstitutional years of major activity restriction being 3.0 for men and 1.3 for women. While women outlived men by 7.5 years (in 1978), their health expectancy difference was only half of that. Females have the longest life but pay for it through more years of restricted functional abilities, although men have a longer period of major disability (3.8 years versus 2.8 years).

A more recent study in Quebec reported a male life expectancy of 70 years, with 60 years of healthfulness, versus a female life expectancy of 78 years, with 61 years of healthfulness.

The Canadian Health and Disability Survey (CHDS) conducted as a supplement to the Canadian Labour Force Surveys of October 1983 and June 1984 was based on almost 65,800 households representing over 126,000 persons. Nineteen screening questions determined mobility, agility, seeing, hearing, speaking and mental handicap. All persons who reported disability were followed up with a personal interview that examined the effect of the disability on the person's life.

Among persons 15 years of age or older, 12.8% were identified by the CHDS as disabled, slightly less than the 14.3% identified in the Canada Health Survey (CHS) of 1978-79 (the CHS figure includes those with mental disabilities while the CHDS does not). Thirty seven percent of disabled adults were 65 and over. In this 65+ age group 39% reported disability. The disabled population varied very little by sex. Over one third of the population with less than grade 9 education reported disability compared to 5% of those with a university degree and 10.5% of those who have all or part of high school but no post secondary education.

Among the 13% of the population 15 and over who reported a functional deficit (which was interpreted to be synonymous with a disability), 65% had problems with mobility, 54% with agility, 26% with hearing, 13% with seeing, 5% with speaking and 8% had other deficits. Three percent of the total population were reported to have a mental handicap. This low figure may be partially a product of the bias of the questions towards physical disability.

Among the 13% disabled, 37% had more than one functional deficit and 14% had more than two. These figures represent 4% and 2%, respectively, of the total population 15 years of age and over.

In 1981 The Canada Fitness Survey (CFS), with a base of 12,000 households and 24,000 people, was carried out "to provide basic information on the fitness levels and lifestyles of Canadians". It is sometimes difficult to know the exact relationship between lifestyle, including fitness, and health but the CFS did tell us a great deal about things that we *think* significantly affect our future health.

Physical fitness and its associated programs will, for many people, reduce morbidity and mortality. For other persons morbidity and mortality will be increased, but the net effect of physical activity is very positive. It seems likely that most persons who participate regularly in recreational physical fitness activities find them enjoyable and emotionally rewarding as well as physically useful. It is, indeed, quite possible that fitness activities are more important as sources of improved quality of life than of lengthened life. There are apparently few studies which compare the effects of fitness programs on people who enjoy them with the effects on persons in the same programs who do not enjoy them.

The CFS indicates that two populations with high morbidity and mortality statistics, the over 40 (and increasing with age) and the socioeconomically disadvantaged, have the lowest involvement in fitness programs and are the least physically fit.

Benefits of physical fitness (and therefore of the activities which bring fitness) include the presence of the energy needed to enjoy other aspects of life. Energy is especially needed in advancing years when an undesirably sedentary lifestyle reduces one's ability to take part in a variety of pleasant activities such as sports, sex, work and travel. These activities also reduce hazardous body changes such as osteoporosis. Physical activity also reduces tension (the 'tranquilizer' effect) and can be a socialization device.

Use of drugs can be considered a measure of health status. A study titled Alcohol and Drug Use Among Ontario Adults in 1984, and Changes since 1982 reported:

— the number of alcohol abstainers went down to 15% but the number of heavy drinkers also fell
— the number of marijuana users did not change but use was less frequent
— 9.3% were using tranquilizers (no change)
— 7.1% of 18-29 years old had used cocaine at least once (one third of the United States utilization rate).

Physical illness can have major impact on the emotional health of both patients and their families. Spouses of ostomy patients exhibit earlier and higher levels of stress than the patients themselves, especially early in the diagnosis/treatment cycle. Later in the cycle, as recovery is slower than expected, the patient copes less well than his or her spouse, and at later stages many household caregivers show signs of emotional burnout.

The Canadian Health Promotion Survey (1985) reported on over 11,000 households, approximately 1000 from each of the provinces and the Yukon/Northwest Territories. An adult contact person was identified in each household. The response rate was over 80%, with most nonresponses being due to unanswered calls or household representatives not available for an interview. The survey method missed households without a phone and persons institutionalized in hospitals or chronic care institutions.

Health knowledge, attitudes, beliefs and behavior were explored. The objective was to find out "what Canadians think, feel and know about health" rather than to collect information about physical health status or lifestyles. Questions examined perceptions of personal health, what people were doing or intended to do to protect or improve health, and the social and health environment in which the individual lived.

The survey made a good effort to escape from the preoccupation with physical health that characterized earlier federal health promotion and health survey activity. The escape was not complete and the report of the survey reflects some confusion. When people were asked about their state of health a great many of them replied in terms of only their physical health, and the majority of key indicators chosen — for example, limitation of activity — are entirely indicators of physical health. Other parts of the survey asked questions about quality of life. Inconsistencies between the respondents' perceptions of physical health and quality of life should have been both expected and understood.

Sixty-one percent of Canadians rated their health as good or excellent. Forty-two percent reported they were very happy and 54% reported they were pretty happy. Happy people reported better health than unhappy people. Other comments arising from this report are in Chapter 2.

Hypertension can be thought of as a threat to health or as ill health. It manifests itself through varying sequelae, each of which has its own diagnosis and therapy and sequelae. Elevated blood pressure increases the risk of vascular disease with increased risk of illness or death from stroke, heart attacks, heart failure and kidney failure. It has been estimated that 5-20% of the adult population has hypertension, that one half to two thirds of those affected are unaware of it, and that half of the cases found are not being adequately treated. Because the cause of hypertension is usually unknown, prevention is not feasible. Treatment, however, can be highly successful and can reduce the long term risks.

The results of the 1984 Health and Activity Limitation Survey will be released in 1988. Statistics Canada has increased its routine data collection about handicapped persons and Canada should, within a few years, have a much more complete picture of the incidence and effects of handicaps among Canadians.

Health Status of Children and Adolescents

The concerns of individuals are a part of their health status, and these concerns vary greatly between age groups. A survey by the Children's Hospital of Eastern Ontario in 1984 of 1,000 teenagers (73% response rate) revealed the following concerns. The percent of respondents who had these concerns is in brackets.

— acne (47%)
— academic difficulties (36%)
— menstrual problems (33% of females)
— family problems (32%)
— nervous and emotional problems (26% — 33% for females and 17% for males)
— "too fat" (26%, again 2:1 female dominance)
— birth control (females 13%, males 5%)
— drugs, alcohol and venereal disease (2%)

With respect to lifestyle features teenagers revealed the following.

— 36% of females and 13% of males smoked regularly
— 15% used recreational drugs
— 49% used alcohol at least occasionally
— 25% of females and 18% of males reported sexual experience

A number of other studies of pre-teenagers and children in their early teens have identified nuclear war as either the largest or the second most important single concern.

In 1984-85 the Canada Health Attitudes and Behaviors Survey of over 30,000 children nine, twelve and fifteen years old reported lifestyles and feelings that are considered to indicate a less than optimal health status. Twenty to thirty per cent of the children reported difficulty sleeping because of worrying, and among 15 year olds 30% used alcohol at least twice a month, 25% were smokers and 20% reported use of cannabis. Sugars and fats dominated diets and activity levels were often very low. Television was more popular than exercise. Children with higher activity levels reported less depression, a happier home life and a more optimistic attitude to life.

Although there is evidence that suicide rates have fluctuated cyclically throughout history, there is no doubt that teenage suicides increased markedly through the 1960's and 1970's. In Alberta from 1964-1979 there was a 400% increase, with this figure being largely a reflection of the increasing number of suicides among young native Canadians. Suicide can be considered an indicator of mental health and quality of life.

A gallup poll in 1982 showed that over 25% of 12-19 year olds have used marijuana, 14% had used it in the past 30 days and 2% used it daily, a slight general decrease from earlier years. In the same survey slightly over 50% of both males and females had used alcohol in the last 30 days.

The Ontario Child Health Survey of 1983, which was based on a sample of over 3000 children, reported on the psychiatric health of children aged 4 to 16 and on their use of mental health services. It documented two types of psychiatric behavior primarily affecting the child; these were neuroses such as sadness, tension, and self-harm, and somatization disorders with physical symptoms but no apparent physical disease. It also documented psychiatric problems with major impact on the environment, i.e. hyperactivity and socially unacceptable conduct such as stealing, violence and bullying (Table 1.1).

Thirteen to twenty-two percent of females and males in each of the age groups were identified as having a psychiatric diagnosis. Diagnostic decisions were based on information from parents and teachers (for the 4-11 year olds) and parents and the youths themselves (for the 12-16 year olds). It was the norm for information from the two sources to present completely different pictures of the child. Psychiatric diagnoses were somewhat more common among urban children than rural children (perhaps because there are more psychiatrists in urban centres).

Infant mortality is almost entirely due to three major factors, crib death (Sudden Infant Death Syndrome or SIDS), congenital abnormalities and prematurity. The infant mortality rate has fallen to below 8 deaths per 1000 live births.

TABLE 1.1
Prevalence of Psychiatric Disorders in Children in Ontario Ages 4-11 and 12-16, 1983 in Percent

	Somatization or Neurosis (Internalizing Disorders)		Hyperactivity or Socially Unacceptable Behavior (Externalizing Disorders)		Both types of Disorders	
Ages	F	M	F	M	F	M
4-11	9.2	6.7	2.7	8.1	1.3	3.6
12-16	15.7	3.9	2.5	11.0	3.5	3.7

Source: *The Ontario Child Health Survey*, 1983

Native Health

The health status of our native population is a disgrace to the nation. Suicide levels in the 15-24 age group are six times the national average. Violence is the cause of 35% of all deaths (15% is considered very high in any population). Inuit women have lung cancer rates 15-30 times greater than that of other Canadians. Some native communities have a high incidence of diabetes. In Alberta in 1982, 23% of native deaths were alcohol related, two to six times the national average (depending on what national figure you accept). Tuberculosis rates in the native population are down but are still 15-25 times those in the rest of the Canadian population.

In 1985 the infant mortality rate for native peoples was 50-60% above the national rate. In the post neonatal period the mortality rate for Canada in general was 3.1 per 1000 while for natives it was 12.2 per 1000, four times greater.

Trends

In 1986 Eve Shulman from the Health Services Directorate of Health and Welfare Canada (HWC) produced a draft report titled Progress in the Health Status of Canadians. This report provided a comprehensive overview of the trends in the physical health of Canadians over the past thirty years. Much of the following summary is found in the Shulman document although most of it is also found elsewhere. There is, unfortunately, much less data describing trends in emotional, mental or psychosocial health than in physical health.

Gains in life expectancy, which occurred at all ages, included a significant reduction in premature deaths of males 35-64 years. Longevity gains in all ages were, to a significant extent, due to a reduction in deaths from cardiovascular disease and motor vehicle accidents (MVA). From the late 1960's to 1983, age standardized mortality rates from cardiovascular disease declined between 15 and 30%.

Following a peak in 1973, death rates from MVA had by 1983 fallen from 40 to 60% in different age groups and sexes but the decline was major in all age groups and for both sexes. The pattern is similar when examined in terms of mortality and injury rates per billion kilometers driven.

Cancer mortality rates, excluding lung cancer have fallen 5% for males and 12% for females in the last 15-20 years, but lung cancer mortality rates have, at

TABLE 1.2
Life Expectancy of Canadians at Birth 1931-1981

	Males	Females	Both Sexes
1931	60.0	62.1	61.6
1941	63.0	66.3	64.6
1951	66.3	70.8	68.6
1961	68.3	74.2	71.3
1971 (70-72)	69.3	76.4	72.9
1981 (80-82)	71.9	79.0	74.9

Source: Official Canadian Life Tables in *Progress in Health Status of Canadians*, HWC, 1986. (Draft Report)

best, stabilized for males while rising sharply for females. The rates for breast cancer remain stable while death rates from cervical cancer have fallen 50% (1950-1980). Female lung cancer deaths will very soon exceed deaths due to breast cancer. The rate of deaths from stroke continue to fall steadily, a trend established 15-20 years ago.

Age standardized mortality rates per 100,000 population for Canadian males in 1982 were 70% higher than those for females. Recent data suggests the gap between the sexes is falling, partly because males are living longer but also because female age standardized mortality rates are rising. Canadian life expectancies (1982) at birth, age 45 and age 65 respectively were for females 78, 36 and 19 years and for males 72, 30 and 14 years.

Maternal mortality has declined from over 100 per 100,000 live births (0.1%) in 1951 to 6.2 per 100,000 (0.006%) in 1981, a drop of 94%. In 1981 there were only 23 maternal deaths in Canada.

Disability rates are almost surely increasing, at least in the elderly, although the terminology in the relevant surveys is not consistent and the amount of increase is uncertain. Only part of our increased longevity will be disability free years. From the Canada Sickness Survey (CSS) in 1951 to the Canada Health Survey (CHS) in 1978-79, the percentage of the elderly with disabilities rose from less than 30% to more than 40%. Dementia, predominantly Alzheimers disease, is now a major factor in all long term care, affecting 1% of the population at age 65 and 20% at age 80.

The commonest less serious and short term health problems reported in the 1951 and 1978-79 surveys changed from trauma, digestive disorders and headache to limb and joint disorders and allergies.

End stage renal disease, in which kidney function can no longer sustain life, continues to occur but the availability of dialysis and kidney transplants has changed the outlook from one of certain death to one of either a normal life or a life dependent on modern technology. Transplants are the preferred treatment in economic and human terms but, despite a steady increase in the number of kidneys available, the waiting list is long. The number of persons on dialysis in Canada rose from 2300 to 2800 between 1981 and 1985. Home dialysis is becoming less popular in most provinces, with fewer than 15% of patients now being treated at home.

Health status and the threats to it are not static. Ulcerative colitis was, a decade or two ago, far more common in children and adolescents than Crohns disease (regional ileitis). Now Crohns disease is as much as 10 times as common as ulcerative colitis. Other diseases have also become more common, for example, anorexia nervosa, lung cancer in women and Hepatitis B.

Between 1969 and 1975 the age adjusted ischemic heart disease (IHD) mortality rate for Canada declined 16.4%. Whether the changes reflect a change in incidence, a change in severity or an improvement in clinical management is not known. In the United States from 1968-1980 the same death rate fell from 231 to 163 per 100,000, a decline of almost 30%.

Acquired immune deficiency syndrome (AIDS) is the new and terrifying element in our spectrum of epidemics. In June 1987 the British Columbia government reported that in 18 months of testing for the human immunodeficiency virus (HIV, formerly referred to as HTLV2), over 8% of 14,000 samples had tested positive. With the number of tests per month rising sharply, the percentage of positives was unchanged. Later in 1987 New York City estimated that 50,000 females in their reproductive years were carrying the virus. In the United States AIDS now causes over 500 deaths per week.

The possibility of an individual suffering from a few selected conditions is shown in Figure 1.2 and Figure 1.3.

Variations in the Health of Different Canadian Population Groups

Native health has been briefly described. Many data also confirm the health differences amongst socioeconomic classes, cultural groups and geographic regions. These differences are discussed in Chapter 2.

FIGURE 1.2
Prevalence of Various Conditions in the Canadian Population

	Rate	**# of cases in Canada**
Disabling Mental Retardation	0.5-1%	100-200,000
Autistic children	1:25000	1000
Some form of epilepsy	1%	200-300,000
Crib death (per 1000 live births)	1-3	
Panic Disorders	1-5% (USA)	0.3-1 million
Teenage pregnancies (per 1000 females 15-19 years)	30-60	
Hypertension (adult population)	5-20%	1-3 million
Alcohol related disability	5-10%	1.3-2.6 million
Cancer		80-100,000
Serious alcohol addiction	2-4%	0.5-1.0 million
Chronic Pain	2-10%	0.5-2.5 million
Parkinsons Disease (over age 55)	1:100	50-60,000
Multiple Sclerosis	1:500 (0.3%)	50,000 — 100,000
Sexually Transmitted Diseases (STD)	1:250 p.a.	100,000 annually
Legally blind	1:500	40-80,000
Alzheimers Disease at age 65	1%	150-200,000
at age 80	20%	
AIDS	Climbing	1700
Positive for AIDS Antibody		25-50,000
Suicide	1: 1000 (USA)	
Sleep disorders	10-30%	7 million
Acne	5-10%	1.5-2 million
Mental/Emotional Ill Health	10-40%	2-10 million
Muscular Dystrophy (1:3000 males)	1:10,000	2500
Significant Hearing Impairment	1-3%	250-750,000

Figure 1.3
Probability of Selected Events Affecting an Individual
(if 1981 experience is maintained)

Cancer of any kind	35%
Skin cancer	8-10%
Colorectal cancer	5-6%
Lung cancer	7-8% (males) 3% (females)
Breast cancer	7-8% of females
Prostatic cancer	5-6% of males
Lymphoid, also bladder cancer	2% each
Uterine cancer	3-4% of females
Stomach cancer	almost 2%
Oral and pancreatic cancer	1% each
All other cancers	10-12%
Accidental death	6% of males; 4% of females
Suicide	1.4% of males, 0.6% females

SOURCES OF INFORMATION ABOUT HEALTH STATUS

It is not always possible to find out what we would like to know about health status but considerable information is available from a great many sources.

1) *Vital Statistics,* in particular death certificates.

Mortality statistics expressed as rates (per 1000 or per 100,000) and using the same diagnostic codes (for example, The International Statistical Classification of Disease and Injury, ICDA) are one of the most commonly used measures of health and disease.

2) *Special Studies*

Many community or regional special studies (needs studies, impact studies, marketing studies), report on some aspect of health status, but their findings are often of questionable quality and usually of only local or regional interest. Many of these reports, as well as many individualized questionnaires, wellness checks or hazard appraisals, suffer from a lack of attention to psychosocial or emotional content. The national studies of greatest consequence have already been summarized earlier in this chapter.

3) *Registries*

All provinces participate in The Canadian National Cancer Incidence Reporting System but they supply data with varying completeness and accuracy. This registry illustrates the simplicity of the registry concept, the complexity of its implementation and the fact that data can be collected for years and used very little. This registry has almost 20 years of quite well standardized data although some provinces, such as Ontario, joined only recently. The implementation of mandatory reporting, or use of reliable sources such as death certificates, can increase the availability of cancer data. Saskatchewan uses a slightly different approach to assure the reporting of cancer: physicians are not paid for cancer care unless the patient is registered with the Saskatchewan Cancer Commission.

The Canadian National Institute for the Blind (CNIB) maintains a registry of the blind population in Canada. The registry contains only persons voluntarily registered with them but the material is well coded and available for use.

A Canadian Renal Failure Registry, maintained by HWC and the Kidney Foundation of Canada, records the pattern, treatment and outcomes of end stage renal disease.

Most disease or disability registries are provincial. The British Columbia Health Surveillance Registry is, in reality, a group of separate registries covering congenital anomalies, genetic defects and several chronic disabilities. It began in 1952 and has undergone several metamorphoses. The Manitoba Infant Deafness Risk Register documents infants at risk of hearing damage. These infants are routinely registered and are followed by regional hearing centers and the Provincial Office of Hearing Conservation. An Ontario Crippled Children's Central Care Registry is maintained by the Easter Seal Society. As with many voluntary registries, the information is not sufficiently complete to provide total incidence or prevalence of handicapping conditions.

Registries must be used if they are to be worthwhile. To be useful, the data, whether local, provincial, national or international, must be accurate, continually updated and available for analysis. The history of registries suggests that they should not be started without considerable study. Once started, they become difficult to abandon even if their usefulness is limited.

DIFFICULTIES WITH DATA

In discussing the state of the nation's health we should appreciate some of the factors which decrease our ability to reach fully accurate conclusions. Provincial reporting is not always standardized, for example, the provincial lists of notifiable diseases vary. In August 1984 AIDS was a reportable disease only in Ontario, Saskatchewan, Alberta and British Columbia. In addition, not all cases of disease are reported even when there is mandatory notification. The more that sexually transmitted diseases (STD) are treated in private offices, the more they will be underreported. In addition, the less importance a practitioner attaches to a condition the more it will tend to be underreported (for example rubella). Reporting may increase if a condition acquires notoriety, as with the 60% increase in reported cases of herpes virus infections in Canada between 1978 and 1983. This increase is probably more a factor of better reporting than it is of increased prevalence of the condition.

Diagnostic and disability reporting are each subject to error. The usefulness of hospital and ambulatory care diagnostic information is limited by the rather random way in which primary diagnosis is sometimes selected in multiproblem patients and by the regular underreporting of alcoholism, psychiatric conditions and suicide. In the reporting of disability there is a tendency for each study or region to develop its own definition of major or minor disability, or its own categorization of mobility or other handicaps. Comparison is, therefore, often difficult.

One's definition of abnormality will, as already mentioned, sharply influence data describing it. What is a normal blood pressure? Certainly clinicians cannot fully agree. What amount of variation in the cervical cells of a pap smear should be accepted as normal, and when should these changes be called questionable or abnormal? How much crookedness should there be in the spine of a child before it is called scoliosis? What pattern of carbohydrate metabolism should exist before a patient is called diabetic or prediabetic? What personality characteristics merit use of the term personality disorder or panic state? The degree of disagreement over what is normal is quite astonishing even when dealing with tangibles such as x-rays or ECGs, and this disagreement can markedly weaken the comparability or equivalence of data.

Because discussion of health status tends to be comparative — that is,one community or population versus another — it is necessary to adjust data so that selected differences in the populations can be taken into account. Examples of important differences would be age, sex or socioeconomic status. The need for standardization of data is easily demonstrated.

Only two decades ago children and adolescents represented up to one half of our total population. Now adults from the baby boom (25-45 years of age) are dominant, and this bulge of young adults will move through the older age groups in the next few decades. Suppose we wished to compare the health status of today's population with that of 20 years ago, and suppose the comparison was based on the incidence of various childhood and adult diseases per 1000 population. One could only know whether health status was better or worse either by studying only one age group or by standardizing the total population at least by age.

Cause and Effect

Unfortunately, even when health status or changes in health status are adequately documented, it is not always easy to identify the causes of inadequate health. For example, the number of deaths from heart attacks (the age standardized mortality rate for ischemic heart disease) has fallen 5-30% in most industrialized countries, including Canada, in the past 15-20 years. The extent to which the decline was due to a decrease in cigarette smoking, reduced consumption of polyunsaturated fats, better exercise patterns, better detection and control of hypertension, better treatment of heart attacks when they occur, or some other factors, is not fully known. We do know, on the basis of major studies which have followed large populations over many years, such as the Framingham studies, that the reduction in cigarette smoking is certainly one of the major factors, but the importance of other factors is unclear. As we discuss determinants of health we will, therefore, often have to be content with semi-confirmed assumptions.

The current interest in the hazards of osteoporosis also demonstrates the frailty of our knowledge base. We know all about the absorption and utilization of Vitamin D and calcium but there is varied advice as to the mix of exercise, diet and medication that best assures a control of decalcification of bone, especially in the post menopausal period. It is often difficult to reduce risk efficiently if one does not know what factors are most important in the production or the elimination of that risk.

SUMMARY

Selected kinds of ill health are now effectively avoided or reduced. Whether we are more healthy as a nation than we were two or three decades ago is unknown but many indicators, especially those related to physical health, indicate improvement. If a healthy state of mind is considered to be the most dominant characteristic of a healthy person then we do not know for certain whether we are becoming more healthy because we have not been collecting the necessary information about expectations, optimism, happiness, peace of mind and contentment. Using mortality rates as one index of health, Canada stands high in world rankings. Though it falls behind a few countries such as Japan and Sweden, it comes ahead of the United States, Britain and France.

The health status of Canadians, and of specific segments of our population, is certainly changing and these changes are, at times, of major significance to those who write policy.

Chapter 2 will look at the factors that are determining our health as individuals and as a population.

Suggested Reading

The Active Health Report — Perspectives on Canada's Health Promotion Survey 1985. Health and Welfare Canada and Supply and Services Canada, 1987.

Canada Health Attitudes & Behavior Survey. Health and Welfare Canada 1984-85.

Canadian Health & Disability Survey 1983-84. Health and Welfare Canada, 1986.

The Health of Canadians — The Report of the 1978-79 Canada Health Survey, Statistics Canada, 1981.

The Canada Fitness Surveys, 1976 and 1981, Statistics Canada, 1983.

Wilkins R., and O. Adams, *Healthfulness of Life*, The Institute for Research on Public Policy, 1983.

Illness and Health Care in Canada; a Report of the 1950-51 Canada Sickness Survey, Department of National Health and Welfare and The Dominion Bureau of Statistics, 1960.

Lapierre, L., *Canadian Women: Profile of Their Health*, Statistics Canada, 1984.

Ableson, J., et al., *Perspectives on Health*, Statistics Canada, 1983

Chapter 2

HAZARDS TO HEALTH

THE CAUSES OF MORBIDITY AND MORTALITY

Why do we become 'sick', or why are we less well than we should be or could be? Which of the factors that limit our health are important, which ones can be controlled, and which ones can be controlled at acceptable emotional and economic cost? We should have at least vague answers to these questions if we wish to take action, either through public policy, education, research or personal response, to successfully improve our collective or individual health.

This chapter will discuss the forces and factors which cause ill health or injury. As we examine these forces and factors (the determinants of health) we will usually be examining factors outside of the 'health' system. We are increasingly aware of the impact of highways, housing, smoking, privacy, unemployment, pollution, education, the courts and job hazards, on both the health of Canadians and on the need for health services. We know that immunization and Pap smears are not the only important kinds of preventive medicine. Every event, decision or action that one can imagine has either an effect on the health of someone or the potential for such an effect, but the real or potential effects of most decisions or actions are small. This chapter will emphasize those things which affect our health in significant and recognized ways.

In looking at the effects on health of a variety of factors it will be immediately clear that both negative and positive effects on our health can flow from the same activity. Work, for example, brings with it many occupational hazards but it also often provides emotional as well as tangible rewards that are good for our health. Even smoking, which is immensely damaging to physical health, must bring pleasures to the smokers or they would not do it. This chapter will examine those factors which increase wellness as well as those which produce illness or injury.

In discussing determinants of health or illness or death, it is often difficult to separate direct from indirect effects. If 80% of lung cancers are caused by smoking, should smoking be listed as the cause of death? If a drunk driver sits in his car with the motor running and dies of CO poisoning, is the cause of death carbon monoxide or alcohol? If a person commits suicide with a gun, is the cause of death a gunshot wound or the factor(s) which led the person to choose suicide? This problem is handled on a death certificate by asking for the immediate cause of death as well as for identification of contributing causes. In our discussion of determinants of health, disease, disability or death there will be no organized effort to separate immediate from indirect causes; both will be considered.

In this chapter, as elsewhere in this book, psychosocial/mental health — our degree of wellness — will be considered to be central to health and to a reasonable quality of life. Factors which affect psychosocial/mental health will, therefore, be given major attention. As pointed out earlier, this approach is extremely different from that found, for example, in publications of Workers Compensation Boards (WCB). Physical health will be considered important because of the extent to which it determines one's psychosocial/mental health and because of its association with length of life.

One's definition of health is central to the identification of determinants or indicators of health or ill health. If one sees longevity as the major objective or measure of health, then attention will first be given to heart disease and cancer. The major causes of death in Canada are, in order of importance, coronary artery disease (CAD), cancer (especially of the lung and breast), stroke, accidents and chronic obstructive lung disease (COLD). If psychosocial health is the primary objective, however, our attention is redirected sharply to unemployment, chronic disability, isolation, lack of power, low self esteem and destructive personal environments. This chapter will look at both types of determinants.

Causes of death and determinants of physical health vary sharply with age. Low birth weight, prematurity and congenital malformations are major causes of death in the first year of life. Sudden Infant Death Syndrome (SIDS) is responsible for about a fifth of infant mortality with an incidence of 1 to 2 per 1,000 births. In children and young adults ages 5-24, accidents and suicide are the leading causes of death. In the mid-life years of 45-59, cancer accounts for half of female deaths. In males of this age group, cancer and coronary heart disease each account for about 30% of deaths. In older years, heart disease becomes more prominent and cancer declines. Stroke and chronic obstructive lung disease become more common after age 70.

The impact of various causes of death can also be compared in terms of potential years of life lost (PYLL. See Figure 2.1). When this measure is used accidents become dominant, especially for males.

It is now common to list four major determinants of health: environment, lifestyles, biology (genetics) and health services. Public policy has recently been said to be a fifth major factor. We are increasingly aware that health workers and the services they deliver are not as crucial to the health of the nation as we thought they were. The major determinants of health will be discussed separately. As part of environment and lifestyles we will explore culture, attitudes, values and philosophies.

ENVIRONMENT AS A DETERMINANT OF HEALTH

Our total environment is a mosaic composed of our cultural, social, technological, psychological, political, economic, occupational and physical environments. These interlocking but distinct environments each have their own impact, or potential for impact, on health. The overlapping of some of these environments leads to use of such terms as psychosocial or socioeconomic; no matter what terms are used the boundaries of the various segments remain vague.

Figure 2.1
Potential Years of Life Lost by Cause*
Canada, 1984

(000's)

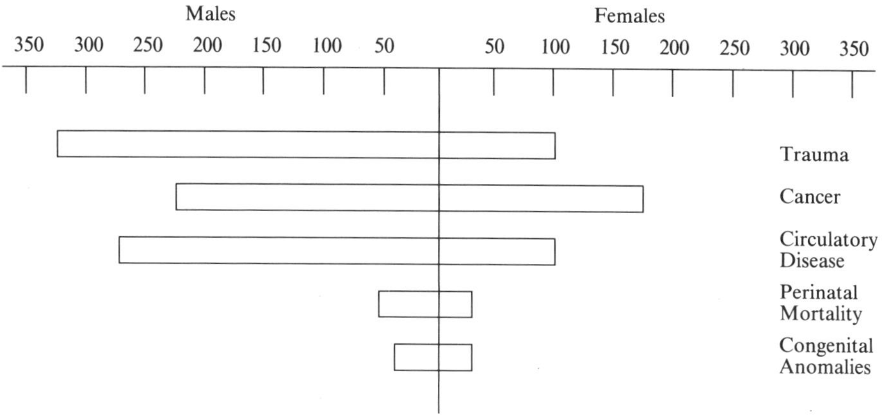

* Using age 75 as expected life span
Source: Ku, Smith, Mao, *Chronic Diseases in Canada*, Dec. 1986.

The Cultural and Psychosocial Environment

The cultural environment encompasses tradition, collective values and religion. To a large extent it determines whether communities will accept, tolerate, reject or be indifferent to the priorities, values, actions or aspirations of an individual. This acceptance, rejection, tolerance or indifference inevitably affects the health of the individual. Within a specific cultural environment the work ethic or a particular set of religious beliefs may be either accepted or rejected. To the extent that the cultural environment rejects the values or objectives of an individual, that individual may suffer emotional stress or physical harm; to the extent that the personal values or intentions of an individual are acceptable to society, he or she may be encouraged and made to feel welcome.

It has been said that events can bring momentary pleasure but that sustained happiness must be found within oneself, and that although it may be difficult to find sustained happiness within, it is impossible to find it anywhere else. If this is the case, and if a healthy state of mind is the most important element within total health, then one of the most important determinants of health is a societal environment which encourages and assists people to have confidence, optimism, self-reliance and the capacity to function in a co-operative and secure manner. These assets will prepare one for the challenging task of enhancing happiness through development of internal strengths and stability.

Our affluent society does not always provide support and acceptance and it does not always promote the development of confidence and self-reliance. It sometimes complains if the world does not respond to its every wish, and individuals rebel if any external force intrudes even slightly into what is perceived to be their domain. As a nation, community or household we often generate sarcasm or anger more readily than tolerance or affection, and we seem to enjoy putting people down more than we enjoy seeing them thrive and grow. These cultural habits do not create an environment conducive to health.

The complexity of our cultural environment and the challenge of working within it are illustrated by our interest in the protection of children from physical abuse. Our wish for child protection will, at times, introduce threats to their mental health as well as threats to the health of involved adults. The answer is not to ignore child abuse; it is to understand that actions which reduce a hazard may introduce other hazards, that human beings charged with any task will sometimes fail, and that some degree of failure must be forgiven. Errors in judgment are inevitable; some cases will be missed, and some will be improperly identified. Social health requires that parents, children and family workers learn that constructive support is at least as important as careful surveillance and that long term social improvement lies much more in the way we encourage healthy actions than in the way we punish those who are perceived to be unhealthy.

Another example of cultural influence is found in the high price we pay for our cultural attachment to winning. Hockey produces many physical injuries (including 4 to 8 spinal cord injuries per year in Canada, almost all of them in amateur players), but it also produces psychological injury. A civilized culture surely should be able to recognize the value and worth of all players, and the importance of the emotional health of all players, rather than rewarding only those who, through effort or innate ability or both, happen to emerge as 'best'. Overemphasis on being *the* winner reduces the likelihood that an individual, a society or a nation will develop a capacity for compromise and co-operation, and these abilities are cornerstones of emotional survival and reasonable psychosocial health.

Culture as a determinant of health can be complex and perverse. Canadians have always responded generously to fund raising by children's hospitals or other child related programs, but in 1976 Canada had the worst or second worst (depending on the data source) child accidental death rate among the developed countries. The English and Swedish rates were less than half of ours while those of the United States and West Germany were almost as bad as ours.

In the last 10 years, however, our death rate per 100,000 children has fallen 35-40%. Automobile accidents continue to dominate with up to 40% being pedestrian/car accidents. Drownings were next at 15%. In 1982 just over 900 children 14 and under and almost 1,400 aged 15-19 died of accidents or violence. Although accidental death rates have gone down some new hazards appeared and some former ones have not been contained. In 1984 in New Brunswick alone there were 13 child deaths associated with the use of all terrain recreational vehicles (ATV's). In Manitoba, between 1979 and 1984, 238 children under 16 years of age were admitted to hospital with injuries from use of minibikes and trail bikes. Nineteen were killed. Our culture sometimes barely notices how accidents are caused but becomes outraged if a child receives second rate health care for the physical injuries arising from the accidents.

Culture is a determinant of health when collective mood affects collective and individual health. Individuals or groups who hate, suspect or despise others can give to their hatred the kind of missionary fervor that justifies violence. At home, on the playing field and on the international scene we see conflict routinely resolved through violence, and our search for the most successful way to be violent often consumes far more energy and resources than our efforts to master the skills fundamental to the peaceful resolution of conflict. The ultimate and most hazardous acceptance of violence is to believe that nuclear war is a realistic final tool for resolution of international conflict.

Our health status, both mental and physical, will improve when our culture decides that hatred is counterproductive to the development of a sharing and caring society, and when we collectively teach and learn nonviolent conflict resolution techniques. The words of Einstein continue to be true: "We shall require a substantial new manner of thinking if mankind is to survive (the nuclear age)".

Culture has probably been the basis for our long-standing and continuing, although decreasing, discrimination against those who are mentally rather than physically ill. In Ontario the deinstitutionalization process was encouraged, not to give the mentally ill a better life, but to save money. Neither the communities nor the discharged patients were ready for the change and the health of no-one was improved. Our culture still tends to see the physically ill and injured as unfortunate and the mentally ill as embarrassing.

Society has not been offended by the fact that the purchasing power of families on public assistance has fallen steadily over the last decade, a decline that must surely have affected the emotional and physical health of the households involved. Our cultural wish for protection against taxation is a stronger force than our interest in the opportunities of low income children and mothers.

Culture continues, although to a gradually decreasing extent, to see death or physical illness or injury as our major hazards. The elderly and disabled are advised, and sometimes forced, to live not where they want to live or in the way they want to live, but where and how it is safest; safety is sometimes ranked ahead of quality of life even if the individual is prepared to take the risk. Society and health workers often go to great lengths to protect themselves against the criticism that someone was hurt, or someone died or became physically ill, because 'we' allowed them to be exposed to danger. Within this philosophy we have spent millions of dollars making sure there are no explosions in our operating rooms and few bacteria in our swimming pools, and we usually investigate everyone with even minor physical complaints. We have made life an end in itself when it should be merely a means to an end. We should live so that we can enjoy life and increase its pleasure for others, not merely so that we can be alive.

Fortunately we can have our cake and eat it too. In August 1982 the schools of medicine at Yale and the University of Manitoba studied 3000 people, all aged 65 and older, to look for links between mental health and survival or between perceptions of health and survival. They found that some people who were in good physical health considered themselves to be in fair or poor health. Others who were physically much sicker saw themselves as well. The surprising finding was that the people who thought their health was poor had a higher chance of dying (even when they were physically healthy) than those who were significantly sicker but saw themselves as healthy. This pattern supports the long accepted belief that tribal medicine men, or the placing of hexes, can have a real impact on people's survival. This study, plus many others, established that a healthy mind is associated not only with a better life but also with a longer one.

Earlier paragraphs have argued that the emotional stability of the adults of tomorrow depends heavily on the emotional environment of the children of today. An environment which promotes confidence, creativity, independence, sharing, reasonable expectations and tolerance in children will be likely to produce mentally healthy adults. After adulthood, however, these individuals continue to live in a social environment that affects their health. If this social environment offers a few successes to preserve confidence, allows for the satisfying of a reasonable number of sensible expectations such as having a job or being loved, and offers a greater volume of positive than negative strokes, then the mental health of the adult will be even more assured. The relative importance of environmental as opposed to inherited factors as determinants of mental health is unclear but environmental factors usually appear to be dominant.

Our ability to measure the adequacy of home environments as a factor in the mental health of children is still poor. The 1983 Ontario Child Health Survey (see Chapter 1) found that family dysfunction had a strong correlation with psychiatric abnormalities in children. The incidence of psychiatric disorders in children was not, however, higher in the presence of early separation from parents, marital disharmony, domestic violence or excessive drinking by one parent. These findings are not in keeping with common assumptions and we need a better understanding of what environmental factors or syndromes represent hazardous family dysfunction.

The Socioeconomic Environment

Economic factors operate at the collective and the individual level. Whether we are speaking of national or personal wealth we know that wealth is a significant determinant of health (Figure 2.2).

Variations in access to hospital care, medical care, community health services and most long term care are not as evident in Canada as in many other countries but they still exist. Beveridge, in his report in Britain in 1943, listed the five major evils that had to be conquered to improve the nation's health — ignorance, squalor, disease, unemployment and want. We know that in Canada in 1987, as

Figure 2.2
Health Expectancy by Income Level, by Sex, Canada, 1978

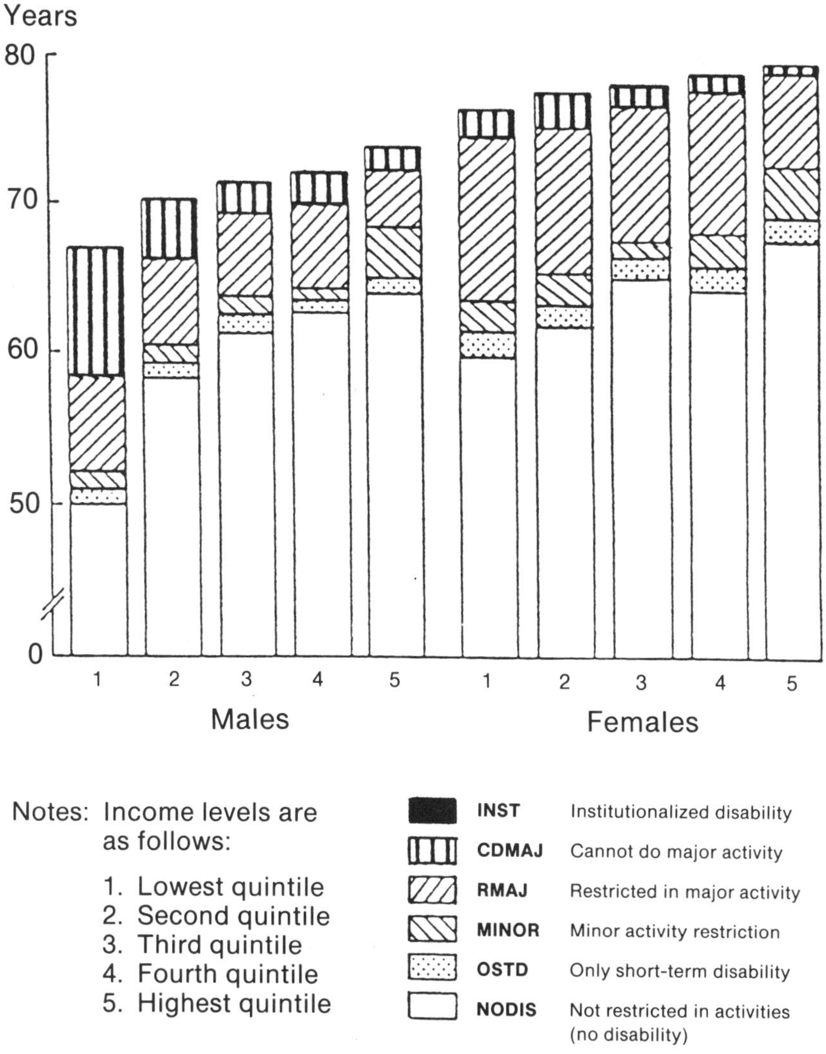

Source: Wilkins and Adams, *Healthfulness of Life*, Institute for Research on Public Policy, 1983.

in Britain in 1943, socioeconomic factors continue to have an influence on health status.

Whether one compares life expectancy, disability free years (health expectancy), or quality adjusted life expectancy (a calculation which takes into account both length of life and the quality of its years) the results always favor higher over lower income groups. Between the highest and the lowest income groups in Canada the difference in the early 1980's was 4.5 years of life and 7.7 years of disability free life.

Individuals and households are often considered to be below the poverty line if food, shelter and clothing consume greater than 58.5% of income. (In the average Canadian household these items consume 38.5% of income.) In 1985 16% of all Canadians, including 48% of those over 60 years of age, were in this group. It is quite proper to consider these as indicators of health status.

The mortality rate for infants born into lowest income families (lowest 20%) is twice that of infants from wealthy families (highest 20%). The bottom 20% of the population in terms of income has 25% of the total health problems. Children in low income households have a higher incidence of psychiatric disorders and of chronic physical disability. Low income is, on occasion, the result of ill health, but there can be no doubt that it also reduces ones level of health. Low income people exercise less, smoke more, use more tranquilizers, are less well nourished, are less likely to use seat belts, are more likely to be hurt at work and contact physicians less often. They do not, however, drink as much alcohol as higher income persons. Improving access to health care does not eliminate differences in the health of various income groups; after 20 years of universal health insurance the poor are still less healthy in Canada than are higher income persons.

Even to the extent that the health of the poor has improved, credit cannot automatically be given to better access to health care. Other factors such as federal programs of income redistribution are also at work. These programs include the following:

1) Old Age Security (OAS) was introduced in 1952 for those aged 70 and over. In 1986 it provided $292/month to 2.5 million persons over the age of 65.
2) Guaranteed Income Supplement (GIS) was introduced in 1967 as a supplement to OAS for persons shown needy by a means test. The GIS provides $350 per individual and $575 per couple. The percentage of those on OAS who qualify for GIS has been slowly dropping and is now below 50%. Many provinces also provide means tested supplements to the elderly but these are much smaller than the payments from the federal government.
3) Spouses Allowance has been available since 1975 for surviving spouses of OAS recipients. In 1986 it provided $520 per person to those aged 60-65. Programs 1, 2 and 3 cost the Federal Government $11.4 billion in 1985.
4) Income Tax Credits (Federal and Provincial).
5) Canada Assistance Plan (CAP) provides Federal cost sharing in support of provincial social services.
6) Special programs for native peoples.
7) War Veterans Allowance.

Unemployment, which is usually thought of as an economic issue, affects much more than income. It produces social pathology and threatens both physical and mental health. It can uncover latent physical and emotional vulnerabilities. It can take the quality out of life through lowered self-esteem and loss of confidence, and through sequelae including alcoholism and interpersonal conflict. It increases utilization of physical and mental health services and of a broad range of income support and other social services.

In terms of magnitude, unemployment must be one of the largest health hazards of the 1980's. When money is spent on job creation or job protection some of that expenditure should be seen as a health expenditure and some as social welfare in the best and most supportive sense. In Malcom Taylor's recent survey of over 2000 physicians, respondents reported having to deal regularly with serious recession-related disorders such as depression and intrafamily conflict. One quarter of the physicians reported having to deal with these problems daily. Health workers in the north or those who deal with our native populations will attest to the role of social and economic factors in health. The social and psychological effects of unemployment include increases in aggression, sleep disorders, nervousness (anxiety), hopelessness (depression), insecurity and alcoholism.

The Physical Environment

The writing and activities which pertain to the health hazards and benefits of our physical environment have been inappropriately titled "environmental health". The incorrect inference is that only the physical components of our environment are of consequence to health. Earlier parts of this chapter have described the importance to our health of our cultural, emotional, social and economic environments.

Workers who are experts in the evaluation and improvement of our physical environment have historically given greatest emphasis to the state of our water, air and land. Some have more recently studied things such as urban design, the physical attributes of the workplace and the impact of technology.

Air Pollution

Some pollutants are widely dispersed in the air and total populations are at risk. These pollutants include such things as sulfates, nitrites, pollens and other allergenic materials. Other pollutants are specific to selected personal activities or to specific locations. Tobacco smoke, silica dust, asbestos fibers and the vaguely identified ingredients of recycled office air (the sick building syndrome) are examples of these less universal hazards.

The known impact of polluted air on our physical health is immense. An average heavy smoker, for example, lives seven years less than the average nonsmoker and incurs four times the health cost of an average nonsmoker. Second-hand smoke affects millions of non-benefitting and unwilling bystanders; tobacco smoke is dangerous at any volume.

It has been estimated that smoking during pregnancy causes 6000 spontaneous abortions per year in Canada and 500 perinatal deaths (stillborn or deaths in the first week). Nicotine reduces fetal oxygen supply by as much as 25%.

Many specific hazardous air pollutants such as silica dust, asbestos fibers and grain dust have been well identified and often well controlled. The effects of others such as those which produce acid rain, the lead in leaded gas, or the herbicides and pesticides that are widely used, are less well known. Destruction of the ozone layer is a new and major threat.

Water Pollution

Pollution by living organisms, including bacteria, viruses and parasites, is still a major problem in developing countries but in Canada is not a major threat to human health. Our public health departments and our municipal water treatment capabilities have assured us of safe drinking water; in fact the water declared unfit for swimming in Canada is often cleaner than water available for washing or even drinking throughout the developing world. It is the chemical pollutants of Canadian waters that now ought to concern us most.

Pollution Probe publications have said that many Canadians are drinking chemical stew, and they are right. Industrially produced contaminants are much less routinely tested for than bacterial contaminants but they are present and, at least on occasion, may be dangerous. They are particularly dangerous because we do not know their long term effects even at current levels. We do, however, know the difficulties inherent in reducing this chemical pollution and we know that we are apparently not going to pursue improvement vigorously.

Improving our water quality will, as with many other efforts to improve our physical environment, lead to conflict. The commerce and industry represented by smelters, pulp mills, farms and investors see protection of our physical environment as a threat to production and profits. Consumers also see threats in pollution control. Pollution abatement can mean direct cost in the form of higher priced gasoline and cars, higher sewage treatment costs and higher electricity costs. It can also lead to inconvenience as we alter our wasteful and polluting approaches to packaging, reduce our use of plastic disposable cups and utensils and change from private to public transportation. Very often the choice is between long term goals and immediate gratification, and 'civilized' populations tend to prefer immediate gratification. Those who seek to protect our long term health and the health of future generations by protecting our physical environment must pursue personal, local, regional, provincial, national, international and global approaches.

Geography, climate and other natural hazards of all sorts are part of our physical environment and are of consequence to health. Skin cancer, for example, is most common in white populations with excessive exposure to the tropical sun, but colorectal cancer is lower in these same regions. Multiple Sclerosis is highly regional, being almost absent in many equatorial regions and occurring most often in selected parts of the temperate zones. Most tropical diseases are relatively uncommon in Canada although most are now diagnosed here occasionally.

The factors in our physical environment that are perceived by the public to be of greatest importance to health change regularly. Strontium 90, polychlorinated biphenyls (PCBs), asbestos, lead, phosphorus, other heavy metals, urea formaldehyde insulation, group homes, ozone and traffic noise have all had their day. Sulphates from acid rain may emerge soon, either on the basis of their direct effects (it has been estimated that over 10% of deaths are accelerated by atmospheric sulfates, and hospital admissions for respiratory problems increase when sulfate levels are high) or their indirect effects (such as an increased presence of lead, mercury and cadmium in the food chain because of leeching associated with acid rain). Future public concern or hysteria could also arise from the greenhouse effect (whatever its cause), from the impact of garbage, from industrial pollution or from the presence of radon gas in basements.

Technology and Health

Technology brings its own special set of threats and benefits to both our physical and psychosocial environments.

Technology is not inherently a bad thing. It can improve and has improved the quality of life. It has given us more leisure time, new forms of pleasure and better physical health. It has sharply reduced the likelihood that we will see our children die, and it can, if used wisely, give us more protection, greater privacy and a greater chance to be independent.

Antibiotics, immunization, birth control and new diagnostic capabilities, for example, are important but the technologies that have had the greatest positive effects on physical health status are those that have not been seen as health technology. These include our water and sewage treatment capabilities, our divided highways, the expanded food production of an acre of land, or the availability of fresh fruit and vegetables all year. On the negative side, technology has brought transportation and industrial pollution of everything and the possibility of nuclear catastrophe.

The greatest hazards of technology may, however, be to our psychosocial health. One reasonable hypothesis proposes that we have, in an emotional sense, become machine dominated. Technology is now seen as our saviour instead of our servant. We have, at times, been so mesmerized with what machines can do that we have lost sight of all the things they cannot do.

At times we also demand machine like performances from people. We set standards which cannot be met. The rigidity and perfection of science is increasingly dominating our dealings with each other and so we all fail because the standards are too high. Because some sports, some high schools and some parents have made failure a cultural crime, and because we all increasingly fail when measured by technocratic or perfectionist standards, more and more people lose the self-image and confidence that is so necessary for good mental health and a reasonable quality of life.

Unrealistic standards and expectations, including those based on our faith in and reliance on technology, are a menace to our health. Realistic expectations require that one understand that life is short, that it always ends in death, that it cannot always bring what one wishes, and that it will, at times, be filled with sorrow and discomfort and bad health. Realistic expectations reduce the number of disappointments. The balanced, mature individual has expectations that are relatively close to what life is actually offering or able to offer. One feature of some neurotic or psychotic individuals is a major difference between expectations and what is realistic. We, therefore, can be made less mentally well by anyone who convinces us that we should seriously hope for things that cannot happen or are very unlikely to happen. Science, including medical science, routinely promises or implies more than it can deliver.

For centuries technology has been impressing us with the pyramids, the Eiffel Tower, the atom bomb, and the space shuttle. Within the health world, we are informed of transplants, open heart surgery, the latest tranquilizer, or an artificial hip. The technocrats can, indeed, do the impossible, and the long list of successes has lead most of us to expect technical perfection. We would be quite annoyed if an elevator did not stop at the right floor. We might even be quite annoyed if it left us with two inches to step either up or down. We certainly are annoyed if the computer over-books an airplane, if cable TV is not completely clear, or if the telephone line is noisy. We have come to expect 100% security, convenience, comfort, and service. When faced with a shortage of energy we collectively ask technology to produce more energy even though we could, with only modest personal adaptation, use much less. We want acid rain controlled but we want it done by producing energy without pollution rather than by producing less energy. We want technocrats to solve problems we can collectively solve ourselves.

For every problem we expect a new process, an instant cure, a better computer, a new kind of technocrat, and a new gadget or theory. For every discomfort we assume that there is a suitable drug or soon will be. For every inconvenience we assume that there is a new kind of shelter or transport or other appropriate gadget or soon will be. For every undesirable activity we assume that there is a mechanical device to replace it or soon will be. Technocrats and their successes have trained us to believe that all our problems will eventually be cured or disposed of by technological breakthroughs, and this faith in technology has led us to stop learning how to remain happy and content in the face of the problems that have not yet been handled by technology or can never be handled by it.

Technology cannot make any of us accept life as it is presented to us and it cannot prepare any of us for whatever sadness we meet. It cannot make us immortal and it cannot teach us to see something good in the world or each other every day. It cannot bring us tolerance, patience, understanding or willingness to be a good loser, it cannot replace the interest and the respect and love that children can bring to elderly parents or the emotional security that parents or teachers or friends can bring to children. A machine is of little help to a frightened or lonely person or an alcoholic. In summary, machines are frequently useful but they are not useful when one is faced with the problems that are most central to a high quality of life. They are frequently seen as the route to a life without problems, but the vision is a mirage. The world is now searching for solutions within technology rather than within people, and in our preoccupation with this search for external resolution of problems we have sometimes failed to retain in ourselves the adaptability and attitudes that are fundamental to good mental health.

Good mental health is most apt to be present in a person with a reasonable set of expectations, with some sense of personal control over one's self and one's environment, with some feeling of self-worth, and with an ability to accept failure in both oneself and in others. Technology has, for some people, decreased their opportunity to have a sense of control. It has led people to have unrealistic expectations. It has fueled the worldwide economic feudalism that threatens the role and independence of individuals, communities and countries.

What technology will do to our health status in the future is for humans to decide, although the most important decisions cannot be made by one individual and often not by the population of only one country or continent. The average individual can only vote (in those countries which are democratic), protest (by sanctions or preference or demonstration if choice is possible and demonstrations allowable) and hope that those with financial, military and political power, often in that order, will be interested in long term as well as short term benefits and in the security and healthfulness of all races, cultures and socioeconomic classes.

Although multinational or global factors dominate when we discuss the role of technology, there are subordinate but still consequential decisions that are under the control of Canada, the provinces, our municipalities, our private sector or individual Canadians. We have decided to have seat belts in our cars and, therefore, we have the opportunity to use them. We will probably soon be driving with our lights on at all times (and technology will turn them on and off without our assistance) and we have still to decide whether we wish all cars to have air-bags. Automobiles are usually the major cause of death, of brain and spinal cord injury and of other forms of trauma between infancy and middle life, and it has been estimated that air-bags to complement seat belts would reduce deaths and injuries by 10-50%. Canada and Canadians can alter the levels and the nature of factory, household, automobile and other emissions or effluent, but only at economic and social cost. Available technologies can be used or ignored -- the choice is sometimes ours.

Different choices bring different positive and negative effects; most choices improve health status in some ways and damage it in others. Policy development is, unfortunately, made difficult by people who want solutions that bring advantages but no disadvantages; we wish our garbage to be disposed of, for instance, but nowhere near where we live. The main point to be made here is that although technology makes options available it is not the villain; if society or individuals make selfish or short sighted choices the error is entirely theirs.

Technological developments have changed us into a society in which a few people and many machines do the former work of thousands and in which computers do our calculations and make our decisions. Wondering what artificial intelligence will be like is passé — the era is here. In-vitro (test-tube) fertilization and the artificial heart get headlines but they are trivial when placed beside the world of genetic engineering. The creation of life itself may soon occur. Already machines guided by computers can create genes while you wait. The DNA helix, our genetic code, can be broken and spliced with defective or unwanted components removed and with useful new segments inserted. The extent to which these emerging skills will determine our health is still unknown.

The rather widespread acceptance of the concept of nuclear war, or of winning such a war, is an incomprehensible example of our failure to deal with the options that have come from new technology and which carry immense implications for the health of everyone. The destruction, the radiation and the ensuing nuclear winter ensure that there will be no winners.

SPECIAL ENVIRONMENTS

Planners and researchers may categorize the environment as a number of specific locations, for example, a workplace, a school, a playground, or a uterus. Each special environment contains specific threats to and supports for both emotional and physical health.

The Workplace

Working conditions affect physical and mental health. Physical health is endangered by such things as noise, dust, equipment, fumes, chemicals, flying or falling objects and fatigue. Mental health may be affected when work demands are excessive, when work is boring and nonrewarding, when shift work is required, or when working conditions are generally unpleasant.

In the work environment people are often the major source of stress for other people. Physicians surveyed by Prof. Malcolm Taylor in 1983 almost universally felt their work was stressful and identified patients as the major source of stress. Only 15% reported government as a problem of consequence. The stressful patients were those with unrealistic expectations, those with social problems the physician could do very little about, those who wished for more information and explanation than the doctor thought was necessary, those who did not follow instructions and those who shopped around. It is quite probable that a fair number of patients also see doctors as a source of stress, but that stress is not work related.

In most occupations which involve sustained human interaction (politics, law enforcement, sales, education, health and social services) the workers are stressed by the people they deal with. Many people might consider unexpected death or physical injury to be the major threat to the health of police officers but the stress of being regularly seen as the 'cop' who hands out tickets or tells your party to quiet down may be a greater cause of ill health.

It has been estimated that at least 550,000 Canadians suffer a significant physical injury at work each year. Many of these are fully preventable. Occupationally induced hearing loss, for example, produces over 1,000 new WCB compensation awards annually despite our knowledge of the hazard and the availability of protective equipment.

Some workplace hazards are well studied and others less so; some are easy to respond to and some not so easy. We usually think of drug interactions, for example, as arising from prescribed and nonprescribed drugs. However, people on medication may come in contact with chemicals at work (in farming, factories or hospitals) that interact with the drugs being taken for therapeutic purposes. The magnitude of the workplace as a threat to health is illustrated by the size of WCB budgets — over $1.6 billion per year in Ontario.

Recent decades have seen quite remarkable reductions in physical injuries on the job. Certain job related physical diseases such as asbestosis have also become less common. Many historically dangerous jobs such as oil drilling, logging and mining have better safety records now, but on a per capita basis these, as well as fishing and farming, remain at the top of the danger list. Some jobs have special physical hazards; nursing care for chronic patients, for instance, produces many back injuries. Good staff education and supervision can reduce these injuries by 50% or more. In some occupations such as nursing stress levels are increasing.

The Schools

The environment in which children, youths and young adults are educated can enhance or damage the intellectual curiosity, the initiative, the creativity and the individuality of each student, and these characteristics are central to the self-image and confidence that are a part of good health.

The Home

Many injuries and deaths caused by falls, fire and domestic violence occur in the home. Home is a place where love and support can strengthen one's health, and where criticism and disinterest can damage it. Often it is a place where television is king. In the absence of strong and positive human interaction the idiot box can be the surrogate parent, and usually a surrogate which specializes in physical and mental violence.

Recreation

Recreation is essential for physical and mental health but it carries risks to both. The mental hazards of our preoccupation with winning were discussed earlier.

Approximately one quarter of all accidental injuries cared for in an emergency department are recreation related. For the 10-24 age group the figure approaches 50%.

The incidence of serious eye injuries, including blindness, has fallen sharply in the last 10 years as participants in hockey, squash, racquetball and war games have increasingly worn eye protection. About 30 eyes per year are still made blind by sports injuries; all or almost all of them are eyes that were not protected by visors, glasses or full face protectors. Unfortunately, the use of adequate head and face protection may contribute to an increased incidence of spinal cord injuries in contact sports such as hockey. Knees and shoulders also remain unable to tolerate the stresses of contact sports, and the brain continues to be unable to withstand the battering of boxing.

The Uterus

Health after birth is partly a product of factors which had their effects before birth. Each year thousands of Canadian children are born damaged by completely avoidable in-utero hazards. The total cost arising from this damage is in the billions. Some of the viral hazards such as rubella (german measles) have been virtually eliminated, as have the effects of the Rh factor, but the toxic effects of tobacco and alcohol are poorly controlled. Tobacco smoke causes low birth weight and less healthy babies. Alcohol is also damaging. The incidence of fetal damage due to alcohol intake by the mother during pregnancy has been estimated at between 0.1% and 0.7% of babies (1 to 7 per 1,000 births) with the figures perhaps rising to 2-5% of births in selected communities. Some of these children suffer major brain damage leading to unproductive lives. The risk is greatest at 4-6 weeks, often before pregnancy is even confirmed.

LIFESTYLE CHOICES AS DETERMINANTS OF HEALTH

It is common knowledge that smoking is part of lifestyle, and that it is dangerous, and that smokers voluntarily choose to do it. The same is true of alcohol consumption and, to a lesser extent, of being obese, of being poorly conditioned, and of being overcritical. When speaking of lifestyle as a determinant of health we are speaking of activities and attitudes that we could have modified if we, as individuals, had chosen to do so. A broad range of injuries and ill health are caused by our lifestyle choices, but there is some uncertainty as to when a disease should be called a lifestyle disease.

We all know lung cancer and coronary artery disease can be wholly or partially the product of smoking or obesity and yet, in some cases, they occur in the absence of smoking or obesity. Are they always lifestyle diseases or are they lifestyle diseases only when they occur in someone with a particular lifestyle? And what about some of the things we have already discussed, such as a tendency towards intolerance or violence? Are these lifestyle diseases? They certainly have lifestyle consequences for others. What about injuries in battle or during a bank robbery; they could have been avoided by staying out of the army or deciding not to be a bank robber? Are they lifestyle diseases? And what about pregnancy and all its hazards and sequelae? Since all are to some degree avoidable, can they sometimes be classified as lifestyle diseases?

The term lifestyle diseases should be exchanged for lifestyle consequences, a lifestyle consequence being something that could have been avoided by choosing an alternative lifestyle that was realistically available. This definition rules out the diseases or consequences that flow from poverty, climate, or working or living conditions that an individual cannot realistically be expected to avoid. Lifestyle consequences is a term which might best be used only with respect to the consequences *to me* of my actions. When my lifestyle is a threat to someone else I become an environmental hazard rather than a lifestyle hazard.

Any discussion of physical ill health and lifestyle should begin with an examination of smoking even though smoking has already been discussed as a source of air pollution. The American Association for Cancer Research estimates that one in every three persons who smoke cigarettes will die from a related effect. Cancers from smoking, which represent 30% of all cancer deaths, are a preventable epidemic. Society absorbs billions of dollars of tobacco-caused social cost.

An HWC survey in 1982 showed that 22% of Canadian teenagers smoke daily with the percentage increasing from 8% at 12-14 years to 39% among 18-19 year olds. Females were more apt to be daily smokers (24% vs 21%) but were less likely to smoke a pack a day or more. A high percentage of smokers and non-smokers were aware of the hazards of smoking.

Smoking is being attacked by means of legislation, social pressure, pressure at work, warning labels and higher prices. However, about 35% of males 15 and over and 32% of females continue to smoke. A combination of chronic cough, impaired taste, discolored teeth and fingers, smokers breath, burned holes in clothes and furniture, $1000-2000 per year of direct cost and 30,000 related deaths per year has not stopped 35% of adult Canadians from smoking; they prefer the benefits of peer approval and of satisfying their systemic craving for nicotine.

A second addiction reinforces the importance of lifestyle as a determinant of health. About 65% of adult Canadians use alcohol at least once a month; about 10% of these will have some alcohol related disability, over half a million are alcohol dependant, and at least 100,000 have a disabling dependency. Thirty percent of suicides, 50% of homicides, over half of our automobile fatalities and perhaps 10% (15-18,000) of our total annual deaths are alcohol related. Besides causing these deaths alcohol is a factor in 50% of divorces and 50% of welfare families, and although tax revenues from alcohol sales in 1983-84 were three and one half to four billion dollars the social costs were probably twice as high. Although the taxes on alcohol appear substantial there was, in the period from 1962 to 1982, almost a 50% reduction in the cost of a litre of absolute alcohol if the cost is expressed as a percentage of personal disposable income. In the same period there was a 30% increase in consumption per person.

Male, young and less educated Canadians have the most unhealthy lifestyles. They are more likely to smoke, to use alcohol in excess, to avoid using seat belts and to be involved in accidents and violence.

Alcohol and tobacco are not the only lifestyle activities of consequence to mental and physical health; there is danger in physical inactivity, inappropriate diets, obesity, abuse of narcotics, unsafe use of all forms of transport and abuse of prescription drugs.

HEREDITY/BIOLOGY

Our genetic pool is a major determinant of physical health status but it is a factor we can usually do nothing about. Genetics as a medical science deals with over 3000 conditions such as Tay-Sachs Disease, sickle cell anemia, hemophilia and phenylketonuria, all of which are deviations from what we call normal. It should also be remembered that our genetic pool is the primary determinant of lifespan, of the capacity of our kidneys and livers to handle toxins, of the pattern of osteoporosis, of the structural inadequacies of our knees, shoulders and backs, and of the adequacy of our immune system. The question of the extent to which emotional/mental health is genetically rather than environmentally determined is largely unknown, but our genetic pool is definitely a factor in a few specific psychiatric conditions.

PUBLIC POLICY AS A DETERMINANT OF HEALTH

The decisions made by governments and governing bodies affect our safety, our opportunities and the mix and character of our social and economic institutions, all of which affect our health. These decisions are the product of the talent and the values of the decision makers and of the pressures acting upon them. Decisions and policies can be seen as products of the social and economic environments and can be discussed under those headings, but it can also be argued that public policies ought to be considered as a separate factor affecting health.

The role of governments and other governing bodies is more fully discussed in later chapters.

Summary

This chapter has looked at the determinants of the health of Canadians and has emphasized the importance of cultural, social, genetic, political and economic factors.

In any discussion of health in Canada we should remember that increasing our material standard of living may not increase our level of health proportionately. Improved health is likely to occur only if we use our affluence to strengthen our concern for each other and to strengthen the optimism and confidence of each of us. At the moment we measure national success in terms of GNP or balance of payments; we should also be developing measures of group tolerance, capacity for compassion, willingness to share and willingness to oppose our drift to increased economic centralization. Good health is difficult to maintain in individuals who must act and live in patterns and communities shaped by forces beyond their control.

This chapter has argued that the total health of Canadians is influenced only minimally by the number of hospital beds or Intensive Care Units (ICU) or specialist physicians, and is influenced heavily by those factors that strengthen and promote such things as mental health, security, nondestructive lifestyles, safer workplaces and a healthier environment.

The actions taken to improve health have changed over time. The first big advances in health status were due to socioeconomic and public health measures including improvements in housing and water supply, the preservation of food, the pasteurization of milk, sewage control, garbage disposal, and control of communicable diseases. These were followed by an acceleration of scientific and technological progress, by the prevention and cure of infectious diseases and by a greater understanding of and interest in mental health problems and endemic chronic diseases. Associated with the onslaught of chronic diseases was the need for new treatment and prevention strategies but especially for new attitudes toward the relative importance of state of mind as opposed to state of body.

A third phase of health protection relates to the burgeoning volume of social and environmental pathology. We are still adapting to these and are not, as yet, skillful at dealing with them or at recognizing how and why they develop.

The major determinants of health are, today as always, outside of the purvue and mandate of the health system. They include the level of employment, the quality of interpersonal interaction, the quality of our social and physical environments and the safety of our workplace. At this point in time we often ignore major threats to health while lavishly supporting selected health services whose impact on health status is much smaller than we believe.

We also give too little attention to mental/emotional health compared to physical injury or illness. The good effects of good teachers and day care staff on the psychosocial health of children are a more important outcome than the physical safety provided by a well designed playground. We also would benefit immensely if the magnitude of various hazards and the potential for their occurrence were taken into consideration before we reacted, and it would offer new hope for humanity if we were at least as vigorous in our attack on hazards under our control as we are in our attacks on other people when they do not fully act against hazards that they control.

Suggested Reading

1. *The Silent Epidemic: Childhood Injuries*, The Canadian Institute of Child Health, 1984.
2. *Booze, Pills and Dope, Reducing Substance Abuse in Canada*, The Standing Committee on National Health and Welfare, Government of Canada, October 1987.
3. Wigle, D.J. and Mao, Y., *Mortality by Income Level in Urban Canada*, Health and Welfare Canada, 1980.
4. *Chronic Diseases in Canada*, a quarterly Health and Welfare Canada publication, but in particular the issue of June 1987.
5. *Poverty Profile*, National Council of Welfare, Ministry of Supply and Services, Canada, 1985.
6. *Progress Against Poverty*, National Council on Welfare April 1987.
7. *Alcohol in Canada. A National Perspective*, Health and Welfare Canada, 2nd Edition 1984.

Chapter 3

ORGANIZATION AND ROLES

INTRODUCTION

Health services in Canada are provincially dominated but there is major federal influence. They are pluralistic but with universal elements. They are the product of a French and an English culture, a 'quiet revolution', an agrarian socialism, a rich economy, an oversupply of physicians and an electorate which assigns a high priority to health services. They are in a constant state of change, if not of turmoil.

This chapter describes the general characteristics of the health services network. It looks at objectives and functions, at organizational characteristics and options, and at the roles of the major players. It also introduces subjects which will be examined in greater detail in later chapters.

PHILOSOPHY

The current philosophical underpinnings of our health services are, to a large extent, a product of former decades. Canada has in theory, and sometimes in practice, opted for (a) egalitarian rather than elitist or market based access to health care (that is, access on the basis of need rather than ability to pay); (b) for the right of every individual to approve or reject recommended care, or to approve or reject a healthy or an unhealthy lifestyle, or to accept or reject almost any form of risk; (c) greater societal response to physical ill health or injury than to mental or psychosocial difficulty; (d) protection of children against public or individual decisions which are not in their best interests; and (e) collective priorities and practices determined increasingly through public policy rather than by providers. There is uncertainty regarding the extent to which access to services should change as potential for benefit changes, although to date the decision has usually been to provide unlimited service if prescribed by a physician. There is freedom of choice of physicians, access to any number of physicians, and physician freedom to reject any patient except in selected situations. It is current practice to give much greater weight to the needs of people who are already receiving services than to those who are waiting in line. There is lip service, but only lip service, to the concept of reducing pressure on the system by actively encouraging self-help or household involvement. The rationing of health care is regularly mentioned, and usually condemned, although the practice is with us and always has been.

GOALS AND FUNCTIONS

Different health services have quite different costs, degrees of sophistication, types of ownership, images with the public and organizational structures. All of the not-for-profit sources of care have as their primary goal the maintenance or improvement of the health status of all or selected members of the community.

The for-profit sector must have profit as its primary goal but if the marketplace is operating as it should then the profit sector will survive only if it also maintains or improves health. There is general public acceptance of the global goal of maintaining or improving health status but there is less of a consensus as one moves from global goals to objectives, activities and programs. The decreasing consensus arises from the varying perceptions of health, from the different priorities given by different people to different elements of health, from the variety of actions that have an effect upon health status, and from the different priorities given by different people to these actions.

One traditional way to categorize the functions or objectives of health services is the clinical/academic list in Figure 3.1.

If these health service objectives are modified it becomes evident that they are extremely similar to the objectives of many other social services and their networks. (Figure 3.2).

The overall goal of a civilized society should be the highest possible health status for present and future populations, with health being first of all a state of mind. This global goal does not imply that the highest quality or the maximum consumable amount of health care or health protection will be available routinely to everyone or to anyone. It does not mean that the life of everyone will be the longest it could possibly be, or that every hazard that can be eliminated

FIGURE 3.1
A CLINICAL/ACADEMIC CATEGORIZATION OF OBJECTIVES AND FUNCTIONS OF HEALTH SERVICES

1. *To detect and diagnose* (including identification and measurement of hazards).
   a) Environmental abnormality (of water, air, food).
   b) Personal diseases, defects, injuries, deficiencies or psychosocial problems.

2. *To treat.*
   a) To cure or attempt to cure.
   b) To delay death or other serious consequences.
   c) To relieve symptoms.

3. *To bring comfort, to care.*

4. *To support:* For example, to provide food, water, shelter or protection.

5. *To medically rehabilitate.*

6. *To do research.*

7. *To train, educate and inform.*
   a) Health workers.
   b) The public.
   c) The patients.

FIGURE 3.2
GOALS OF THE HEALTH SYSTEM

1. Prolongation of life (through prevention of premature death).
2. Minimization of departures from physiologic or functional norms.
3. Minimization of discomfort.
4. Minimization of disability (mental, emotional, physical, social).
5. Promotion of high level wellness or self fulfillment (internal satisfaction).
6. Promotion of high level satisfaction with the environment (external satisfaction).
7. Extension of (increased) resistance to ill health and the creation of reserve capacity.
8. Increased participation of all clients in health matters.

will be. The global goal, if it is accepted, implies that there will be a collective willingness to share risk and resources in such a way that the health patterns of the community, that is, of the total population, will be as good as they can be. As one part of the vast social and economic network of activities that affect health, health services should contribute to the attainment of that global social goal to the maximum extent possible with the resources that are available. Health services should also avoid seeking more resources when those resources will have a greater positive effect on health status if they are consumed elsewhere.

The goal of the publicly funded health services network (the major part of the health system) is, therefore, to exert influence and provide services at the places and times, in the amount, quality and sequence, with the efficiency, and with the degree of safety, that are consistent with (a) the priorities assigned by society, (b) the total availability of resources and (c) the consumers' wishes. The Canadian population has repeatedly reiterated, in elections and in opinion polls, its wish for equal and excellent access of all Canadians to those health services that are publicly funded. Services privately funded will, as with other services purchased in the marketplace, reflect the wishes and wealth of a buyer and the willingness of a seller subject only to whatever constraints society chooses to apply.

Global goals are easy to write because they rely on the rhetoric of motherhood and apple pie for impact. Unfortunately, what they mean and how they should be transformed into specific policies and actions with specific objectives and targets is not so clear. Several governments have recently attempted to respond to the current need for better defined national and provincial health objectives. Despite the usual absence of a reasonably clear blueprint for action we do have a complex health system that consumes resources in an organized way to produce various outputs.

TYPES OF SERVICES

The types of services that should be considered as health services are often difficult to identify rationally, but a few qualify easily.

Acute care services, which for the most part provide either diagnosis, care and/or cure, are usually thought of as short term and episodic. They are provided from, or in, a vast array of noninstitutional and institutional sources, such as offices, emergency rooms, outpatient clinics, hospital beds, health centers, homes and schools. They respond to physical, mental and emotional problems.

Acute care services merge imperceptibly into chronic or long term care (LTC) services. For example, hay fever, diabetes, hypertension and arthritis are certainly chronic illnesses but they are usually cared for in short term care locations by health care providers who are not part of what is usually thought of as the long term care system.

Health services often include social services, recreation services, transportation, education, income assistance, vocational rehabilitation and/or help with household chores or maintenance, but each of these is also routinely provided quite separately from health services. It also is difficult to decide how to categorize care provided by oneself, by household members or by friends. If these are considered health care services they will be very statistically dominant.

THE MAJOR NATIONAL MODELS

There are three basic national or provincial approaches to the organization of health services. These are the national health services model, the public insurance model and the entrepreneurial/market model.

In a national health system (NHS) or national health service model (the name is not important but the concept is a major option), a government, usually through a ministry of health, organizes and delivers health services. Russia, Cuba and Great Britain have chosen this model. An NHS tends to be centralized but it may sometimes be quite decentralized as in Sweden and Finland.

Canada has a few examples which illustrate the NHS model but they represent only a minority of our health services network. Examples include the major psychiatric facilities which in most provinces are still owned and operated by the province, public health services in some provinces, the provincial laboratory networks, provincial ambulance systems (financed, organized, planned, evaluated and delivered by a government) and the childrens' dental services program in Saskatchewan which operated from 1974 to 1987. At the federal level the armed forces medical services and the services to Indians and Inuit are also examples of the NHS model. Most Canadian health services, however, are not organized this way.

Most Canadian health services are publicly financed but are administered and delivered by someone other than government. Canada, in general, has chosen the public insurance model. The Canadian public insurance umbrella, through which services are paid for by a provincial government, universally covers physician and hospital services with ambulances, dentistry, chiropractors, optometrists, podiatrists, long term care, drugs, private physiotherapy and home care having differing degrees of coverage in different provinces.

Governments usually finance, regulate and sometimes plan health care services but delivery is usually carried out by non-governmental for-profit or not-for-profit agencies. The agency and the workers who actually deliver the services are not a part of, or employed by, the ministry of health or any other ministry.

The third health service model is the entrepreneurial model in which the government does not play a role as a provider or a funder of health services. The United States is probably closer to this model than to the public insurance model but in the United States, as in Canada, there are elements of each of the three basic models.

THE FEDERAL GOVERNMENT

The *British North America (BNA) Act* of 1867 and subsequent interpretations of it gave the provinces jurisdiction over most health services. The federal government was given jurisdiction over health services only for those specific populations mentioned in the BNA Act. These include native peoples, the armed forces, the RCMP, immigrants or refugees at certain stages in the immigration process, those living in the Northwest Territories and the Yukon and a few other small groups.

Several federal departments are involved in the planning and delivery of health care. The Department of National Health and Welfare (DNHW), also called Health and Welfare Canada (HWC), through its Medical Services Branch provides services to one third of a million Inuit and status Indians. HWC has financed many special studies including the Royal Commission whose 1964 report helped establish national medicare. Through an Ottawa production centre and warehouse HWC offers emergency health supplies, including total hospitals, and maintains regularly updated emergency equipment and supplies stored throughout Canada. HWC also provides specialized laboratory and epidemiological services through its Centre for Disease Control (CDC), drug and equipment testing through its Food and Drug Directorate and its Bureau on Medical Devices, occupational health services to a broad network of federal government employees, consulting services in many environmental, occupational and health care fields, expanding programs in the field of health promotion, and research funding of over $170 million annually to the Medical Research Council (MRC) and of $13 million annually to the National Health Research and Development Program. Through its welfare side HWC delivers old age pensions and other income maintenance programs that are frequently fundamental to independence and good health. In 1974 a HWC Minister, the Honorable Marc Lalonde, published a book, *A New Perspective on the Health of Canadians*, which received worldwide recognition because of its call for a reorientation of health services towards health promotion.

The Department of National Defence (DND), through facilities on military bases or at the National Defence Medical Centre in Ottawa, provides services to the armed forces, the RCMP, veterans, members of parliament, senators, foreign students funded by Canada, visiting dignitaries and selected senior civil servants and representatives of the crown. The Department of Veterans Affairs (DVA) at one time had a network of veterans hospitals but these have now largely been converted to civilian hospitals. DVA is, therefore, now more of a paymaster than a deliverer of service.

Atomic Energy of Canada (AEC) controls the use of all radioactive equipment and supplies. Correctional Service Canada (CSC) spends $40 to 50 million a year providing health care for the inmates of federal custodial institutions. Partly for health inspection purposes the Department of Manpower and Immigration maintains immigrant stations at major ports and airports as well as in selected locations outside Canada. Other federal ministries such as Labor and Environment have functions closely or directly related to health care delivery, and Statistics Canada is a major producer of and repository for a broad range of health and health services information. The Canadian International Development Agency (CIDA) and the International Development Research Centre (IDRC) provide a variety of health programs and services as part of their assistance to less developed countries.

The above list mentions most federal health service activity but does not begin to list all of the ways in which federal activities directly affect health, nor does it fully illustrate the difficulties inherent in determining federal versus provincial jurisdiction. For instance, the transportation of toxic materials can be interprovincial and, therefore, is controlled by the federal Ministry of Transport. To a constitutional expert the activity is transportation but people and municipalities tend to think of it as a health matter.

The health services over which the federal government has constitutional jurisdiction serve over half a million Canadians, and other services provided by HWC and Statistics Canada are also of national importance, but the influence of the federal government has, perhaps, been most felt when federal money has been used to affect policy in areas of provincial jurisdiction.

In 1867, when the provinces were given jurisdiction over them, education and social services were not very expensive. Expensive functions such as defence and much of transportation were assigned to the federal government and, therefore, the most lucrative revenue producing taxation methods were reserved for the federal government. As the cost of education, health and other social services increased they became increasingly unaffordable for the provinces and the federal government became able to influence provincial policies through offers of financial aid.

The withholding of financial aid was not the first choice of the federal government as a tool to influence national health. World War II had shown that an unacceptably high percentage of Canadian recruits were medically unfit for military service, and both the Beveridge Report in Britain and the Marsh Report in Canada had recommended the establishment of national health systems. At the Conference on Reconstruction during World War II the federal government proposed a national approach to health services funding and planning, a proposal that required provincial support and an amendment to the constitution. The provinces, however, would not agree to give up their control over health services.

Constitutional amendments which allow the federal government to act in an area of provincial jurisdiction are not always rejected by the provinces. In 1940 and 1951, for example, the provinces consented to Federal implementation of national unemployment insurance and universal old age security respectively, but the provinces preferred to retain direct control over health services.

Having lost its bid for a federally operated health insurance program the Federal Government then sought other ways to contribute to and influence health services and their costs. The following three devices have been most commonly used:

1. Federally financed and operated services which are useful to the provinces, for example, laboratories and health promotion. These direct federal expenditures on health were discussed earlier in this chapter.
2. Conditional grants. These grants are available only if used for specified purposes and in specified ways. There are two main types of conditional grants.
   a) Funds available without provincial government expenditures although various other conditions must be met: The Canada Assistance Plan (CAP) is one example. Through CAP fifty percent federal funding is available for a broad range of rehabilitative, social support and community based programs so long as the other half is provided by other than a federal source. Many programs which are funded through CAP have the second half of the necessary funds raised locally with the provincial government contributing nothing. The vocational rehabilitation of disabled persons (VRDP) arrangements and the new 1987 drug abuse expenditures are also in this category. At least half of the $4 billion in annual CAP payments (1984-85) and much of the $400 million in VRDP contributions go to support what we call health services, including home support services, homes for special care, rehabilitation programs and assessment and referral programs. In 1984 about 2,000,000 Canadians received income assistance under CAP and 500,000 received social services.
   b) Funds available only when there is an associated provincial government expenditure and when other conditions are met. Such arrangements are known as cost sharing. Hospital insurance and medicare were in this category from their inception to 1977. *The Hospital Insurance and Diagnostic Services Act* (HIDSA — Bill 360) was passed in 1957 and came into force on July 1, 1958. It required (i) that a minimum but broad range of hospital inpatient services be insured, with outpatient coverage being optional, (ii) that there be standardized national reporting, (iii) that services be available on equal terms and conditions and (iv) that basic standards be met. In return provinces received a per capita payment for each insured person. The

payment was a composite of 25% of national per capita costs plus 25% of provincial per capita costs. Through this formula high cost provinces received less than 50% of their program costs; the opposite held true for low cost provinces.

The medicare legislation which came into force in 1968 required public administration, coverage of a comprehensive range of physician services, coverage of at least 95% of the population (later raised to 100%), portability between provinces and reasonable compensation for physicians, all of which were principles put forward in the 1964 Hall Commission report. The financial formula was slightly different from that applied to hospital services and was once again designed to assure that poor provinces would be more generously assisted that the wealthier provinces.

3. The third device used by the federal government to help the provinces is the unconditional grant. These funds increase provincial revenue but have no strings attached.

   The *Hospital Insurance and Diagnostic Services Act* of 1957 and the *Medical Care Act* of 1966 are still seen as the vehicles through which universal health insurance was brought to Canada. They are, perhaps, our most famous pieces of health legislation but they are now largely historical documents. Federal-provincial fiscal arrangements in the two famous statutes were replaced in 1977 by the *Federal Provincial Fiscal Arrangements and Established Programs Financing Act*, (EPF), and by the *Canada Health Act* of 1984. These two acts spell out the terms and conditions prerequisite to receipt of federal financial assistance subsequent to 1977 and 1984 respectively.

The unconditional transfer of federal funds to the provinces is not new but under EPF these unconditional transfers were sharply increased. Actually, it can quite properly be argued that transfer payments under EPF are not unconditional because of the conditions stipulated in the *Canada Health Act* in particular; nevertheless the degree of federal control certainly decreased significantly in 1977. EPF terminated federal responsibility for a fixed portion of provincial expenditures for selected health services, and for practical purposes eliminated federal control over provincial medicare and hospitals. It also reduced federal financial risk. As compensation the provinces were given a per capita block grant, per capita payments tied to the gross national product, fourteen additional points of personal income tax, one additional point of corporate income tax, and full flexibility to financially support various health services to whatever extent they wished.

From 1977 to 1984 quite predictable sums were transferred from the federal government to the provincial treasuries with the provincial governments being, for practical purposes, able to spend these monies in any way they wished. The amounts transferred continued to rise but not as rapidly as they would have risen if the 1977 cost-sharing arrangement was still in place (Table 3.1).

TABLE 3.1
FEDERAL GOVERNMENT CONTRIBUTION TO PROVINCES IN LIEU OF FORMER COST-SHARING PAYMENTS FOR HEALTH SERVICES; 1977-78 TO 1983-84
(In $ millions)

Year	Contribution	% Increase Over Previous Year
1977-78	4,673	—
1978-79	5,345	14.4
1979-80	6,094	14.0
1980-81	6,814	11.8
1981-82	7,731	13.5
1982-83	8,512	10.1
1983-84*	9,354	9.9

*Provisional
Source: Adapted from *Preserving Universal Medicare*, Health and Welfare Canada, 1983, p. 29.

Thirty five years ago about two thirds of personal income tax points (revenue) came to the federal government. As part of the process of helping provinces, the federal government has regularly increased the provincial share.

The *Canada Health Act* (1984) once again required certain performance from the provinces if all promised federal funds (under EPF) were to be received. Requirements included coverage of 100% of the population and direct charges for insured services only under a limited number of circumstances. User fees and physician extra billing became tied to provincial penalties; the province lost one dollar of EPF payment for every dollar of user fees or extra billing.

Federal legislation can also significantly affect delivery of health care without any change in federal/provincial fiscal relations. For example, the 1971 bill legalizing abortion had a direct effect on hospital functions, medical staff organization, hospital board decisions, health care costs and the emotional and physical health of many women.

Health Services to Native Peoples

There are various interpretations of the statutes and treaties which establish federal responsibility for health care to the Indians and Inuit, and there is disagreement about the range of responsibility and who is entitled to care. However, a relatively unchallenged relationship, based on a combination of contract, precedent, legal decision and acceptance of obligation, exists between the native peoples and the federal government. This relationship includes an obligation for health and other social services, although the federal government continues to regularly seek devices through which native peoples can, at least for the purposes of health care, be seen as provincial residents. Provinces have varied in their willingness to accept natives as regular beneficiaries under provincial medical and hospital insurance, but in most provinces this administrative absorption has occurred.

For the last 30-40 years health services to native peoples have been financed through and often delivered by the Medical Services Branch (MSB) of the Department of National Health and Welfare. This branch maintains nursing stations, health stations, health centres, clinics and small hospitals. MSB also trains and employs indigenous health workers. MSB pays directly for care provided by health workers and institutions outside of the MSB network. The 1981 MSB beneficiaries included over 300,000 registered (status) Indians and about one fifth as many Inuit.

Services operated or funded by MSB include a wide range of preventive, diagnostic, treatment and educational programs in the fields of dentistry, medical care, public health and environmental health. Some programs such as the National Native Alcohol and Addictions Program (NNAAP) are operated by national and local native organizations, and there is currently a major push towards transfer to bands or native councils of administrative responsibility for health services. The transfer of function is being impeded by disagreement over the amount of money that will be available to the native authorities, by uncertainty regarding the role of provincial governments, by the lack of skills in some native communities and by the question of how much federal control will remain after transfer.

In several provinces medical schools contract to supply services to northern communities. For example, since 1969 the University of Manitoba has been responsible for maintaining medical services in Churchill, Norway House, Hodgson and a number of other smaller communities in northern Manitoba and in the Northwest Territories.

In summary, the federal government influences the health of Canadians through (a) health services within its jurisdiction, (b) healthy public policy in all areas of federal jurisdiction, and (c) pressure on the provinces to act in healthy rather than unhealthy ways in their areas of jurisdiction.

PROVINCIAL GOVERNMENTS

Each province can, almost to the extent it wishes, be directly responsible for all or any part of priority setting, policy selection, planning, financing, regulating, administration, resource allocation, evaluation, standard setting and delivery of any type of health service. These services include physicians services, dental services, ambulances, hospitals and public health. Provincial jurisdiction is quite absolute, subject only to rights enshrined in the *Charter of Rights* and other components of our constitution, and to the exclusion of the limited areas of federal jurisdiction. Each province theoretically could choose any of the macro-organizational models discussed earlier. To varying degrees the various provinces have chosen, by act or omission, to delegate certain managerial and delivery functions to quasi-governmental (special purpose), voluntary, professional or commercial entities, but all provincial governments now have also chosen to be directly active to at least some extent in most major aspects of health care.

All provinces, through one or more departments and statutes, take a direct interest in the standards and costs of most health care, with hospitals, physicians' services, public health, home care, long term care institutions and ambulances being most routinely under scrutiny and control. Drugs, dental services and the supply of health manpower receive varying attention. Some activities such as chiropractics and optometry receive funding but are otherwise largely ignored. In most of the smaller provinces most of the public health programs are administered by the provincial department of health or its equivalent. Psychiatric hospitals are also primarily provincially owned and operated. Provincial governments tend to require standardized reporting with respect to selected aspects of institutional or other operations and care delivery.

Health Insurance Programs

All provinces operate health insurance programs either from within a ministry, which is the commonest approach, or through some separate agency very closely linked to the minister of health. The public insurance agency always covers hospital services and physician services because public administration was a condition of federal financing, but it may also cover all or some drugs, ambulance services, long term care, dental services, prosthetics, glasses, home care, optometry and chiropractics.

Health care insurance operates within the same principles as any other insurance. It is a means whereby people replace unpredictable major expense by predictable regular expense. A beneficiary facing a risk makes regular payments to an insurer who agrees to meet the unpredictable costs if they materialize. Public health insurance differs somewhat in that it is usually compulsory and the beneficiary may make all payments through the tax system. When health care costs are paid out of general revenue the payments made by each person vary with their level of taxation rather than their level of risk.

Public insurance systems have major advantages for most taxpayers. Their administration costs are very low compared to those of private and competing insurance companies. Multiple carriers are inefficient and bring no benefits to users. Governments have excellent data which increases their ability to identify unreasonable billing patterns. Governments, as the only major paying agency, are in a better position to regulate payment amounts and patterns of practice by using negotiation as well as statutory powers. Because the programs have public service as their motive the user need not worry about losing insurance coverage if costs are high; the insurance will not be cancelled. There is a much reduced likelihood of major expenses falling to the user as was common with the exclusions, deductions and indemnity payments that were common in profit based plans. Because billing forms (claims forms) are standardized, physician payment is rapid as well as inexpensive, especially when the bill is submitted to the government directly from the provider rather than via the patient. With the abolition of extra billing the patient reimbursement mode of payment is now almost a thing of the past.

In 1934 the Canadian Medical Association asked the federal and provincial governments to institute general medical care insurance, and in a vague way repeated their support for such a proposal in 1943. By the 1950's, however, the CMA and provincial medical associations had changed their position and had become supporters of universal insurance administered by physicians rather than the government. They wished the government role to be restricted to paying all or part of the premiums of persons in financial need.

Provincial and federal governments affect health programs and institutions through many statutes and regulations other than those administered by the department of health. Laws and regulations governing such things as minimum wages, vacation pay, affirmative action, equal pay for work of equal value, the rights to and process of certification, collective bargaining and conflict resolution, payroll deductions, discrimination, collection of sales taxes, quality of construction, Workers Compensation Board (WCB) participation, invasion of privacy and public safety apply throughout the health services network unless all or parts of it are specifically exempted.

All provinces are more dominant in planning and financing health services (both capital and operational) than in administration or evaluation. Provinces usually standardize statistical, financial and other reporting and these provincial data are sometimes also nationally standardized, as with hospital data. All provinces define by statute the status and the self governing powers and responsibilities of the various professions; one such statute is the *Health Disciplines Act* in Ontario.

Provincial governments all have one or more departments directly related to health care organization, financing and delivery. Some provinces, like Ontario and Saskatchewan, have only a ministry of health which deals with all health services and little else. Other provinces such as Quebec and Manitoba have health and social services in one ministry. Other provinces have more than one department dealing with health, with one or more of these departments usually also responsible for all or part of social services. Departmental titles and functions regularly change. Within a ministry there can be more than one deputy minister, as was the case in Health and Welfare Canada in the 1970's.

There are, in almost all provinces, also a series of quasi-public bodies of varying importance. These bodies usually report to the minister or deputy minister and, occasionally, to the cabinet. They perform tasks which could be, and in other provinces often are, carried out from within a department of government.

The Quebec Model

The organization of health and social services in Quebec is sufficiently different from the rest of the country to merit separate attention (further comments are found in Chapter 8).

In the 1960's under Premier Lesage the quiet revolution converted the Quebec education system from a primarily parochial (religious) system to a system similar to that in other provinces. In the 1970's the quiet revolution was applied to the health and social services systems but the product was unlike the systems in other provinces.

In 1970 the second and enlarged version of the Castonguay-Nepveu Report was published and before the year ended Castonguay was Minister of Health. In the same year the Quebec Ministries of Health and of Welfare were combined to form the Ministry of Social Affairs (Ministère des Affaires Sociales, which was later renamed Ministère des Affaires Sociales et de la Santé). This 1970 amalgamation of Ministries was the first step towards implementation of the Castonguay-Nepveu Report.

In 1972 *Bill 65* reorganized and regionalized health and social services. It established a province wide network of twelve regional councils, later to become eleven, each with 21 members. Four of these members were to be elected by the mayors of the municipalities of the region, two would be named by the ministry as representatives of regional socioeconomic groups, three representatives would come from universities and community colleges (CEGEP's) and three would be from each of the four categories of institutions within each regional system.

The four categories of health and social service organizations into which most existing and future institutions would fit were the local community service centers (Centre Local des Services Communautaires — CLSC), the social service centers, the hospital centers and the reception centres (Centres d'Accueil), which include group homes and halfway houses (Figure 3.3).

Bill 65 described in detail the composition of the boards of the four categories of institutions and in each case the boards included one or more representatives of neighboring institutions, the regional council, the professional staff, the other staff and the public. The public representatives are elected at an annual meeting. The spirit of the Castonguay-Nepveu Report, which had recommended a high degree of local participation and of regional control, was not fully evident. *Bill 65* opted for a minority role for unaffiliated local representatives on all boards and gave regional councils very little power. The government clearly believed, probably correctly, that a radical redistribution of function and the introduction of new structures would be more likely to succeed if there was a strong central hand at the helm.

Among the hospitals within each region there was and is one or more 'designated' hospital centre or centres which, through their departments of community health (Départements de santé communautaire — DSC), were given responsibility for epidemiological studies and planning. These functions in other provinces usually rest with the public health departments. There is no separate public health agency in the Quebec system, the functions having been merged with other functions and carried out primarily by the DSC in designated hospitals and by the CLSCs. Some functions, such as those of public health inspectors, were transferred completely out of the health agencies and into such departments as environment, agriculture and fisheries and food, or to agencies dealing with such things as work safety.

FIGURE 3.3
THE ORGANIZATION OF HEALTH AND SOCIAL SERVICES IN QUEBEC

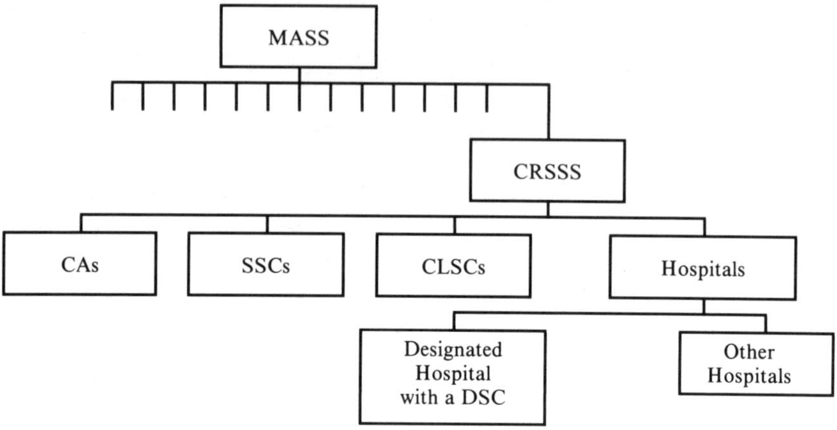

MASS — Ministry of Social Affairs and Health
CRSSS — Regional Health and Social Services Council
CA — Reception Centers (Centre d'Acceuil)
SSC — Social Service Centre
CLSC — Local Community Health Centre
DSC — Department of Community Health

The Quebec system is a network of population based facilities and programs, each with a specific population for which they are responsible and to which they are at least somewhat accountable. Each institution and program has a responsibility to offer a specified range of services to its specified population. The situation is analogous to a police force, an Ontario public health unit or a school with a designated service area, and is quite different from the usual hospital or grocery store which provide services to those who come in rather than having a mandate to serve a specified population. The boundaries do not restrict client access to other physicians and hospitals but they do give the institutions an obligation to be available to the population in their area.

Quebec created a network of agencies responsible for social services and for primary, secondary and tertiary health care, for home care, public health, emergency care, health planning, health promotion, long term care and episodic care, for physical health and emotional health. In the Castonguay concept the regional network measured local needs, set local priorities and delivered a broad range of services to the extent possible given the resources available. Unfortunately, the private practitioners were sufficiently entrenched and powerful to resist merging and, therefore, the integrated network is incomplete.

The merging of mental health with other services was not immediate but is quite fully accomplished now.

Other provinces have implemented, in a less comprehensive way, similar integrated regional systems. Many parts of rural Manitoba are served by LTC facilities, public health services, home care services and community hospitals all under one board. Alberta has a small number of rural communities, High Level is one example, with a similar arrangement. Quebec, however, is unique in its province wide plan and the breadth of the health and social services integration.

The current role of the federal and provincial governments has been determined by tradition (and our provinces do not all have the same traditions), by law (in particular the *BNA Act* and its successors), by experience (for example the failure of the private sector to deliver health care to the high risk part of the population), by the imbalance between provincial responsibilities and financing capabilities, and by public demand. There is no typical provincial or municipal role. Role varies with political philosophy and with culture, with population characteristics, with economic capacity and other factors.

MUNICIPAL GOVERNMENTS

Municipalities are the creatures of provinces. Their roles in health care can, therefore, be defined by and constrained by provincial decisions. Most provinces have not assigned major health care functions to municipalities but municipalities have contributed to the Canadian pattern of publicly rather than privately controlled health care. Many western municipalities had municipally based doctor and hospital plans in the early part of the century and many major urban municipalities in Canada have always directly administered public health services through a public health department. This organizational pattern may become more common. In Ontario several large municipalities including Halton, Toronto and Ottawa have, in the last decade, taken over public health functions that were formerly under the control of a separate public health board.

Total municipal expenditures in Canada in 1986 were about $45 billion, of which up to 15% in any single municipality was for health and social services, but mostly for social services. The amounts, and the emphasis on health and on social services, vary greatly from province to province and municipality to municipality.

Prior to universal hospital insurance many municipalities regularly contributed to the operating and capital costs of hospitals. Contributions to operating costs largely ceased in 1958, but municipal contributions to capital costs continued in some provinces and this practice is currently expanding. Toronto City Council in 1987 voted $3 million a year for health services and earmarked all of it for hospital capital costs.

QUASI-PUBLIC (QUASI-GOVERNMENTAL) AGENCIES (also sometimes called Special Purpose Bodies or Crown Corporations)

Quasi-public agencies are created by governments of all levels to perform some specific regulatory, educational, policy making, evaluative or managerial function that government prefers not to do itself. The function is moved outside of the government bureaucracy although usually not fully beyond government influence. Quasi-public agencies are usually created by statute although some, such as the District Health Councils in Ontario, are created by Order in Council. Most have executive functions but others, such as the Ontario Council of Health, are only advisory.

Moving functions out of government is often said to be a good thing because it removes political influence, the implication being that political influence is a bad thing. Not only is politics usually still at work, but there is also often a reduction of accountability to the public or to users and an increased insensitivity to outside concerns. The proposition that separation from government will reduce bureaucratic characteristics is seldom born out, while coordination is apt to be more difficult.

There is, in organizational terms, only an invisible line between quasi-public agencies or special purpose bodies, and voluntary agencies. These two categories are best thought of as a spectrum rather than two distinct organizational forms. The spectrum extends from very close ties to government to complete separation from government, from ability to generate all revenue to having no revenue generating capability at all, from a high degree of public accountability to very little, from a high degree of public visibility and openness to being extremely insular and secretive, from having an open ended spending ability to being on a very constrained budget, and from being fully dependent on government financing to receiving no money from government.

A number of quasi-governmental agencies that once had major operating responsibilities have been abandoned, two examples are the Ontario Hospital Services Commission and the Saskatchewan Medical Care Insurance Commission. Others remain, including the Manitoba Health Services Commission and the Quebec Health Insurance Board (La Régie). Many governments and electorates see these special purpose bodies as an inappropriate transfer of public policy and administration functions to the control of non-elected persons.

Some agencies such as The Addictions Research Foundation in Ontario have only advisory or educational functions. Councils of this type have a history of self-imollation; they tend to eventually become sufficiently critical of government to be disbanded or lose funding. They function best, and survive longest, when their area of advice is clearly defined (often technical), their mandate is clearly stated and their mandate is primarily education or research. Prior to appointment to the boards of these agencies, nominees should be clear as to the agenda they are expected to deal with, the level of governmental contact available to them (the minister, the deputy-minister, other staff, the cabinet), the resources that will be available (for instance, can special studies be done), and the expected schedule of meetings and payment. Members can then know whether the agency is likely to exert the kind of influence that is consistent with their wishes.

Provincial Colleges of Physicians and Surgeons and equivalent other professional organizations are also quasi-governmental agencies. They are created by statute to perform functions which are delegated to them by the province including the licensing, regulation and discipline of their members. They are funded by fees paid by their members.

THE PRIVATE NONPROFIT SECTOR

Boards of the private nonprofit agencies may be elected or appointed. They usually manage a corporate entity and are responsible for planning and/or operational decisions for a hospital or CHC. They are legally independent although often considerably controlled by government regulation or financing arrangements as well as being less formally constrained by precedent, public perception and social values. These boards operate agencies that usually provide either health services or health and other social services. Examples include Alcoholics Anonymous, community health centres, group homes, long term care placement agencies, Childrens Aid Societies, senior citizen centres, and halfway houses. A small number, such as Social Planning Councils, exist primarily or exclusively to plan. Hospital boards are similar to other independent boards in many ways but operate under an unusually high degree of ministerial control.

Private nonprofit agencies or facilities can be quite parochial and, therefore, are less easily fitted into an overall regional or community plan. On the positive side they may be able to mobilize local support in the form of volunteers and money. Efficiency is seldom measured. Quality is also seldom evaluated except by means of the hospital accreditation process.

Workers Compensation Boards (WCB) are health related agencies that fit poorly into any of the listed categories. They have their own statute but a minister is usually politically responsible for their activities. They exist to provide aid to workers suffering from work related injuries or diseases or their sequelae. They were created in the early part of the twentieth century to protect employers from the hazard of being sued by workers who were injured on the job. They have a history of being technocratic, bureaucratic and autocratic although they have, over the years, become somewhat more worker oriented. Workers have, until recently, been unable to sue for damages arising from negligence at the workplace but they are eligible for long term care and income support even if the negligence is theirs. Recent senior court decisions giving workers or their families the right to sue employers may bring about major changes in the entire WCB operation.

A WCB is a big business — for example it spends about $150 per capita per year in Ontario. These costs are financed entirely by employers who pay a percentage of payroll varying from 1-20% depending on the accident experience of each category of employer. There may or may not be experience rating of individual employers, that is, rates may or may not be higher for employers with a bad safety record. One quarter to one third of WCB expenditures are for health care.

Voluntary agencies are nonprofit and nongovernmental. They range from quite organizationally complex (the Canadian Red Cross) to very simple (an unincorporated self help group). They can be small and local (Meals on Wheels) or large and national (Canadian Cancer Society, Victorian Order of Nurses). They may be largely publicly funded (Canadian Red Cross) or receive no public funding (Alcoholics Anonymous). Their function may be primarily or entirely education and research (Canadian Heart Foundation), service delivery (group home) or political action (anti and pro-abortion groups or the Canadian Health Coalition). They are often concerned with a specific disease or condition such as cancer, heart, mental health, muscular dystrophy, paraplegia, arthritis or hemophilia. They may be clearly identified with health services or may have health matters as only one part of a broader mandate (the Canadian Labor Congress and the National Anti-Poverty Association). This vast network of nonprofit agencies is important and powerful in the Canadian health services mosaic.

Charitable institutions were operating hospitals and institutions for the disabled and the dying hundreds of years ago and their example is perpetuated in religious and voluntary institutions and programs. Before national compulsory hospital or medical care insurance was introduced the hospital associations and the physician organizations were the largest carriers of hospital and medical care insurance respectively. They were, in a competitive market, quite easily able to offer more attractive insurance than the for-profit sector.

Nongovernmental boards and agencies organized at the federal or provincial level are likely to have separately incorporated regional or local chapters. These local or regional chapters usually have some degree of management autonomy but also have close structural ties with the central body (Victorian Order of Nurses, Canadian Red Cross, Planned Parenthood).

Public policy has altered the nature and role of several national voluntary agencies. Publicly operated home care programs altered the role of the Victorian Order of Nurses (VON), of previously existing cancer treatment programs and of the Arthritis Society, for example. Further conflicts and changes are likely to emerge. Changing disease patterns have produced changes in some diagnostically specific agencies; the Anti-Tuberculosis League, for instance, became the Canadian Lung Association. The emergence of the consumer age with a reduction of acceptance of paternalistic programming altered the power balance in the Canadian National Institute for the Blind (CNIB).

The policy and management roles typical of the voluntary (private nonprofit) sector often reflect history and values more than anything else. Choices are apt to be made on the basis of the way governments or communities feel about smallness versus bigness, uniqueness versus standardization, profit versus non-profit, consumer versus provider control, centralization versus decentralization or government versus the private sector. One thing seems certain; these agencies are here to stay.

THE PRIVATE-FOR-PROFIT SECTOR

In Canada the private-for-profit sector has been much less dominant than in the United States. It has played a particularly small role in hospitals and health insurance. This restricted role is much more a product of experience and of culture than of political ideology. Even before the appearance of government sponsored universal insurance most insured Canadians used a not-for-profit carrier.

The for-profit sector, however, remains active in our health services network, and the subject of the extent to which its role should be expanded — that is, the extent to which health care should be privatized — is under active examination. Its involvement is usually in one or more of the following ways:

1) As an outsider who has a contract with a specific institution or program to provide a specified service:
   a) Advice. This is the role played by most consultants.
   b) Management. A for-profit firm may be hired to manage a total institution or program, or any part of it. When management of a total institution is contracted out it may be combined with an infusion of private capital, as in Hawkesbury, Ontario and Wetaskiwin, Alberta, although there may be no financing associated with the management contract as was the case with the Extendicare contract to manage the hospital in Athabaska, Alberta. The contracting out of the management function has received far more attention than it deserves. It is merely a variation of a widely accepted concept.
   c) Hotel services such as housekeeping, laundry, dietary and parking.
   d) Administrative services such as payroll management, occupational health and fund raising.
   e) Clinical (patient care) services. A small number of community agencies buy nursing and other care from for-profit sources. In theory, a hospital or other health care agency could contract out its laboratory, pharmacy and radiology department, and probably others.

   This contracting out is often cheaper but, unfortunately, the savings are almost, if not entirely, made at the expense of poorly paid non-union and often part-time workers who replace full-time workers earning decent wages.
2) As owners and operators of sources of health care such as nursing homes, ambulances, special hospitals, pharmacies, agencies providing services in the home, laboratories and the manufacturers and fitters of orthotic or prosthetic devices.
3) As a banker. The provision of capital is, as has been noted, sometimes tied to an ongoing management role. In other cases payback is based on a share of revenue rather than an interest rate. An example is the construction by Extendicare of LTC beds at the Queensway General Hospital in Toronto.

   When the private sector provides capital for hospital construction there is weakening of one of the provincial government devices for control of institutional costs. The government is less able to control the timing of the construction.

4) As partners with nonprofit agencies in some other mutually advantageous arrangement such as the agreement between University Hospital, London, Ontario and Hospital Corporation of America (HCA). In this agreement the hospital gains access to the purchasing power of HCA and HCA gains preferential access to the hospital for care for selected patients. (Patient care costs in Canada are significantly lower than in the United States and HCA saves money by having some of its patients come to the London hospital for elective care.) In 1986 the Toronto General Hospital entered into a similar, mutually advantageous arrangement when Travenol Canada financed a $750,000 intravenous drug administration centre within the hospital in return for a fee-for-service contract to deliver the 300,000 intravenous drug doses which in 1985 cost $4.5 million.

There is, within the chronic care system, one recent transfer of function from the nonprofit or governmental sector to the private sector which has gone relatively unnoticed but which would have major impact if extended. Institutionalization was, until a few years ago, the standard solution when the level or complexity of care required by any individual exceeded what was available from household members or home care programs. This is still the practice for the disabled elderly but younger severely physically disabled persons, such as quadriplegics, now routinely live in their own residential units and receive 24 hour services from staff who are somewhere nearby. The health and social support services are publicly funded but the disabled persons are tenants with leases who obtain their housing through the same arrangements as the rest of us. This housing would, a few years ago, have been part of a long term care institution but may now be provided by the private sector. (See Chapter 14)

The extent to which health services should be provided by the for-profit sector is uncertain. Profit is most clearly a hazard when competition that is useful to the consumer is absent, when quality is very difficult to measure or when caseloads or service mix can be manipulated to avoid unattractive components, which must then be borne by non-profit providers. Profit is most defensible when competition exists that is useful to the consumer and when product specifications can be clearly written.

Health services buy large quantities of supplies and services from the private sector (food, equipment, linen) but this is not usually referred to as the privatization of health services.

Whether or not private practitioners (dentists, physicians, chiropractors) should be included in this listing of for-profit sources of health care is a matter of opinion but in this chapter they are not included. The most distinguishing characteristic of the profit sector is the concept of return on investment. Fee-for-service practitioners are distinguished from other workers by their method of payment but it is inappropriate and sometimes unnecessarily provocative to consider their offices to be equivalent to places of business.

PROVIDER ORGANIZATIONS

Major health worker groups (nurses, physicians, physiotherapists, laboratory technicians), some facility types (hospitals) and most major service areas (mental health, public health) have national, provincial and often regional or local organizations. The most important of these organizations are at the provincial level because health is a provincial matter. Provincial professional associations are of two types — those which perform licensing/certification and regulatory duties as assigned by statute, and those which perform trade union functions. Not all professions are represented by both types of organizations. Provincial institutions and programs are in some provinces served by a single umbrella association, usually called a health association. In other provinces the various associations such as the hospital association and the public health association remain separate.

Provincial institutional associations can be active in many ways. The Ontario Hospital Association, for example, offers Ontario Blue Cross (a non-profit $200 million a year supplementary insurance program covering 60% of Ontarians), a liability insurance program operational since 1987 in response to the 1985-86 crisis in premiums and availability, a provincial hospital computer service, a hospital purchasing program, a variety of personnel insurance programs, a hospital occupational health and safety service (funded by WCB), support for multi-institutional province wide collective bargaining and a large menu of educational and advisory services. Regional organizations like the Hospital Council of Metropolitan Toronto (HCMT) may offer similar services. The HCMT operates, or has initiated, a consulting service, group purchasing, a drug information service, two laundry services, an instructional media service, a nursing registry, a specialty food shop, a high technology maintenance program and a research support service.

The Ontario College of Physicians and Surgeons has, for almost a decade, conducted a peer review program in which physicians are visited by a review team. This ambitious program has statutory backing; participation is not voluntary. The College in British Columbia is contemplating a similar review but only of physicians without hospital privileges.

Some provider organizations are quite ideological, including antinuclear war groups (Physicians for Social Responsibility (PSR), International Physicians for Prevention of Nuclear War (IPPNW), or Nurses for Peace), Medical Reform Groups (left wing) and the Committee of Independent Physicians (right wing).

Although provincial provider organizations have the broadest range of functions there are a number of important national organizations. Almost all physicians, for example, buy their medical malpractice insurance through a physician operated nonprofit insurance company, the Canadian Medical Protective Association (CMPA). The CMPA has always been dominant in Canada but in 1986 physician enrollment increased rapidly, to 48,591, due primarily to a withdrawal of private insurance from this market. In 1986 the CMPA paid out over 17 million dollars to settle 155 claims and paid out over eleven million dollars in legal fees related to approximately 900 lawsuits and a somewhat larger number of inquiries.

In recent years the CMPA has moved to variable fees. Prior to that all types of doctors paid the same fee. The high risk groups of physicians (obstetricians, anaesthetists, neurosurgeons, orthopedic surgeons and cardiovascular surgeons) paid a 1987 premium of $8,250 (in 1984 it was $1,950). General practitioners who also see obstetrical patients paid $1,675 in 1987 (up from $900 in 1984). Many provinces have made special payments to physicians to cover the higher insurance costs.

Provincial Medical Associations play quite variable roles in the claims review procedures of the provincial insurance plans.

Most professional and institutional organizations have a code of ethics or conduct. This code is voluntary in such organizations as hospital or hospital administrator associations and is mostly window dressing, but the codes can be of importance in those self-governing professions who have been assigned responsibility for public protection. The vigor with which professions enforce their ethical codes through member discipline varies from absent to moderate. Physician organizations now probably perform best (after years of concentrating on advertising practices and whether members talked to chiropractors) with the degree of professional rigor seeming to be at least somewhat related to the degree of governmental and public scrutiny. Professions about which few questions are asked such as chiropractors and optometrists appear to be quite internally unregulated. Some physician organizations now have active and expensive programs to detect and respond to drug and alcohol abuse, public complaints, aberrant billing, unusual practice habits and the quality of office records and equipment. Some professional organizations such as the Canadian College of Health Service Executives and the College of Family Physicians of Canada require evidence of involvement in continuing education if there is to be continued membership. The latter organization is also currently developing a software package for evaluation of a physician's practice, and this evaluation may become part of the recertification process.

Professional organizations regularly conduct educational/lobbying activities. In 1985 the British Columbia Medical Association launched a 3 year $2 million project including a 26 week TV series on health services and the physicians' role in them. Chiropractors have for years conducted back clinics in schools and elsewhere.

Governments, at least in principle, seek professional regulatory arrangements that protect the public by enforcement of professional standards and by describing the scope of activities that are within the competence of different professionals. The regulatory arrangements often assign responsibilities to the professionals themselves; in Ontario there are currently 18 self governing health professions and that number may soon rise to 25. The public interest would seem to be best protected by professions that work co-operatively with other professions and that encourage cost control as well as good patient care. Unfortunately, independent professions more frequently oppose co-operation and vigorously defend their turf even when tasks would be better and/or more cheaply performed by other workers.

COMMUNITIES AND CONSUMERS

The consumer age has changed health services. Consumers increasingly believe the health services network exists to work for them, and the services have been obliged to be more responsive, less paternalistic (or maternalistic) and more sensitive. Changes have occurred in patients' rights statements and legislation, in obtaining access to records, and in the composition and roles of boards of trustees. Through influence on public policy, consumers could, if they chose, limit resource availability and utilization, control professional supply and function, determine rates of pay, and directly influence if not control a broad range of professional decisions.

Consumers have always been able to complain to caregivers, institutions, the police, the media or anyone else, but they historically seldom complained and were seldom listened to if they did. Complaints now are not only more apt to receive attention but they are being delivered in more ways. Patient satisfaction surveys and questionnaires are routine and institutional ombudsmen are increasingly available to help identify patient problems or abuse and to implement acceptable response. Self-help or advocacy groups are now common, insurance is usually obtained through a public agency, which may be more apt to investigate and react to a consumer complaint, legislation and court decisions have spelled out the rights of patients to information and choice, and professional complaints committees and higher appeal mechanisms have public members. The existence of these devices encourages institutions and individual caregivers to be aware of the wishes, preferences and values of patients. Boards, discipline committees, payment agencies and courts now routinely decide whether professional or institutional service and conduct is adequate or merits discipline.

The rise in public participation and influence can be endorsed as a means of strengthening democracy through the production of a more informed and less cynical population and because the process identifies indigenous leaders. It also can counter-balance the power of professionals and bureaucrats and more decisively insert the priorities of users and payers into the decision making process. However, despite all of the above changes and optimistic verbiage, the professionals still often manage to ignore, intimidate or co-opt the consumer process.

CAREGIVERS AS ADMINISTRATORS/PLANNERS

The primary role of caregivers is obviously to give care, but while continuing in this function they also have a role in the planning, administration and evaluation of health care services. Many caregivers become department heads, committee members and advisors to management while continuing to personally provide care, and there is uncertainty as to the training that is most appropriate for these management roles and whether to, or how to, pay for this work.

In 1984 Quebec made it mandatory that practicing physicians be represented in hospital management and payment for selected medical administrative tasks became routine. Sunnybrook Hospital in Toronto has adopted a decentralized administration in which clinicians become directly responsible for departmental global budgets. Other professionals (nurses, physiotherapists) have routinely been represented in planning and administration by their senior salaried members, although when a professional becomes predominantly an administrator with little or no involvement in direct patient care that individual should be seen as (and should see himself or herself as) an administrator rather than as a caregiver.

The training of practicing health care professionals, especially physicians, for administrative participation is receiving increasing attention because of the impact of physician decisions on costs and client outcomes. The Canadian Medical Association and the Canadian College of Health Service Executives co-sponsor a travelling modular executive training program (1-2 weeks) for physicians. The Program in Health Administration at the University of Montreal also offers such courses, as do some provincial hospital and health associations. Physicians and other senior health executives may also participate in continuing education at the Banff School of Management.

Throughout this chapter the focus has been on the organization of Canadian health services. One significant fact should be remembered: health care is under provincial jurisdiction. This jurisdiction includes resource allocation, the management of health professions, and the ability to influence provider organizations. The next four chapters will discuss the resources, costs, quality and dynamics within the provincial health systems.

Chapter 4

RESOURCES

Resources will be discussed only under the two general headings of human resources and physical resources. These two plus information combine to produce health care. Money is only a tool useful for buying these resources.

HUMAN RESOURCES

Human resources will be looked at in terms of numbers (manpower), education and research, each of which influence the knowledge and skills that produce health care. The required knowledge covers a broad spectrum of clinical, social, epidemiological, demographic, economic, cultural, administrative, and environmental information. The required skills are technical and behavioral and include human relations, communications, prevention, diagnosis, patient care, rehabilitation, education, research, management, planning, community development, decision-making, problem solving, social marketing, program evaluation, risk analysis and priority setting. Knowledge is important because our level of knowledge has a significant impact on what we do and cannot do, although there is ample evidence that what is done by practitioners and by users/consumers is often not consistent with the knowledge that exists. Skills allow knowledge to have effect. Both knowledge and skills tend to be implemented through human resources.

Manpower

Health workers represent 6-8% of our labour force. In Ontario alone over 200,000 people work in the health sector. Of these, about 75% work in hospitals.

The supply of manpower is often expressed as a population to worker ratio, a ratio which is seldom precise. It varies with the extent to which one includes part-time workers, unemployed workers, retired workers, persons qualified but not licenced or registered and persons filling positions for which they are not fully qualified. Figures vary markedly if one counts available versus employed or active workers. For example, 15 to 30% of nurses, are, at any given time, either not working in nursing or are only partially employed in nursing. Similarly, in 1986 a federal-provincial committee identified 21,000 family physicians in Canada; a report by the College of Family Physicians of Canada (CFPC) in the same year claimed the proper figure was between 15,000 and 16,000. The disparity is almost surely due to different definitions of 'family physician', with the Committee counting all physicians not certified as specialists and the CFPC counting only physicians actually engaged in family practice.

Tables 4.1 and 4.2 document the supply and the trends in that supply of many types of health workers. Most worker groups have been growing a great deal faster than the total population, and for most health care occupations this trend is continuing. Physician supply, for example, expanded rapidly in 1985 and 1986 despite an awareness since the middle 1970's that Canada has too many physicians. In 1985 over 1400 new physicians were registered in Ontario for a net gain of over 1000 and a 6% increase in physician supply, and in 1986 the net gain was almost as large. Medical school enrollment in Canada doubled between 1965 and 1983-4 to over 1800 entering each year.

Some supply changes are difficult to understand. With total births down 40% from 1968 to 1980 the supply of pediatricians climbed from 3.35% of all physicians to 3.63%.

Another factor contributing to oversupply has been an influx of foreign medical graduates (FMGs). Prior to about 1974 physicians were among the highly favored immigrants. In the 1960's and early 1970's the number of foreign medical graduates licenced in Canada was approximately equal to the number

TABLE 4.1
POPULATION PER HEALTH WORKER BY TYPE OF WORKER, 1971-76-81

	1971	1976	1981
Audiologists/Speech Therapists	....	22,134	15,002
Medical & Biological Engineers	....	110,884	77,528
Chiropractors	20,176	16,274	11,666
Dental Nurses & Assistants	14,264	7,915	11,295
Dental Hygienists	25,571	11,970	5,941
Dentists	2,913	2,465	2,133
Dieticians	12,673	8,732	5,846
Electroencephalograph Tech.	....	70,015	75,614
Health Record Administrators	15,540	11,277	10,712
Health Service Executives	....	19,345	14,812
Medical Laboratory Tech.	2,128	1,146	1,314
Medical Radiation Tech.	4,692	2,893	2,536
Nurses, Registered	149	129	119
Nursing Assistants, Licensed	446	323	277
Occupational Therapists	20,937	15,399	13,228
Opticians	16,075*	10,063	8,987
Optometrists	13,784	12,334	11,016
Orderlies (in hospitals)	1,897*	1,555	1,403
Pharmacists	1,916	1,578	1,438
Physicians	659	577	538
Physiotherapists	7,515	4,623	4,304
Podiatrists	176,501	154,499	94,590
Public Health Inspectors	29,348*	28,717	25,414
Respiratory Technologists	46,587	17,704	12,700
Social Workers	4,608*	4,533	3,532

a. The population of Canada for the years selected was: 1971, 21,709,600, 1976, 23,174,800, 1981, 24,498,900.
b. The * symbol indicates that 1971 data were not available and that either 1973 or 1974 data were used.

Source: *Canada Health Manpower Inventory* (1982). These data were extracted from all 25 sections of the inventory.

TABLE 4.2
NUMBER OF HEALTH PERSONNEL IN CANADA BY TYPE OF WORKER
1971-76-81

	1971	1976	1981
Audiologists/Speech Therapists	....	1,047	1,633
Medical & Biological Engineers	....	209	316
Chiropractors	1,076	1,424	2,100
Dental Nurses & Assistants	1,522	2,928	2,169
Dental Hygenists	849	1,936	4,124
Dentists	7,453	9,401	11,484
Dieticians	1,713	2,654	4,191
Electroencephalograph Tech.	....	331	324
Health Record Administrators	1,397	2,055	2,287
Health Service Executives	....	1,198	1,654
Medical Laboratory Tech.	10,202	16,368	18,649
Medical Radiation Tech.	4,627	8,012	9,660
Nurses, Registered	145,683	179,567	206,184
Nursing Assistants, Licensed	48,716	71,641	88,344
Occupational Therapists	1,062	1,505	1,852
Opticians	1,404*	2,303	2,726
Optometrists	1,575	1,879	2,224
Orderlies (in hospitals)	11,447	14,901	17,456
Pharmacists	11,330	14,687	17,039
Physicians	32,942	40,130	45,542
Physiotherapists	2,287	3,591	4,453
Podiatrists	123	150	259
Public Health Inspectors	769*	807	964
Respiratory Technologists	466	1,309	1,929
Social Workers	4,966*	5,112	6,936

Source: *Canada Health Manpower Inventory* (1982), data extracted from all classifications.

of MDs produced by Canadian medical schools — about 900 of each per year. Due to federal-provincial discussions, immigration procedures were changed in early 1975 and the number of FMGs entering Canada was reduced by 75-80%. Those who did manage to enter the country, however, continued to have a reasonably good chance of eventually practicing medicine here.

In the 1980's the number of physician immigrants again increased and the number of FMGs who became licenced also increased despite the administration of a general qualifying exam and then the insistence upon one or more years of mandatory internship. This trend may once again now be downward. In 1987 only 20 out of 453 FMGs who sought internships or residency placements through the Canadian Intern Matching Service were given positions. Some provinces have restricted the number of provincially funded internship positions that can be filled by FMGs, and hospitals in some provinces are not allowed to offer unfunded residencies as they did in the past. The extent to which FMGs are offered internships in provinces in which they have traditionally been the major source of rural doctors will largely determine how many of them will be licenced in Canada in future.

If one interprets these data to suggest an oversupply of doctors, and almost everyone now believes this is the case, then control is indicated. It is not in the interest of medical schools to reduce intake, and one cannot reasonably expect tertiary care physicians voluntarily to support the reduction of the numbers of interns and residents. These 'house staff' are important sources of in-hospital professional labor. The problems posed by doctor oversupply must, therefore, be addressed by a government initiated reduction in enrollment in our medical schools and a reduced rate of licensure of foreign medical graduates.

In recent years there has been some response to the physician oversupply. Québec and Manitoba have, for several years, reduced first year medical school enrollment, and the number of annual medical school entrants in Canada had, by 1987, dropped about 4% below the peak year of 1983-84.

History, power, disinterest, technology, scarcity, economics, politics, and geography have helped to determine our present mix of health workers. Florence Nightingale created the generalist nurse that we are still graduating from nursing schools today. Nurse anesthetists established their competence fifty years ago but they could not survive in Canada in the face of the organized and male power of physicians who wished to control the discipline; to date midwives have been excluded from medical practice, through the same process. Respiratory Technologists appeared for uncertain reasons; nurses could have absorbed this new component of patient care if they had been interested or the cylinders of gas had been lighter or there had been more male nurses. Our need to provide care to small isolated northern settlements led to the special training of nurses; in the south, however, the physicians again exercised their power and relegated the nurse practitioner to limited functions in even more limited locations. In Saskatchewan economics led to the creation of a childrens' dental program dependent on the dental therapist; politics in a later era gave the program back to the more expensive, but more politically favored, privately practicing dentist. A scarcity of trained laboratory technologists at the time of the introduction of mass cervical screening (Pap smears) led to the use of job specific technicians to do the work. Yet, despite a similar shortage of physiotherapists and the proven adequacy of physiotherapy aides we have very few aide training programs because physiotherapists do not approve.

New worker groups continue to be recognized. The next arrivals may be midwives and osteopaths. Existing workers such as ambulance attendants and clinical nurse specialists are expanding their areas of competence and activity. Unspecialized dentists are moving rapidly into orthodontics and oral surgery.

There has been a rather random pattern in the appearance of new kinds of professional or semiprofessional health workers who work in association with physicians or dentists. Orthopedic technicians who repair or apply casts were welcomed by the interns and surgeons who previously put on the casts. Dental hygienists are routinely employed to perform examinations and preventive functions formerly performed by dentists. However, at the same time, physicians are objecting to the appearance of midwives, and dentists have opposed expanded roles and freedoms for denturists. The mixture of acceptances and rejection is a practical one that should surprise no one. New workers, or new roles for existing workers, are usually welcomed if they will reduce physician/dentist work without loss of physician/dentist fee-for-service income; if there is a threat to income the new workers or new roles tend to be opposed.

The question of the future role of the registered nursing assistant (RNA) is a matter of importance. Nursing associations have proposed that no one but a registered nurse (RN) should provide direct nursing care, a proposal with conceptual, economic and social consequences. Conceptually, we should defend the idea of high volume work being done, when possible, by the least skilled person who can do it adequately, and we should promote the idea of assigning skilled persons to the level of work for which they are prepared. Financially, we should want to keep the lower cost RNA, and socially we should resist changes which reduce the employment opportunities for semi-skilled, often middle-aged and usually female workers. This battle is far from over although some active treatment hospitals have already reduced their employment of RNAs.

The male-female mix of health care workers is also changing. Canadian health administration schools have many more female than male graduates and females are approaching or have reached parity in many medical schools. (They represented 60% of incoming McMaster students in 1983).

This dynamism in the health manpower field is not new. Decades ago nurses began to expand their areas of competence, cervical cytology technicians appeared to handle the large volume of specimens generated by Pap smear programs and physician specialists appeared in response to the explosion of clinical and technical knowledge and capability. There is nothing to suggest that the same rate of change will not continue.

Decisions about manpower requiremens tend to have been made either on the basis of population/worker ratios which were usually created on the back of an envelope, or by universities guided primarily by professor or university self-interest. Two other much better methods are available and are occasionally used:

(a) Estimation of the volume of services required. This method involves finding out the usual worker productivity in the situations under consideration and then calculating manpower needs.

(b) Estimation of caseloads. This method involves categorizing caseloads by volume of service required, estimating the caseload that a worker can handle, and then estimating manpower needs.

When faced with new tasks to be done, or greater volumes of an old task, one may expand the supply of existing kinds of workers, give existing workers new training, or create a new kind of health worker. One's choice will depend on many factors including public acceptance, political feasibility, whether new statutes will be needed, the power of those who will object to new workers or changes in functions, the availability (supply) of existing workers and the costs inherent in the options.

Education of Health Workers

Health-worker training in Canada is usually partly academic and partly practical. The academic portion leading to a degree or diploma is usually provided by an educational center which is within the jurisdiction of a department of education. The academic program usually includes practical training as well as academic material but the academic experience is also commonly supplemented by a quite separate and often mandatory period of apprenticeship after graduation. Within these general specifications there is considerable variation.

A registered nurse (RN), for instance, may be a graduate of a 2 or 3 year community college program or a 3 or 4 year baccalaureate program but no post-diploma or post-baccalaureate apprenticeship is required for professional licensure. Nurses with baccalaureate nursing degrees represented 6% of all nurses in 1971 and 9% in 1981. During the baccalaureate program the student may usually, at her or his choice, concentrate on one field of nursing such as public health, psychiatry, pediatrics or geriatrics. Besides the academic exam, the graduate nurse may need to pass a provincial exam to be eligible for provincial licensure or certification.

The one year postgraduate certificate programs which were formerly common in public health nursing and psychiatric nursing, for instance, have now been largely abandoned due to increased attention to these nursing fields within the academic RN programs. (Prior to the 1960's, nursing education was usually based in a general hospital where psychiatric and public health nursing experience were often not available.) There is, unfortunately, considerable evidence that the new graduate nurse is not adequately prepared for many of the tasks that will be assigned, including work in the operating room, the emergency room and the intensive care units. This is a significant problem considering the fact that 80% of all nurses are employed in hospitals and that there are only a few large scale post RN programs offering specialized clinical training.

The great majority of new nurses continue to be graduates of non-baccalaureate programs, but the Canadian Nurses Association (CNA), with the support of provincial nursing associations, has announced its wish that all nurses should, by the year 2000, be graduates of a baccalaureate program. This objective, which seems reasonable in light of the stature of nurses and the responsability given to them, can be met as long as there is (a) early planning for a massive expansion of university nursing faculties and other resources and (b) acceptance of the need to lower the current admission standards of university nursing programs. Most of the necessary faculty should be available in the existing community college programs, but faculty with the academic credentials usually required will be in short supply.

There appear to be no insurmountable financial, cultural, conceptual or logistic problems associated with the change to baccalaureate training for nurses. The major financial hazard lies in increasing training costs because university education is longer and more expensive per year than community college training. The pay differential between a baccalaureate and non-baccalaureate nurse is small and nurse pay scales are already commensurate with or better than those associated with other baccalaureate graduates. Employment costs should, therefore, change very little. Nevertheless, despite the apparent feasibility and appropriateness of the CNA proposal there has been little hospital or governmental support for the idea of converting to the baccalaureate model.

Medical students enter 33-36 months of medical training (spread over either 3 or 4 years) after a minimum of 2 pre-medical university years. Some medical schools require an undergraduate degree prior to entry into medicine. Many medical school entrants (as high as 50% or more in some universities), have earned a masters degree or a Ph.D. before entering the medical program. A few medical schools, such as the one at the University of Saskatchewan, make a point of accepting very few students with more than a baccalaureate degree.

McMaster University medical school deserves special mention. From its inception in the mid 1960's under the leadership of Dr. John Evans, it rejected the classical medical school pattern of quite unreasonable domination by such basic sciences as biochemistry, anatomy, bacteriology and pathology. McMaster followed the pattern pioneered by Western Reserve University in Cleveland and introduced students to patients at the beginning of their first year. The problem solving process is emphasized, as is the idea of consideration of the complete patient rather than primarily the disease. Traditional medical schools have been highly critical of McMaster but testing has found McMaster graduates to be at least the equal of the graduates of other schools. The traditional schools — and most medical programs still fall into this category — have frequently allowed their preoccupation with the basic sciences to obstruct the addition to the curriculum of adequate amounts of instruction on important subjects. These new areas of instruction include geriatrics, public health, health promotion, communication with patients, the ability to practice as part of a medical team, knowledge of the economic and policy climate in which physicians will practice and the management of pain. In 1987 Harvard medical school announced its intention to implement the McMaster model, and Johns Hopkins recently announced a screening process that will not use the Medical College Aptitude Test (MCAT) and will, therefore, give less emphasis to a science background.

In addition to deficiencies in curriculum, which may lead to deficiencies in the skills of some graduates, medical schools are also sometimes inadequately or inappropriately active in the field of continuing medical education. Many field trials and research projects, with Dalhousie University leading the way in Canada a decade ago, have noted the lack of effect of the classical 1 to 3 day conference on the practice habits of physicians. Change has been shown to occur most commonly if educational experiences are centered in the actual care of patients within a physician's practice, but the short conference remains the usual continuing education model.

The last few years have seen a sharp increase in interest in training physicians for medical administrative duties. Whether short courses are suitable remains to be seen, but such courses are currently being offered. It is almost 30 years since Oswald Hall, one of Canada's earliest medical sociologists, described the clinician who becomes an administrator as "an amateur in a structure peopled by professionals among whom (the physician) is a layman". Because this statement is still accurate, activities which prepare the clinician to make administrative decisions are welcome.

After completing their 3 or 4 years of medical school, all Canadian medical graduates write their university MD examinations and their Licentiate of the Medical Council of Canada (LMCC) examinations. Having an LMCC confirms the graduate as academically acceptable in all provinces. All provinces also require at least one (and not more than 2) years of approved internship training before granting a licence to practice to a physician. Educational licensure is granted during the interval between completing university training and qualifying for a licence to practice.

Physicians who wish to be recognized specialists (Fellows) must complete training approved by The Royal College of Physicians and Surgeons (RCPS), which approves most specialist training or by the College of Family Physicians of Canada (CFPC). The CFPC approves family practice training programs. Three years of approved training in family practice qualifies one for fellowship in that specialty.

After 5 years of approved specialist training and successful completion of an exam (which 15-25% fail), a physician becomes a Fellow of the Royal College of Surgeons of Canada, FRCS(C), or of the Royal College of Physicians of Canada, FRCP(C). This training program, which leads to the most prestigious designations a physician can earn, is not affiliated with a university. The fellowship award is not a university degree; it is a designation granted by peers. Fellowship allows a physician to bill at specialist rates and is the major pre-requisite to being granted major hospital privileges in most hospitals. Within specialities there is a trend towards greater and greater subspecialization. The generalist specialist in internal medicine, for example, is now largely replaced by physicians specializing in such subspecialties as rheumatology, endocrinology, hematology, allergy, cardiology and diabetes.

Nurses should learn from this pattern of peer sponsored post-academic training. Governments, health care institutions (including hospitals), and the public are not particularly concerned about how competence is acquired or who approves it; they merely wish it to be there. Nursing leaders who strongly push an expansion of clinical masters degrees in nursing would do their profession a service if they chose instead to concentrate on the development of a multitude of hospital based post baccalaureate nurse specialist programs. This is the pattern which produced the internationally renouned British midwife and the neurosurgical nurses trained at the Montreal Neurological Institute. The current practice is for nurse graduates to acquire special skills while on the job and, although this undoubtedly results in good competence after several years in the same clinical setting, it would be of benefit to all if the special skills could be more thoroughly acquired through supervised and formal post RN programs taken before attempting to provide sophisticated nursing care.

Most health workers receive at least part of their training in a university or community college, but Canadian trained chiropractors and optometrists are graduates of unaffiliated schools of chiropractic and optometry.

The licencing of foreign medical graduates was discussed earlier. In Ontario, at least, there is to be a phasing out of unfunded residencies, from 63 in 1985 to 45 in 1987 and then continuing reduction. To partially compensate for the elimination of these unfunded positions, Ontario, in 1987-88, funded 24 new FMG pre-internships of 36 weeks. All entrants must have completed their LMCC exams. Successful completion of the 36 week internship will assure access to the two more funded years of training that are necessary for licensure in Ontario. The pre-internship program will eventually accept 48 FMGs annually, all of whom must have lived in Ontario for 2 years.

Although the work world has changed for all types of health care personnel, perhaps that of the health administrator has changed the most. At one time the administrator was a physician or nurse who incidentally ran the hospital or clinic or health unit. Now he or she is a full time career professional whose field of expertise is administration. The good health administrator is skilled in communication and communicates regularly with users, workers, communities, governments, the press and other health care agencies. He or she understands product and program evaluation, appreciates the rights and roles of users, workers, and politicians, understands conflict resolution and problem solving in situations of uncertainty, knows a fair bit about computers, personnel management and financial management and accepts responsibility for decisions while being certain to involve others in them. He or she also understands the need for and the possibilities for non-monetary motivation, appreciates the impossibility of providing optimal health care to all people but tolerates abuse from people who do not get it, deals constructively with planners and civil servants who are struggling with equally difficult decisions and equally untenable options, works in today's context with today's problems while preparing for new problems and new rules, and attempts to accommodate diverse ethical positions on endless and volatile issues.

Two unexpected and already described educational features are unique to the health system. The first is the phenomenon by which the physicians with the highest income and who are the most honored professional group in society(the physician specialists), receive their specialist training and designation through a professionally controlled process rather than through a university. The second feature is the fact that the great majority of nurses are not university graduates at all.

Research

Applied Canadian health care research assigns almost all of its resources to the examination of superspecialized physical health questions. Behavioral and mental health research are minor areas of activity. Measurement and improvement of the quality of life get little attention. Cost-containment, cost-effectiveness, priority setting (resource allocation), optimal health care delivery arrangements, manpower needs, efficiency, case finding, coordination and other important policy, planning and administrative questions are largely ignored. We know very little about the relative extent to which individual or collective health status changes when resources are used for one activity rather than another. We talk about the importance of knowing the impact or outcome of various policies or practices but are not spending health research money on either measuring impacts or producing the data necessary for later measurement. We spend large sums looking for chemical or technical ways to cure cancer and considerably less studying changes in lifestyle, in the work places or in the environment that would sharply decrease the incidence of cancer. We are more apt to document lifestyles or patterns of utilization than to study how to alter these lifestyles or patterns of utilization.

Unless research granting bodies, or the political masters above them, begin to devise and enforce new research priorities we will continue to allocate funds primarily in keeping with the social theorem 'them that has, gets.' The scientific community that has the capacity to write technically good research submissions is the one that gets most of the money. As long as methodological excellence is considered to be more important than the significance of the question being examined, and this is the current situation, we will continue to expand and entrench research patterns established 25 years ago. Recent appropriate initiatives include attention to AIDS, the establishment at McMaster University of a centre for the study of health economics and policy, and the setting up of a data linkage project in Hamilton in which family practice units, hospital emergency rooms, psychiatric clinics and hospital bed registries will share on-line patient data; however, such examples of applied research in important areas are too few.

Tens of millions of dollars a year are spent in Canada on cancer research but over the past decades the prognosis for a number of the common and deadly cancers has changed very little. Survival rates associated with most intestinal cancers, including esophagus, stomach, colon, pancreas and rectum, have only marginally improved. Breast cancer 5 year survival rates have improved a bit but probably because of earlier diagnosis. The disease is still not manageable when lymph nodes are involved. Lung cancer survival rates remain poor but research into the prevention of lung cancer, which is within our grasp, continues to be less attractive to researchers than chemotherapy or cell cultures.

There is a great deal of clinical information that we use badly and a great scarcity of the kind of administrative information that we need. It is sometimes believed that if we know the cause, distribution and impact of diseases and injury, good policy and planning will automatically follow. Partly because of this misconception, we collect and analyze population and clinical data rather than study operating and policy problems. Most of our current applied research is in the form of studies commissioned by government, committees or task forces. It is usually done by consultants. Our university based capacity to do administrative research is quite limited and funding for such research is equally limited.

Study of the organization and management of health services, and of the options available, would be especially useful to a country with significant geographic diversity and with authority vested in the provinces. With better information different provinces might choose different options.

In 1986 the Ontario Minister of Health described the rapid increases in costs and volumes of various elements of health care. He said there was a need to know "precisely which diagnostic and treatment services are appropriate in given situations," and that "more research on results being achieved is necessary."These statements are consistent with the mandate of the new research center at McMaster University but the breadth and excellence of health services research that is urgently needed will require the establishment of many similar centers. In the mid 1960's, in response to recommendations of a Royal Commission, the federal government dedicated $100 million to an upgrading of medical education and clinical research. The same kind of bold initiative is needed now to study and improve health services organization and delivery.

Ministers of health, and perhaps ministries of health, do not appear to be aware of how seldom health professionals really know the relative value of the services they give. In mid 1986 British Columbia announced a $120 million health improvement fund. Providers of services were invited to compete for the funds by submitting competitive innovative proposals, but the invitation then targeted organ transplants, advanced cancer treatment and care of AIDS patients as areas of special interest. The fund will, within at least the first two of these service areas, produce little that is innovative. Governments would be much better served by a research fund which supported innovative or non-innovative efforts by hospitals or others to improve their ability to allocate resources. This kind of support would encourage everyone to examine the relative benefits of different actions so that we might know what would happen if the money were not spent, and what would happen to outcomes if either more or less money were spent per case.

The Medical Research Council (MRC) budget for 1987-88 rose 6.2% to $171.7 million. Whether its revenues will continue to rise in the future depends on the success of a recent government decision to solicit more private sector support for MRC research. The public expenditures via MRC on clinical research are approximately equalled by funds raised for research by voluntary organizations and other philanthropic sources. The budget for the National Health Research Development Program (NHRDP) is about 10% that of MRC. Very few private nonprofit dollars are spent on nonclinical research.

The volume of research done by university based physicians may also be in jeopardy from a reported trend toward requiring medical professors to generate more money from clinical work. Cutbacks in university budgets have been reported to be forcing clinical departments to support more of their research from clinical income.

Even the subjects given emphasis in patient based research need review. Superspecialized therapies and marginally better diagnostic tools must increasingly share center stage with important epidemiological studies. Few issues or problems of consequence can now be studied with small budgets or by a single agency. If we wish to learn about the role of diet, environment or trace elements in health we need longitudinal and expensive population studies. Canada has extensive experience with the national reporting of diagnostic and utilization data. This experience and the associated skills now must be applied to the collection of data which will clarify relationships between personal and environmental factors and the quality of our health.

The National Breast Screening Study (NBSS) involves 90,000 women aged 40-59 in 15 Canadian centers. Repeated examinations, including mammography, may clarify the role of early screening in breast cancer detection, and tell us whether early detection changes the course of the disease. A similar study is underway in the United States. No previous studies have produced unequivocal evidence that women in these age groups benefit from early diagnosis.

In 1976 the report of the CMA group studying annual physical examinations recommended that the traditionally encouraged annual exam was not indicated for a large part of the older child and younger adult population. Similar kinds of studies, many of which will be complex and expensive, are needed so that we may know whether other traditional and high volume activities should also be dropped or given less emphasis.

PHYSICAL RESOURCES

Physical resources include facilities, supplies, equipment and organs for transplant. Their supply varies with the supply of money but also with culture, philosophy, tradition and history.

For the last 10-15 years there has been a steady reduction in the acute treatment hospital bed supply per 1000 population, a trend that has occurred at quite different times and rates in different provinces but which has occurred everywhere. (Table 4.3 suggests otherwise but these figures include long term care beds in acute treatment hospitals). In 1982 British Columbia closed nearly 10% of acute treatment beds and reduced provincial hospital expenditures by $60 million. The 1984 Newfoundland Royal Commission on hospitals and nursing home costs recommended closure of at least 300 acute care beds. Beginning in 1978 Ontario reduced the ratio of recommended acute treatment beds from 5.0 (urban) and 5.5 (northern) per 1000 population to 3.5 (urban) and 4.0 (northern). In 1986 Alberta announced an objective of 4.0 beds per 1000 instead of the existing 5.2. Data describing the supply, nature, ownership and distribution of hospitals are shown in Tables 4.3, 4.4 and 4.5.

Hospital reporting and definitions are standardized across Canada. 'General' beds are those designated medical, surgical, obstetrical (maternity), intensive or

TABLE 4.3
HOSPITAL BEDS* PER 1000 POPULATION BY PROVINCE 1977-78 AND 1984-85

	1977-78	1984-85
Canada	6.75	6.56
Newfoundland	5.70	5.47
Prince Edward Island	6.35	5.96
Nova Scotia	6.13	6.12
New Brunswick	6.20	6.05
Quebec	7.63	8.07
Ontario	5.87	5.44
Manitoba	6.13	6.15
Saskatchewan	8.46	7.00
Alberta	7.57	7.15
British Columbia	7.23	6.75
Northwest Territories	2.07	3.61

*These figures include all beds within acute treatment hospitals including long term (chronic) care beds. In 1973 these chronic beds represented 15.4% of the total;by 1977-78 the figure had risen to 20.7% and to 24.3% by 1982-83. Quebec hospitals have the highest percentage of chronic care beds.

Source: Derived from the *Canadian Hospital Association Directory*, 1986.

TABLE 4.4
HOSPITALS AND BEDS BY TYPE 1986*

	Public General		Public Special		Profit (Proprietary)		Federal		Total
	No	%	No	%	No	%	No	%	No
Hospitals	879	71	245	20	58	5	50	4	1,232
Beds in those hospitals	127,000	68	51,500	28	3,700	2.5	2,700	1.5	185,000

*Six hospitals with a total of about 1,000 beds appeared to be wrongly classified and have been omitted. These data are summarized from larger tables.

Source: *Canadian Hospital Association Directory*, 1986.

TABLE 4.5
HOSPITALS AND BEDS BY OWNERSHIP 1986

	Hospitals		Beds	
	#	%	#	%
Lay	509	41.1	94,449	50.8
Religious	130	10.5	23,116	12.4
Municipal	331	26.7	23,991	12.9
Provincial	160	12.9	37,849	20.4
Proprietary (profit)	58	4.7	3,679	2.0
Federal	50	4.0	2,673	1.4
TOTAL	1,238	100.0	185,757	100.0

Source: *Canadian Hospital Association Directory*, 1986.

coronary care, pediatric, gynecological, ear-nose-throat (ENT or otorhinolaryngological) or eye (ophthalmological). 'Special' beds or hospitals are those designated as psychiatric, chronic, extended care, auxiliary, mental retardation, rehabilitation, convalescent, contagious, tuberculosis and respiratory, isolation, orthopedic and arthritic. There is considerable overlap between some general and special categories — orthopedic and surgical, for instance — and this ambiguity weakens the accuracy of the terms and the associated data. Bed totals do not include bassinets and incubators.

The footnote to table 4.3 reports the growth of chronic beds in general hospitals. There has been an even larger increase in the supply of chronic (long term) beds in long term care institutions. In keeping with this trend the government of Ontario, in 1987, approved over 4400 new institutional beds of which 1375 (31%) were acute care beds and 3081 (69%) were for chronic care. Approval of so many long term care institutional beds in preference to optional forms of housing for the chronically disabled is unfortunate at a point in time when the feasibility of the residential options has been proven and the users often express a preference for noninstitutional living.

Besides hospitals and long term care facilities, institutional and residential resources also include detoxification centres, infirmaries in universities and correctional institutions, and a large number of group homes, halfway houses, and free-standing abortion clinics of the kind that are common and accepted in Quebec but which are struggling for existence elsewhere. Ontario has recently funded a 12 bed hospice in Toronto for AIDS patients.Emergency equipment includes vehicles, airplanes, boats, communication systems, and standby emergency supplies. Later chapters will look more closely at specific kinds of institutional resources.

Although there are many examples of the increasing sophistication of health care technology (lithotripers, CAT scanners) there are also many examples of investigations being simplified by other technology. Small office based laboratory tools are rapidly becoming cheap and reliable. More and more biochemical, bacteriological and hematology tests can be done immediately and a return office visit may be avoided. In the United States 30% of lab work is now done in the doctor's office. Insurance agencies should be developing policies which will invite use of this new office based technology without misuse.

Reliable equipment for self diagnosis is also rapidly appearing on the market. Although some of this equipment is of questionable quality at this time, the technology is rapidly improving. The ethics and medical implications of self-administered tests for a broad range of diseases including AIDS, gonorrhoea, hepatitis and gout are under discussion. There is medical objection although there have been few if any problems with the availability of self-administered pregnancy tests, BP examinations and urine tests for sugar.

Computers have changed health care and its delivery. They have brought better office procedures, easier and more accurate billing, faster handling of laboratory specimens and reporting of the results, on-line data bases that may make libraries redundant, and analysis of patterns of practice. The beginning of the biggest and most challenging clinical development, computer assisted diagnosis and treatment, has arrived. Computer based simulations have for some time been a major part of medical teaching but future diagnosis and prescribing will almost surely become partly a computer function. The computer will process data and evaluate alternative diagnoses and therapies with a skill equal to or greater than that of most health workers in most complex circumstances. The machine age is here and many health workers, especially physicians, will have their work world altered by it.

Organs for transplant are a new category of physical resources. The supply, whether of kidneys, hearts or anything else that cannot regenerate, is routinely less than the demand. In 1987 the supply of organs for transplant was smaller even than the year before despite efforts to alter retrieval patterns. There are active campaigns to increase access to organs, including the Canadian Medical Association drive to encourage physicians to promote organ donation. Scholars are studying the 'organ market place' and are evaluating various imaginative techniques to increase supply or optimally allocate what is available. In Belgium, as of 1987, organs may be taken for transplant without the consent of the patient or the family.

Very sophisticated and international organ matching services, such as the Multiple Organ Retrieval and Exchange Program (MORE) in Ontario, or the national Organ Waiting List (OWL) based in Winnipeg, have increased the likelihood that organs that are available will be used. There is, however, still greater need for public awareness and greater co-operation from physicians and hospitals. Kidney donations rose 300% in Ontario from 1976 to 1984 but patients who would be more economically and better served by a transplant continue to be on dialysis. In 1986 about 1000 persons were awaiting a kidney in Ontario despite the over 850 transplants that were performed in that year.

Suggested Reading

Canada Health Manpower Inventory, Statistics Canada, 1982.
Fulton, M.J., *The Regulation of Emerging Health Occupations*, Canadian Hospital Association, 1988.

Chapter 5

COSTS AND FINANCING

SOCIAL EXPENDITURES

Social spending in Canada, which includes expenditures on health, rose from 12.1% of Gross Domestic Product (GDP) in 1960 to 21.7% in 1981, with 1960-1975 being years of rapid increase (9.5% per year). From 1975-1981 the rate of increase was 2.9% per year, smaller than the growth of the GDP. Throughout the period 1960-1981 Canada was consistently more generous in its social spending than Japan or the United States but was behind major European countries. Pensions in developed countries represent the largest percentage of social expenditure with health and education services being next most expensive and unemployment insurance costs the smallest of the big four.

Although health services are not the largest component of social spending in Canada, they are a $25-30 billion industry. Health expenditures represent 25-35% of total provincial government budgets, and three quarters of these expenditures are for institutional and physician services. In 1986, Ontario spent $9 billion on publicly financed health care for eight million residents. These costs are not typical of other parts of the world. The United Kingdom, in the same year, spent the equivalent of $38 billion Canadian on its National Health Service for 50 million residents. For a more comprehensive set of services, the United Kingdom spent only two thirds as much per capita, whereas in equivalent dollars the United States spent 40% more per capita than Canada but got less.

When Canada introduced national universal health and hospital insurance, a variety of critics warned of runaway costs. Costs did, indeed, rise rapidly in the 1960's but during the 1970's Canadian health expenditures stayed close to 7% of Gross National Product (GNP) while the percent of GNP consumed by health services continued to climb in the United States (Table 5.1). During the prolonged recession of the early 1980's, when GNP in Canada rose very slowly or not at all, hospital and physician costs continued to rise and, therefore, consumed a rapidly increasing percentage of the GNP. From 1981-1982 the percent of GNP attributable to these costs jumped 0.8%. By 1983 health care costs in Canada had risen to a peak of 8.8% of GNP and it had become clear that the policies that kept costs at a constant percentage of GNP in the 1970's did not work in periods of economic stagnation. The growth of health services costs continues whether or not the GNP also grows. The financial demands of institutional and personal providers of care have, to date, been politically unmanageable.

Despite the increase in the percentage of GNP devoted to health care, from 5.5% (1960) to 7.1% (1970) to 7.2% (1978) and to a plateau of 8.5-8.8% (1982-1985), the pressure for additional funds for health services continues to increase. The critics of universal programs no longer complain about the threat of uncontrollable costs; they speak of underfunding. User fees are being vigorously

TABLE 5.1
HEALTH EXPENDITURES AS PERCENTAGES OF GROSS NATIONAL PRODUCT, CANADA AND THE UNITED STATES, 1960-1985

Year	Canada	U.S.A.
1960	5.6	5.2
1965	6.2	6.0
1970	7.3	7.4
1975	7.2	8.3
1980	7.5	9.5
1983	8.8	10.2(1982)
1985*	8.6*	10.6*

Source: *National Health Expenditures in Canada* 1970-1982, and *National Health Expenditures in Canada* 1975-1985, Health and Welfare Canada.
* Provisional

proposed and hospital fund-raising campaigns have once again become common.

Per capita health expenditures in Canada grew from $357 in 1972 to $1220 in 1982, an increase of 240%. In constant 1970 dollars the growth was from $340 to $445, an increase of 31%. In the same period, total national health expenditures grew, in constant dollars, about 48%, and population grew about 14%. In actual dollars, national expenditures on health grew almost 300%.

Although health costs continue to rise, the federal government has, through the *Established Programs Financing Act* (EPF) of 1977, stabilized the federal contribution to those costs. After introduction of EPF, federal transfer payments to the provinces fell from 4.7% of GNP in 1975 to 4.3% in 1980, with a rise to 4.4% in 1983.

Sources of Health Funding

Health care costs are met from five sources with the importance of the five sources varying by province. The contributions, by source, are 27% to 36% from the federal government, 38% to 50% from the provinces, 0 to 5% from local government, 0.4-1.3% from WCB, and 17 to 29% from private sources (Table 5.2). Interprovincial variations are not predictable. Alberta, the bastion of individual responsibility, has the lowest contribution from private sources. Quebec and Alberta, at 49% and 50% respectively, have the highest provincial contributions.

Health Care Costs

In both 1975 and 1984 (provisional data), health care costs as a percentage of gross provincial domestic product were the highest in the Atlantic provinces. All were above 11% in 1984. Alberta had the lowest percentage in both years at 5.4 and 6.4% respectively.Ontario, Saskatchewan and British Columbia were next lowest in each of the years although the order changed somewhat (Table 5.3).

TABLE 5.2
CONTRIBUTIONS TO HEALTH EXPENDITURES BY SECTOR, CANADA AND THE PROVINCES, 1983 IN PERCENT

	Federal Government Direct	Provincial Government: From Federal Government	Provincial Government: Direct	Provincial Government: To Local Government	Local Government Excluding Transfer From Prov.	WCB	Private
Canada	2.9	27.7	42.4	0.6	1.7	0.9	23.7
Newfoundland	2.5	33.0	42.6	0.0	0.1	1.1	20.8
Prince Edward Island	2.6	33.9	42.0	0.0	0.0	0.5	20.9
Nova Scotia	5.0	31.5	39.8	0.0	1.0	0.7	22.0
New Brunswick	2.7	31.1	40.7	0.0	0.2	1.2	24.0
Quebec	2.2	29.3	48.0	0.1	0.1	0.9	19.5
Ontario	2.4	27.4	37.5	1.1	1.3	0.9	29.4
Manitoba	8.0	27.2	41.9	0.1	1.2	0.5	21.1
Saskatchewan	4.0	28.8	42.1	0.2	5.3	0.4	19.2
Alberta	2.1	24.6	49.6	0.6	4.7	1.1	17.3
British Columbia	2.1	25.5	41.3	0.6	3.7	1.3	25.5
Territories	49.7	20.7	26.1	0.0	0.2	0.5	2.9

Source: Table 80, *National Health Expenditures in Canada* 1975-1985, Health and Welfare Canada 1987.

Care provided by institutions consumed 61% of the health dollar in 1976, excluding physician payments associated with care in institutions. Provisional figures for 1985 suggest a drop to 56.1% (Table 5.4).

The costs of general hospitals make up about 75% of the institutional costs. Institutional costs as a proportion of total health care costs increased steadily in the period preceding 1976 and have fallen steadily since then. TB and mental

TABLE 5.3
HEALTH CARE AS A PERCENTAGE OF GROSS DOMESTIC PRODUCT, CANADA AND THE PROVINCES, 1977-78 AND 1984-85

	1977-78	**1984-85**
Canada	7.26	8.53
Newfoundland	11.08	11.91
Prince Edward Island	11.44	12.36
Nova Scotia	10.10	11.19
New Brunswick	8.65	11.59
Quebec	8.27	9.47
Ontario	6.88	8.07
Manitoba	7.83	9.69
Saskatchewan	6.48	8.44
Alberta	5.39	6.41
British Columbia	7.19	9.10
Northwest Territories	7.71	11.16

Source: *National Health Expenditures in Canada* 1975-1985, Health and Welfare Canada, 1987. Page 16.

TABLE 5.4
HEALTH CARE EXPENDITURES BY TYPE OF SERVICE
1970-1985

	1970	1976		1979		1982	1985*
	(a)	(a)	(b)	(a)	(b)	(b)	(b)
General and Allied Special Hospitals	36.6	40.8	—	40.4	—	—	—
Mental Hospitals	6.5	4.6	—	2.1	—	—	—
TB Hospitals	0.4	0.0	—	0.0	—	—	—
Federal Hospitals	1.5	1.0	—	0.8	—	—	—
All Hospitals	45.0	46.4	45.1	43.3	41.9	42.0	40.4
Homes for Special Care (Other Institutions)	7.2	10.2	10.1	12.0	11.8	11.6	11.3
All Institutions (Operating Costs)	52.2	56.6	56.2	55.3	53.7	53.6	51.7
Capital Costs	5.8	4.6	4.6	4.3	4.3	5.5	4.4
All Institutions (Operating and Capital Costs)	58.0	61.2	60.8	59.6	58.0	59.1	56.1
Physicians	16.6	14.9	15.4	14.9	15.5	14.9	15.7
Dentists	4.2	4.9	5.0	5.8	5.7	5.3	5.5
Chiropractors	0.5	0.5	0.5	0.6	0.6	0.7	0.7
Optometrists	0.7	0.6	0.3	0.5	0.3	0.3	0.3
Other Professional Services	0.4	0.3	0.3	0.4	0.3	0.3	0.4
Ambulances	—	—	0.5	—	0.6	0.7	0.8
Prescribed Drugs	5.9	4.7	4.7	4.8	4.7	5.1	5.5
Non Prescribed Drugs	5.3	4.4	3.8	4.4	4.3	3.8	4.7
Eyeglasses	0.9	1.1	1.4	1.1	1.4	1.5	1.6
Other Appliances	0.4	0.4	0.4	0.4	0.4	0.4	0.6
Public Health	3.2	3.4	4.3	3.7	3.9	4.0	4.2
Home Care	—	—	0.4	—	0.5	0.5	0.5
Research	1.1	1.0	0.8	1.1	0.9	0.9	0.9
Prepayment Administration	1.6	1.5	1.5	1.4	1.4	1.3	1.3
Other	1.1	1.2	1.1	1.3	1.4	1.3	1.2

Source: (a) From *National Health Expenditures in Canada* 1970-1982, Health and Welfare Canada, 1984. Table 5, Page 35.
(b) From *National Health Expenditures in Canada* 1975-1985, Health and Welfare Canada, Table 9, Page 35.

Note: Data in the two federal reports are sometimes different. Differences are due to changes in classifications and sorting of data.

* Provisional

hospital costs have declined steadily for three decades, whereas the cost of homes for special care has grown sharply. To arrive at the full cost of institutional care, one should add at least one quarter of the payments made to physicians because at least this proportion of their revenue, and probably considerably more, is related to hospital work.

The operating costs in public general and allied special hospitals, also referred to as acute treatment short term hospitals, rose from about $62 per patient day in 1971 to about $275 in 1984-85. In 1971 dollars the increase is from $62 to about $90, a 45% increase. (These figures represent total hospital operating budgets divided by number of days of inpatient care and therefore unfairly assign emergency and outpatient services costs to inpatient care. They also are affected by the mix of acute care and long stay beds.)

Costs of noninstitutional and institutional services can be expressed as costs per day, week or month of care, or as costs per unit of service. A home visit by a nurse, for example, costs $20-40, each client visit to a senior citizen or drop in center costs $5-10, a day at a detoxification center costs $60-150, and costs of an Ottawa psychogeriatric clinic are in the order of $150 per client month.

Institutions still consume the largest portion of new dollars available for health care. In the period from 1975-1985 hospitals received 38.6% of the increase and other institutions received 11.9%. Physicians accounted for 15.7% of the increase and drugs 10.7%.

Expenditures on physician services in the period 1970-1982 gradually decreased as a percentage of total health expenditures (down to 14.9%) and then rose again to match 1975 levels (15.7%). In the period 1970-1985, the proportion of the health dollar assigned to dental care increased until 1980 (at 5.7%), and has now fallen slightly. Drugs represent about 10% of total health service costs and this 10% is quite evenly divided between prescription and nonprescription items.

It is useful to remember the relative sizes of different areas of expenditure when discussing cost control or resource reallocation. A 5% reduction in institutional expenditures could, for example, allow a 100% increase in public health expenditures and a 10% reduction in expenditures on drugs would allow a doubling of our expenditures on research. Two forces may accelerate such reallocation, namely the pressure of AIDS and the evidence produced by cost-effectiveness studies.

The HWC budget for 1987-88 was $29.21 billion, up 5% from the previous year. Old age pensions and family allowances accounted for $17.22 billion, up 6.6% from the previous year. Although there were budget increases for most areas of health expenditure, there were reductions in the budget of the Centre for Occupational Health and Safety (down 1% with staff down to 130 from 143) and in Medical Services Branch (budget down 4.1% and staff down from 3040 to 2710). Transfer payments for provincial and territorial insurance programs rose 3.1% to $6.84 billion.

The expenditure patterns in individual provinces often vary significantly from the national pattern (Table 5.5). Some of the variations arise from provincial organizational and reporting differences. Comparisons are, therefore, hazardous. Reported home care expenditures varied from zero to 1.2%, but the inaccuracies become obvious when we note that Quebec and Alberta report no expenditure on home care when both offer this service extensively. The pattern of growth in per capita costs of major areas of expenditure is shown in Table 5.6.

Provincial health insurance plans are major sources of income for most physicians. Physicians receive 93-94% of Ontario Health Insurance Plan (OHIP) payments to professionals (Table 5.7). Of these physician payments, 3 to 4% are for out-of-country services and for physicians on salary or capitation. Physicians also receive payments from WCB, private patients and a variety of other third party payers.

TABLE 5.5
SELECTED CATEGORIES OF HEALTH EXPENDITURES AS PERCENTAGES OF TOTAL HEALTH EXPENDITURES, CANADA AND THE PROVINCES, 1983

Prov.	Hospital Operating Costs	Other Institutions' Operating Costs	Physicians	Dentists	Drugs	Capital Exp.	Ambulance	Public Health
Nfld.	47.7	11.6	10.3	2.2	11.1	6.6	0.6	2.7
P.E.I.	43.2	12.6	12.0	4.5	14.7	1.1	0.6	6.0
N.S.	48.5	8.2	14.2	4.8	13.3	2.9	0.5	2.6
N.B.	45.0	13.5	12.7	3.2	11.2	6.0	0.1	3.9
Que.	48.8	12.4	13.6	3.8	7.6	3.7	0.4	3.4
Ont.	38.8	11.4	16.8	6.2	10.3	4.4	0.9	3.1
Man.	40.0	14.0	12.7	5.1	9.1	4.9	0.6	5.1
Sask.	36.3	20.2	12.0	4.9	10.1	3.8	0.4	4.4
Alta.	38.8	9.3	14.3	4.0	7.0	12.1	0.2	6.1
B.C.	37.0	10.1	19.4	8.0	8.7	4.6	1.2	4.2
Can.	41.7	11.7	15.3	5.3	9.1	4.8	0.7	3.8

Source: *National Health Expenditures in Canada* 1975-85, Health and Welfare Canada, page 18.

Health-related costs tend to rise faster than can be fully accounted for by inflation. In 1986 the health care component of the Consumer Price Index (CPI) rose 5.6% while the total CPI rose only 3.9%, and this was a year in which health cost increases were smaller than usual. Weekly average earnings of salaried workers in the health care sector rose only 3.6% in 1986. Most of the increase in expenditures is absorbed by provincial governments.

TABLE 5.6
ANNUAL PERCENTAGE RATES OF INCREASE IN HEALTH EXPENDITURES PER PERSON FOR VARIOUS CATEGORIES OF CARE, CANADA, 1960 TO 1970 AND 1970 TO 1982(a)

Category	Per Capita 1960	Per Capita 1970	Per Capita 1982	Yearly Per Cent Increase 1960-1970	Yearly Per Cent Increase 1970-1982
	($)	($)	($)	(%)	(%)
Homes for Special Care	6.85	21.03	166.99	11.9	18.8
Dentists	6.12	12.43	68.24	7.3	15.3
General and Allied Special Hospitals	33.59	107.45	488.49	12.3	13.4
Capital	10.99	17.11	64.29	4.5	11.7
Physicians	19.82	48.81	179.02	9.4	11.4
Drugs and Appliances	17.33	36.55	132.83	8.1	11.4
Total (b)	119.30	293.37	1,220.18	9.4	12.6

(a) 1982 data are preliminary
(b) Total includes all categories

Source: *National Health Expenditures in Canada* 1970-1982, Health and Welfare Canada, page 14.

TABLE 5.7
PAYMENTS BY OHIP BY TYPE OF SERVICE AND BY IN AND OUT OF PROVINCE 1984-1985

To Ontario Professionals		95.4%
Physicians*	90.2%	
Dental	0.4%	
Chiropractic	2.2%	
Optometric	1.7%	
Physiotherapy	0.7%	
Chiropody	0.2%	
Osteopathy (less than 0.1%)	—	
Out of Province Payments (including some payments to hospitals)		4.6%
	100%	

* Primarily fee-for-service (FFS) payments but includes capitation payments and payments from V.D. clinics and other minor sources of care.

Source: *Practitioner Care Statistics, OHIP, 1984-85 (Pre-Audit),* Ontario Ministry of Health.

As already described, the federal government, through a number of mechanisms, provides provinces with funds equivalent to approximately half of the costs of hospital and physician services. The provinces differ in how they finance their share of health care costs, but general revenue is the source of most funds for most insured services in most provinces.

Alberta and British Columbia, and other provinces to a lesser extent, had, until the *Canada Health Act* and its associated penalties appeared, always had a number of hospital user fees. In British Columbia these fees represented 7.6% of daily hospital costs in 1955 but this figure had dropped to 2.6% of total costs in 1983. The 1984 fees included a charge of $4.00 for attendance at a hospital emergency department, $7.50 for an outpatient visit or day surgery, and a $7.50 daily fee while in hospital.

Ontario, Alberta, British Columbia and the Yukon have health insurance premiums. Alberta premiums in 1986 were roughly $170 for an individual and $340 for a family. Those in Ontario were higher at over $400 for an individual and $816 for a family. About one third of Ontario residents were exempted from the premium.

After the introduction of universal hospital insurance, municipalities felt they were permanently relieved of responsibility for hospital capital and operating costs, but in response to pressure from hospitals some municipalities are once again contributing to hospital costs. This trend is likely to continue although it should not. The residential property tax is fully needed for other expenditures that are also important to health; these include recreation, urban planning, police and fire protection, sewage, water and garbage services, daycare and low income housing.

Tables 5.4 and 5.5 illustrate the cost of various types of health care. There is ongoing discussion of whether further expenditures on institutions and physicians is a reasonable way for society to spend its money, and the basic conclusion is that to improve or maintain the health status of the nation we should direct money to activities and workers other than hospitals and doctors. The level of per capita provincial health care costs does not predict provincial life expectancy.

If the costs of hospitals and physicians are controlled, there will be continuing complaints about, and effects from, longer hospital waiting lists and the absence of the latest technology. We should accept these problems, however, because expenditures in other areas will produce greater improvements in the health status of Canadians. Evidence is mounting that other expenditures bring more social return per dollar spent than hospital or physician expenditures. It is reasonable to conclude that these two sources of traditional health care are already overfunded (in relative terms) rather than underfunded.

INSURANCE PROGRAMS FOR HOSPITAL AND PHYSICIAN SERVICES

Most Canadians take hospital and medical care insurance for granted, but they should not. When any health service (or any other kind of service) is being insured, there are a number of quite different options available, and only a series of historical accidents coupled with a large measure of social concern led us to have the health insurance arrangements we have. A look at some of the options available to policy makers in 1946, at the time of the introduction of Saskatchewan's hospital insurance, and in 1962 and 1968 (when Medicare was born and expanded), will allow Canadians to consider whether there are other arrangements they would have liked better or whether they should be thankful for choices made earlier.

The policy writers who create insurance programs have to decide who is to be covered by the insurance; that is, they must decide who will be beneficiaries or be eligible to be beneficiaries. Health care insurance can be sold the same way fire insurance and dental insurance are sold today. Those persons who pay the premiums, or have the premiums paid on their behalf, are covered. The rest are not. Forty years ago this laissez-faire model applied throughout Canada. Premium costs might be paid by an employer as part of a collective bargaining agreement or by government on behalf of selected populations such as the elderly, the young or the poor, or by individuals alone or as part of a group. However, the picture began to change when Saskatchewan introduced universal hospital insurance in 1946.

In 1962-64, when the Hall Commission was preparing the report that introduced national medicare, many briefs from medical associations, insurance companies and others recommended that government should only pay the premiums of persons who could not afford to pay the premiums themselves. The Hall Commission chose to recommend the Saskatchewan pattern in which essentially the entire population was covered regardless of age, income or state of health. Under private insurance sold by for-profit insurance companies, it was routine for the company to refuse to renew health insurance contracts if the health of the beneficiary was deteriorating. Our Canadian arrangement assures us that if we get sicker there is no danger that our health insurance will be cancelled.

Besides deciding who is the beneficiary, policy makers must decide what kinds of services will be insured. Early private insurance sometimes listed all the things that were covered; if a particular problem or operation was not on the list, the patient had to pay his or her own bill. Sometimes there would be a cash payment to the patient when he or she had received a particular type of care. This was and is known as indemnity insurance. (If you had two or three insurance policies you could make money being sick, and having all your childrens' tonsils out was a financial godsend.) The better insurance plans, however, including most of the nonprofit plans in place before the universal plans arrived, covered most of the services that are covered now; that is, almost all admissions to hospital and almost all physicians' services were insured. The insurance did not then, and usually does not now, pay bills for which someone else was or is responsible. For example it did not pay for injuries for which someone's car insurance would pay, or services covered by WCB. Other uninsured services theoretically include medicals to go to camp or to renew a driver's licence but such examinations are often disguised by some kind of diagnosis and, thus, can be billed to the public insurance plan.

The issue of uninsured services is once again becoming important as provinces seek ways to control medicare costs and a few physicians react to their loss of the right to extra bill. These physicians are beginning to charge for such services as writing referral letters, giving telephone advice and ordering repeat prescriptions because these services are not considered to be within the list of insured services.

The definition of terms is important; even terms which appear quite well understood may require clarification. Hospital services may mean only inpatient care, may mean inpatient and outpatient care, may exclude psychiatric care, or may be defined as 'care which cannot be provided anywhere but in a hospital.' They may or may not include care in the emergency room and the day surgery unit; outpatient x-rays or laboratory work may or may not be covered. In the United States, where there are literally hundreds of different kinds of insurance policies, very complex computer programs are used to tell the hospital, the patient and the provider of care which services are covered by a particular insurance policy.

By 1986 five of the Canadian provincially operated health insurance programs covered at least a portion of chiropractor, podiatry/chiropodist and optometry costs. The services of osteopathic physicians were usually excluded. There was variable coverage of services provided by private physiotherapists and acupuncturists. Services provided by dentists tended to be covered if they were also commonly provided by physicians. Maxillofacial surgery is an example of such a service.

Coverage outside of one's province of residence is routine in Canada although Québec, in 1982, reduced its coverage to emergencies only. Payment is usually made, as a maximum, at the rate that would have been paid if the services had been provided in one's home province. Special contracts or arrangements sometimes apply in communities such as Ottawa-Hull where tertiary care for the residents in one province is routinely sought in another province, or in Lloydminster where a provincial border bisects the town.

There have always been provincial variations in the range of insured services and the number of these has recently increased. In some provinces immunization in physicians offices is not an insured service; families are expected to receive these services from public health personnel or to pay for them privately. Cosmetic surgery may be fully or only partially covered. Alberta and British Columbia, in particular, have recently reduced their coverage of a number of services related to family planning, including giving advice on contraception.

Policy makers designing insurance programs must make choices regarding direct patient payment at the time of service. These direct payments are, at various times, called utilization fees, deterrent fees, co-insurance, user fees, deductibles, extra billing or balance billing. Objections to physician extra billing, as shown by the widespread support for the *Canada Health Act*, (which banned extra billing by physicians), would suggest that Canadians are fundamentally opposed to these payments. These fees are still quite common, however, and include resident fees in long term care institutions, client payments towards drug costs in Saskatchewan, extra billing by chiropractors, extra billing when physicians provide services to patients from outside their province, and charges for ambulance services.

Arguments used to support the use of direct patient payments, (instead of first dollar coverage), include the following:

1. These payments reduce premiums or taxes. This argument is sound as long as the co-insurance fee is subtracted from the total payment or fee that would have been paid to the provider. For example, if the fee for an ordinary house call by a physician is $18 and the patient is expected to pay $5 then the insurance plan would pay the doctor $13. If the patient cannot pay or if competition makes it wise for the physician not to charge the $5, then the total cost of health care goes down, but in all situations the funds required to operate the insurance program are reduced by $5 per visit.
2. People will not appreciate the care they receive unless they pay something for it. This is an entirely political/philosophical argument which the voters of Canada have largely rejected but which is still supported by a minority of the population.
3. Payments at the time of service will keep people from seeking unnecessary care. This is an argument that is not defensible for most medical care. For people with a modest amount of disposable income the

deterrent fee is of no consequence, for the working poor the fee becomes a barrier to care and, for those in selected groups such as the very poor and the elderly, the fee is of no consequence because it is routinely waived. When Saskatchewan had such fees in the 1960's and early 1970's, the use of services by low income residents decreased. In 1987 New Brunswick reported a 12% increase in outpatient and emergency room visits after the removal of a user fee. Experience in other countries indicates that demand for eye glasses and drugs is altered by a requirement for patient payment.

Deterrent fees can be best defended for services shown to be likely to be seriously abused and in situations where the patient has control over choice.

4. In the special case of long term institutional care, people should have to pay for their room and board wherever they live, especially when they are receiving publicly financed pensions. Thus, a monthly payment is collected in long term care facilities in all provinces.

The form of co-insurance in which patients pay all or part of costs to some sort of maximum per year (a deductible) can be administratively cumbersome. A full refund may be paid to users when a prescribed ceiling per person or per household is reached. A continuous co-insurance fee of a fixed amount per prescription, or a fixed percentage of costs, is much simpler. Protection beyond an annual maximum is known as catastrophic coverage. It can apply to a broad range of services or to one service only.

Co-insurance fees sometimes have a more noticeable effect on utilization when they are first imposed or removed than they do later on. They appear to have no effect when the patients pay the fee but physicians make the decisions. British Columbia and Alberta had hospital fees for 20 to 30 years and their patterns of hospital use were no different from those of other provinces where there were no patient payments. Roemer's Law applies: 'A built bed is a filled bed.'

Participation in health insurance plans run by government can be voluntary or compulsory. When it is voluntary some people will not join because they choose to pay their own medical bills, some will not join because they cannot pay the premiums and others will not join because they have no assets and assume they will get needed care anyway (which they will). The voluntary versus compulsory argument can be completely avoided by paying for health care out of taxes (general revenue) and offering the same set of health services to all residents.

Single Versus Multiple Carriers of Insurance

Competition is in the public interest if it reduces price without lowering quality but when many companies compete in the health insurance market there are increases in price and, even at best, no effect on quality. When physicians and hospitals set the rates and insurance companies compete for clients, and this is the case when a variety of for-profit companies are selling health insurance, the consumer is the loser. Several arguments favor having all health insurance (including WCB medical care functions) handled by a single public agency:

a) The government is best able to represent the public (the consumer) in discussions with the providers of health care services on such questions as price, quality and distribution.
b) Administration in both the physician's office and in the central insurance program is simplified. Administration costs in the United States, with multiple carriers and contracts, are 5-10 times those of our Canadian system.
c) There is better capacity in the insurance agency for evaluation and research.
d) There is more uniform and more complete statistical documentation of patterns of service.
e) The use of a single program covering all of the population eliminates all discussion about whether people should be rejected, or charged higher premiums, because they are likely to consume a great deal of care.

The choice of a single carrier usually settles the question of whether the insurance program should be run by government or a for-profit agency. Monopolies should, to the extent that they are the rational choice, be in public rather than private hands. Either way they invite inefficiency and insensitivity to users but in public hands there is, at least, some degree of accountability. Deciding whether to operate the public plan from within a ministry or through a crown corporation (such as The Manitoba Health Services Commission) is less important but the political accountability of a department is greater than that of a crown corporation. Many quasi-public (special purpose) bodies which formerly administered health insurance programs have now disappeared.

Many of the above comments apply only to an insurance arrangement that must adapt to the fee-for-service method of physician payment. When capitation is a real option, as it is with the health maintenance organizations in the United States, then multiple competing carriers can lower costs. In capitation the providers, or an agency representing providers, agree to deliver a prescribed spectrum of care for a fixed amount per person per year, and competing agencies can lower the price. When fee-for-service is the method of physician payment, the volume and value of services that will have to be paid for is unknown. The same principles apply to hospital insurance, where global budgeting is a better approach than per diem or fee-for-service payments.

In a discussion about health insurance even five years ago, it would have been necessary to write about all the physician payment options available, including direct billing, billing the patient only, billing the government and also extra billing, billing some artificial intermediary, and using different billing arrangements for different patients at the physician's discretion.

Provincial action in provinces such as Quebec and British Columbia removed this chaos years ago and the *Canada Health Act* cleared up the chaos in the rest of the provinces.

Features that Canadians Wish to See in their Health Insurance Program

1. No payment by the patient directly to the providers of service at the time of service.
2. Coverage of a broad range of services provided by a variety of providers in a variety of locations.
3. No loss of coverage when costs are high, and no cancellation of insurance when future costs are likely to be high.
4. A program open to all persons.
5. A reasonable quality of care with quality measured in terms of clinical adequacy, continuity of care, accessibility and acceptability.
6. Freedom of choice of providers and receivers of care.
7. Simple and inexpensive administration — a minimum of red tape. Consumers want a program designed to keep things simple for the patient and the doctor.
8. Continuous coverage on moving from one province to another (portability).
9. Good value for money spent.

UTILIZATION

Age and sex are closely correlated with the use of health care services. Babies, the elderly and females aged 15-45 are heavy users of health care. Before age 5 males use more health services than females. From 5-14 years and after age 45, males and females consume relatively equal amounts of care per capita whether measured in number of services or cost in dollars.

In most provinces, 80-85% of the population see a physician at least once a year. For optometrists and chiropractors the figures are 10-20% and 5-15% respectively.

Utilization of health services is usually expressed as numbers of contacts per person, per 1000 or per 100,000 per year. The number of physician contacts per person per year in Canada has risen from less than three, thirty years ago, to around 10-12 in recent years, and the increase is continuing. In the period 1982-84 the number of medical services per patient in Alberta rose by over 15%.

The number of admissions to hospitals per 1000 fell from 167 in 1973 to 148 in 1980-81. The number of days of acute hospital care per 1000 also fell, but the amount of the decrease is not easily identified because of the mixing of acute and long term days of care; many hospitals provide both types. The number of hospital admissions per 1000 involving surgical procedures and treatments rose from 82 in 1971 to 89 in 1980-81 (with major fluctuations in between) despite a reduction in the availability of surgical beds. Shortened lengths of stay for inpatient surgery have more than made up for the reduced bed supply. In addition to the increase in hospital surgery there has also been a steady increase in the number of surgical procedures performed as day surgery, outpatient surgery and office surgery.

Utilization of LTC institutions is increasing steadily per 1000 total population but there is not much recent change in utilization if expressed as use per 1000 population over 65, and in some locales such as Ottawa-Carleton, there has been a decrease in the percentage of those over 65 who are in institutions.

Home support services have grown rapidly from their formal beginnings in the 1950's. Emergency visits and the use of ambulances continue to grow.

Other services are also being provided more often. Between 1976 and 1981-82 the rate of billings in Saskatchewan for psychotherapy rose 38%, for consultations 25%, for office visits 20% and for laboratory services 8%, while home and emergency visits remained steady and diagnostic radiology services decreased 10%. In Ontario, the volume of tests performed in private laboratories rose 54% in the first 5 years of the 1980's.

Even the rates of established individual procedures are rather unpredictable. In 1968 less than 5% of Canadian births were by caesarian section; this statistic rose to 12% in 1977 and to 20% or more in many centers. There is now a national effort, led by the Society of Obstetricians and Gynecologists of Canada, to reverse the trend.

Physicians have a startling capacity to alter utilization. In most major centers it is customary to find 5-6 cases per 1000 newborns who require treatment for congenital dislocation of the hip, but one orthopedic surgeon in Vancouver for years found 12-15 cases per 1000, in what appeared to be a comparable population, who required treatment.

Physician approaches to common ailments also vary greatly and bring quite different levels of utilization and cost. Examples include hemorrhoids, where therapy options include high fibre diet, ligation, injection, topical medication, cryosurgery and surgical removal; or mild to moderate seasonal allergies, where the choices are long term desensitization with injections or use of medication during the allergy season. Use of diagnostic procedures is also unpredictable. In Alberta, between 1979-80 and 1980-81, there was a 22% increase in the volume of urinalyses billed to the provincial insurance plan. The volume of Pap smears varies with the source of advice followed and the habits of the practitioner, as does the use of ultrasound in pregnancy, the use of fetal monitoring during labor, the volume of mammographies or the frequency of CAT scans for patients with headaches. In at least two of these cases — fetal monitoring and the use of ultrasound in pregnancy — the patterns of use are inconsistent with the recommendations of the Society of Obstetricians and Gynecologists of Canada. In cancer treatment there is immense disagreement regarding when to use radiation, radical surgery, chemotherapy, or conservative surgery for a multiplicity of types of cancer, and the costs and side effects vary greatly as therapy changes. Manitoba studies found regional hysterectomy rates varied by as much as 100%. In the management of hypertension (high blood pressure), overtreatment is frequently reported.

Excluding obstetrical and newborn days of care, 54% of total hospital days in 1982-83 were consumed by females. Persons 65 years or over accounted for over one fifth of hospital separations and over one half of all hospital days. Persons 75 years and over, who represented 4% of the population, accounted for 10% of separations and almost one third of hospital days. The age group 45-64, which made up approximately 20% of the population, accounted for approximately 20% of separations and hospital days. The volume of use of hospitals by the elderly increased primarily because this age group has become larger but partly because they were using hospitals 38% more per 100,000 in 1982-83 than in 1961. Dr. Robert Evans, in 1988, reported a major concentration of care in the year before death, regardless of age.

Major provincial variations in average hospital length of stay (Table 5.8) are, to a significant extent, merely a reflection of the degree to which acute treatment hospitals in the various provinces operate long term care beds.

The number of reported abortions in Canadian provinces per 100 live births varies from 5% to 26%, with British Columbia having the highest rate. In the last 10 years the total number of abortions performed has slowly increased, the percentage performed in the first 13 weeks of pregnancy has decreased, and the percentage performed on persons less than 20 years of age has gone down by one quarter.

TABLE 5.8
SEPARATIONS,* DAYS OF CARE AND AVERAGE LENGTH OF STAY IN ACUTE TREATMENT SHORT STAY HOSPITALS BY PROVINCE 1982-83, EXCLUDING NEWBORNS

	Separations per 1,000	Days of Care per 1,000	Average Length of stay
Canada	146	1730	11.8
Newfoundland	162	1380	8.5
Prince Edward Island	193	1504	7.8
Nova Scotia	168	1594	9.5
New Brunswick	168	1724	10.3
Quebec	112	1700	15.2
Ontario	148	1690	11.4
Manitoba	160	1763	11.0
Saskatchewan	210	1665	7.0
Alberta	175	1884	10.8
British Columbia	149	1930	12.9

*These data include separations of out-of-province patients. These usually constitute 1-2% of cases but are 5% in Manitoba.

Source: *Hospital Morbidity 1981-82 and 1982-83*, Statistics Canada, 1986.

The extent to which health services utilization is a product of mental or emotional problems is uncertain, but many primary care health workers have identified psychosocial problems as the cause of over half of their patient contacts. This pattern applies to all socioeconomic classes.

Suggested Reading

Evans, R.G., *Strained Mercy, The Economics of Health Care in Canada*, Butterworth, Toronto, 1984.

Chapter 6

THE QUALITY OF HEALTH CARE

QUALITY ISSUES

The quality of health care is the product of many decisions. It is measured through many techniques used by many people and agencies.

The Multifactorial Nature of Health Care Outcomes

Some of the difficulties associated with evaluation of health care activities are more easily understood after recognition of the major factors that determine patient outcomes. These outcomes are a product of:

1. The basic mental and/or physical healthiness of the individual at the time of the health care intervention.
2. The basic healthiness of the psychosocial, economic and physical environment of the individual. Will the environment, both during health care and afterwards, promote or impede recovery?
3. The nature of the medical problem. Is it treatable, untreatable or in no need of treatment and, if it is treatable, is it at an early stage or a late stage? (For the great majority of health problems, the outcome is largely or completely determined by these first three factors.)
4. Whether the correct diagnosis(es) is (are) made, and whether additional incorrect diagnoses are made.
5. Whether correct treatment is prescribed. This factor includes prescribing the correct treatment for conditions that exist as well as avoiding prescribing treatment that is unnecessary.
6. Whether the patient contributes fully to the diagnosis/treatment/recovery process. The degree of patient compliance will depend considerably on environmental factors but is commonly under some degree of individual control.

It is evident that health care does not always have much to do with whether a patient recovers or even feels better.

It follows that measuring the quality of health services is not synonymous with measuring patient outcomes although outcome measures are, at times, the best way to decide whether health services are of adequate quality. As has already been stated, patient outcomes are determined by patient genetics, physical health, psychosocial health, intelligence and willingness and ability to implement activities that support health, and by the social and economic environment, as well as by the quality of the health services.

How Good Is Our Health Care?

The simple truth is that we do not know whether our health care services are doing all that they should or can do to improve health status. We do not know the relative importance of health services or of specific elements of different services. Medical schools presumably believe physicians are appropriately educated but many others disagree. Physicians have a rather low opinion of chiropractors but patients disagree. Our professional associations and clinical leaders in universities regularly make recommendations regarding what to do, or not do, but large numbers of physicians do not follow their advice. Fetal monitoring and the use of ultrasound in pregnancy have been mentioned as examples of this phenomenon.

Many studies have described the imperfections of our health services. A 1979-81 study based in sixteen major clinical centers reported that one quarter of biopsies of malignant bone and soft tissue tumors were inadequately performed or interpreted. In 18% of cases, treatment was less than adequate because of the diagnostic error. In 4% of cases, the inaccurate diagnosis led to an unwarranted amputation.

In many other instances, the usefulness of health services is not known. For many years, for example, it has been routine to perform carotid endarterectomies as a protection against strokes. This surgery was performed when the major arteries in the neck and leading to the brain were found to be narrowed by arteriosclerosis (the same process that produces narrowing in the arteries of the heart and leads to heart attacks). In the operation, the artery is cleared so that the channel is more normal. Many of these operations are done each year in Canada at a cost of many millions of dollars. The operation definitely improves the size of the channel in the artery, but we do not know whether or not it prevents strokes any better than taking one or two aspirin tablets daily, or whether either of these is worth doing. An earlier evaluation of the procedure that was done about 15 years ago was inconclusive. A major North American study in 50 Canadian and American centers was started in 1987 to decide whether the surgery was a waste of time or whether it should continue. This example is quite typical of many situations in which things are done without scientific proof that they are the best things to do, or even that they are helpful.

One similar neurosurgical procedure has already been evaluated. For years, neurosurgeons performed operations called the extracranial-intracranial arterial bypass on the arteries of the neck and skull for the purpose of reducing the risk of stroke. These operations were done because they became technically possible and because they seemed like a good idea. Finally a large and at least modestly scientifically valid international study (ending in 1986) reported that the surgery either did no good at all or actually increased the risk of stroke. Scientific study of many other kinds of surgery may lead to the same finding and probably will meet the same degree of rejection as this particular study met. Surgeons are not quick to abandon procedures to which they have become either psychologically or financially attached.

Many studies have shown inappropriate prescription of antibiotics and other drugs. A large study of cimetidine prescriptions (one of the ulcer wonder drugs of the last decade and one of the drugs most commonly prescribed in North

America) showed that in only 14% of the cases was this drug appropriate for the problems of the patient.

Surgical patterns are equally disturbing. They vary on the basis of medical culture and physician interest as well as users' preference and pathology. Users of health care should be aware of how likely it is that some part of their health care may be unnecessary or inappropriate and, therefore, unable to improve health status.

All of the above studies examined the clinical usefulness of services received. To fully evaluate the quality of total community health care, it is also necessary to know the extent to which necessary services are not received, the extent to which resources have been allocated to the most cost-effective actions, the extent to which patient rights have been honored, the extent to which users have been exposed to avoidable hazard, the level of efficiency with which resources have been used, the extent to which social values and priorities have been honored and, in the final analysis, whether the health care interventions are optimally altering the present and future health status of the community.

The remainder of this chapter will look at various aspects of the quality of health care.

THE MEASUREMENT OF QUALITY: THE GENERAL PRINCIPLES

Quality is a characteristic. Programs, procedures, patient care, a piece of equipment, a process, a department, an examination, a policy or an activity each have an inherent level of quality.

Evaluation is the making of a judgement about the adequacy of the quality of something. The judgment can be completely intuitive (as when one 'likes' a painting or a caregiver), it can be based on reliable, relevant, weighted, objective and perhaps quantified and carefully analyzed information, or it can lie anywhere between these extremes.

The process of evaluation always consists of the same basic steps whether one is dealing with a simple situation or a very complex one. There must be something to be evaluated, one or more indicators (criteria) that will be used to identify the quality of what is being assessed, units of measurement for each indicator and one or more standards against which the findings will be compared. There must be a process for applying the units of measurement to the indicators and a comparison of the findings and the standard(s). The evaluation will be imperfect, and perhaps useless, if any of these elements or processes are missing or cannot be carried out.

Indicators and criteria are often categorized as pertaining to either input (structure), process (throughput or performance), output (outcome or product), or impact. Criteria are often considered to be more general than indicators. If the criteria for evaluation of a nurse included 'the degree to which the nurse carries out patient care plans,' then one or more indicators would be used to tell whether or not the plans were being carried out.

The terms output, intermediate output, outcomes and impact may be defined and used differently. Confusion arises from the fact that a developed x-ray film is the output of the radiology department but is input into the complex of activities and services that make up patient care. The x-ray film is sometimes called an intermediate output. Outcome is a term which often is reserved for effect on a patient, a population or a system, while impact even more routinely has this connotation. When considering outcomes or impact it is desirable to consider both the negative and the positive outcomes or impacts.

Two examples may indicate a few of the points that have been made. Both of these examples could be made more simple (although not much more), and both could easily be made more complex.

a) Evaluation of a nurse.

The indicators chosen could be qualifications (an input measure), and/or punctuality (a process measure), and/or the frequency of drug dispensing errors (a process measure). Outcome or impact measures are usually inappropriate because outcomes are usually the product of many persons' efforts and activities and, therefore, are difficult to relate to the nurse. Patient satisfaction is sometimes the only relevant and valid outcome measure, and certainly often is the only outcome measure easily available. If punctuality is chosen as a criterion, the indicator could be the number of times late or the number of minutes late. Whichever is chosen, there must be a process (or processes) by which one learns how often the nurse is late and/or how late.

b) Evaluation of a community health services network.

This evaluation can consider or ignore acceptability, availability, regional co-operation, accessibility, efficiency, efficacy, cost-effectiveness, relative cost-effectiveness, priority setting, ethics, scope or effects on health status. Evaluation can, but should not, be based on measurement of inputs such as manpower or the supply or range of facilities and services. It can look at elements of process such as patient referral or the adequacy of record keeping, or it can look at outcomes or impacts such as effects on the health status of the community. Mortality rates or morbidity patterns are appropriate measures of community health services only when sophisticated operational research accurately identifies the extent to which the health services have affected mortality and disability.

Evaluation of quality is filled with possibilities for misunderstanding or arriving at inappropriate conclusions. It is, for example, difficult to evaluate anything on behalf of someone else. Health professionals often decide what is best for a patient but if the patient is asked he or she often chooses different actions and futures. Patients may attach quite different degrees of importance to a good life or an independent as opposed to a long life. One patient may have quite different feelings about convenience, safety, comfort and protection of their family ties or income than does another.

Evaluation results may be positive or negative depending on the perspective of the evaluator. Evaluation conclusions may be complimentary when the technical quality of a procedure is being examined, even if that procedure may be completely abandoned if examined in terms of usefulness. Patient care in an intensive care unit may be considered excellent but one might find that inadequate diagnosis or transportation caused the crisis, in which case the overall health services network becomes inadequate. Technological care may be excellent but psychosocial and emotional care very poor; the extent to which the care is seen as adequate or inadequate will vary with the importance attached to each element of care and to the standards set for each element. In other cases, the outcome of care may be excellent but the care itself will be found to be poor; the patient was exposed to unnecessary hazard or cost.

In the two decades after the second world war, it was assumed that increasing the supply of resources was the answer to all problems. By the mid 1960's the reverse was considered to be true. Reducing the supply of acute treatment hospital beds was seen as necessary for a balanced and cost-effective health care network and now a reduction in physician supply is advocated and needed for the same reason.

Although many programs, especially peer review programs, examine the quality of individual professionals, there are few programs which systematically examine total professions in terms of the appropriateness of their curricula or assigned roles. If such a systematic examination were carried out, it is likely that nurses, family physicians and a variety of specialists or physicians in subspecialties would be trained differently and used differently.

In deciding what to evaluate, or how to evaluate it, it is important to remember that everything affects quality and everything can be evaluated. In the face of the impossible task of validly and, perhaps, repetitively evaluating everything, one must try to give priority to questions and situations of major importance.

Generally speaking, evaluation does not include identification of why things are or are not of good quality. When quality is found to be inadequate, it is the job of managers to decide whether correction is indicated and, if it is, to find out why quality is poor and how to improve it.

Characteristics of a Good Evaluation Process

Outcome and degree of exposure to risk are usually the primary concerns of a patient (although such things as acceptability, convenience, discomfort and cost can also be important variables), and they are the best measures of the quality of care of a population. Technicians may be of high quality, administration may be of high quality, staff-to-patient ratios may be excellent and facilities may be the best; however, collective patient care quality can be truly expressed only in terms of how well the patients did in comparison to how well they might have done, or how much hazard they were exposed to in comparison to how little they might have been exposed to.

In the evaluation of the quality of health services, we tend to concentrate too much on measures of input and too little on process, output and impact. Impact measures are essential to evaluation of the quality of a system, or of the care provided to a community. Process measures are important because they are often the most appropriate for evaluation of the care given to an individual patient.

When evaluating quality of care, one has to carefully define what is being evaluated and over what period of time. Does the evaluation encompass one episode of illness, one part of the episode or a period extending beyond an illness? Is one evaluating a program, a service, an activity, a person or a function?

Two cautionary comments are important. Firstly, we quite commonly set standards and evaluate quality in terms of a single service, a single episode of illness, the part played by a single individual, or some other quite circumscribed event or activity. This approach is acceptable as long as it is remembered that total patient care is not being measured. Secondly, when we evaluate something other than direct patient effect, such as the quality of a laboratory or a patient record, we are only measuring something that we believe affects a patient's safety and health outcome.

It is obvious that the task of evaluating health care is complex. The roles and techniques are often untried or unclear, but a few characteristics appear to be desirable features of most evaluation exercises:

1. Ethical acceptability.
2. Emphasis on outcome indicators, or input/process indicators that have an established relationship to outcomes.
3. Attention to the efficiency and cost-effectiveness of the evaluation process itself. Only significant data should be collected, evaluation should be repeated only at sensible intervals, and cost should be in proportion to the importance of what is being evaluated.
4. Reasonable replicability and acceptability.
5. Use of indicators and standards that reflect the concerns and opinions of all interested parties including users, providers, planners/administrators and payers.
6. Use of indicators that, in a balanced way, represent all important features or characteristics of the thing being evaluated, preventing undue emphasis on ethical aspects, quantifiable data, user opinions, technical processes or other specific features representing only some of the factors that are important to quality.
7. Use of a built-in pattern of repetition on either a regular basis or in response to identified warning signals such as a rise in patient, caregiver or community complaints.

TECHNIQUES AND TOOLS USED IN EVALUATION OF HEALTH CARE

Because quality is a product of an immense range of policy, administrative and clinical decisions, and because protecting quality requires an equally varied set of actions, each of a vast array of tools and techniques is at times appropriate:

1) The information in medical records is often used to measure the quality of patient care. Medical records are the basis for, or are used in, the medical audit (prospective and retrospective), the nursing audit, the reports produced by the Hospital Medical Records Institute (HMRI) and the Professional Activity Study (PAS), the tracer disease concept, the peer review process of some Colleges of Physicians and Surgeons and comparison of the effectiveness or cost-effectiveness of different approaches to a problem.

2) Population data derived from surveys can document levels of immunization, the incidence and prevalence of handicaps or disease, the degree to which health care is considered to be unsatisfactory and levels of unmet need. Continuing (longitudinal) population studies such as that based in Framingham, Massachusetts, look for relationships between health (or ill health) and a broad range of population factors. They have contributed greatly to our certainty that environment, lifestyle and heredity are more important to community health status than are health services, but they have not primarily evaluated health services nor did they intend to.

3) Direct observation is used to evaluate the quality of trainees and providers of care. It is also used in the hospital accreditation process and is part of the peer review program of the Ontario College of Physicians and Surgeons, in which office equipment and environment are examined along with office medical records.

4) Analysis of data on claim forms submitted to provincial insurance plans is occasionally used to find medical practice patterns that are thought to be undesirable, although the primary function of the analysis is identification of unusual billing patterns. These data, in combination with other data, can also be used to examine utilization patterns and to detect inequitable access to health care.

5) Cost-effectiveness studies report the extent to which expenditures result in changes in health status. There are, unfortunately, very few of these. Studies or information systems which deal only with cost, such as the new hospital MIS developed by the Canadian Hospital Association, do not tell us anything about effectiveness.

6) Despite a tendency toward preoccupation with physical health rather than total health, some researchers have produced new and more encompassing evaluation tools. These instruments tend to look primarily at physical abnormality and physical ability or performance but they may also document behavior, mental health (state of mind), and complaints/symptoms. The broad instruments include The Rand Health Insurance Study Measures (Rand), The Index of Well Being (IWB), The Sickness Impact Profile (SIP), The Nottingham Health Profile (NHP) and the Duke UNC Profile (DUHP). None are in widespread use in Canada at this time but all should be conceptually of interest to those who wish to measure health status and then study how to improve it.

7) Comparisons of performance and previously established criteria are common. Examples include the tracer diseases concept, Sentinel Health Event

Systems, patient surveys that examine the appropriateness of patient location and prospective patient care audits.

Quality Assurance (QA)

Quality Assurance is a new term. Its meaning is unclear, although usage is general. Many institutions have QA coordinators and committees, but job descriptions and mandates vary immensely. One common theme is that quality must be the responsibility of all departments and of senior management, and that a broad approach to it is desirable.

Quality assurance is composed of two related but distinctly separate activities (Figure 6.1). The first of these is quality measurement (or evaluation), the second is quality control. Measurement can be performed by either in-house or external personnel. Quality control can be partly accomplished through external regulation or assistance but, to a large extent, it must be accomplished through in-house actions and decisions. Measurement has already been disussed.

QA should look at both the negative and positive effects of what is done. It should measure quality and implement procedures to improve it. It should give highest priority to deficits that can be corrected and which have a proven and substantive effect on outcomes.

Quality Control

After quality measurement activities have led to awareness of the quality of total health care, of some part of it, or of something related to it, action to improve or maintain quality can then be considered. Quality control is that part of the QA process that begins after quality has been measured. The two phases of QA are not always easily separated; the same activity often evaluates and then improves performance.

Everything affects quality, but many things affect it very little. Consequently, improvements should not be automatically sought just because imperfection is found. Factors which are commonly upgraded or maintained as part of quality control include the following:

1. the quality of the workers which, in turn, is thought to be a product of the inherent quality of those who become health workers, the quality of their formal education, the availability of good role models, the adequacy of continuing education, the adequacy of certification and recertification programs and the relevance of worker skills to the task being performed.
2. the quality of the environment in which activities are performed. This factor, in turn, is the product of the policies and procedures in place, the quality of equipment, facilities and back up staff, and the appropriateness of the location in which activities are being performed. The environment includes more than just the health service environment; it includes social service networks and the nature of educational, urban, justice and employment systems.
3. the degree of compliance of the system, and all parts of it, with the values and ethics of users and communities.

FIGURE 6.1
THE QUALITY ASSURANCE PROCESS

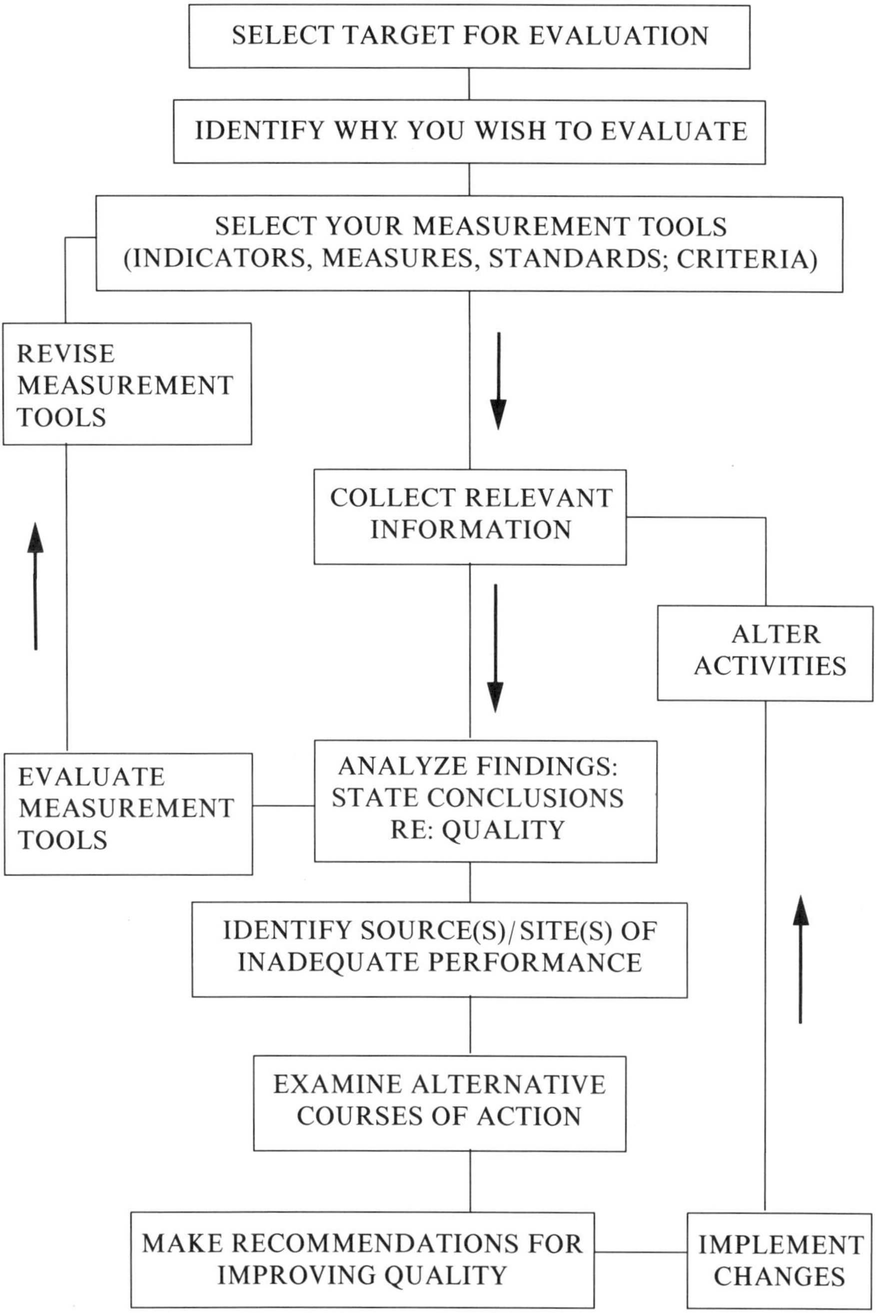

4. the technical quality of the work that is performed, which is a product of the worker and the environment.
5. the adequacy with which the patient or other affected persons are informed and involved (which is one aspect of ethics).
6. the quality and appropriateness of the clinical and administrative decisions made. These include such things as the timing and quantity of activities performed, which in turn are the products of the quality of the judgment and ethics of the workers, the availability of resources, and the quality of policies and of the process of resource allocation. Decisions also govern acceptability and accessibility of services, as when physicians, either individually or through hospital admission policies, determine which patients will be admitted to hospital.
7. the quality of the evaluation activities. Evaluation activities in themselves tend to improve quality of process and quality of decision making. Surveillance, whether it is of major surgery, billing practices, bed allocation, response to patients' complaints or the allocation of resources, is likely to reduce the volume of inappropriate activity. A more fundamental argument supporting the need for good evaluation programs is the fact that it is difficult to correct poor quality if it has not been identified.

Decisions and actions aimed at improving the quality of health services usually attempt to alter the supply of resources, upgrade available resources, allocate resources more optimally or improve the utilization of resources. The most global of these decisions will be made by policy creators, planners and administrators. Caregivers will continue to dominate at the personal level.

The allocation or reallocation of money is one of the important tools for improvement of the quality of health care outcomes. Inability to control the costs in any major expenditure area is, therefore, a threat to quality improvement everywhere.

Many programs are aimed at better use of resources, and better resource use should mean better quality of care. For example, patient categorization in hospitals allows nursing staff to be better distributed to wards. Placement coordination services and regional patient assessment processes improve the matching of patients with programs or facilities. Operating room scheduling can minimize disruption of physician office time. The delivery of care through multidisciplinary teams can allocate work more efficiently and conserve patient resources. The amalgamation of obstetrical units or the designation of only a small number of hospitals as appropriate for highly specialized services also improves quality.

Provincial and federal statutes are fundamental to many quality control activities. The mandatory reporting and follow-up of selected diseases reduces their likelihood of being a hazard to the community. Provincially required certification, licensing and discipline improve the quality of workers. The restriction of certain duties to certain professionals such as dentists and physicians is thought to protect quality but negative impacts of these rules may be as great as the positive ones. Drug licencing and the use of federal legislation to ban unsafe equipment are other examples, as are regulations governing the granting of hospital privileges to physicians and dentists.

Resource allocation is, perhaps, the area of greatest weakness in our quality control, and our resource allocation will remain weak until we know a great deal more about the benefits of various health services. We have good examples but not enough of them. The annual physical check up was actively promoted until an extensive 1975-76 study by the Canadian Medical Association led to the proposition that, for many years of one's life, the annual physical is not a good use of resources. Nurses took the temperature of all patients in hospital 2 to 4 times a day until someone examined the practice in the early 1960's and said it was a waste of time. Similar comments have been made about fetal monitoring and the use of ultra sound in pregnancy. In terms of quality improvement, there is nothing so beneficial as stopping something that either produces no benefits or is actually a hazard.

PATIENTS' RIGHTS

One of the measures of the quality of health care is the extent to which it respects patients' rights.

Perhaps the most important right, and one which is honored most of the time, is the right to refuse to do what a health professional recommends. This concept of informed consent is longstanding but is still evolving. At one time, a general consent form, usually signed at the time of admission to hospital, gave the physicians and institutions permission to proceed virtually as they pleased. Later, it became necessary for the consent to specifically authorize designated procedures. More recently, informed consent required that the patient not only understand what was being proposed but also be fully informed about the risks associated with the intended services.

A new requirement has recently been added. An Appeal Court judgment in 1986 confirmed that merely describing the risks of what the caregiver wanted to do was not enough. Caregivers now must explain the available alternative courses of action to a patient so that an informed choice can be made. In this case, an award was made to a patient who became disabled following surgery. The surgery was found to have been adequately performed but the option of nonsurgical therapy was not presented or explained to the patient. The fact that the possibility of major disability was not clearly spelled out was also criticized. Informed consent cannot now be considered to have been given until all clinical options have been described by the practitioner and understood by the patient.

The necessity for patient agreement when the patient is mentally competent is absolute, but the question of what procedure to follow when the patient may be mentally incompetent is more difficult. Mental health legislation must attempt to protect the rights of the individual while also allowing physicians to institute therapy in selected circumstances without patient consent.

Patients probably believe and expect their medical information to be confidential, but they should be aware of the situations in which this confidentiality will not be preserved. Hospital and office medical records, or portions of them, can become partially or fully public through subpoena by a court, through a request from the Canadian Security Intelligence Service, through the compulsory reporting of a variety of reportable diseases, through the compulsory reporting of vital statistics, or through information provided to medical care insurance agencies so that payment will be received by the person providing service. The use of computers has not reduced the confidentiality of patient information.

Patients in different provinces have quite different degrees of access to their medical records. In Quebec, access at all times is assured by law but in most provinces patients have access to their records and related documents only at the discretion of an institution or physician or on the order of a court.

In the last few years a number of provinces have passed legislation preventing personal or legal access of patients to peer review documents.These documents are the product of one professional examining the work of another. When the confidentiality of these records is not assured, it is difficult to find physicians who will adequately perform the peer appraisal process.

When patients consider any aspect of care to be inadequate, they have the right to initiate a civil lawsuit. The incidence of successful suits is likely to increase with an increasing acceptance of American precedents, with the use of juries instead of judges in some provinces, with more generous time limits for commencement of an action and with general use of contingency fees (which are already in use in most provinces).

In theory, patients have the right not to be coerced by process or professionals but, in practice, patients are routinely placed in a take-it-or-leave-it situation or are in other ways convinced they should do what the system recommends. This coercion is particularly the case with the physically disabled, most of whom are elderly, and it is also common with minority groups.

Health care providers and administrators should actively seek to adapt their decisions and services to the religious and cultural preferences of clients. The beliefs and the culture of health care workers should not take precedence. Religious beliefs may alter diet (Jewish, Moslem, Seventh Day Adventist), days of work (Jewish, Seventh Day Adventists) or dress at work. Autopsies, organ donation, circumcision and the disposal of amputated limbs may have restrictions or protocols. Rituals vary at birth and at death (Roman Catholic, Episcopalian, Eastern Orthodox). Blood transfusions and use of blood products may be prohibited (Jehovah's Witnesses).

WORKERS' RIGHTS

Workers in health care, as with workers everywhere, should have the right to reasonable working conditions including safety and absence of discrimination. The most contentious current safety issue is the risk involved in contact with patients with AIDS or AIDS antibodies. Some American hospitals are now routinely testing a majority of admitted patients for AIDS so that staff may know when to be particularly careful regarding contact with body fluids.

Health and Welfare Canada has, for several years, sought individuals exposed to HIV (AIDS virus) by needle puncture wound or exposure to body fluids. The first 30 instances followed did not lead to infection. By the end of 1987, however, at least 9 cases of AIDS in health workers in North America had been traced to work-related contact. The risk of Hepatitis B is potentially much greater but immunization is available. Hepatitis B is also contracted through contact with body fluids and the incidence of Hepatitis B in health workers is 5 to 6 times that of the population at large. Over 1% of all hospital admissions are Hepatitis B carriers. A Toronto surgeon died of the disease in 1985, an event which sharply increased the use of Hepatitis B vaccine by health workers.

Other features of worker safety are no different from those in other industries. Hazards include noise, radiation, back injuries, burnout (especially in intensive care and palliative care units), toxic fumes and injury from clients. Workers should also be assured of the confidentiality of employee health records although this protection may not be required by law.

SUMMARY

When it was generally believed that every health problem would be resolved as soon as enough resources were available, there was little or no evaluation. All energies went into gathering more resources. Now we know health care cannot be given endless resources but we also know evaluation costs money, so now we do not evaluate because we want to spend every dollar delivering care, whether or not that care needs delivery or whether or not other services would be a better buy.

Planners and administrators who control resource allocation must allocate some of their scarce resources to research, including nonclinical studies, if they are to improve the usefulness of health care. Those who allocate resources must know the relationship between specific health care activities and the health status of individuals and communities or allocation will continue to follow historical patterns or the winds of medical politics.

The cost (in dollars) of various services or episodes of care in hospital is now well known or can be known. Costs outside of hospital are not so constantly examined but are also quite well known. There is, occasionally, reasonably good data about selected groups of patients, for example high risk pregnancies, and sometimes adequate data describing changes in the health of the group over time. There is virtually never a clear understanding of the extent to which health care is responsible for whatever changes have occurred in the population, and there is even less likelihood that we know what would have happened if health care resources had been cut back or increased by 10% or 50%. Actions based on the known efficacy or/and cost-effectiveness of various health activities will only become possible when we document the health of a population at one point in time, measure it again at a later point in time, know the health resources and activities that were applied in between the two points in time, and are reasonably certain of the part played by the health activities in whatever health changes occurred.

It is not easy to be optimistic when writing about the evaluation of health services. We have very few answers for that most important question, *What is the relative usefulness of the various things on which we spend our money?*

Suggested Reading:

Einsenberg, J.M., *Doctor's Decisions and the Cost of Medical Care, The Reasons for Doctors' Practise Patterns and Ways to Change Them*, Health Administration Press, Ann Arbor, Michigan, 1986.

Mizetic, B.Z., H.G. Pauli and P.-G. Svennson (eds), *Scientific Approaches to Health and Health Care*, World Health Organization, Copenhagen, 1986.

Stoddart, G. et. al., *The Economic Evaluation of Health Care*, Oxford Press, 1987.

Chapter 7

THE DYNAMICS OF HEALTH CARE

INTRODUCTION

Chapters 3, 4, 5 and 6 described organization, resources, cost, utilization and quality. This chapter will discuss interactions and interrelationships. The earlier chapters described the players and the products, while Chapter 7 discusses where and how these players and products show harmony, stress, innovation and inertia. Chapters 3, 4, 5 and 6 concentrated on the nuts and bolts, the static structures and recent experiences. Chapter 7 looks at major processes within the network.

POWER

Power implies the ability to control or influence events. It allows the offering of rewards (incentives) or the application of penalties (disincentives or coercion). In the health care network, power is widely dispersed among caregivers, other workers, institutions, consumers, communities, taxpayers, profit and nonprofit private corporations and all levels of government. The recent increase in grass roots' power and of providers other than physicians has altered the traditional distribution of power.

Power has several important characteristics. It is, for practical purposes, of little importance unless used. Power is most effective when it is acknowledged by others; for instance, a physician's order on a hospital chart will only lead to action if a nurse or other hospital worker believes the physician is entitled to write the order and if the worker believes someone would apply sanctions if the order were not carried out. Health care is a field in which influence (informal power) is often more 'powerful' than the legal authority to legislate or regulate. Power can be acquired or lost; it can be centralized or decentralized. Generally speaking, there is only so much of it to be distributed and to the extent that one person increases his or her power, someone else loses power.

Power does not flow only from constitutions, statutes and elections. The highly personal and often frightening nature of ill health or injury, the miracles of modern medicine and the high (often unreasonable) levels of expectation in the public have created an environment in which logic and mandate may be no match for the power of a charismatic politician or professional. It is an environment in which those who wish to have influence must often understand the political and behavioral elements of decision making better than they know how to handle data, conduct research or scientifically evaluate the options.

Individual caregivers have power based on their expertise, their ability to withhold or supply needed care, the information they control, statutes or regulations, a culture in which the client/patient and/or the family believes the caregiver should be in charge and make decisions, or on some combination of these factors. Any individual can have power through oratorical or other charismatic skills. Canadian governments derive their power from the public acceptance of our democratic traditions in which governments may, within their areas of jurisdiction, pass laws and see that they are enforced. By virtue of their policy-writing mandate governments, boards and administrators can, in their respective areas of control, start, reduce, expand or stop programs. All parties can exert influence beyond their areas of jurisdiction through activities such as lobbying, harassment, passing resolutions, sending letters to the editor or complaining, but these extra-parliamentary processes are particularly important to individuals and communities who lack formal power. Courts have power because governments, culture and tradition have given it to them. Bureaucrats have power through their expertise, their direct access to political policy makers and their capacity to obstruct, sabotage or ignore policies with which they do not agree. Throughout health services there are innumerable networks with power based in their internal loyalty, these might include the 'old boys network' — that is, the graduates of a particular university or school or members of the same occupational, religious, ethnic or political group. These groups and all others can also be powerful if they are able to offer money or withhold it, and people can have power because of the information they control.

In Canada, whether one is a politician, an administrator, a caregiver or a consumer, one's capacity to change health services or health policy is routinely dependant on the support of others. An understanding of networking, group dynamics and participatory leadership are routinely useful, if not essential. Changes being proposed must, in principle, be acceptable to, and preferably attractive to, a variety of social or bureaucratic entities, and the details of the proposal should be hammered out in a mood of compromise so that the necessary range of allies can be retained.

The amount of change that can be caused or prevented by a person, group, institution or government depends, not only on the amount of formal or informal power held or available, but also on the skill with which it is used and the skill with which the power of opposing forces is neutralized. The governments of Saskatchewan in 1962 and Ontario in 1986 could have averted or emasculated their doctor strikes by showing early sensitivity to minor issues which eventually led large numbers of physicians to support the militant minority. The governments failed to neutralize the power of their opponents. Physicians, as a group, routinely demonstrate poor tactics, insufferable self-righteousness and a lack of acceptance of social change. Their lack of understanding of issues and their lack of tactical skills has regularly resulted in physicians having minimal influence in situations in which they have major interest and in which their sensible participation would be helpful to all parties. A poor understanding of process reduces their power.

Increasing one's influence is not necessarily complicated or difficult. The desirability of seeking allies (creating networks) has already been mentioned. In addition, individuals or groups can promote themselves or their representatives as members of boards or committees or as candidates for political office. Merely understanding the committee process, including when and how to present motions, how to become secretary and write the minutes, or how to present information so that it attracts allies can sharply increase the chance that preferred ideas will be all or partly implemented. Understanding the world of the media, including its appreciation of good copy, the importance and timing of deadlines, the impact of courtesy and convenience and the desirability of fair and equal treatment, can improve one's opportunities for influence. It is helpful to appreciate that influence is greatest in situations in which one's stature is established, whether this is a classroom, an office or an operating room. Also, messages are best received if delivered by someone who is acceptable to the recipient.

In seeking to have influence or exercise power, it is best to have a plan, with each step along the way having options. Without planned options, it is more difficult to adapt quickly to changes in allies or environment. One must know the subject, anticipate questions and prepare answers, be flexible so that opportunities can be used to advantage, and understand the rules according to which one must operate. One should give credit freely to those who offer support; a motivated ally or colleague is much better than a jealous one. One should set an example with energy and attention to detail, in particular, to the human relations details.

In the end, despite the importance of money and formal power and tradition, events usually happen through people talking to people, and the 'people' skills are, therefore, still vital to affecting events. Co-operation, flexibility, sharing (of the workload and the credits), reliability, patience, tenacity and tolerance all contribute to the kind of reputation that carries its own inherent power.

Competition for territory and power within the health services network is intense. Hospitals see themselves as the hub and routinely wish for more and more of the system to be within their orbit. Within the hospital family, the tertiary care (university teaching) hospitals constitute a form of royalty. These hospitals and their superspecialists see themselves as the elite whose services deserve limitless access to funds and growth, a position put forward in 1984 in a Medical Research Council submission to Health and Welfare Canada. Nursing homes see themselves as the 'keystone' in long-term care, a position vigorously rejected by almost (if not all) other parts of the LTC network. Community health centers (by many names) remain an optimistic group who see themselves as the logical entry point and gatekeeper to medical treatment.

Many health workers are anxious to climb the ladder or, at least, to defend their rung. Physicians pretend chiropractors and optometrists do not exist and equally vigorously continue to believe that nurses, physiotherapists, psychologists and pharmacists are merely useful responders to the orders of doctors. Dentists continue to battle with denturists and dental therapists, and family physicians continue to struggle to preserve a meaningful but perhaps shrinking place in the health care team.

Physicians are much less dominant in health policy development than they were, and somewhat less dominant in patient care, but their powers remain massive. They, and only they, can admit and discharge patients from hospital. They do almost all the prescribing. They have almost total control over access to diagnostic and therapeutic tools including almost all of the high technology tools. They are perceived by patients as the primary holders of the key to life despite the importance of other caregivers and the dominance of non health factors and environments in the equation of health. They have great financial ability to defend themselves; in 1984 a small minority of right-wing physicians in Ontario quickly and easily raised $250,000 to support a legal challenge to legislation opposing extra billing.

A few examples may show how difficult it is to predict who, or what, will be most powerful in a given situation or at a particular moment in time.

Physicians tried to stop chiropractors from being given statutory recognition, but they could not. Nurses, through their associations, their clinical importance and their large numbers should dominate in matters of nursing policy but their objections to formally trained nursing assistants were ignored by governments and educators. In 1987, hospitals, provincial governments, consumer groups and most of the public opposed patent law changes that would raise the price of drugs in Canada but the political clout of the pharmaceutical industry was greater and new legislation was approved by the House of Commons. A new and unexpected player, the Senate, complicated the process but the outcome was only delayed, not changed. When the Ottawa Civic Hospital planned a major building program in 1978-79 but neglected to discuss traffic, parking and other such issues with the neighborhood, the hospital found it could not get a building permit; the entire project had to be redrawn. The community association and a sympathetic city hall were more powerful than the hospital. The unanimous passage of the Canada Health Act in 1985 demonstrated the power of the extra-parliamentary processes. Opinion polls, petitions and public discussion convinced even traditionally conservative MPs, who personally approved of extra-billing, that extra-billing must go. These examples are not meant to have anything in common; they merely demonstrate the existence of a wide range of players in situations of conflict and the unpredictability of the outcomes.

Of all the players who wield power, the provincial governments are probably the most important, but because there are so many players, victory, or partial victory, usually goes to those who have most carefully done their lobbying, built their networks, and neutralized major opponents. Good tactics, the art of compromise, and the talents of good leadership are often more important to success than good data or legal/administrative control although it will almost always be very persuasive to be able to offer money or to withhold it.

POLICY AND PLANNING

Policies represent intent and may represent practice. They are not recommendations. They are statements of what is to be done. They infer a capacity to implement. They may or may not say much about how the stated intent should be carried out.

The processes of policy creation and of planning are often difficult to separate. They both occur at many levels and places in the health system. A policy is a decision that has been made whereas planning refers more to the process through which the decision was selected or the process by which it is implemented.

Statutes (laws) relevant to health are enacted only by federal and provincial governments but the list of bodies which write health policy includes institutional boards of trustees, children's aid societies, boards of health, boards of education, municipal governments, some regional planning agencies and all those other boards, councils and executives of profit and nonprofit agencies which establish rules about financing and resource allocation.

The legislative stages of public policy adoption are highly visible but policy often passes through a complicated, tortuous and time consuming multistage process before ending in a legislature or other forum able to approve policy. A policy proposal can originate within government or from outside; it can come from special interests, from special studies or inquiries, from the example of other jurisdictions, from a coroner's inquest or a court, from citizens or civil servants. Proposals tend to be examined, initially, in one department and reviewed by one minister. If supported at this level, they may then go to a cabinet committee (or more than one) and to various departments, for financial, social, political or organizational evaluation.

The role of the informal caregiver and the voluntary agencies as creators and shapers of programs that later become universally accepted is impressive. Palliative care, programs for persons with Alzheimer's disease, sheltered housing for the disabled and home-support services of various kinds exist because someone in the community saw a need and responded to it. Family-centered maternity care will, as with the other examples listed, eventually also arrive, but often despite rather than because of initiatives in the offices with a designated responsibility for policy and planning.

After passage of an act in a legislature, it becomes law when proclaimed. There may be a considerable delay between third reading in the legislature and actual proclamation, sometimes so that the regulations under the act can be written. Statutes may set out only the general principles, with the details being written into the regulations. Statutes are difficult to amend but regulations can be easily altered. Statutes can only be amended by a legislature whereas regulations can be changed by Order in Council or a minister.

Advisory groups, regardless of their permanence or reputation, do not write policy. The Economic Council of Canada or a new National Health Council (as proposed in the 1984 report of the Canadian Medical Association Task Force on Allocation of Health Care Resources) may make recommendations and be quoted often, but these recommendations are not policy and most of them do not become policy. In 1980, an Ontario Royal Commission into the Confidentiality of Health Information brought forth 179 recommendations; by 1987, only one of these had become law. Task forces, commissions and other such bodies have the habit of producing reports which include very long lists of impractical and unpriorized recommendations, a habit which may help explain why so few recommendations become policy.

Health services statutes and their related regulations tend to affect one or more of the following.

1) Quality and safety. These are affected by legislation (and their regulations) governing such things as the running of hospitals and nursing homes, the handling of radioactive substances, the disposal of toxic wastes, and professional quality assessment.
2) Professional entry or function. Licencing regulations limit the entry of individuals to specified professional groups and, to varying extents, prevent other persons from performing certain of the acts that are performed by the licenced group, for example, physicians and dentists. Certification is associated with entry restriction but does not convey exclusive functional domain, for example, nurses and physiotherapists. Others who do not qualify for certification can legally perform these duties.
3) Rate or price regulation. Rates of payment — that is, fees, sessional payments and salaries — can be determined by the government. Governments can vary rates of pay on the basis of location or other factors.
4) Income regulation. Governments can place ceilings on incomes per year or month, from a particular paying agency.
5) Institutional authority to deliver services as with, for example, hospital legislation enabling the building of a new hospital.
6) Matters of ethics or human rights. The 1985 Canadian Charter of Rights, for example, outlaws discrimination while establishing some grounds for exemption. The exact impact of the Charter of Rights on health services is not likely to be known for some time.

Policies are a reflection of the values and priorities of those who influenced and authored them. In 1984, the government of Ontario found $45 million to bail out a financially sinking, luxury lodge in northern Ontario. At the same time, it could not find $45 thousand to bail out the Kenora (Ontario) Children's Aid Society overwhelmed with the products of family breakdown in that northern community. Also at the same time, there was almost no help available for hundreds of ex-psychiatric patients recently discharged from Toronto psychiatric institutions. The values and priorities of policy makers have a direct effect on the services available to people. Several provinces are actively attempting to set out overall goals which will provide a framework within which policies and plans can be created.

Individuals or groups who wish to influence policy should become thoroughly acquainted with the key committees and other agencies or persons who are important in the policy development processes in their own provinces. They should also be aware of the various steps in both the statutory and the Order-in-Council process. Influence may be exerted at all points along the way, even at the end of the process when regulations are being drafted in support of legislation. One should know whether the regulations will be issued on the authority of cabinet, a cabinet committee, a single minister or some identified agency or board.

The policy creation process in Canada is influenced by the concepts of democracy, pluralism and federalism, each of which reduce the ease with which leaders can do as they please. In our society, there are well-defined 'limits to governing', especially when all interested players understand the process and play the game in the way that is their right.

The process of policy selection (creation) or planning may be very sophisticated or very simple. It can be highly intuitive, as with a committee discussion where expert opinion and group dynamics determine the choice, or it can be highly quantitative with use of hard data, statistical analyses and complex simulations. Either way can be appropriate or inappropriate; both approaches should include the steps of clarifying objectives, identifying alternative ways to achieve the objectives and evaluating the various alternatives. With the emergence of good planning techniques and well-trained planners, the quality of the policy selection process is improving. Practical politics seem to demand that we usually build on or modify what exists rather than abandoning what exists and replacing it with something quite different; our present process is usually called disjointed incrementalism.

Health planning at one time often consisted merely of selection of quite arbitrary resource to population ratios such as one public health nurse per 5000 population or 6 acute treatment beds per 1000 population. This arbitrary selecting is still done but is now partly replaced by needs planning in which the needs of a population are documented and plans are then developed to meet those needs. As with all change, however, the conversion to needs based planning has not been without its pitfalls.

In the 1980's in Ontario, needs studies were seen as a necessary prerequisite to a wide series of actions. Inadequate information derived from poorly conducted local studies was, and continues to be, regularly used instead of good information produced through much better studies performed in comparable communities. Needs studies prepare one for planning; they are not the essence of planning. Deciding what to do in response to specified problems is planning; information from a variety of sources merely helps one decide what to do. The essence of planning is the identification and evaluation of available alternatives, an evaluation which should include consideration of technical, economic and socio-political factors. The value and role of needs studies have been regularly misunderstood by some and this misconception has interfered with good planning.

Other factors also reduce the quality of our current health planning. Our responses are too often reactive rather than proactive; many decisions are of the firefighting variety. We also do not know enough about the effects of various services and expenditures on the health of communities. Health planning has, to a large extent, assumed that if physicians think an action is useful then it is, in fact, useful, an assumption that has lead us into many high cost, high volume activities that probably have modest if any effect on either the quantity or quality of the life or health of a community.

Municipal and regional governments are usually seen as very minor players in health planning but their areas of jurisdiction include land use (zoning), the availability and routing of general and special public transportation, the planning of traffic patterns, handling and disposal of toxic wastes, adaptation of facilities to the physically handicapped, establishing parking requirements, assigning heritage designations and the appointment of trustees. Local governments also usually influence or control the degree to which the community is served by a broad range of health related social services and institutions such as public housing, day care, recreation, half-way houses, and group homes, and these decisions have an impact on health planning. Local governments can also finance health services, especially capital costs. This role was largely abandoned to provincial governments for many years but is again emerging.

COMMUNICATION

Communication is absolutely necessary to the delivery of reasonably adequate health care. Providers need up-to-date information so that care plans can be prepared and followed. Consumers must be provided with information if they are to give an informed consent and participate fully in the preventive, diagnostic and therapeutic process. Planners and administrators must be constantly in contact with users, providers and other players. Communities and taxpayers are entitled to know what is being done, for what benefit and within what value system. Two-way or multi-way communication is a prerequisite to appropriate decision making throughout the health services network.

This two-way communication has, in health services as everywhere else, been revolutionized by computers. Terminals in offices, at the bedside and throughout the network have reduced errors in data transmission, made diagnostic information available to clinicians more quickly, linked geographically dispersed caregivers, and reduced staff requirements. Computers can protect confidentiality and privacy when proper access controls are in place. However, even with the computer contribution, the bulk of patient-provider communication is still unautomated.

Our health care providers are not usually well prepared for communication with people who speak different languages or have a markedly different culture. Not enough time is spent preparing providers for the task of obtaining information from, or sharing decision making with, the deaf, the mildly confused, the temporarily frightened, the chronically or acutely stressed or those with limited communication or intellectual skills, nor are health workers accustomed to working with interpreters. An examination of curriculae would, unfortunately, show more attention to biochemistry or bacteriology that is unlikely to be used, than to communication skills that are needed daily.

Exchange of information between the caregivers involved in the care of a patient in hospital is relatively easy because there is usually only one patient chart and the information in it is available to all caregivers, but the same level of information exchange between legally and geographically separate sources of ambulatory care is much more difficult to achieve.

Medical records are important legal, financial and patient care documents. In a hospital, they bring together the observations and opinions of many persons whereas in offices they may reflect only the activities of one caregiver; nevertheless, in both cases they confirm what was done, provide a rationale for the chosen course of action and support a request for payment when fee-for-service is the method of payment. They also show, with varying degrees of precision, the resources consumed by a patient.

In the traditional medical record, each type of professional has his or her own portion of the record; that is, the nurses' notes are separated from the physicians' notes and orders. In the Problem Oriented Medical Record (POMR or POR), the notes are separated on the basis of the problem that is being studied. The POMR is easier to digest, easier to summarize and easier to use in research or quality review but is probably still less widely used than the traditional format.

Diagnostic or symptom information tends to be recorded according to the International Classification of Diseases and Injuries (ICDA-latest edition) or the International Classification of Health Problems in Primary Care (ICHPPC). The Emerl Diagnostic Book (E-Book) is a summary of ICHPPC that is sometimes used to describe the profile of an ambulatory care practice.

LABOR-MANAGEMENT RELATIONS

Prior to the appearence of public insurance programs very few Canadian health care workers were unionized and the majority were poorly paid compared to similar workers outside the health sector. With unionization, however, and most health sector workers are now unionized, pay scales rose rapidly. Nurses, for example, achieved 40-75% pay increases in several provinces with the signing of their first negotiated contract, and a number of other worker groups had similar successes. Salaries and wages throughout the health care industry are now comparable to those paid elsewhere.

In most provinces, collective bargaining occurs only between the ministry and provincial unions. In Ontario, bargaining is not a provincial function but hospitals voluntarily act collectively to establish master contracts. In most provinces, strikes by hospital workers are illegal.

Physicians in several provinces are now officially unionized with the provincial medical associations (or the two separate specialist and family practitioner 'syndicates' in Quebec) as the bargaining units. The Quebec Medical Association, with both specialist and nonspecialist members, has tried, unsuccessfully, to replace the two separate syndicates as the bargaining agent for all physicians.

Physicians negotiate fees or incomes through a variety of mechanisms. Nova Scotia, Manitoba and British Columbia have tried to settle disputes through binding arbitration but are now wary of this process. The arbitration awards were unacceptably generous. In most provinces, the final fee increases are determined by government after discussions with the physician representatives. There may or may not be a mutually accepted fee increase; usually physician demands are not met.

MANAGEMENT INFORMATION SYSTEMS (MIS)

The managing of information has always been one of the great challenges of administrators; another is the management of people. The relative importance of these two functions varies from time to time and place to place, but the management of people is often much easier and better done if information is being well handled.

Information selection, collection, storage, retrieval and use have always been important. In recent years, computers have allowed the difficult to become mundane, the impossible to become routine and the previously unimagined to be merely difficult. These changes have been as revolutionary in health services as in other industries.

The development of MIS for the nonclinical side of health services is no longer news. Schedules for patient rooms, patient visits, operating rooms or public health nurses, inventory distribution and control, routine reports regarding patient census, patient transfers or surgical activity, personnel files, financial records and other operational data are now routinely computer handled.

Patient care has also been affected by the computer. Machine reading of electrocardiograms has long been routine and computers are fundamental to new imaging processes such as computerized axial tomography (CAT), positron emission tomography (PET) and nuclear magnetic resonance (NMR). Regular patient assessment allows more efficient allocation of nursing staff on the basis of workload (although some of these programs are still manual). Quality control through prospective medical audits may also be computer based, and a variety of students sharpen their diagnostic and treatment skills through computer assisted education. An increasing number of hospitals have terminals in all patient care locations and all laboratories and pharmacies, forming a network that allows instant access in many locations to the latest information about a patient. Computer programs are increasingly being used in pharmacies and elsewhere to identify potential drug incompatibilities or interactive effects, and other pharmacy-based programs are identifying patients who are double doctoring for the purpose of drug abuse or trafficking. Care providers, through their terminals, can be told when medications or other activities are due or have been given. Computer-based management information systems are still, unfortunately, seldom able to tell us how much a patient was helped by the services received, but this failure reflects human inadequacy rather than a problem with hardware.

Computers can, and increasingly will, be used to examine patient information, provide a list of possible diagnoses, identify the most likely one and suggest further investigation. They will, in the future, evaluate different therapies and suggest a preferred therapy. For the foreseeable future, the final decisions will always rest with a physician or other professional but the computer will become a valuable assistant and monitor.

The computer-based communication network will also continue to expand. Obstetrical records in physicians' offices will routinely be available to hospitals by way of a common data base. The hospital will have access to an up-to-date medical record as soon as the patient appears at the hospital. Physicians and others will, through their office terminals, stay aware of the progress of their patients, both in hospital and under the care of home care personnel. Computers will, on discharge, produce patient summaries for immediate delivery to the workers or institutions who will continue care. Immediate consultation with geographically separated specialists is increasingly available.

The progress made in our use of computers can lead us to believe that all MIS problems will be resolved by the next generation of computers. Unfortunately, individuals must still decide what data to collect and what not to collect, and administrators are poorly trained for this task. Some professions and institutions still wish to be individualistic and parochial; requests for standardization and co-operation are not always welcome. We are still far from developing the kind of continuous personal medical record that will integrate and summarize medical events throughout an individual's life. Until this type of information is available, we will have difficulty evaluating the cost-effectiveness of many preventive, diagnostic and therapeutic activities. Until we alter the information being collected, it will tend to tell us much more about the physical health of the patient than about emotional health or quality of life.

Health care MIS are constantly improving. Hospital data are standardized nationally and are summarized annually by Statistics Canada. The Hospital Medical Records Institute (HMRI) in Toronto, and the Professional Activity Study (PAS) in Michigan, but HMRI in particular, provide additional regular and ad hoc reports on activity in most Canadian hospitals. The CHA, with provincial and federal collaboration and funding, is nearing the end of a major project to improve hospital financial reporting. Use of at least portions of the new system is already mandatory in several provinces. Unfortunately, there are few equivalent projects outside of hospitals. The reporting of medical care, psychiatric care, public health activities and long term care is not yet standardized across the country.

Failings in information systems tend to be caused by the failures of managers rather than of MIS technocrats. Managers must have clearly stated objectives and know how to identify which data will be useful (and not useful), or the MIS is likely to collect and skillfully handle data which will not, when it is fully reported, answer the questions most important to the managers and planners.

Until we have industry-wide information systems which tell us what benefits were provided in return for known services, it will not be possible to fully allocate resources in ways that bring optimum benefit for the resources consumed.

COORDINATION AND INTEGRATION

These words are often used together although they are quite different. Coordination helps separated (discrete) administrative units or care delivery teams to work together. Integration is defined as a fusion of either two or more administrative units or two or more information systems, inventories, or other such services. 'Coordinated' units may be in the same organization, as is the case with departments in a hospital, or they may be in quite different organizations as is the case with a public health unit and a community health center. Both integration and coordination can occur at the point of delivery of service or at any higher level in the administrative hierarchy.

Integration is routinely a centralizing phenomenon, whereas successful coordination is frequently almost a prerequisite to the preservation of a decentralized arrangement in which functionally related but organizationally separate units must work together. The health services network exists to serve individuals and groups of individuals whose problems do not fit into convenient boxes — they cross bureaucratic and professional boundaries. The problems are emotional, physical, functional, cerebral, spiritual and financial, or all of these in the same person at the same time. It would be organizationally convenient if the problems of the person could be separated into parts and each part handed out to a particular system — a bit to a priest, a bit to a lawyer, a bit to a welfare office, a bit to a marriage counsellor, a bit to an ambulance, and so on. Unfortunately, bureaucracies and professionals are trained to cope only with specific problems and, therefore, they sometimes chop people into a set of discrete problems, each one the property of a particular agency or worker or statute. This dissociation is a major hazard to quality and convenience when the problems are interacting, as they usually are, and the hazard is reduced only by the coordination of agencies and professionals.

The purposes of coordination and integration include:

1) Providing improved service delivery, especially to multiproblem patients or families. These clients with complex problems, such as alcoholics and the severely disabled or ill (whether acute or chronic), require a variable and often sophisticated mix of health services with or without other social services.
2) Providing improved productivity through job sharing, information sharing, or simplified transfer of tasks or patients.
3) Decreasing opportunities for client manipulation of the system. This objective has, to date, been limited primarily to situations in which a client could obtain similar social support services from multiple sources, but future cost-control objectives may lead to greater interest in modification of utilization of health care.

4) Achieving better planning through a capacity to affect a greater number of components of a network, and a greater capacity to standardize data and procedures.
5) Achieving greater likelihood of conflict resolution within the service network or bureaucracy.

Integration has the added advantage of reducing or eliminating legal barriers to information transfer.

Prerequisites to successful coordination include the official and personal support of highest level bureaucrats, a willingness by all parties to become acquainted with the goals, fears, culture and operations of other parties, absence of serious levels of mistrust or competition, a willingness to develop new skills including those of consensus seeking, conflict resolution and negotiation, and a willingness to accept delays and failures so that common goals may eventually be better served. Another desirable prerequisite is the availability of successful role models or examples from which to learn, but these are, especially at the service delivery level, few and far between.

Although coordination and integration often seek the same ends they must, because of their inherent differences, use quite different techniques to attain those ends. They are also used in quite different circumstances; integration is used when merging or fusion is practical, whereas coordination can be useful and can be carried out almost anywhere at almost any time.

Techniques which promote coordintion include:

1) Multiagency committees or boards.
   Examples include federal-provincial committees of ministers of health or deputy ministers of health, special federal-provincial technical advisory committees dealing with such subjects as manpower, laboratory services or health insurance, and committees of regional planning bodies. The old voluntary hospital planning councils, the Halifax-Dartmouth Mental Health Planning Board and social planning councils are other examples.
   These multiagency committees may be standing or ad hoc, may be highly formal or quite informal, may exist at all levels of bureaucracy or community, and may be voluntary or mandatory.
2) The case conference.
   This forum is quite analogous to the multiagency committee but it operates at the point of delivery of care. It brings together a number of skills and points of view that are important in the solution of a problem or the provision of care to a patient and it improves the coordination of the many disciplines involved in the care of the patient.
3) Secondment of staff.
   There have been many examples of public health nurses playing a liaison and referral function in hospitals, physicians' offices and CHCs, and some multiservice centers will have on-site staff who are employees of provincial welfare programs, mental health agencies or children's aid societies. This arrangement, which encourages coordination, allows staff from several

agencies to work together in a single office without unduly disturbing established and, perhaps, parochial agencies.

4) Interlocking board memberships.
   In Quebec, board member exchange is mandatory for hospitals, regional planning councils, CLSCs and other components of the regional health and social services network.
5) Devices for information exchange.
   A study in Edmonton a few years ago asked 40 health and social agencies to comment on interagency liaison and coordination. Lack of information regarding the policies, resources and services of other agencies was reported as the biggest single area of concern, and many other researchers and participants at conferences have expressed the same opinion. Information availability and transfer is improved by such things as having a central community information service, adherence to a standard set of definitions and to a standard format for data collection, the production of simple but informative annual reports and the regular holding of regional or local conferences and seminars.
6) Formal agreements.
   Coordination is easier and better when the rules are produced by, acceptable to and accepted by all parties, as is the case with the agreements between educational and service units which assure field based training for professional and technical students.

Examples of integration are also common and include:

1) LTC patient placement services with the authority to control placement. Functions formerly served by independent admissions offices are now centralized.
2) Multiinstitutional organizations (MIO). These usually consist of two or more hospitals but also often include LTC facilities, ambulatory care units and public health programs. MIOs are now common throughout Canada with the western provinces leading the way. Health Science Centers were an early phase of institutional amalgamation.
3) The merging of the departments of health and of social services into one department.
4) The merging of small public health units in Ontario into county or multi-county units.

All large institutions and other bureaucracies are examples of integration although they are not always thought of as such. They represent the integration of such diverse functions as emergency services, hotel services, business services, education, psychiatric services and diagnostic services. When cared for in the community, patients who are quite similar to many institutional inpatients receive their care from multiple sources that are not only not integrated but often not coordinated.

The concepts of coordination and integration are inherent in such terms as 'one-stop shopping' and 'single-point-of-entry.' The general hospital is an example of an institution bringing many types of services together rather than having many types of workers deliver care to the patient from organizationally separate units. In this instance the unification (integration, centralization) was primarily for technological and administrative reasons rather than for client convenience, but inpatient hospital care certainly illustrates the one-stop shopping principle.

Community health centers and a variety of multiservice centers are, in a similar way, designed to bring a mix of health and social service professionals to one spot under one management with the client being the major winner. Group medical practices also bring convenience to the client through the adjacency of a mix of medical specialties and easy internal referral; there may or may not be easy access to other health professionals and there is seldom an association with social service personnel.

The 'single point of entry' concept commonly refers to an arrangement in which persons in need of continuing care are referred to and assessed by a standardized process based in a single agency. After review, the person is referred to the appropriate community based or institutional program for ongoing care. This arrangement is a great improvement over unintegrated options in which many types of agencies, programs and institutions use their own (often unique) referral and assessment practices.

Despite the acknowledged importance of coordination it is often inadequate. It is often impeded by:

(1) geographic dispersion such as the separation of the offices and laboratories that provide services.

(2) obvious or latent competition between agencies or individuals whose co-operation is important to the client. There can, for example, be competition between hospitals, between physicians or between agencies providing similar services such as prenatal classes or home support services. Client or community interest becomes secondary to institutional or worker self interest.

(3) unwillingness to share information.

(4) unwillingness to change. Coordination may require adaptation, sometimes with a sharing of functions or even the loss of specific functions. Counselling, for example, may move from physicians to social workers and psychologists. Coordination may also require a modification of currently used vocabulary and reporting. All of these changes may be resisted.

(5) interprofessional hostility or disdain such as that which exists between physicians and chiropractors, physiotherapists and athletic therapists or chiropodists and podiatrists.

(6) different priorities and objectives. Highly technological workers may rank client needs much differently than someone whose service area is housing, advocacy, spiritual health, employment or long term care.

(7) differences in self-image and external image. Health care workers, especially acute care workers, often have a higher social profile and status than social service or long term care workers.
(8) the fee-for-service payment system. Practitioners on fee-for-service find it difficult to coordinate or co-operate with other workers and agencies because their income is tied entirely to what they do and who they see. Shared services or transferred services may result in lower income or to difficulties with a paying agency.
(9) legal obstruction to easy exchange of information or delegation of functions.

Almost all of the factors that impede coordination also impede integration, but the list of impediments to integration also includes objections to an integrated patient record (such as is able to be used in a hospital), objections to loss of 'freedom' and a desire for corporate survival.

People and agencies may be reluctant to put the public interest ahead of their own. Personal freedom, personal income, agency survival and both agency and professional jurisdiction are not usually surrendered easily even if the change will improve the access, convenience, quality and/or cost-effectiveness of some service needed by some client or groups of clients.

Health service users need institutions and programs that communicate and co-operate but this need is often not met. The users need workers who form teams that can respond to multiproblem situations, but this need is also often not met.

DELIVERY OF CARE

The last half century has seen a large portion of health care become increasingly multidisciplinary and technological. The all-purpose physician working with an all-purpose nurse is no longer dominant. Most care is now delivered by a physician who works with a particular set of problems or patients, a nurse who works in only one clinical area, and a continually expanding cadre of other specialized health workers.

Some things have not changed. Physicians still often work alone. Nurses still usually have little if any specialized training. The workers within the traditional medical team still have minimal contact with the caregivers who are outside the medical model. Much health care remains relatively uncomplicated. Health workers who, in previous decades, were exposed to tuberculosis and septicemia and, then, to hepatitis as a condition of work, must now, in the same way, and hopefully with the same attitude, deal with exposure to AIDS.

The specialization of physicians has had many effects. Medical care insurance statistics suggest that one quarter to one half of all primary care is now provided by specialists. The percentage is much higher in pediatrics and in obstetrics. The rate of participation of the family physician in obstetrics has been falling for decades. Major increases in liability insurance for physicians performing deliveries has recently accelerated the trend. Specialists now provide two thirds of routine obstetrical care. Major surgery in large urban centers is now done almost exclusively by specialists, and the trend is pronounced even in rural and small urban centres.

Medical students are taught primarily by specialists and then, as interns and residents, work almost exclusively with specialists. The role of family physicians in Canadian health care has been protected somewhat by a widely established and governmentally encouraged network of family practice training programs that are based largely in university affiliated primary care (non hospital) group practices, but their future is uncertain.

Most formal health care is delivered within the medical model, a model in which the physician is the monarch. Other professionals who routinely work within the medical model almost always do so with the understanding that the right to diagnose and to prescribe is legally a physician's prerogative. This situation shows little likelihood of changing although the Royal College of General Practitioners in Britain recently proposed that nurses working in association with family physicians should have the authority to prescribe, or to alter the dosage of, a very limited list of drugs and biologicals.

Health care workers (such as chiropractors, optometrists, chiropodists and dentists) who usually operate outside the circumferance of the physician umbrella, have their own level of decision making rights, routinely including diagnosis and treatment, embodied in their own legislation.

The dental care arena was, at one time, as hierarchical as the medical model. Other workers including dental hygienists and denturists acted only under the direction of dentists. In recent years, however, denturists, dental technicians and dental therapists have, through legislation (which varies considerably among provinces), gained significant independence in providing diagnosis, therapy and technical service, a sensible trend which seemed secure until the Saskatchewan government, in 1987, decided to partly re-establish the historical model of dentist dominance.

Despite the legal, professional and historical underpinnings which support the independence of the physician as a decision maker, there are various situations in which other forces significantly intrude into decisions associated with the delivery of care. Financing decisions, such as those defining insured services, influence who receives care and where, hospital admission and discharge committees influence who gets admitted and how long they stay, peer review processes move care towards whatever is the current professional preference and hospital ethics committees influence the performance of providers when patients' rights are at stake. Most health care workers increasingly work within rules laid down by their profession or by some government or governing body.

The Care Delivery Team

As it became more and more unlikely that one person would have all of the skills necessary to care for a patient, the need for teamwork increased and several quite different types of teams emerged.

Sometimes the team is composed of equals, as when a group of medical and dental specialists plan and implement the care of a child with a cleft palate. Each specialist (pediatrician, anesthetist, plastic surgeon, dental surgeon) brings his or her own specific expertise. These types of teams are common when technologically complex care is delivered in tertiary care teaching hospitals.

Another type of team is composed of people who are not usually perceived as equals. Such a team might include one or more physician(s), physiotherapist(s), nurse(s), social worker(s) and speech therapist(s). With this mixed group there are two models. In one, the physician is the leader either with or without everyone's support. Other members bring their expertise to the discussion but they know that the physician (the psychiatrist, physiatrist, pediatrician or other physician), will make the final decision. In other mixed teams (the second model), all members expect to be able to dominate in their own areas of expertise and to play a greater role in the final decision. Each person is recognized as someone with a unique body of wisdom and skills which can, for a particular client, at certain points in time, be more important than the wisdom and skills of other members of the team. In this model each professional will, in his or her turn, become the team leader and/or the dominant member. Each could also be the formal leader/coordinator of the team.

This democratic or consensus type of team is a model frequently referred to but seldom practiced. Clinical professionals, especially physicians, do not usually have much training in group dynamics, conciliation, communication, compromise or sharing, and whenever physicians reject the consensus model it tends not to exist. This model may be admired in theory but there are very few operating models to watch. Major progress towards this type of team is unlikely until educators create learning situations where it is used daily.

There are two important members of the team not mentioned yet — the patient and his or her family (or significant others). Patients who are mentally competent adults should be regularly involved. Other persons should be involved if the patient so wishes, if the other individuals will be significantly affected by the decisions being made, or the patient is not competent to play a full role.

Prerequisites for the multidisciplinary team

a) People must know what other people can do, what others see as their realm of expertise, how others keep records and what terminology others use.
b) There is a need for mutual trust, which includes a willingness to share patients and information and a willingness to accept that the skills of others are greater in certain functional areas.
c) All members of the team must not only be able to participate in decision making but they must be expected to.
d) All members must regularly see their opinions represented in what is done or they will, probably correctly, assume that their expertise, opinions and recommendations are of minimal importance.

e) Workers must have an opportunity to learn how to work within a team. Good intentions are not enough; there are skills to be learned and behavioral knowledge to be acquired.

Impediments to Team Work

Factors impeding the existence or success of multidisciplinary egalitarian teams include parochial curriculum development, the absence of role models, historical animosities, the way institutions are organized, fee-for-service payment, disputes over jurisdiction, and the kinds of personal insecurities, jealousies or incompatibilities that can interfere with any form of group decision making and production. The disputes over jurisdiction are greatest when specific duties either can be, or it is assumed that they can be, adequately performed by more than one type of worker and both or all wish to perform them; counselling is an example.

Organizational structure can impede team formation and function. Social workers tend to work in social work departments, public health nurses work in public health nursing departments, and so on. This arrangement obliges teams to be multidepartmental as well as multidisciplinary. Co-operation is made easier if the organizational units are multidisciplinary such as is the case in multiservice centers or community health centers.

For some workers, the team approach means a loss of dominance, for others there is loss of or sharing of a function, and for still others there will be new insecurities because of a need to work at a higher level of competence. Professionals performing semi-skilled tasks may, in the team situation, find those tasks assigned to semi-skilled workers who are also in the team. The professional is expected to provide a higher level of professional evaluation and advice. This request can be a threat to a physician or physiotherapist who has, for years, been functionally underemployed.

To administrators, the team approach means attending many meetings in order to write rules, to amend rules, to resolve conflict, to write protocols, to educate each other, and to assess or reassess clients and produce care plans. If the calling of meetings or conferences is uncontrolled they can seriously reduce the time available for patient care. The administrator may also need, and may need to be able to teach, coordination and conflict resolution skills.

It is necessary to decide how likely it is that a particular client needs review by a team. There should be a rational trade-off between the possibility that some needed professional will not be consulted and the possibility that professional time will be wasted, and it seems likely that the triage model should often be used instead of holding case conferences. Assessment on first contact would include assessment of the need for multidisciplinary review. The triage officer would, in less complicated cases, make referral to the few persons relevant to the clients' needs.

Teams can also produce problems for patients. The patient may, for instance, have trouble determining who is in charge and who is his or her primary contact.

It often is desirable that one worker be designated as the person to whom the client and family will look for information or advocacy; this model has been used for decades at the Mayo Clinic. The contact person could be a social worker, nurse, physician, or any other professional or advocate.

One recurring theme in many discussions of health care is the need for more emphasis on community care. This de-emphasis of institutional care, in particular of acute treatment hospital care, is desirable for therapeutic, economic, and perhaps even philosophical reasons. It is economically desirable because hospitals may care for people who could more cheaply be cared for elsewhere. It is therapeutically desirable because hospitals are often dangerous places for pre-school children (who can be psychologically damaged), for mothers and their newborn (who in the period after delivery are more likely to pick up infections in hospital than at home), for the elderly (who often do not fit well into the paternalistic, high-speed and unfamiliar environment of a hospital), and for the mentally ill (who in many instances should be in a more normal therapeutic and social milieu). De-emphasis of hospitals is economically indicated because, without sharp limits on bed supply, hospitals will consume dollars that will benefit the health of the country more if spent elsewhere. Philosophically, hospitals are hazardous to the extent that they perpetuate the myth of the technological panacea.

SUMMARY OF PART A

Our Canadian health services network is dominated and characterized by a number of features, trends and problems or issues. The following lists reflect personal bias as well as the current state of affairs.

Philosophies and Priorities:

- health services are primarily nonprofit;
- there is equal and unlimited patient access to health care services that are under the public umbrella;
- there is increasing willingness to decrease the formerly almost absolute degree of physician autonomy;
- there is freedom of choice of provider by users, and of users by providers;
- there is increasing discussion of the importance of quality of life;
- there is public rejection of cost at time of service;
- there is an emphasis on expensive types and sources of care;
- there is increased attention to health promotion and health maintenance including an attempt to acquaint Canadians with the extent to which their health is the product of their own individual actions and, therefore, is their own responsibility;
- physical health problems have a higher priority than mental health problems.

Organization and Administration:

- Canada is an example of the public insurance model;
- there are ten independent provincial health care networks, plus the federally determined arrangements in the Yukon and Northwest Territories and in areas of federal jurisdiction;
- administration of health services takes place predominantly at the local level and predominantly through nonprofit, independent boards;
- private practitioners remain uncoordinated and highly independent;
- provincial approaches to public health and mental health are quite variable, with Quebec being unique;
- progress towards coordination, or integration, of health services and other social services is variable, with Quebec being most advanced;
- urban family physicians increasingly have no hospital affiliation;
- the medical model is dominant.

Policy and Planning:

- planning decisions are usually centralized at the provincial level;
- there is variable but often significant use of quasi-public agencies for policy development and advice;
- regional planning agencies are increasingly responsible for agency functions and coordination;
- there is no private insurance of services under the public umbrella; that is, a monopsony exists;
- federal influence through financial leverage is less evident since the EPF legislation in 1977.

Financing and Costs:

- the percentage of our health dollar that is spent on institutional care continues to increase;
- there has been a serious but only modestly successful attempt to control hospital costs;
- public programs are financed primarily through general revenues, with premiums still being charged (1987) in Ontario, Alberta, British Columbia and the Yukon.

Resources:

- there has been a rapid and undesirable increase in physician supply;
- acute treatment hospital bed supply per 1,000 appears to have stabilized after 15 years of decline;
- there has, to date, been successful preservation of the family physician, with one third of new physicians continuing to remain in family practice;
- professional roles continue to change;
- there is a major shortage of nonclinical health services research and researchers;

— there is a perception, probably over-stated, of a high degree of obsolescence in major hospitals.

Utilization:

— the number of physician contacts per person per year by fee-for-service physicians continues to climb;
— hospital utilization (days of inpatient care per 1,000 per year) has stabilized;
— the number of surgical procedures per year per 1,000 continues to rise;
— the volume of laboratory investigations continues to rise.

Problems and Issues Include:

— a system still dominated by the concept of cure; and a patient group increasingly dominated by degenerative diseases that cannot be cured;
— an emphasis on physical perfection and quantity of life, with death as the enemy, and a continuing although perhaps slightly reduced neglect of emotional distress, environmental stress and the quality of life;
— a system dominated by the medical model (a unidisciplinary domination promoted by fee-for-service and characterized by episodic and fragmented care);
— health services which are primarily reactive rather than proactive. Services are regularly provided, often in large volume, because some individual or group or public policy failed to prevent easily preventable disease or injury;
— information systems and payment arrangements that are inappropriate for health care networks which must increasingly deliver multidisciplinary and long term care;
— an incompatibility between paternalistic providers (who tend to wish to decide what kind of care the user gets as well as from whom, where and at what cost), and the modern trend towards user decision making based on complete information.
— conflict between individual needs or benefits and collective needs or benefits. The public has, in the past, been told, and providers still often believe, that the objective is 'the best health care for everyone.' To meet this objective is now impossible and not socially desirable because of the massive trade-offs required. Perfect care for anyone usually means a decreased amount of care for someone else who is also in need;
— a major gap between what the system is capable of (with the resources available) and what is delivered;
— great uncertainty and ambiguity about consumer and community roles, including confusion with respect to technocracy versus democracy;
— an increasing governmental interest in the quality of health care but professional objection to quality review by anyone but practicing peers;

— a wish for an integrated system but privately controlled segments of the system that plan and operate independently;
— ignorance as to which things are worth doing or which are most useful, which makes it difficult to reduce resource consumption rationally. This situation will remain until information systems are markedly improved.

Historical Trend

In the years prior to WWII, health care was a personal or a charitable function. Following WWII, Canadian governments quickly selected health care as an area for public policy and their interest has been sustained. In the 1950's and 1960's, the top priorities were the removal of financial barriers to health care and the expansion of human and institutional resources. By the end of the 1970's, cost containment was the top priority; the numbers of hospital beds and of newly licensed foreign medical graduates were sharply curtailed but the number of long term care facilities and domestic medical graduates proved hard to control. Regional planning was well established. The 1980's brought great interest in better costing, further constraints on the licensing of foreign medical graduates, timid reductions in medical school enrollments, abolition of physician extra-billing, the introduction in British Columbia of controls on physician location, an expansion of collective bargaining by physicians, some cutbacks in the range of insured services, an expansion of noninstitutional services, especially in long term care, and, perhaps, the real beginnings of acceptance of the importance of new areas of prevention such as controlling smoking and other substance abuse.

Canada has opted for more public administration, more universality, less competition and a smaller private sector role than the United States, and a smaller government role in administration of the delivery of care than in Great Britain. Canada, like the United States, has a mixture of government, nonprofit agencies and institutions, and for-profit agencies involved in care delivery.

In examining the preoccupation of our health services with physical health rather than mental health, it is difficult to know whether our system shapes public values and priorities or vice versa. Does society give its highest priorities to physical health care and the elimination of physical health hazards because that is the orientation of our technocratic professionals and bureaucrats; or do the health professionals and bureaucrats have their current preoccupations and skills because they reflect the society that produced them?

This is the end of Part A of this book, which has offered a broad perspective of health and health care in Canada. Part B will look in greater detail at major components of the Canadian health services network.

PREAMBLE to PART B

CANADIAN HEALTH SERVICES BY TYPE

Part A examined what we mean by health and ill health, how healthy or unhealthy Canadians are, factors making us healthy or unhealthy, and the basic characteristics of health services in Canada. Part B explores the major types of health services.

In Part A we had difficulty defining health or disease, and had difficulty defining health services. Throughout Part B the definitional problems will continue. What, for example, is a preventive health service, or what is a community health service? There is no clear boundary between mental health services and hospital services, or between community services and long term care. Noninstitutional services will often be referred to as community health services (CHS), a network which encompasses long term care services, mental health services, occupational health services and many other kinds of services.

Part B continues to acknowledge that many of the activities which eliminate or reduce ill health fall under the auspices of transportation, agriculture, justice, finance, education, consumer affairs, and the CBC. Many rehabilitative activities are vocational and are carried out within the world of labor or education, while many important diagnostic activities deal with the physical or psychosocial environment and are carried out by workers and departments other than health workers and health departments.

Sometimes health services are very easy to categorize. Everyone knows that hospitals, physicians and ambulances deliver health services. However, much of the diagnosis and treatment of emotional illness or injury, or correction of psychosocial distress, is delivered by the clergy, school teachers, social service agencies, recreation staff, social networks and half-way houses and these are not usually thought of as health services. When emotional health services are being discussed, it would be unwise and unreasonable to completely ignore services and activities in the home, the schools, the workplaces and the communities that so directly cause, prevent and treat mental ill health, but it is also not feasible to attempt to fully examine these traditionally nonhealth services in any detail in this book.

The categorization of diagnostic services is also imprecise. Some diagnostic services such as the examination of human urine, blood and tissues are almost always thought of as health services. Diagnostic services in which the specimens are air, water or food, however, may or may not be performed within what we think of as the health system. They are also routinely performed by departments of the environment and of labor and by industry.

Discussing preventive services brings a different problem. Health services (such as our immunization programs) still prevent many infectious diseases but, in general, the prevention of both mental and physical ill health takes place in schools, on the highways, in the workplace, in the chimneys of our smelters and powerhouses, in sewage treatment plants, through our interpersonal relations and through the examples and attitudes that shape our lives. Staying within the boundaries of traditional health services, therefore, will sharply restrict our discussion of prevention.

From this commentary, it should be clear that there is no easy or concise definition of health services. This book does not discuss all the services important to the prevention, diagnosis and treatment of ill health. For practical purposes the sale, prescription, testing and approval of drugs are considered health services; the manufacture of drugs is not. Programs to prevent measles and polio are in; programs to prevent brucellosis and bovine tuberculosis are out. (The department of agriculture inspectors and the veterinarians are more important here than any health workers.) Chronic care (long stay) hospitals are in; nursing homes are on the edge (sometimes in and sometimes out) and residential homes are out. Highways and automobiles are out but ambulances are in. It has not been possible to provide any absolute and sensible rules that will tell us when something is a health service. The services that Canadian society has chosen to place within the worlds of mental health, physical health and public health are rather a random lot.

Health services are delivered by an impressive array of traditional and nontraditional health workers plus a vast array of other workers including snow shovellers, hairdressers, friendly visitors, credit counsellors, volunteer drivers and marriage counsellors. The noninstitutional list of workers includes many health care workers outside the medical model such as chiropractors, optometrists, osteopaths, nonphysician acupuncturists and traditional healers.

Desirable Features of Health Services in Canada

Before examining institutional and noninstitutional services as they presently exist, one might wonder what fundamental features this service network should have. The following list does not describe features one can actually find but, rather, outlines a set of expectations that a client might consider reasonable. These features can be kept in mind as the next nine chapters describe the health services that actually exist. It would seem desirable that our health services network:

1) Contain a broad spectrum of preventive, diagnostic, response (therapy) and follow-up services which addresses the hazards and pathology of individuals and groups.
2) Offer services that represent the attitudes, values and philosophies of the community being served rather than of providers or any other group.
3) Assure accountability of all sources of care and all decision makers to the consumers/community. Only if there is accountability can responsiveness be demanded. Responsiveness to the values of the community or the user can be reasonably assured only if power is vested in the community and the user. Without consumer/community power the rules, policies and priorities may reflect the values of only the providers, institutional managers or the bureaucrats.

4) Use a coordinated community and/or regional approach to planning, implementing and operating health and health related services.
5) Include financial and organizational arrangements which:
   a) encourage accessibility as required
   b) encourage mobility within the system as required
   c) minimize the difficulties of a multiproblem person or family who concurrently requires a number of different services.
6) Conduct a continuing program of area-wide evaluation which looks at mental and physical health outcomes, at cost-effectiveness, at efficiency, at the priority setting (resource allocation) process used, at evidence of free movement of clients and information and at other health service features considered important by the community.
7) Use a formal, ongoing priority setting process which assigns priorities on the basis of effects on, or degree of protection of, the health status of the community.

In summary, the network that a community might most admire would reflect the values of society and be responsive to society. To accomplish these overall goals, one would need regional planning, coordinated delivery, formal and consumer dominated priority setting, and evaluation processes that use community health status as the yardstick.

What One Might Wish to Know about each Health Service

Ideally, Part B would review all significant health services and programs with respect to a prescribed set of features such as:

1) History and evolution. Why are things as they are?
2) Philosophy.
3) Goals and Objectives. These would be expected to reflect the chosen philosophy and to include targets with respect to scheduling, cost and outcomes.
4) Authority and Power. Do they arise from a statute, a charter, a by-law, or an Order-in-Council and, if so, from what level of government or what office? Does authority have primarily a formal base or does it arise primarily from tradition (history) or popular support?
5) Planning. Who does it? How many actors play a role? Is it centralized or decentralized, short-range, long-range or both? What techniques are used?
6) Organization. How are the services usually organized? To whom does the organization report? What factors determine organizational form? What relationships exist with other services?
7) Financing. Is this service financed collectively or individually — for instance by general tax revenues or premiums or user fees? Is it prepaid or paid for at time of service? What is the role of private capital?
8) Budgeting. Who controls the budget? How is it produced?

9) Administration. What are the characteristics of the policy and of the executive body if there is one? What is the administrative philosophy? In what areas is administrative autonomy limited and by whom?
10) Evaluation. Who, if anyone, is responsible for quality measurement and assurance? What evaluative techniques are used? Is quality at an acceptable level? Is quality defined broadly or narrowly? Are outcome measures being used?
11) Clientele and case loads. Is there a prescribed population base or client group? What factors impede access? What percent of potential clientele are served?
12) Cost. What is the cost per year, per service, per client episode or per unit of outcome?
13) External forces or constraints. Are these of consequence? Are there waiting lists?
14) Major problems. What are they?
15) Changes. Are any occurring or expected?
16) Major variations. Which of these are possible? Which are in existence elsewhere?

If one understood all of the above, one would have a good background from which to approach planning and the making of operational choices. Such a background would usually be sufficient to allow one to see if things were happening as they should — that is, whether procedures and policies were being followed — and compare performance to that of other agencies or to one's own experience in previous years.

After a service/activity/agency has been described, there are a number of more important evaluation and policy questions to be asked.

1) What impact is this activity or service having on the health status of the community?
2) What should be changed? What optional objectives, organization, financing and staffing are available? Would one of these options (or more than one) be better than what exists? Should utilization changes be encouraged? What would happen if this activity were doubled or cut in half, or increased or decreased by 10%?
3) If there are things that should be changed — how do we get them changed? Changes do not occur spontaneously just because they are desirable.

Lack of time, space and knowledge prevents serious discussion of all of these questions, but if this book prepares you for their examination, its purpose will have been accomplished.

Chapter 8

REGIONALIZATION

THE EVOLUTION OF REGIONALIZATION

Health programs and facilities were once quite independent. To varying degrees, they raised their own money and did their own planning. This autonomy has now been largely replaced by multiagency or regional arrangements that fall within the vague and ill-defined concept of regionalization. Because regionalization means quite different things to different people, and different things to the same people at different points in time, it is a term which can be a source of confusion for those who plan, administer and finance health services.

Alberta has, for some time, been regionalizing its hospital boards. Instead of each hospital having its own board, one board administers a number of institutions. One budget has replaced a number of budgets and one executive director/president replaces several. In this example there is no significant change in hospital financing, planning or evaluation, but legal responsibility is centralized with probable changes in personnel management, resource allocation and other functions.

In many urban areas there has been regionalization of a number of clinical specialty services such as cardiac surgery, hemodialysis, pediatrics and obstetrics. There is no change in the number of organizationally separate institutions but a particular service which was formerly provided from several sites is now provided at only one.

When a number of institutions lose their in-house laundries and a new and quite separate organization is formed to provide this service to all, this change is also called regionalization. Not only is an activity centralized but a new regional financing and management arrangement is put in place.

When a provincial or federal ministry of health, or some part of a ministry, creates regional offices, this creation is again called regionalization. There may have been little or no change in policy, organization, or function.

In Quebec in the 1970's, both institutional and noninstitutional services were affected by regionalization. Functions were changed, a number of traditional programs disappeared, many new boards and agencies came into being and planning, financing and administration processes were significantly revised.

In Ontario, the old Regional Hospital Planning Councils have been replaced by another type of purely advisory body — the District Health Councils. The DHCs have no executive authority over any health services but they give advice on the planning of a broad range of health services. They are only advisory and are concerned only with planning, but they also are an example of regionalization.

In Prince Edward Island public health services were decentralized to four regions, each with a population of 30-40,000. Some of the units created were similar in size to those that were abolished through centralization of public health services in Ontario two decades ago. In both Prince Edward Island and Ontario the change was referred to as regionalization.

We are currently regionalizing emergency services in Ontario through the categorization of emergency rooms. Some emergency departments will provide the most complex kinds of care and some will remain open only 14-18 hours per day. In this example of regionalization, it is probable that no organization charts will be altered although functions will change and some global budgets will be adjusted.

The examples reveal little if any pattern. Regionalization can deal (even when we stay within Canada) with populations of 30,000 to 2,000,000. It can affect one health service or program or many health services or programs. It can affect the delivery, planning, financing, administration, or evaluation of care, or any combination of these plus any number of specialized administrative functions such as management information systems (MIS), quality control and education. It can affect only one type of patient (renal failure patients, hemophiliacs), one specific activity (computers or collective bargaining) or a broad range of both care and management functions (Québec CRSSS; Manitoba rural health and social service boards). It can involve major authority transfer (regional public health units, multihospital boards) or none at all (District Health Councils in Ontario). It can lead to smaller units being amalgamated (the food commissariat in Ottawa), to completely new units being created (the Greater Vancouver Mental Health Service), or, very rarely, to new and smaller units being created to replace a larger one (the creation of community based public health and social service centers). Sometimes decision making or some other activity moves to another community but stays in the same organization (for example the creation of the regional offices of the Department of Indian and Northern Affairs), and sometimes it stays in the same community but moves to another organization, as with a regional laundry. There appears to be no limit to the variations possible within the theme of regionalization.

Institutions, agencies and communities often believe that, with regionalization, there will be decentralization of provincial powers. This seldom happens. Regionalization is much more likely to lead to increased centralization, as is the case when enlarged hospital boards or public health units are created or laundries are amalgamated.

If there is any common thread throughout these examples, it is the tendency for something to move to a larger or smaller unit. This common thread suggests one definition of regionalization that is very simple: regionalization is the centralization or decentralization of something. This definition is, admittedly, almost too vague to be useful, but anything more specific becomes inaccurate.

It may now be clear that if someone speaks about regionalization one cannot know exactly what is meant unless a number of matters are clarified. The following questions might well be asked.

1. What are the objectives of the regionalization?

2. If a new organizational entity is being created, what redistribution of authority, influence or function will occur? Who gains, and who loses influence, authority or function? Will any existing organizational entities disappear? There is a fairly finite amount of authority available for distribution among various people, governments or institutions. Therefore, whenever a new regional organization is created with authority that authority comes from someone else, and until it is clear who are to be the winners and losers the creators cannot know who their allies or enemies will be.
3. What services does the regionalization affect? Are they clinical (patient care) or nonclinical services? Nonclinical services include the hotel services (laundry, food, housekeeping), the business services (accounting, computers, purchasing, personnel) and the physical plant services (maintenance, heating). Will the regionalization exercise affect only one service or more than one, that is, what is its scope? It could be quite broad, as with the regional councils in Québec, or it could be limited to only one service such as obstetrics, drug purchasing, computers or neurosurgery.
4. If a new organizational entity is being created, to what administrative functions will its decisions be related? Will it deal with planning, capital financing, operational financing, administration, evaluation, other functions, or some combination of these?
5. Is the regionalization related to (a) a defined geographic area or (b) to a specified group of institutions or (c) a specific type of patient or other population?
6. Are any assets changing ownership?
7. Is the change financially significant? If so, are costs expected to increase or decrease? What is the size of the budget and where will the money come from?
8. Who initiated the regionalization, who took part in the planning and policy selection process, and how long has it been under study or in place?
9. If a new organizational entity (authority) is created, what is its form? Does it have an appointed or an elected board? What are its relationships to other organizational entities?
10. What organizational options were considered or should now be considered? Could the proposed functions have been given to an existing agency or government? Could regional health planning functions, for example, have been given to a regional municipality already responsible for the planning and operation of long term care facilities, public housing, social services, transportation and urban design, and which may already have a health and/or social policy (or services) committee?

At least most of the important questions have now been asked. The answers any person prefers will vary with such things as whether he or she supports consumer rather than technocrat control, whether he or she thinks senior policy makers should be appointed versus elected, whether he or she thinks we already have too many special purpose bodies, and whether he or she believes accountability and responsibility should go together. Whatever the preferred answers, one cannot have a reasonably clear understanding of the nature of a particular example of regionalization until one has asked at least a great many of the listed questions.

It may be helpful now to express some of the preceding material in a slightly different way.

THE VARIABILITY OF THE CHARACTERISTICS OF REGIONAL AUTHORITIES, AGENCIES, COMMISSIONS, BOARDS, COUNCILS, DEPARTMENTS, COMMITTEES OR PROGRAMS

This summary of the options available will confirm the idea that the term *regionalization* is extremely encompassing and is too vague to be useful.

1. Objectives and Philosophy

The motivation for regionalization can be social, technological, managerial, political or some combination of these. The objectives and philosophies of different examples of regionalization may be overlapping or in conflict. No example can meet all of the objectives in the following list because some of them are opposites.

a) Development of policies and programs which reflect the character and priorities of the region.
b) Reduction in intraregional disparities in such areas as access, cost, availability and quality.
c) Provision of greater opportunity for and degree of consumer and community influence and control. (Sometimes stated much more strongly as local control rather than central control.)
d) Reduction in the parochialism found in individual programs and facilities.
e) Attainment of financial savings through economies of scale, reduction of undesirable duplication, and reduction in undesirable competition.
f) Easier movement and referral of patients.
g) Increased standardization.
h) Better information flow.
i) Integration/coordination of related services.
j) Better distribution of personnel and facilities.
k) Development of better quality control techniques.
l) Better staff training.
m) Attainment of the 'critical mass' of cases (or services) that is necessary if quality and efficiency are to be satisfactory. This critical mass attracts competent staff, allows this staff to remain competent, makes it more likely that equipment will be up-to-date, promotes research, and encourages a motivating professional atmosphere.
n) Reduction in the power of some central agency through the creation of a smaller jurisdiction and the delegation to that jurisdiction of some of the powers that were formerly exercised centrally.

o) Development of a regional approach to such functions as priority setting, planning, delivery and administration, by bringing a broad range of services and administrative functions under one regional jurisdiction.
p) The rationalization of services (whatever that means).
q) Provision of greater career opportunities for staff.
r) The creation of one agency responsible for servicing a specified population with a broad range of services.
s) The creation of a system whereby consumers may more easily interact with administrators and planners.

2. **Optional Sources of Authority for Regionalization**
   a) A statute, such as the ones which established the consolidated Boards of Health in Ontario or the CRSSS in Québec.
   b) An Order in Council, such as was used to establish each District Health Council in Ontario.
   c) A decision of a minister or a bureaucrat, such as that which centralizes the intern and resident payroll function in one regional hospital or which gives a particular laboratory responsibility for certain tests.
   d) Letters patent, which might establish a separate corporation such as a regional laundry.
   e) A decision by another regional body.

3. **Degree of Influence or Authority of the Regional Body**
   a) It can be purely advisory, perhaps with an advocacy function, as is the case with the Ottawa-Carleton Council on Aging and the Social Planning Council.
   b) It can be purely advisory but have major influence assured by government policy, as with an Ontario District Health Council.
   c) It can have limited decision making authority, as does the Québec Regional Health and Social Services Council (CRSSS).
   d) It can have major decision making authority, as do the Ontario Boards of Education and the Ontario Boards of Health.

4. **Methods of Selection of Members of a Regional Board, Commission, Council, or Committee**
   a) Election by a total regional constituency, as occurs with a regional and municipal government and with most boards of education.
   b) Election by a membership, as occurs with the Ottawa-Carleton Placement Coordination Service.
   c) Appointment by a minister (as with appointments to a District Health Council in Ontario), by designated agencies (as is the case with the Ottawa-Carleton regional food services and regional laundry) or by someone else designated in law. The agencies which are to be represented on a board or council may be named in a charter, a statute or the regulations under a statute.

d) By any combination of the above.

5. **Methods of Financing**
   a) Budget from one or more levels of government (as is the case with Boards of Health, DHC, CRSSS).
   b) Fees from users (as with regional food services or regional laundries).
   c) Government grants.
   d) Philanthropy.
   e) By direct taxation, as is the case with Union Hospital Districts in Saskatchewan or boards of education in several provinces.

   In some cases of regionalization no new financing is required.

6. **Devices for Intraregional Liaison and Consensus Seeking**
   a) Interlocking board memberships. Quebec offers the only formalized and province-wide example.
   b) Regional committees with multiagency representation. Once again Quebec offers the only example which is province wide and proscribed by law, but other examples are common. The DHCs in Ontario usually have a number of such committees which advise with respect to either types of service such as long term care or categories of consumers such as children.
   c) The extraparliamentary and less formal processes, which include lobbying, submitting briefs and writing letters.

TECHNIQUES FOR INSTITUTIONAL OR PROGRAM OBSTRUCTION OF REGIONAL APPROACHES

Regionalization is not always welcomed, nor is it always passively received. There are techniques by which agencies or groups show their displeasure:

1. End runs to the province. This term is applied to instances in which agencies who do not get what they want at the regional level go directly to the ministry for approval.
2. Lack of co-operation, as when institutions fail to participate on committees and boards, fail to provide information or fail to perform assigned functions, or when they proceed with institutional initiatives that are inconsistent with regional plans or with assigned functions.

   Lack of co-operation is perhaps the most commonly used and the most damaging of the techniques available to institutions, and the larger and more dominent institutions use it best. The Ottawa Civic Hospital has such political and community power that a few years ago it quite easily created a tertiary level neonatal unit even although the Health Sciences Centre Campus had been designated as the site for this level of service. In the early 1970's, the Civic damaged chances for a regional computer network by refusing to participate. Even smaller institutions will often use private funds to buy equipment that has not been approved at the regional or provincial level.

Fortunately, there are other large institutions, such as those in Hamilton, which have shown that regional co-operation can occur and that unique and admirable innovations can come from it. Twenty years ago, for example, the Hamilton hospitals, without government prodding, created a regional laboratory services network.

3. Use of the media. Common approaches include scare tactics such as releasing misleading descriptions of waiting times or the length of waiting lists, dramatizing deaths that might have been avoided, distorting facts through the exploitation of anecdotal events that are inconsistent with norms, or making appeals which imply that institutions are the only defender of some patient group. When such strategies are used the provincal, regional or municipal governments are often portrayed as callous and disinterested.

PREREQUISITES OR DEVICES FOR STRENGTHENING REGIONAL APPROACHES (or which make them more likely to be successful).

Provincial support is the most important prerequisite. Advisory regional planning bodies, such as DHCs in Ontario, can only be successful if the ministry refuses to recognize attempts at end runs, and if the ministry provides adequate operating funds and start up funds. Support among local health administrators is equally important. The Hamilton example has already been cited. The process also works better if leaders have good consensus seeking skills, can maintain broad local involvement, and know how to find solutions that bring rewards to at least most of the major players.

AREA WIDE (REGIONAL) HEALTH PLANNING AGENCIES

Planning is one of the functions with which regionalization is closely associated. The desirability of comprehensive area wide (regional) health planning is no longer questioned, but because major tertiary care services require a population base of one million or close to it (some countries use a minimum base of two to three million), many provinces cannot regionalize tertiary care planning. Regions with populations of less than one million or thereabouts can play a role in planning certain kinds of services such as those which provide less sophisticated long term care or primary care, but they find it difficult to plan a total health services network except in co-operation with other geographic units.

From 1945-1965 area-wide comprehensive health planning was largely carried out by voluntary hospital planning councils. Though they were a useful evolutionary phase they could not handle situations in which decisions were unacceptable to one or more of their members. These voluntary models were gradually replaced by government sponsored regional planning arrangements with the province often quite unavoidably being the planning region.

Only Ontario and Québec have an established network of regional health planning agencies with comprehensive mandates, but even in these provinces (especially in Ontario) all major planning decisions are still made at the provincial level.

The suggestion that provinces should provide global budgets to regions so that the regions can then plan and finance a total health services network is popular, but unrealistic. Provincial legislatures are likely to continue to aim for a reasonable degree of balance and similarity between health and social services in the various parts of the province and they will, therefore, either retain direct control over both capital and operational spending or they will write such detailed and binding guidelines that the regions have only very limited discretionary spending powers (as is the case with respect to Boards of Health in Ontario). Local authorities traditionally want control over local spending even when they did not raise the money. Provinces, on the other hand, do not like to raise money and then not control how it is spent. In other words, local authorities like unconditional grants but the provinces usually will not transfer much money without strings attached.

There is strong support for the idea that too much administrative centralization reduces the likelihood that there will be adaptation to differences in local needs and priorities. Centralization also brings less communication between the users and the administrators, and demotivates local managers and planners. However, the centralization of planning and financing, especially the latter, can reduce regional disparities. In Canada the province is often the most sensible level at which to make many planning decisions that can quite reasonably be decentralized (regionalized) in larger jurisdictions such as China or even California or Great Britain.

When considering the usual local wish for autonomy — meaning the freedom to spend provincial money in accordance with local rather than provincial priorities — it is useful to remember the administrative and democratic doctrines which suggest that there should be a close relationship between authority (responsibility) and accountability. Provincial legislators are responsible to the taxpayers for the taxes that provinces collect; they also have constitutional jurisdiction over and, therefore, responsibility for health and other social services. Local influence over planning decisions is highly desirable, and local responsibility for administration can be well defended, but at some point regions and communities must expect to be constrained by provincial philosophies and objectives expressed through statutes, directives, guidelines, and budgets.

Provinces can legally transfer to regions or municipalities whatever powers and costs they wish. A share of educational costs is often raised locally and the same could apply to health care. In practical terms, however, there must be a limit to how much taxation the province can transfer to the local level and to property taxes. Given this limit, it does not seem likely that local financing of health services will increase significantly.

Major Organizational Options for Health Planning Agencies

Health planning agencies are commonly under the control of an appointed board. This board has the characteristic of seeming to be nonpolitical, a trait which is supposed to be an advantage but which, in fact, merely tends to assure absence of accountability. At one time it was thought that these boards should be composed primarily of persons with technical expertise, but such a composition would now be seen as relatively incompatible with our belief in the value of consumer influence. Boards now usually consist primarily of consumer and provider representatives.

A second option that has, fortunately, not been encouraged is a regionally elected health board equivalent to an elected board of education. The last thing needed is another regional policy-making body to compete with municipal government, transportation commissions, police commissions, boards of education, utilities commissions, children's aid societies and housing authorities for territory and power.

A third option is the incorporation of the health planning function into existing regional or metropolitan governments, an option that receives far too little consideration. A regional government already has a number of operating departments responsible for such things as welfare, roads, day care, social services, public transportation, utilities, police, fire and recreation. By definition it serves a significant and defined population and area. Its planning department deals with land use, housing, economic development and personal services. It is functionally quite equivalent to the government of a mini-province although education and health are usually excluded from its mandate. The planning and delivery of health services (and of education services) would fit logically and easily into its areas of power (subject to provincial constraints).

By operating within the boundaries of regional government, health care planners would have a greater opportunity to coordinate the planning and operating of health services with other public services. As a part of regional government, the health branch would be accountable through an elected body to the people within the region. A number of major urban municipalities and metropolitan areas in Canada are already responsible for the public health services and public health planning provided elsewhere by appointed boards of health or by ministries of health, and expansion of those health responsibilities should be considered.

District Health Councils (DHCs) in Ontario

The first DHCs were established in 1973. By 1986 there were 26 of them serving almost all of the province. The establishment of DHCs was promoted by the province but they were not set up until there was a request from the region.

They are established by Order-in-Council, that is, at the request of the Minister of Health, with the support of the cabinet and with the approval of the Lieutenant Governor, and they report directly to the Minister. They have 15 to 20 members usually appointed for 3 year terms. Members are appointed by the Minister of Health and include representatives of consumers, providers and the regional municipality. The DHCs serve regions with populations ranging from 150,000 to 2,000,000. Annual basic budgets, as provided by the Ontario Ministry of Health, are at one of two levels. Depending on whether the population served is under or over 200,000, the budget is sufficient to hire approximately 4 or 6 professional staff. Additional funds are granted on a project basis. The budgets are quite inadequate for the responsibilities assigned.

The mandate of DHCs is to advise the Minister of Health on the planning and coordination of health services. They are expected to identify needs, set priorities, plan a comprehensive health care program, coordinate health services, evaluate and promote co-operation within the regional network and make recommendations regarding all of these. The councils may initiate studies themselves or may respond to proposals made by agencies or institutions.

Proposals considered by the DHCs tend to come from one or more of a series of task forces or committees usually representing a major user group or service type; examples include primary (ambulatory) care, mental health, hospitals, long term (continuing) care, pediatric services and health promotion/disease prevention. Ad hoc subcommittees are created as needed.

In some Ontario communities, the DHCs replaced Regional Hospital Planning Councils but, in Toronto, the Metropolitan Toronto Hospital Planning Council continues to operate. Duplication and competition seem inevitable. Overlap is probably further increased by the presence of OCATH (Ontario Council of Administrators of Teaching Hospitals).

District Health Councils should be considered at least a qualified success. They have led to major discussion between regional sources of care and have produced many fine studies. All DHCs undertake priority review exercises, usually annually, and may review hundreds of submissions (140 to 160 in Ottawa-Carleton). In the priority-setting exercise, each proposal is assessed with respect to such features as need, value for money, ease of implementation and extent of fit with council and ministry priorities.

With the maturing of DHCs, there appears to be a tendency towards increased provider domination. This trend is quite contrary to the concept within which DHCs were created. Perhaps provider representatives stay in the network whereas the community representatives come and go. Perhaps the more permanent members have co-opted the system. If a reasonable balance of power is to be maintained providers must become less dominant on DHCs and their committees, and perhaps provider representatives should be excluded from Council membership. In the early years, hospitals were unhappy with the appearance of DHCs and fought or ignored them; now they have decided to gain control. Providers, especially hospitals, have no difficulty exerting major influence when they wish.

Conseil Régional de la Santé et des Services Sociaux in Québec (CRSSS)

Regional councils were a key element in the restructuring of health and social services that began in Québec in 1972 with the passage of Bill 65. The regional councils, of which there are eleven (one less than originally proposed), develop regional objectives, measure need, establish priorities, are responsible for coordination of the sources of health and social services, evaluate outcomes, to a variable but usually quite limited extent approve capital and operating expenditures, and provide advice to the Minister as required.

The nature and role of Councils is spelled out in the statute which created the regionalized network (Figure 8.1). The Councils have 15 or more members (initially there were 22) representing post secondary educational institutions, voluntary agencies, municipalities, socioeconomic groups, the health and social service facilities (one from each of the four types), and professional providers of care. The executive director of the CRSSS is also a member. There are many mandatory committees and commissions (15 to 20) and other such bodies may be established. In the statute, great emphasis is placed on the need for objectives and plans.

Social Service Centers provide social services to institutionalized and noninstitutionalized persons and groups. A CLSC, in theory, provides a broad range of primary health care and social services but often offers very few physician services. 'Reception centers' include half-way houses, day care centers, rehabilitation centers and long term care institutions. Of the hospitals, 32 have been designated by the ministry as sites for departments of community health (DCH), or, in French, département de santé communautaire (DSC). These departments do much of the public health planning for the region.

All the councils make recommendations to the ministry regarding new capital expenditures. In recent years the councils have been given the power to approve certain expenditures without provincial review and some councils have been given major control over regional expenditures or over selected special projects, for example, in 1982 the CRSSS for metropolitan Montreal was entrusted with the establishment of a coordinating center for emergency services. Operating budgets and staff complements of the regional councils in Québec are many times larger than those of DHCs in Ontario. The Councils play a major role in assigning functions to the various sources of care and in assuring coordination of these units. Only private practitioners are fully outside of their area of influence.

Other Regional Planning Examples

Regional public health units deliver a broad range of services but they also act as regional planning agencies who, in some instances, conduct innovative priority setting and other exercises. These units do not exist in all provinces. In Québec they do not exist because public health activities have been assigned to other organizations, primarily to CLSCs and to departments of community health (DSCs) in regionally designated hospitals. In some other provinces they do not exist, or exist only in larger cities, because all or some executive responsibility for public health services rests with the provincial health department.

Health Sciences Centers were a favored centralization/integration tool of the 1960's and 1970's. In the presence of major federal funding through the Health

Figure 8.1
Regional Network of Health and Social Service Institutions in Québec

- Department of Health and Social Affairs (Département de santé et des affaires sociales)
  - Regional Health and Social Services Council (RHSSC) (Conseil régionaux de la santé et des services sociaux — CRSSS)

    (There are eleven of these regional councils, each of which has responsibility for the following four major categories of institutions)
    - Hospitals
      - Acute Care
      - Long Term Care
      - Special (e.g. psychiatric)
    - Social Service Centres
    - Local Community Health Centers (Centres locaux des services communautaires - CLSC)
    - Reception Centers (Centres d'accueil)

Resources Fund, ($100 million available to upgrade research and clinical teaching), and encouraged by provincial governments who were concerned about the cost of tertiary care, many university affiliated hospitals moved toward an administrative and planning merger with or without physical consolidation. General hospitals, special hospitals (for children, for example), long term care facilities and universities entered into agreements tailor made to the situation but all sharing the common feature of a new superagency which blunted or eliminated the image and autonomy of the formerly independent units. Most of these fusions were accomplished with difficulty and for some the unrest has continued.

In some instances — for example, the development of the Health Science Complex in Kingston, Ontario in 1972 — the creation of a new level of planning co-operation and operational coordination was the result of a Ministry of Health decision not to deal with any requests for new projects until they had been recommended by a formal council representing all major players. The participating institutions (Kingston General Hospital, Hotel Dieu Hospital, Ongwanada LTC childrens' facility, St. Mary's on the Lake chronic hospital, the Family Practice Unit and Queens University) have all retained their names and a significant degree of administrative independence but there is now a common planning body which deals with all major functional allocation questions and major capital projects. The two general hospitals have a common medical staff and a common process for granting and renewing medical staff privileges. (An original proposal to merge the two hospitals has not proceeded.)

THE ADVANTAGES AND DISADVANTAGES OF REGIONALIZATION

It has been suggested that regionalization is the centralization or decentralization of something. The 'something' may be power, an administrative function, a type of care or some other activity. Movement or change is implied.

Why might we want or not want this centralization or decentralization?

Advantages of Decentralization (a list that can, with modest rewording, become the disadvantages of centralization)

In any given situation only some of these advantages will apply.

1) Increased local (institutional or personal) autonomy.
2) Greater adaptation to regional uniqueness; greater sensitivity to local needs.
3) Greater opportunity for consumer influence or control.
4) Increased sense of control on the part of individual agencies and/or workers.
5) More personalized service.
6) Smaller bureaucracy to deal with; a bureaucracy that will be more responsive to users. Greater user acceptance.
7) Greater opportunity for integration of services at the point of delivery.
8) Dispersion of employment to smaller centers.
9) Greater local initiative, greater local loyalty and contribution to programs and greater ability to attract volunteers and donations.
10) Delivery of care in an equally adequate but less expensive way.
11) The involvement of large numbers of local leaders to strengthen the democratic process.

Disadvantages of Decentralization (these can be easily converted into the advantages of centralization). In any given situation only some of these disadvantages will apply.

1) Disadvantages that accrue only when volume falls below the critical mass, including:
   a) increase in unit cost due to loss of economies of scale;
   b) decreases in quality due to difficulty in attracting specialists, maintaining skills when service volume is low, justifying purchase of up-to-date equipment, providing 24 hour coverage, doing research and obtaining peer support;
   c) decreases in the number of specialized administrative services such as data handling, in-service education and employee group benefit packages.
2) Greater possibility of decentralized units developing goals that oppose those of the larger jurisdiction; greater potential for undesirable duplication and competition.

3) Loss of political accountability. The people spending the money are less likely to be the ones who must collect it.
4) Possibilities of conflict between the decentralized units and the parent government(s). This conflict is not likely to be tolerated over time if the central authority is politically embarrassed or unable to retain the degree of control it desires.
5) Increased difficulty coordinating such activities as information flow and patient transfers.
6) Increased likelihood of regional disparities.
7) Decreased in-house employee career opportunities.
8) Greater difficulty in ensuring standard approaches to such functions as data collection, quality control and program evaluation.

In the light of these strengths and weaknesses of centralization and decentralization one should be able to examine a situation in the context of a prescribed set of goals and decide whether changes are in order.

Factors Suggesting a Need for Centralization

1. Inadequate quality due to lack of a critical mass.
2. High unit costs due to low volume. This problem is most easily correctable when there are within a reasonable distance other low volume units which could be closed.
3. Inability to satisfy overall goals with respect to such things as standardized data collection (for example, encounter forms), standard setting and evaluation, range of services, integration of services into a larger system, accessability and identifying priorities and acting on them.
4. Regional disparities. Correction of regional economic disparities lies in centralized financing. Manpower maldistribution is most easily corrected through use of centrally created policies and programs.
5. Inappropriate or inadequate flow of patients between components of the health services networks. Optimal patient movement can be impeded by such things as the restrictive and undesirable relationships which existed between specific general hospitals and specific long term care institutions prior to the appearance of central assessment and coordination programs.

Factors Suggesting There May Be Benefits In Decentralization

Some of these can be found earlier in the chapter.

1. Community displeasure or cynicism with centralized decision makers or care givers.
2. Significant cultural, demographic or other relevant regional or community differences that are apt to receive better response from smaller units or bureaucracies.
3. Volumes of activity far beyond the level at which there can be reasonable costs and quality.

Services and Functions That Have Been Centralized To At Least Some Extent

1. Financing and administration of ambulance services in most provinces.
2. Departmental functions in large institutions or in multiinstitutional arrangements. These include laundry, food services, computer networks, purchasing, laboratory services, biomedical engineering, printing, consultant services and medical records.
3. Medical staff organization as in Guelph and Kingston.
4. Senior administration (administrative mergers) as in Victoria Hospital Corporation, London, most Health Sciences Centres and many multi-hospital boards in British Columbia and Alberta.
5. Basic clinical services such as obstetrics and pediatrics.
6. Specialized clinical services or facilities such as poison information centers, burn units, dialysis units, organ transplant units, blood transfusion collection, processing and distribution, forensic units, trauma centers and cardiac surgery units.
7. Prescribed packages of clinical and nonclinical services as occurred at the Shaughnessy — Grace — Children's (CGS) in Vancouver. Under this arrangement there has been physical integration, a shared approach to certain identified services and preservation of three boards.
8. Planning, as in the case of regional planning agencies and all provincial ministries.
9. The financing of health care.
10. The financing and operation of hospitals such as provincial psychiatric institutions.
11. Patient placement in LTC facilities and programmes.
12. Emergency response systems such as central dispatch for ambulances, central bed registries and regional disaster plans.
13. Educational programming including resident and intern placement, continuing education programming, approval of new graduate programs and the use of one hospital as paymaster for all interns and residents in a region.
14. Collective bargaining.
15. Unions (unaffiliated local unions are now uncommon).
16. The evaluation and funding of research as with MRC, NHRDP, SSHRC, NSERC, CHF and CCS.
17. The distribution of charitable funds by such agencies as the United Way and social planning councils.
18. Employee pension plans.
19. The setting of professional and institutional standards.
20. Public health units.
21. Evaluation programs such as CCHFA (formerly CCHA) or the Ontario physician peer review program.

Services and Functions That Have Been Decentralized To At Least Some Extent

1. Administration of provincial psychiatric hospitals.
2. Care delivery, as in instances where psychiatric patients and mentally retarded persons have moved from large institutions to smaller institutions or to group homes, or from geographically centralized places to many places. A further example is the change from nursing care by ward to nursing care teams or primary care nursing.
3. Emergency care through satellite emergency units.
4. Administration of mental health services in Vancouver.
5. Measurement and priorization of community needs as in DHCs or CRSSS.

SUMMARY

The concept of regionalization is not new. In Roman times a decentralization/regionalization process reduced the administrative problems of an unwieldy empire. In recent times regionalization has attempted to bring order, efficiency and sometimes responsiveness to a chaos of uncoordinated actors.

Regional planning is a natural and logical response to the problems of specialization and of scarce resources. Without it, quality of care would go down and the cost of care would go up, both in principle and in practice, although individual examples can probably be found to disprove this general statement.

Even when regional planning bodies are entirely advisory one should not consider them unimportant. They are useful devices for achieving local consensus, producing greater agency appreciation of total community need and giving advice to provincial ministries which reflects the priorities and needs of the region (or of whoever has the greatest influence within the regional body).

In general, regional planning bodies will fail, or be only marginally successful, unless they have strong and continuing philosophical support from the province, are provided with an appropriate budget, can acquire staff with at least modest competence, and can find in at least some community agencies and facilities the necessary leaders who will actively support the regional approach.

The concept of regionalization requires that we struggle with the problem of the extent to which we wish to allow or prevent regional disparities in ideology, wealth, priorities, demography, and health. At the international level we solve the problem by abandoning the concept of equity, but within Canada, or a province, there is less willingness to tolerate major inequities. Our constitution assures opportunities for provincial diversity and national pluralism, but federal initiatives have promoted national equity and reduced the pluralism and diversity. Within provinces the conflicts are the same but on a smaller scale. Local control and the encouragement of regional difference seem always to carry some threat to equity between regions.

EPILOGUE

In the period 1920-1950, innumerable major reports dealt with the idea of regionalization, and some of their wording and recommendations are as sensible now as they were then.

Summary of the Report of the Committee on the Costs of Medical Care (CCMC), United States, 1932

This CCMC Report made five major recommendations. It recommended:

1. Organized Group Practice, preferably hospital based.
   a) There should be one or more nonprofit medical centers in all communities with a population of over 15,000. There would be a local community board for each center.
   b) The hospital-based organized medical groups would integrate preventive and therapeutic services on a continuing basis in home, office and hospital (but excluding serious mental care and TB).
   c) Physicians, dentists and auxiliary personnel would be part of the community medical center.
   d) Services available would include home nursing, home care, medical social work, provision of drugs, appliances, eyeglasses, ambulance services and institutional care for the long term ill and the convalescent.
   e) Small communities should affiliate with a medical center and have satellite sources of care.
2. National availability of basic public health services including school health services, screening and health education — all part of the total program offered by the community health centers.
3. Prepayment through either personal premiums, with or without employer assistance, or tax funds, or a combination of the two.
4. Area-wide planning and coordination involving the local level and the state level.
5. Trained health administrators and better training for all health manpower.

Many reports released in the first half of the century discussed a network of coordinated and formally linked but discrete facilities serving a defined area. There was repeated endorsement of many of the things we still talk about such as an integrated network of regionalized services, identified health service areas, regional planning, decentralization of decision making, equitable distribution and efficiency.

"The more things change the more they stay the same."

Suggested Reading

Gosselin, Roger, "Decentralization/regionalization in Health Care: The Quebec Experience". *HCM Review*, Winter 1984, p. 7-25.

Chapter 9

HEALTH PROMOTION

DEFINITIONS OF HEALTH PROMOTION

Earlier chapters have reinforced the idea that health is the product of a broad spectrum of factors including a decent standard of living, good working conditions, opportunities for education, preservation of psyche, one's genotype, a clean physical environment, social support for families and individuals, a responsible lifestyle, and a reasonable spectrum of health care. Acceptance of all of these as determinants of health requires that health promotion protect and improve our mental as well as our physical health, and that it act upon a broad mix of social, physical and personal environments. Health promotion will, of necessity, affect such varied health influences as the purity of our air, the pH of lakes and streams, the safety of vehicles and highways, the mood in our schools, the availability of rewarding employment, the levels of immunization and the consumption of harmful substances.

'Health promotion' is one of the modern terms. The World Health Organization and Health and Welfare Canada are pursuing it with vigor and volumes are written about it, but it appears to mean different things to different people and to contain the ideas inherent in some other commonly used terms. To what extent, for example, are health promotion, health education and preventive medicine the same or different? Suffice it to say that health educators are health promoters, as are those who deliver preventive services. This semantic footwork does not, however, deal adequately with the challenge of what is meant by the term 'health promotion'. The following definitions represent some of those which have been offered in the past decade.

a) Health promotion is the encouragement of, or implementation of, ways and conditions of living that promote health. Within this definition all social, ecological, cultural and economic determinants of health are eligible for change so that there may be improved emotional, physical, social, economic, mental or spiritual health. This definition includes health protection in its broadest sense including activities which increase opportunities to improve health and respond to threats to health. This definition encompasses the concept of 'healthy public policy'. It invites action with respect to all determinants of health including income, shelter, food, information, opportunities for choice and a sense of control.

b) Health promotion is the provision of information which allows personal choice and encourages personal responsibility for a healthier future. Health promotion within this definition is quite passive and personal. Education is the tool. This definition protects individual rights by emphasizing only the giving of information and it excludes factors not under individual control.

c) Health promotion assists people to make healthy choices among goods, services, personal habits and personal attitudes. This definition encompasses the use of a variety of incentives and disincentives to promote the various choices.

d) Health promotion is a collective effort to maintain and/or attain health. The commitment to collective activities has been made explicit.

e) "Health promotion is the process of enabling people to increase control over, and to improve, their health. It is, thus, much wider than health education, and encompasses all of the things we do to promote health. Disease prevention is directed at specific diseases, and aims to prevent negative changes in health, whereas health promotion aims to promote positive changes. The two approaches are thus complementary, working on opposite sides of the health ledger. This definition can be read to imply both individual and collective action. (Health Goals for Ontario)"

From these definitions, it is evident that health promotion can be understood to be individual or collective, persuasive or coercive, active or passive, limited or open-ended. It can give special attention to environment, lifestyle, health services or all of these. It can be implemented within a part of the health sector, throughout the health sector or throughout all social and economic sectors.

Despite the many definitions in use, it is practical and reasonable to reduce definitional choices to two:

1) *Health Promotion refers only to activities directed towards changing the behavior of individuals*, focusing on their lifestyles (a variation of definitions (b) and (c) given earlier). When this definition is used, health promotion programs or activities tend to concentrate on educating, primarily with respect to only those hazards which are, to at least a significant extent, under the control of the individual; examples are smoking, lack of exercise and poor diet. Circumstances and hazards that are outside of the control of the individual acting alone are, therefore, excluded. These include bad urban planning, large-scale environmental pollution, unhealthy public policy, treatment of municipal water supplies, the threat of nuclear war, and stresses at work. Acting within the objective of altering personal behavior, health care workers show a tendency to deal predominantly with threats to life or physical health. Neither the Society of Prospective Medicine, for example, or the Health and Welfare Canada (HWC) Health Hazard Appraisal Program (Evalu-Life), give noticeable attention to hazards affecting the quality of life.

2) *Health Promotion encompasses everything that promotes health*, such as policy development, social and economic programs, healthier workplaces, environmental improvement, and health and social services. This is the World Health Organization (WHO) definition. This broad approach encompasses the healthy public policy concept which states that the primary goal of all policy and planning, and of all governments, should be the preservation of or creation of a healthy population. The creation of policies with respect to health services (those services that respond to illness or injury) is only a small part of the policy spectrum although it too plays its part in preserving a healthy population.

The two definitions are significantly different, the first one being much more limited than the second. One's preference for one definition over the other can be clarified by deciding what kinds of policies and actions are appropriately called health promotion. Consider the following policies and actions:

a) The HWC program on smoking reduction.
b) The police crackdown on persons who are not wearing seat belts in cars.
c) New provincial legislation regarding safety in the workplace.
d) The burning of American cities by disadvantaged blacks in the 1960's (with the subsequent accelerated development of policies promoting racial equality and affirmative action).
e) The public housing program which produced 200,000 units of subsidized housing in Canada in the period from 1964-1979.
f) Dividing the highway between Quebec City and Windsor, or between Montreal and Ottawa.
g) Creating jobs for those who wish to work.

Within the broadest of definitions, all of the above are health promotion programs. The final clarification needed, and not available, deals with the relationship among occupational health services, environmental health services, primary care, hospital services, and health promotion. The nature of the relationship obviously depends on which definition of health promotion is chosen.

Throughout this book, health promotion (HP) will be considered to be a broad and encompassing term. It will include wellness promotion and risk reduction whether these are achieved by personal or collective action. It will include all those actions designed to improve or protect health or which were amended in light of consideration of impact on health and, therefore, will include environmental health, improved lifestyles, healthy public policy, occupational health, and health services. Despite our preference for this very broad definition of HP, it is desirable to be aware of the HP activities to date and to note the extent to which past and current HP activities reflect a narrower definition.

PROGRAMS TO CHANGE BEHAVIOR — THE ORIGINAL EMPHASIS

The design and development of most health promotion programs are based in the narrow definition of HP. These programs respond to our knowledge that particular behaviours lead to an increased probability of morbidity or mortality. These programs are based on the medical literature that identifies links such as the following:

a) Smoking is linked to a greatly increased risk of lung cancer, and of other cancers including those of the mouth, throat and bronchus, of emphysema, of chronic obstructive lung disease and of coronary artery disease.
b) Obesity influences the onset and course of hypertension, diabetes and coronary artery disease, increases the risk of surgery and is often associated with a low self-image.

c) Homosexuality with multiple partners, and intravenous drugs administered with shared needles, increase the risk of AIDS.

d) Alcohol abuse increases the incidence of cirrhosis of the liver, spouse abuse, child abuse, and family breakdown with its associated social sequelae.

These programs relate far more to physical than psychosocial hazards. The list does not include most behaviors that increase the probability of reduced quality of life for oneself or for others. Critical, nonsupportive or frightening parents and primary school teachers almost surely increase the likelihood of society producing not only insecure children, but insecure adults. Domineering inflexible supervisors damage the quality of life of those who work under them. These behaviors certainly affect health. Advocates of health promotion must encourage escape from the original narrow definition and expand both the tools of HP and the spectrum of hazards that are to be controlled.

THE NEW HEALTH PROMOTION: HEALTHY PUBLIC POLICY

The most recent perception of health promotion is built around the concept of healthy public policy. Housing, recreation, education, employment and social services are accepted as important to the health status of the population. Powerlessness and poverty become at least as central to our search for health as are carcinogens, genetic engineering or transplants. Social disorders such as violence, vandalism or other products of anger, or escapism in any form, join AIDS, accidents and Alzheimers disease as recognized signs of the need for appropriate health promotion activities. The promotion of better parenting, higher self-esteem, greater personal adaptability or greater independence are all properly labelled as health promotion.

The art of using all areas of policy as tools to improve health is still in its infancy but examples of successes can be found. A mix of consumer groups, industry representatives and government agencies and boards tackled the hazard of clothing burns to children. There were, prior to changes in policy, more than 20 serious burns and several deaths per year from this cause. An earlier attempt to reduce this hazard, by means of a public education program costing one million dollars, produced no noticeable results. In 1987, after holding many meetings, a number of changes were made in regulations under the *Hazardous Products Act* regarding children's sleepwear. It is assumed these technical changes in the flammability of fabrics will reduce the number of serious burns. In this simple, cause-effect situation, regulation is better than education, quite the reverse of the approach that will succeed when attitudes and traditions must be altered.

A few of the more recent programs for Canadian native peoples reflect our new perception of how to seek better health. Recent priorities as expressed by native groups seeking control over their own health and social services, have placed the need for parenting skills, counselling, long term employment, housing and recreation alongside the need for adequate medical services. Front-line health care personnel such as nurses are being trained to be community development personnel as well as health workers. In our search for ways to reduce the rates of suicide and violence among native adolescents, it appears likely that a sensitive school curriculum built around native culture, teaching practices which build links between the community and the school and housing arrangements which, where necessary, reflect traditional relationships rather than suburbia may be more successful than the importation of nonnative mental health workers.

Screening programs that have sharply reduced the sequelae of congenital hypothyroidism, phenylketonuria, tuberculosis, cancer of the cervix, hypertension, and congenital dislocation of the hip are examples of healthy public policy. These programs were easily introduced because they were highly technical, were provided through the health services network, were culturally acceptable, were politically neutral or positive, and were offensive to no-one. Most future successes will have to occur in much more complex and, often, partially negative environments.

Other important examples of healthy public policy have been put in place with only modest notice of their impressive impact on health; examples are the decisions to divide high-volume highways and to eliminate railroad level crossings. These policies have sometimes been put in place primarily for transportation and economic reasons, but their impact on health may be the greatest product. In a similar way, lower speed limits were introduced and enforced because of an energy crisis but reductions in traffic accident injuries and deaths were a healthy by-product.

Airbags in automobiles as protective devices to complement seat belts have been proven to be technologically effective and it has been estimated that installation of airbags in all cars would prevent half of the brain injury cases caused by automobile accidents (and automobile accidents cause 50% of head injuries requiring hospitalization). Installation of airbags would cost $150-250 per car; some of this cost would be directly offset by lowered insurance rates and more (perhaps all) would be offset by reduced medical care and social support costs.

Relatively inexpensive health promotion programs in Florida aimed at preventing spinal cord injuries caused by diving into shallow water ("Feet First, First Time") appear to be directly responsible for a 60-80% reduction in spinal cord injuries arising from diving. This HP program cost $200,000 while the average cost of care and support for only one spinal cord injured person is many times that amount. The avoidance of even one case would, therefore, make such a program cost-effective.

Sometimes policy intended to promote health is not a success. A relationship between saccharin and bladder cancer in rats led to restrictions on the use of saccharin when no substitute was immediately available, restrictions which were unfortunate for diabetics or those struggling with obesity. Many subsequent studies failed to find any relationship between the use of saccharin and the incidence of cancer in humans.

Despite the Constitution, which places health under provincial jurisdiction, the Department of National Health and Welfare has emerged as a major source of rapidly evolving health promotion activities. In 1983, the promotion of healthy living and protection against disease and environmental risk were identified as two areas of concentration for the federal ministry. The others were income security, social services support and universal access to high quality health services. The Health Promotion Directorate of HWC was described as having three objectives:

—To promote wellness or good health.
— To encourage avoidance of unnecessary health risks.
— To assist those with handicaps or chronic diseases in learning skills for coping with their circumstances.

Six Lifestyle Issues were given highest priority:

— Nutrition
— Smoking
— Alcohol
— Drug abuse
— Safety
— Mental health

Four strategies were proposed:

— Informing the public.
— Promoting a social climate that supports a healthy lifestyle.
— Supporting self-help and citizen participation in health promotion.
— Promoting HP practices in public programs in health care, and social services.

Since 1983 HWC, adhering to the concept of healthy public policy, has moved rapidly toward much greater emphasis on health promotion. This emphasis is in keeping with the direction of the World Health Organization and practices in a number of European countries. Recent HWC publications include *The Active Health Report — Perspectives on Canada's* (1985) *Health Promotion Survey*, published in 1987. Canada also contributed to *The Ottawa Charter for Health Promotion*, produced by the WHO at the end of the first International Conference on Health Promotion in Ottawa in 1986. The Ottawa Charter is an evolutionary document which strengthened WHO and Canadian commitment to broadly based multisectoral strategies encompassing community action and personal skill development.

In federal health promotion activities, as in most other health promotion activities, there are many optional approaches available because of the many factors and sequences relevant to many health hazards (Figure 9.1).

The Other New Emphasis Needed — The Promotion of Mental Health

Besides a shift to collective actions which promote health (the use of healthy public policy) there must also be a shift which brings balanced attention to both mental and physical health.

The first step needed is the elevation of mental health itself in our scale of values. Until we see state of mind as more important than sexual prowess, gaining wealth, being best or having a beautiful body we are unlikely to give much attention to protecting or improving mental health.

Figure 9.1
The Ill Health/Health Promotion Relationship

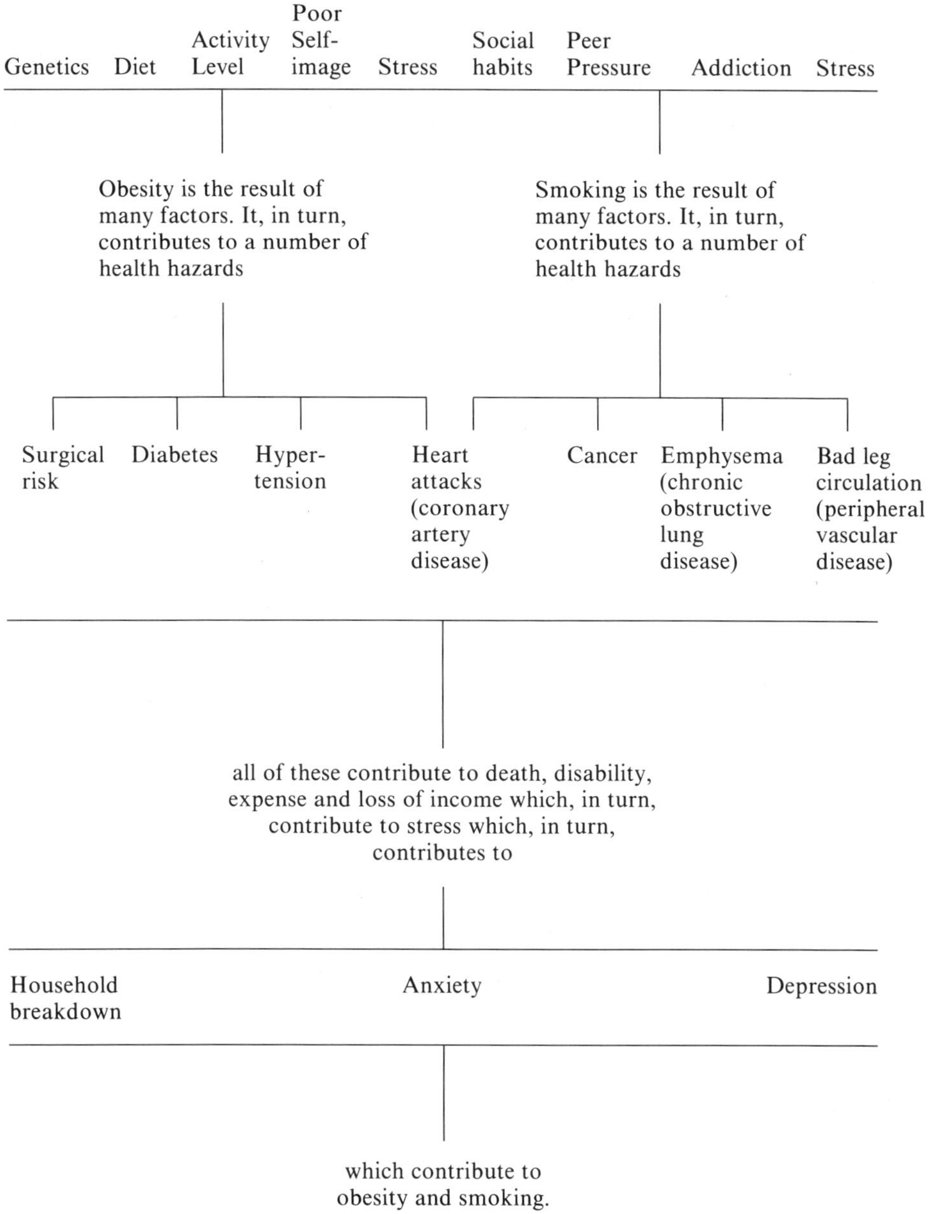

Health promotion can attack the chain of events at any point or many points.

The promotion of mental health should begin in early childhood. We know that isolation, neglect and abuse promote psychosocial disability, and that role models make lasting impressions. Parenting skills have been proven to be of central importance to the mental health of children. Programs or techniques which assist parents to learn how to minimize fear and guilt and transmit a sense of trust and interest, and which transmit these last two with consistency, are fundamental health promotion activities, as are those changes which expose children to better role models. Activities and programs of this type include parent preschool resource centers, family life education programs and others which help parents be better at their job of parenting.

Promoting the mental health of children also requires consideration of other influences. Most children spend more hours in front of TV, at school, or with peers at other locations, than they spend with parents. Television, school teachers, sports or other coaches, and older peers can provide undesirable role models, and these role models both create and reinforce unhealthy behavior. Aggression and related behavior can, for example, be identified in preschool years and it tends to persist unless reduced by planned intervention in the form of such things as reduced contact with violence on TV, rewards for nonviolent behavior, and advice to parents on how to respond to aggressive behavior. Studies have shown that aggressive toddlers retain those characteristics through their teens and into adulthood, and eventually have a higher than average incidence of unlawful and socially unacceptable behavior, unless their environment is permanently improved. Parental disinterest and inconsistency may be the commonest roots of mental pathology in children; failure to alter parent skills and attitudes, or those of other central figures, therefore, appears to sharply limit the usefulness of changes which are external.

Health promotion expenditures probably are most cost-effective in the preschool years. It is much less expensive to improve the social and emotional environment of a 2, 3 or 4 year old than to repair a damaged teenage psyche.

The incidence of unease in children has been illustrated by the degree of use of a free and confidential telephone counselling service launched in Britain in 1986. In the first 9 months, the program received 8000 attempted calls per day and responded to 700 of these. Sexual abuse is the largest category of complaint followed by physical abuse, problems with parents, bullying and pregnancy.

One skill quite fundamental to the improvement of our individual and collective mental health is that of conflict resolution. Pretending conflict does not exist, which has become an almost institutionalized skill in some parts of Canadian society, creates more problems than it avoids, and problem resolution in the absence of developed conflict resolution skills may implement a solution that is conflict creating rather than conflict reducing. When relative power is the dominant feature in problem solving, whether at the international or personal level, the exercise merely enshrines a historical pattern that can lead to individual or national destruction.

A DESIRABLE DICHOTOMY: WELLNESS PROMOTION AND RISK REDUCTION

Health promotion has two major functions — wellness promotion and risk reduction. There is an important concept behind this dichotomy.

Wellness promotion is the side of the health ledger which improves the quality of life. It makes us look forward to tomorrow with greater optimism and to enjoy today more fully. Risk reduction is directed at the prevention of specific diseases or injuries. We have opted for the term *risk reduction* rather than the commonly used *disease prevention*, because health is threatened by injury as well as disease and because risk reduction more accurately can include primary, secondary and tertiary prevention.

Clearly separating the objective of seeking positive changes from the objective of avoiding health hazards is desirable, but it is helpful to recall that some programs or activities serve both objectives and, therefore, do not fall neatly into one camp or the other. All risk reduction, whether disease prevention or injury prevention, is health promoting, and wellness promotion — the act of increasing wellness — often leads to reductions in risk. Certainly neither wellness promotion nor risk reduction is the special domain of the health services sector; both must be accomplished with the aid of the full spectrum of governments and socioeconomic sectors. Both wellness promotion and risk reduction become, therefore, legitimate goals for every ministry of government. This multisectoral approach is encompassed by the term healthy public policy and is central to such ideas as the rapidly expanding healthy cities project.

If one considers the term health promotion to include the concept of improving wellness, it must be remembered that many, if not most of the activities and programs called health promotion have, to this point in time, been implemented with the objective of reducing disease. Wellness promotion is a newcomer. Anti-smoking campaigns are directed to reductions in lung cancer and coronary artery disease, exercise programs are promoted to improve cardiovascular performance (although there often is a by-product of improved wellness), and weight control programs are usually encouraged to reduce the likelihood of diabetes, cardiovascular disease and surgical complications (again with improved self-image as either a by-product or incentive). It seems likely that, at least for the immediate future, the term health promotion will be commonly used by some in a relatively narrow sense whereas to others it will be a very inclusive term including wellness promotion and risk reduction.

Risk Reduction

Risk reduction is accomplished by:

1) Eradicating or reducing the magnitude of a hazard, for example, the purification of water, the avoidance of sports coaches who are disinterested in mediocre athletes, or increasing the safety of a workplace.
2) Altering the individual so that hazards are either no threat at all (for example, polio immunization) or are better handled (such as educational experiences which increase one's stress coping abilities).

3) Early diagnosis. This activity includes screening programs for target populations such as infants (for example, for phenylketonuria,congenital dislocation of the hip, or mental retardation), women of reproductive age or older (for cancer of the breast or cervix), adults of all ages (for hypertension), multipartner gays and I.V. drug users (for AIDS virus antibody), and members of single-parent, low-income families (for lack of stimulation, inadequate nutrition, or evidence of poorly managed stress).

   In all examples proposed, except that of AIDS, the purpose of screening is to initiate early treatment that can prolong life and/or increase its quality. (At the time of writing, no effective treatment for AIDS is available. Screening continues, however, in an effort to control the epidemic spread of the disease.)

4) Optimal treatment and rehabilitation. These reduce the hazard of an illness or injury.

These four approaches to risk reduction constitute what are commonly called primary prevention (the first two), secondary prevention (the third) and tertiary prevention (the last).

Most primary prevention through changes in the environment takes place outside of the health sector. Prevention of silicosis or grain handlers' diseases, for example, requires action by departments of labor, agriculture, environment or mines. The prevention of depression or suicide may require income support, changes in social networks, opportunities for employment, or better rehabilitation after being in jail. Even the prevention of dental caries, typhoid fever or tuberculosis depend more on hygiene, housing, education, nutrition, municipal water quality and good sewage handling than on the actions of health workers, although health professionals have an important role.

Disease prevention is a major component of risk reduction. It is, by definition, also a part of primary prevention. Primary prevention of physical illness is often accomplished by the health services network through immunization programs, health education or genetic counselling, but primary prevention of mental/emotional illness is more likely to occur in the home, the school or the workplace and under the auspices of many workers, institutions and programs that are not part of the health system.

Secondary prevention or presymptomatic diagnosis is primarily, if not completely, the responsibility of health workers when the diagnostic tests are being applied to humans or their tissues or fluids, but diagnostic testing that is important to health is now also routinely applied to water, foodstuffs, scientific devices, the stratosphere, air in the workplace, and equipment of all types, and these evaluations are usually not performed by 'health' workers.

Rehabilitation, one of the dominant components of tertiary prevention, occurs within the health sector to the extent that medical rehabilitation personnel such as physiotherapists are involved. However, when job training or retraining (vocational rehabilitation) is needed, departments of education or manpower provide the necessary services, and when financial or social rehabilitation is needed other departments come into play. Effective treatment is predominantly provided by health personnel when treatment is carried out at the individual level or for a group of individuals, but when one of the environments is being treated in the interest of the health of the community, the task usually falls to workers in departments of social services, labor, justice, education, transport, agriculture or others.

Presymptomatic Diagnosis (Secondary Prevention)

Presymptomatic diagnosis is desirable if treatment is more effective at this stage. Because there are no symptoms the disease must be sought — a process called screening.

Mass screening seeks to identify a previously unrecognized disease or defect through the application of relatively standardized procedures to large numbers of people or situations. Often screening is limited to high risk populations such as VD or TB contacts, or all members of a family with an identified hereditary disease. Some screening programs are aimed at all members of a population such as older adults (who may have glaucoma), blacks (who may have sickle cell anemia) or adult females (who may have cervical cancer).

Screening separates the screened individuals into two groups — those who probably do not have the sought after disease or defect, and those who probably do. Screening usually does not firmly establish a diagnosis; it suggests one. Positive or suspicious findings must usually be confirmed by other tests before a firm diagnosis is made. In multiple screening, more than one test is applied since more than one disease is being sought.

Screening is also routinely done on an individual basis. A person may appear on his or her own initiative with a request for investigation with respect to a particular disease, or for a general check up. The health worker may, with the consent of the patient, carry out investigations unrelated to why the person came. We also screen individuals when they seek life insurance or an operator's licence.

When will screening be appropriate? The following questions need to be addressed:

1) What is the nature of the disease or defect?
   a) Is it of significance to either the patient or the general public?
   b) What is the interval between being detectable but asymptomatic and the appearance of symptoms? If this interval is short, then screening will have to be very frequent or be of little use.
   c) Does it matter in terms of prognosis or cost whether the disease or defect is detected before it is symptomatic or otherwise noticeable?
   d) If it is found, and can be corrected or treated, will it be treated or corrected? Dental caries in low income populations, for example, can be easily found but tend not to be treated, and continued testing of the acidification of lakes will not be productive until there is a greater will to act on the causes.
   e) How common is the condition? How many of the tests will be positive?

2) Is there an effective screening test?
   a) What is the incidence of false negatives? How often will the sought-for disease or defect be present but reports be normal? (The test is said to be highly sensitive when there are few or no false negatives.)
   b) What is the incidence of false positives? How specific is the test, and what are the implications of a false positive? What happens when a test is positive; will there be great anxiety, immediate treatment, ostracism or major but unnecessary changes in life style or other things?
   c) Will the test perform consistently? How vulnerable is the test to temperature, variability, contaminants, patient noncompliance or other factors?
   d) Is there a need for special facilities, equipment or workers?
   e) What is the cost per test?
   f) What is the patient acceptability? People are less likely to accept screening tests that are uncomfortable, painful, time consuming, hazardous or require repeat visits.
3) How feasible is implementation of a screening program?

   This question needs to be answered only if sections 1 and 2 indicate that screening is worth considering.
   a) What is the cost per case found? What is the cost-benefit ratio?
   b) Who would plan, finance, administer and evaluate the program?
   c) What are the start-up costs? How long will it take to implement the program? What is the likelihood that new developments will make the program obsolete before it is started?
   d) Can one predict a case load? What proportion of the potential case load will enter the system?
   e) How will the new program affect and interact with other health services?

These questions allow the evaluation and implementation of a screening proposal. They also typify a problem solving process that has wide application.

Man Is Irrational

Humans are capable of becoming hysterical about minor or nonexistent risks while ignoring large and avoidable ones. People tend to give greater attention to new risks or newly perceived risks such as video display terminals, urea formaldehyde insulation, and genital herpes, than to risks to which they have become accustomed including smoking, travel in automobiles, and riding bicycles. They also react more strongly to risks they do not understand or that are imposed by some outside source (Three Mile Island and AIDS), and they react more strongly when children are involved (Reyes syndrome). Individuals tend to tolerate large risks that arise from their own choices (smoking and mountain climbing), while vigorously rejecting much smaller risks arising from the actions of others (traffic noise and group homes in the neighborhood). There is exceptionally low tolerance for risks within the health services network and a very high tolerance of physical hazards in selected workplaces such as forests, mines or farms. There is a very low tolerance of selected environmental contaminants, such as asbestos or formaldehyde, and a high tolerance of emotionally destructive environments. Here are some examples.

1) Seven eighths of the population did not use seat belts regularly when they became standard equipment in cars. Three quarters still did not use them regularly after it became legally mandatory. It took vigorous enforcement to induce the majority of car occupants to regularly buckle up.
2) Thousands of Canadian houses were dismantled in the 1970's and early 1980's because they were insulated with urea formaldehyde foam insulation (UFFI). The by-products of the UFFI were thought to be hazardous to physical health; the fear, which studies say was unfounded, certainly became hazardous to mental health.
3) In those same UFFI-lined homes, thousands of people continued to be threatened and injured by wet and slippery floors, by unsafe scatter rugs, by endlessly consumed black coffee, by cigarette smoke, by tap water set at scalding temperatures and by dozens of other factors always or often under the control of the householder and more statistically important than UFFI; but only UFFI produced panic.
4) In 1985, Ontario discovered chemical contaminants in a number of wines and, in 1987, broken glass was found in wine. There were no reports of blindness or renal failure, but a great wine testing binge resulted. No-one, of course, wants chemicals or glass in imported wines but it would be nice to think our drinking water might get at least the same degree of regular attention and protection. When it is examined, hazardous contaminants are often found, especially in water from Lake Ontario and Lake Erie.
5) When water in Ontario has more than 100 fecal coliforms per millilitre, it is considered unsafe for swimming. Municipalities close the beaches when this level is exceeded. Thousands of people lose the pleasure of being in the water because there is a possibility of minor illness. (For decades the Ontario standard was 200 fecal coliforms per 100 ml and England, for years, had no standard at all). A few years ago when beaches in Ottawa were closed, three boys on bicycles coming back from a swim in a rural quarry (an unsupervised and untested swimming hole) were all killed by a drunk driver. It would have been better to have given them a safer place in town by being less fussy about a few coliforms which do not kill anyone.

All of these examples can be boiled down to the fact that the way people, including professionals, see hazards does not seem to have very much to do with how dangerous the hazards are. No matter what one does, life is full of risks. All we can reasonably aim for are good information, open discussion and then an opportunity for individual and collective action against selected risks.

In our drive for healthy public policy as the central theme of health promotion, we should note that too much research and too much health worker education and writing deals with statistically unimportant physical health hazards. Deaths due to faulty crib design, for example, are more apt to be studied than how we should screen school teachers to select those who will be optimistic, supportive and positive in their classrooms. No one wishes to see children die or be damaged by faulty cribs but the volume of real and potential damage from teachers who are emotionally unsuited for their jobs, and the benefits from teachers who are emotionally suited for their jobs, is much larger and, therefore, should get more attention. (In the period 1976-1984 there were 3 infant deaths in Canada due to faulty crib design.)

One foreign experience demonstrates how public policy decisions relate to risk. Upper atmosphere experiments in northern Sweden required the firing of rockets whose remnants would fall in sparsely populated regions. To avoid the risk of a reindeer herder being hit by a piece of falling rocket, all herders were evacuated by helicopter. A simple calculation suggested the risk of injury or death in a helicopter accident to be 100 times greater than the likelihood of being hit by a piece of falling rocket. Risk in the political world must be evaluated in terms of the cultural or political acceptability as well as the statistical probability and, in this case, a helicopter crash occurring while the government was trying to protect someone was considered to be more socially acceptable than the much smaller risk of being hit by a falling rocket. The attitudes of populations and individuals may make action necessary even when evidence and rationale suggest that the best thing to do is nothing.

To test your own feelings about various risks, and how you will react to specific policy proposals, consider the following:

1) Boxing versus prostitution

   A ban on boxing has been recommended by many medical societies. Brain damage is routine, but large civilized audiences pay large sums to watch the brain damage occur. The benefits to the participants are primarily psychological although a few make a decent living. In response to concerns regarding serious injury, the sport requires that medical examinations be performed, and that doctors be at the ring side. Prostitution, on the other hand, is also widely practiced, is only semi-legal and, if carried out with the degree of regulation and supervision required in boxing, would bring few physical hazards to either participant and would bring benefits to both. Which of these combinations of risks and benefits is most tolerable (to you), and why?

2) Blood transfusions and hepatitis

   Two to five percent of individuals who receive blood transfusions contract hepatitis (usually non-A and non-B hepatitis and, therefore, not usually serious). Many of these transfusions are not medically indicated. Why is the risk of hepatitis tolerated so quietly?

3) War games

   In 1985 the Canadian Ophthalmological Association reported that, in the 12 preceding months, war games (in which teams of players shoot at each other with supposedly harmless guns) had, in Ontario and Québec, produced 29 serious eye injuries and had caused legal blindness in one eye in 14 persons. A substantial risk could not offset the urge to be macho and violent. Should the games be declared illegal?

4) Failure to immunize
The *Canada Health Survey* (1978-79) reported 237,000 females 20 to 34 years of age without rubella immunization. The risk of birth defects was not enough to cause these individuals to seek a no-cost, very low-risk program of immunization. In 1978-79, 4.5 million Canadians were without adequate protection against polio. These people opted for a serious risk (polio) rather than a painless, safe, no-cost procedure (immunization) available in every community.

5) Coal tar deposits
Relics of old gasification plants have been found in two locations in Ottawa. Their discovery led to great concern about carcinogens and toxic gases, which in turn lead to the hiring of expensive consultants, the carrying out of expensive clean-ups, the writing of frantic toxicology reports and the temporary re-routing of pedestrian traffic. All of this trouble occurred despite the lack of evidence of real danger. It is unlikely that the coal tar deposits produce fumes at anywhere near the level of the gasoline fumes breathed-in routinely by the gas attendant putting gas in gas tanks, but rationale and hard evidence are no match for an unfounded perception of risk.

As a society, we are inconsistent in how we react to various threats to life, but we are even less consistent when our concern about the quality of our lives is compared to our concern over physical health. We are outraged by the physical abuse of a child but tolerate authoritarian schools and mindless TV programming that inhibit or annihilate the independance and the creativity of thousands of children. We continue to often want too much, to expect too much and to share too little — all of which lead to frustration, tension, aggressiveness, possessiveness and reduced mental health.

We are often competitive; we seem more willing to walk over someone than to co-operate with him or her, more anxious to do better than the average than to be the average. Both of these traits carry risks in terms of rejection or failure or criticism, and each of these is a serious threat to the quality of our lives.

Health promotion and healthy public policy must accept that the alteration of perceptions and of culture may be a prerequisite to altering people's responses to risk. Health promotion personnel must become students of public suasion. They must become even more aware of the factors that have major effect on the perceptions of people — for example, advertising — and use the same tools to attain different ends. Long term risk must be made to seem more immediate; the danger of smoking is an example.

Regardless of how much personal irresponsibility (smoking, alcohol abuse, careless driving or boating) has preceded appearance at the hospital door, or at death's door, it is customary to expect immediate and perfect care. The rule seems to be that if you are responding to my problem or hazard, I will demand that every risk be eliminated; if I must respond to my problem or hazard, almost any degree of risk is tolerable. This comment is, of course, unfair to the millions of responsible Canadians who wear their seat belts, drive carefully, and do not smoke, but it does apply to many others who damage their children through needless criticism or who destroy coronary arteries with carbon monoxide or livers with alcohol, but who complain about critical teachers or lack of a 911 emergency telephone system.

FACTORS DELAYING INCREASED ATTENTION TO HEALTH PROMOTION

Several factors have slowed the development of health promotion, including the power of existing attitudes and bureaucracies. The concept of cure dominates in medical schools, hospitals and physicians' offices, and these cost centers are seen by much of the public as the source of good health. In this context it is difficult to find political support or money for health promotion. (With leadership, however, progress can be made, as has been the case with the Toronto health department.) The presence and power of special interest groups such as the tobacco lobby, the gun lobby, the alcohol lobby, or those citizens who oppose group homes in their neighborhood — the 'not in my back yard' syndrome — also impede progress.

Lack of good research indicating the extent to which health promotion efforts are likely to alter the morbidity or mortality associated with various risks means health promotion specialists do not know the relative effectiveness of different approaches. There is even an absence of information regarding the magnitude of various risks. We do not have a reasonably clear understanding of the extent to which many factors promote or threaten our mental, physical or social health.

PRINCIPLES THAT SHOULD GOVERN HEALTH PROMOTION PROGRAMS

What is the optimal role for health and community workers who are interested in risk reduction and wellness promotion as mechanisms for improving the health of Canadians? Toward what should they aim; and how do they reach their goals? The following list presents several principles and options:

1) There must be devices available which ensure that people or populations being affected have an opportunity to complain and exert influence — in essence, to participate.
2) Programs cannot usually be prepackaged for wide distribution. They must be adapted to prevailing cultures and to social and economic conditions.
3) There should be frequent re-evaluation of programs in the light of new information. It is likely that there will be a regular need to drop programs that are either ineffective or are less cost-effective than others.
4) Planning and delivery must anticipate the effect of powerful lobbies.
5) All actions should be consistent with, or part of, the healthy public policy concept.

6) There should be an appropriate balance between our attention to emotional and physical risks.
7) There must be co-operation with the large network of public and private groups and agencies which also exist so the public may be healthy. Technocrats must acknowledge the right of communities to set their own goals and should see the blurring of public health boundaries and the expansion of the health team as an opportunity, not a humiliation or an attack. Acceptance of the importance of nonhealth agencies to health will inevitably lead to the revisions of public health legislation that are necessary if our modern epidemics are to be mastered.
8) The public must be provided with information which will allow it to make an informed choice concerning activities and risks. Persons at risk need to know the seriousness of the risk compared to other risks, how common it is compared to other risks, and how to evaluate it. People need to know that tobacco and alcohol during pregnancy are a greater risk to the unborn than crib death is to the newborn, and that both of them are greater risks than cancer in infancy. They need to know that teenage accidents are a much greater risk than teenage cancer, and our generosity toward cancer research for young cancer victims should be exceeded by our attention to accidents.
9) Members of the public should be helped to resist the temptation to pay major attention to risks that arise from the actions of someone else while largely ignoring risks that arise from their own actions (and the health and community workers must also follow this rule).
10) Health care workers should avoid being paternalistic. They should not decide what is important for other people. Other peoples' lives are their own, and remain their own no matter how much the worker might like to take charge.

If we can agree on these most basic goals or principles, how do we proceed to implement programs for a healthier population?

When evaluating a risk, or considering a response to risk, it is essential to look for negative as well as positive sequelae, and it is wise to consider emotional, ethical, social and economic as well as physical consequences. Greater physical freedom for the confused or the physically unstable may bring greater physical risks but may be a prerequisite to a better quality of life. Attempts to make children aware of the hazards of strangers (street proofing) may produce a child suspicious of and frightened of the world. A person with coronary artery disease or diabetes can become so preoccupied with the hazards of the disease (a preoccupation that can be encouraged by health professionals), that there is little notice of the joy and opportunities that are still available. The search for safety and longevity can damage health as well as protect it.

Professionals who seek to protect adults from risk must recognize that health professionals are advisors, not lawmakers. The right of patients to receive information, to access their files, and to decide about their care, are increasingly enshrined. If lifestyle consequences are to be altered by behaviour modification (social learning techniques), the people being affected have the right to demand participation in both the design and the application of the social learning programs. Brains should be available for washing only if the washee agrees, and coercion should be frowned upon.

DEVELOPING A HEALTH PROMOTION STRATEGY

Countries/provinces should have some idea of what health status they expect in their populations, and they should give regular and serious attention to what national policies will best attain the desired goals. The WHO has given this task considerable thought, as has Canada. The WHO, in 1977, set the goal of "Health for All by the Year 2000," and the Alma Ata Conference in 1978 identified clean water, communicable disease control, and the primary community health services model as major elements of a strategy based on intersectoral action and public participation. The high technology model was deemed inappropriate. The strategies proposed by the WHO are not fully relevant to the developed countries but the overall goal is attractive. Canada went through the infectious disease control phase half a century ago; it then entered and is still in the age of chronic disease control. We have now entered the age of managing social pathology.

In the area of chronic disease control, we are advanced in terms of drugs and therapy, and we are advancing in terms of our psychosocial support systems. However, with respect to social pathology problems, we have barely begun to think about the control of epidemics of anxiety, suspicion and abuse of power. We are dealing, in a preliminary way, with physical environmental problems (for example, lead in gas, the Love Canal, and acid rain) but the pathology in our social and occupational/economic relationships is not yet a common target.

In the period from 1978-1984, thirty-two European countries acting within the WHO framework increased the political focus of HP, shifted attention from technical to political expertise and made the equity issue part of the agenda. There is a commitment to reduce inequities by 25% by the year 2000.

The 1986 first International Conference on Health Promotion in Ottawa produced the *Ottawa Charter for Health Promotion* which proposed social, ecological and political strategies for HP. Major political battles are imminent as healthy public policy alternatives, including the drive for healthy cities, come into conflict with issues such as economic growth, corporate profits, the rights of business and the convenience of the public.

Identification of policy areas that should have top priority requires:

1) a good understanding of the health status being sought, and of the relative importance to be attached to the various aspects of that health, for example, psychosocial versus physical health,
2) an understanding of the current state of the health of the population and of the abilities and interests of the population regarding health and health practices,
3) an identification of major policy alternatives that are available, and

4) analysis of the expected social, political and economic impact and acceptability of each policy alternative.

Aids to Health Workers Who Must Implement HP Programs

1) Provide people with understandable information and then assist them to proceed towards whatever changes in attitude and action they choose; some of these may be major cultural changes. Learn to be a change agent as well as a deliverer of services. Speak for, work for and do what is possible to personally illustrate the lifestyles and perspectives identified as desirable. These may include co-operation before aggressiveness, the development of perspective with respect to risk, the control of expectations, the promotion of tolerance, the idea of industrial democracy or the acceptance of death as a normal event. The changes being sought are most likely to come about if new approaches are used, and efforts are sustained over time.
2) Accept that lifestyle consequences arise from collective as well as individual actions and attitudes and, therefore, be involved in influencing social change beyond the individual level. It is difficult to ask for tolerance and limited expectations from most people if selected groups continue to expand their control and power. A person who accepts the proposition that material rewards are not the only important ones will have less difficulty dealing with the stresses of climbing the competitive and materialistic ladder.
3) Increasingly work with nonhealth personnel such as school teachers who are crucial to total public health.
4) Identify and concentrate on specific local problems as well as on general national problems.
5) Determine priorities on the basis of three major constraints or factors: (a) the goals and objectives one has set, (b) the magnitude and consequences of various threats to health and (c) the extent to which these threats can be reduced.
6) Learn to achieve change through involvement rather than through doctrine, through promotion of healthy adaptation rather than through scare tactics.
7) Acknowledge the right of the individual to ignore advice, if that is their wish. Some health problems or hazards should be endured so that the individual may support values more important than longevity or physical health. Remember that there will be major and perpetual conflict between social choices and individual choices and that this conflict is usually appropriate. Remember that people will do those things they think will bring the most benefit to them or to their family or community. The benefits may be in the form of wealth, comfort, power, freedom, beauty and peace of mind, as well as physical health.

The lifestyle that one prefers is usually essential to the quality of one's life; one could go so far as to say that preferred lifestyle is synonymous with quality of life. It would be reasonable for a client to say, "When you tamper with my lifestyle you tamper with me. My perception of reasonable risk may be quite different from yours and usually my perception will or should determine what I do or am able to do. Your rights as a representative of society will hopefully only very seldom override my rights as an individual. Certainly, as you stimulate me to follow lifestyles that are 'healthy', I hope you will always do so in a fashion that would be acceptable to you if it happened to you. In the end, my lifestyle should be chosen by me, not by you."

It is the task of health workers, however, to propose change, and therefore they must be aware of the different approaches which can be used to alter lifestyle. Traditional health education is one, legislation is another, tax incentives are another; but rational argument must underpin whatever tools are used. Health workers should be at ease with the techniques of motivation, of reinforcement and of positive stroking, as well as of statistical validation, cost-benefit analysis and the shaping of public policy.

Health workers and agencies should not hesitate to confront the health system or its leaders when the goals or principles listed earlier are threatened. There should be rejection of a search for quantity of life ahead of quality of life (our health system frequently has the wrong primary objective). There should be rejection of any tendency to concentrate resources on problems with great technical complexity to the detriment of other more important areas of need. There should be opposition to proposals which encourage false public expectations, and there should be rejection of the historical tendency to say, "Bring your problems to me and I will tell you what to do." This paternalistic and dictatorial proposition should now be replaced by, "Let us study problems together and see what each of us should do."

Dilemmas

1) At what point do health promotion activities directed towards behavioral change become 'brainwashing' or become so coercive or intimidating that they are incompatible with a free society? When do these activities unacceptably infringe on personal rights, in particular, the right to be exposed to hazards when the individual so wishes? At what point does health promotion zeal become grounds for criticism instead of praise?
2) To what extent, and in what circumstances, should programs aimed at altering individuals be favored over programs aimed at changing the environment or the system? When would emphasis on personal responsibility lead to an undesirable underemphasis on collective responsibilities?
3) When should incentives be used, and when should disincentives be used, and who should make these decisions? Should persons suffering from diseases or injuries they could have avoided be penalized? Should persons taking 'inappropriate' risks be penalized, and should persons who consciously avoid major risks be rewarded?

4) When should there be only the provision of information and when should other action also be taken?
5) To what extent should the field of health promotion be associated with one particular bureaucracy or professional group?
6) Are we creating a Spartan culture of healthism? Are we developing authoritarian prescriptions for health, and an even lower self-image for the unwell? (If we are, it is because health is being perceived as physical health and not primarily as a state of mind.)

Summary

Two major evolutionary changes are needed if health promotion is to fulfill its great promise. Firstly, the preoccupation with physical health must give way to a balanced emphasis on psychosocial as well as physical hazards. Secondly, the early emphasis on individual responsibility and change must give way to the larger world of healthy public policy.

Nancy Milio, author of the best seller *Promoting Health Through Public Policy*, has stated that human health does not just happen. It is created or destroyed by a myriad of decisions made by individuals. The likelihood of policy decisions improving the health status of a community or nation increases when the policy writers agree with the WHO that the health of their people should be the primary goal of all governments.

If we accept the general theme that spending more money on the acute care medical system is not the best way to better health, then we must have some other strategy, and that strategy is health promotion rooted in the concept of healthy public policy. *The Ottawa Charter for Health Promotion (1986)* states, "The fundamental conditions and resources for health are peace, shelter, education, food, income, a stable eco-system, sustainable resources, social justice and equity." Within this concept, health promotion becomes a gargantuan task worthy of the efforts of us all.

Suggested Reading

1) Spasoff, R. et al., *Health Goals for Ontario*, Government of Ontario, 1987.
2) Milio, Nancy, *Promoting Health Through Public Policy*, Canadian Public Health Association, Ottawa, 1987.
3) *Health Promotion, an International Journal*, Oxford University Press.

Chapter 10

MENTAL HEALTH SERVICES

INTRODUCTION

If health is first of all a state of mind, and that is our definition, then mental health is of primary importance and mental health services have a special place in the health services network. Although the definition of good mental health will vary with the values of the beholder, it could be described as a state of mind that allows the individual to develop abilities, pursue goals, meet needs and cope with life's problems without undue stress (modified from Heseltine, 1983).

This chapter discusses the public and professional perceptions of mental health, the population who have need of mental health services, or whose mental health is at risk and needs protection, and the policies, programs and institutions that comprise the mental health services network. For pragmatic purposes, the term mental health services will be applied only to those programs and activities which are usually referred to as mental health services.

Mental health services are a health service sector that has emerged from complete neglect but that is still struggling to consolidate public acceptance. The age of the large, low-cost, rural and hidden institution in which incarceration was often for life is past but the stature and the level of financing of mental health care still lag behind those of physical health care.

In 1960, 0.4% of Canadians were in mental institutions and half of them had been institutionalized for more than seven years. By the 1980's, two thirds of psychiatric admissions lasted less than two weeks and many of the institutions were gone or were much smaller. These changes have been accompanied by major reassignment of function among institutions and programs, a reassignment which was, perhaps, made easier by an accident of history.

In 1955-58, when the *Hospital Insurance and Diagnostic Services Act* (HIDSA) was being prepared, passed and enacted, the federal government specifically excluded cost sharing for psychiatric services because those services were already being provided at provincial expense. The new *Act* was intended to expand health care access, not to transfer existing provincial expenditures to the federal treasury. Because of this decision there were, for a time, few if any major expansions or improvements to our psychiatric hospitals, a very fortuitous neglect when one considers how rapidly these institutions lost favor during the late 1960's and 1970's. If psychiatric expenditures had been cost shared in 1958, we would probably have expanded the already excessive supply of these isolated, crowded and soon-to-be-rejected institutional dinosaurs.

THE CLIENTS/USERS OF MENTAL HEALTH SERVICES AND THEIR PATTERNS OF ILL HEALTH

Inadequate mental health is usually characterized by loss of a sense of reality, by socially unacceptable behavior, or by inability to cope. The clients may be individuals or groups of individuals (usually families). Mental or emotional illness may be associated with psychosis but the great majority of those who need and use mental health services are not psychotic.

Cummings (1979) proposed four functional categories of people who seek (or might seek) mental health services. Each category requires a somewhat different capability in the health services that deal with it. This functional categorization is non-diagnostic and is quite different from one based on categories such as cerebral dysfunction, psychosis, mental retardation, personality disorder or social pathology. The four functional categories are:

1) The long term and significantly disabled (for example, the chronic psychotics).
2) The short term seriously disabled (for example, the acute psychotics or those who react severely to situational factors).
3) The distressed (for example, the significantly neurotic or those finding it quite difficult to cope).
4) The dissatisfied (for example, the bored, alienated, unhappy — neither disabled nor ill).

There is much less need for formal intervention in category four than in three, and the need tends to be less urgent in the last two categories than in the first two. The extent to which formal mental health services are required increases as coping abilities decrease and as the incidence of socially unacceptable behavior increases.

Although the general categories described are useful in program development, there are client groups that are difficult to categorize and plan for. There is, for example, a substantial group of almost unemployable persons who do not exhibit gross signs of chronic mental illness. They have few if any skills, minimal if any initiative and a strong expectation of failure (having failed many times). They may tolerate stress poorly. They may or may not be quite content with a life on public assistance. They may share a highly developed belief that society should be generous with a broad range of economic, social and technological supports. They certainly do not subscribe to the work ethic as we describe it. They exhibit a high incidence of substance abuse, child abuse and family breakdown and probably have an above average birth rate. Where do these populations fit? What social pathology exists, which of it should be responded to, and which responses are justifiable? How much of this picture represents poor mental health? Individuals such as these would be categorized differently by different mental health workers.

Estimates of the prevalence of inadequate mental health usually tend to be between 10% and 30% of the general population. Heseltine, in 1983, suggested 25%, whereas, in 1978, the Canadian Mental Health Association (CMHA) suggested between 12% and 17%.

The Ontario study by Heseltine (1983) proposed that of the 25% of the population with a diagnosable psychiatric condition, at least 90% will be seen and handled by nonspecialist services. Most will contact a family physician.

Over half of these will be given a mental health diagnosis such as anxiety or depression. Less than one tenth of the group with a diagnosable psychiatric condition will be referred for specialist attention. There is, however, little evidence to suggest that this referral rate is either too high or too low.

Of the 1-2% of the total population who have a chronic mental illness requiring ongoing attention, one third are schizophrenic, one third have organic brain syndrome and one third have other diagnoses. Although 10-15% of the general population will be hospitalized at least once in their lives with an emotional or mental illness, it is the chronically ill who dominate institutional statistics. Among the 10-15% of persons who are admitted at least once, common diagnoses include alcoholism, schizophrenia, affective disorders and neuroses.

Child psychiatry is a rapidly growing specialty as is psychogeriatrics. Major problems and sequelae in children include hyperactivity, eating disorders, adolescent depression, suicide and sexual abuse. Two to six percent of young females are raped, 80% by males whom they know and who are often members of their families.

The chronically mentally ill are now seldom permanently institutionalized (as was common a few decades ago), but they tend to be continuously in need of support. Ten to twenty percent of persons receiving provincial disability allowances in Ontario for medical reasons have a psychiatric diagnosis. Another, perhaps larger group are on municipal welfare roles. There is often need for assistance with housing as well as a need for regular counselling, social programs, medication and professional review. Employment may be possible only in sheltered situations. Household members or other close associates may also benefit from counselling and other forms of support.

Although there does not appear to be an increase in the incidence of psychotic illness, there certainly has been greater notice of nonpsychotic emotional problems such as insecurity, anxiety and depression. An increasing number of users are receiving services from an expanding list of health workers for problems which, in earlier decades, were apparently largely ignored.

CHARACTERISTICS AND PERCEPTIONS OF MENTAL ILLNESS

Almost all mental ill health is multifactorial. Only in a minority of cases can one clearly identify an organic (physical) cause (in which case the condition can be said to represent physical ill health with mental/emotional symptoms), or clearly associate one event or factor with the emotional problem, as is the case in some reactive depressions. Contributing causes may not all be readily visible and the relative importance of the various causes may be even less known, but many personal and environmental factors tend to have contributed to a person's mental ill health. Although this vague relationship between cause and effect can be seen as a deterrent to effective prevention and treatment, it can also be seen as a help in the sense that any number of actions or changes may significantly improve or protect individual mental health.

Public and professional perceptions of the relative importance of mental health and mental health servcies are best illustrated by a look at a few policies and practices:

1) Only a small percentage of Medical Research Council funds, certainly less than 5% and perhaps less than 2%, are assigned to mental or psychosocial research.
2) Demands by physicians and by the public for increased funding of acute treatment general hospitals are infinitely more aggressive than demands for increased funding for mental health services.
3) Child abuse legislation in Ontario makes it a crime to mentally or physically abuse children and requires reporting by health professionals of all cases of suspected abuse. Cases reported, however, are almost exclusively cases of suspected physical abuse.
4) HWC produced a Health Hazard Appraisal exercise in which an individual is asked a number of questions. These questions relate almost entirely to physical health and the only conclusion reached is the predicted life expectancy of the subject. The quality of life and mental health, and the hazards to each, are not considered.
5) Involuntary admission to and retention in psychiatric facilities is now routinely examined by means of a series of mandatory assessments and reviews. These protections did not exist a few decades ago.
6) Group homes or half-way houses for the physically disabled tend to be more acceptable to residential neighborhoods than those which house alcoholics or the chronically mentally ill.
7) There is much greater general public support for the idea of community-based care for persons with mental illness than there was a few decades ago.
8) Mental health services are now seen to have a therapeutic and preventive dimension whereas in earlier decades their primary role was the protection of the public against dangerous lunatics.
9) Large numbers of individuals with diagnosable mental health problems appear not to be receiving professional help, whereas failure to receive attention for physical health problems is much less common.

Of the above examples, numbers 5, 7 and 8 illustrate a trend towards acceptance of mentally ill persons as persons who deserve social concern and support. The other six examples illustrate the weakness of that support.

MENTAL HEALTH SERVICES, PROGRAMS AND FACILITIES

These services fall into the same general categories as physical health services — that is, into institutional and noninstitutional, emergency and elective, short term and long term, and preventive, diagnostic, therapeutic, palliative (symptomatic) and rehabilitative categories.

Prevention

The general principles of primary and secondary prevention were discussed in the health promotion chapter and examples were given. However, a few points are worthy of repetition or expansion in this discussion of mental health services.

In protecting mental health, it is not always easy to know what we are trying to prevent. A small fracture or a minor pneumonia are not desirable, but some degree of stress and a reaction to it are natural and almost surely desirable. It may not be desirable to be excessively and aggressively competitive, but it would probably be impossible to find a consensus regarding the amount of competitiveness that should be encouraged or considered normal in a child. The same could be said about suspicion, daydreaming, ambition, selfishness and impatience.

Luckily, the areas of disagreement are not numerous enough to preclude preventive programs because there is likely to be general agreement that all of the listed characteristics are abnormal if carried to an extreme. Preventive programs that assist children and adults to tolerate the differences of others and to modify their own performances so that they are more easily tolerated by others are likely to be both widely supported and successful.

Mental health protection can and does occur everywhere. The home and the school environments are probably most important because the personality of the adult is largely shaped during childhood. However, the environments of our workplaces, communities, recreation sites and jails, to name a few, are also important in the preservation of reasonable mental health, as are the actions of individuals.

All people with significant power, including administrators, have a unique opportunity to practice mental health protection. Administrators can be sympathetic or unsympathetic to the problems of their subordinates. Responses to conduct or performance can emphasize either criticism or praise. Rules can be applied consistently and predictably or with bias and without pattern. Unattainable levels of performance or perfection can be demanded.

Caregivers, regardless of the nature of their services, can also promote or damage the mental health of their clients. The way news is delivered, the degree of respect shown for client opinions, the tolerance with which client fear or anger are handled, the patience with which instructions are explained — all affect the self-image and the level of stress of the client.

Health care institutions are a potential threat to the mental health of young children and selected adult populations. For children, the hazardous ages are the infant and preschool years. Preventive activities include using home care instead of institutional care (some children's hospitals seldom refer children to home care programs), encouraging parents to remain with young children as much as possible and preferably constantly, involving parents in the care of the sick or injured child, and developing institutional procedures that minimize the adaptation needed from the child. The child is already under stress and the provision of care should be as nonfrightening as possible. For selected adults, in particular the depressed, demented and frail elderly, the same general rules apply. Familiar events, surroundings and faces are usually preferable. New routines, new corridors and new noises can evoke physical and emotional deterioration which might have been more easily prevented than cured.

One type of low-cost, community-based preventive mental health service deserves mention. Many communities now have one or more centers to which mothers and their infants or preschool children can come. These centers support mothers who are staying at home with their children. These mothers often have inadequate personal support networks, they may not have had experience with small children and they may be on low and fixed incomes. These centers offer a combination of counselling, peer support, education, short term day care and emotional support to help the mothers to tolerate the stresses of parenting. The way this successful preventive model must struggle for funding and recognition is another example of our social preference for treating illness rather than preventing it.

This practice often leads to our spending considerable sums later on. For example, we may spend $20-40,000 a year to care for an emotionally disturbed teenager who has come from an identifiable high-risk group. He or she may be from a low-income, single-parent family or may have been greatly influenced by unattractive role models such as an unhealthy peer group. Not all of these high-risk children, or of any other group of children, can be kept mentally healthy, but major expenditures on good life experiences and opportunities for children have the potential to be cost-effective as well as civilized.

The lines between services delivering primary prevention, secondary prevention and therapy are not clear in the world of mental and psychosocial health. Distress centers help people remain stable and out of care (a primary prevention role), while, at the same time, advising some people to go elsewhere for help (a diagnostic/secondary prevention role) and also actually being curative for some others (a therapeutic or tertiary prevention role). Social drop-in centers for the homeless, the poor, the lonely and the rejected perform the same full spectrum of functions, especially when their range of services includes providing food, socialization and counselling.

Diagnosis

The product of the diagnostic process is the declaration that abnormality (pathology) exists, that it does not exist, or that it may exist. If the diagnostic tests that are available are very good at separating the normal from the abnormal, very few cases will fall into the 'uncertain' category. For instance, x-rays do quite a good job of confirming the presence or absence of fractures.

When one is trying to establish the presence of poor mental health, however, the tests are not sensitive and findings are often interpreted quite differently by different people. How sad does one have to be to fall outside of the normal range, and how does one know? There are tests that suggest how depressed an individual is, or how suicidal or paranoid he or she may be, but the margins of normalcy are unclear. The diagnosis of mental ill health is primarily a process of applying professional judgment to a series of observations and answers, a process which often produces quite different conclusions from different diagnosticians. The likelihood of disagreement is increased by the extent to which the acceptability of conduct varies with the situation. Loud and destructive behavior that might be tolerated or even considered appropriate on Grey Cup day might be considered proof of mental illness in other circumstances.

The diagnosis of mental ill health appears to be made at two levels. Society has a collective opinion as to whether individuals' answers or performances indicate mental illness. When people exhibit socially unacceptable levels of suspicion, intolerance, anger, retaliation or hysteria, they are apt to be labelled as mentally ill. If a high enough percentage of a population are convinced that homosexual practices are a sign of mental ill health, then the prevention and diagnosis of homosexuality become part of the prevention and diagnosis of mental ill health. The same social rejection and response can be applied to political affiliations, to parents who spank their children, or to persons who belong to a minority religious group. Society often makes a diagnostic comment through its statements regarding what is acceptable or normal.

At the second level, mental health is evaluated by professionals who, although constrained and influenced by social norms, will also be interested in less visible characteristics. Is the client able to cope; is he or she a menace to him or herself or to others; is the intensity of response (for example, to a group home or to an AIDS patient in school) an indication of a more deeply-seated personality defect.

A diagnosis of physical ill health is often based on identified anatomical or physiological abnormality, as is the case with cleft palate, Wilms' tumor, diabetes or hemophilia. Other physical health diagnoses are less precise and merely describe the patient's symptom or set of symptoms; examples might be migraine, colitis, multiple sclerosis, cystitis, Reyes syndrome and arthritis. In the world of mental health, the descriptive and imprecise diagnoses are very dominant. Diagnostic classifications are inherently imprecise and include such conditions as personality disorders, affective disorders and psychoneuroses. Even with these imprecise terms, practitioners often cannot agree on which term should apply to a particular patient.

Therapeutic Services, Programs and Facilities

As with physical illness, treatment of mental illness has, as its desired outcome, either the alleviation of undesirable symptoms or the control or elimination of disease. When the diseases are poorly defined, when symptoms cannot be quantified and when the symptoms at some level become 'normal', it is not only difficult to know when to start treatment but is also difficult to know when treatment should be stopped. There is considerable possibility of both overservicing and underservicing, although each is difficult to prove. When conditions are the product of many factors, and when improvement can arise from a variety of changes within the individual and the environment, it is also often difficult to know the extent to which improvement is the result of the treatment versus other factors. Despite these uncertainties associated with diagnosis and treatment, there is no doubt about the usefulness of most formal mental health programs and therapies. When the patient can cope moderately well and is able to be tolerated by society, treatment is usually stopped or reduced to a maintenance level.

When the cause of illness is unknown, treatment is less apt to be scientific and successful. The degree of cure or improvement is also difficult to measure, and all of these factors increase the likelihood that there will be disagreement as to the preferred method of treatment.

The therapy for mental illness is quite different from its physical health counterpart. In mental illness, sick role theory usually does not apply. The classical sick role, which often does apply in physical health services, requires that the patient place himself or herself into the hands of the system and passively wait for care or cure. In mental illness, however, the patient and all persons of significance in his or her environment must usually actively contribute to the recovery process and to the maintenance of recovery if outcomes are to be satisfactory. In mental illness, as in other chronic illnesses, improved function is as likely to be found in providing assistance to help the person adapt as it is in removal of a cause.

Mental health treatment tends to be delivered by multidisciplinary teams within a therapeutic milieu. This is an ecological concept which recognizes environment as part of both illness and recovery. In this ecology, any number of individuals or factors may be an important part of therapy. At any particular time and with respect to a particular patient, the most important team member may be a psychologist, psychiatric nurse, social worker, family member, psychiatrist, nursing assistant or remedial gymnast. Mental health teams should, ideally, be much less hierarchical than physical health teams but one can easily find psychiatrists' kingdoms in which a hierarchy definitely exists.

Physical health services and workers tend to say, "Give yourself to me and I will cure you and care for you". Often, this approach works. Mental health services and workers often say, or should say, "Sit down with me and we will try to find a way in which all of us working together can improve the health of those in need of help." To the extent that mental health workers are paternalistic or discourage family and client participation, the system may partially fail. In mental health the 'therapeutic milieu' includes the household, the workplace or school, and the social network of those in need of assistance.

Inpatient mental health services are provided by psychiatric hospitals and general hospitals with psychiatric units. Residential care — that is, a living-in arrangement combined with some level of counselling and supervision — is provided in a general category commonly called Homes for Special Care. This category includes homes for the aged, nursing homes, boarding homes, special treatment centers for children, group homes (including homes for ex-psychiatric patients, battered wives and disturbed adolescents) and half-way houses. Mental health assessment and therapy in many forms is available through many nonprofit and a smaller number of for-profit agencies. Most large educational institutions and many churches and other agencies offer programs on family-life education, assertiveness training and life skills, for example, all of which should be seen as part of the mental health services network. A small number of psychiatric facilities, the forensic centers, have the special function of caring for persons who are a major threat to society or themselves.

A mental health services network will be faced with crises as well as less urgent demands and many communities are not nearly as well prepared for emotional or psychiatric crises as they are for injuries or other physical emergencies. A good crisis intervention service should be able to respond quickly with an almost unlimited short term volume of resources available 24 hours a day and seven days a week. Housing, multidisciplinary specialized staff, financial aid and continuous care may be necessary to prevent further rapid deterioration. Community-based mental health crisis intervention requires institutional back-up and it must be able to support households as well as individuals. The crisis intervention teams should work closely with the police. (Police are often the first to know of the crisis. They are among those who need and welcome good professional back-up. The psychiatric workers will, in turn, on occasion need good police back-up). Good crisis intervention markedly changes the pattern of institutionalization and frequently shortens length of stay when institutional care is unavoidable.

In the physical health field we insist on the broadest imaginable level and mix of emergency services being available. Mental health workers regularly work with quite primitive crisis response capability.

Psychiatric units in general hospitals, of which there are 350-400 in Canada, have replaced isolated, large, psychiatric hospitals as the dominant site of short term, active psychiatric care. The beds in psychiatric wards in general hospitals represent 4-5% of all acute treatment, general hospital beds. Despite the move towards providing care in psychiatric wards in general hospitals, the large psychiatric hospital is still an important source of care which, in 1979-80, provided twice as many days of care as psychiatric wards in general hospitals. Psychiatric hospitals and units routinely offer both inpatient and outpatient care, and occasionally operate outreach programs or satellite clinics. Two thirds of the increase in the number of psychiatric facilities in the last 20 years has been due to the appearance of psychiatric units in general hospitals; the other third has been mostly special treatment centers for children.

In Canada at the end of the 1970's, we were down to a national figure of somewhere under 1 (0.8 or 0.9) psychiatric beds per 1000 people. Patient census on any day was down to about 0.7 per 1000 because the institutions were operating at about 80% capacity. Besides admissions to psychiatric beds, there is an unknown number of psychiatric and psychosocial admissions to general medical, pediatric or other beds.

Different provinces have gone through the same trends somewhat differently (Table 10.1). In the late 1960's, Québec had 3.6 psychiatric rated beds per 1,000, the highest number in the country, and many institutions exceeded their rated capacity by 50 to 75%. By 1978-79, Québec had reduced its psychiatric bed supply to 0.6 per 1000 and the patient population in psychiatric institutions had fallen by up to 90%. Other provinces had gone through the same deinstitutionalization process, with Saskatchewan being first.

The decrease in facility size and number was associated with a major improvement in all aspects of facility services; that is, more institutions had more and better staff and offered better therapy, improvements which meant marked increases in per diem costs. The move was from warehousing to therapy, from public protection to concern for the recovery of and the rights of the client. The decrease in beds was also accompanied by a growth in outpatient services; for instance, there was a 300% increase in outpatient services in Ontario from 1961-70.

Not all provinces have changed as much as Québec and Saskatchewan. For example, New Brunswick had, by the end of the 1970's, cut its bed numbers by only about one half and the institutions remained full. Preference for one provincial experience over that of some other province will depend on the extent to which provincial policy makers and administrators think people should live in the community and the extent to which community back-up is available to people after discharge.

In Ontario in the period from 1961-1976, the daily patient census in psychiatric hospitals fell from 18,000 to 5,000, a fall of 70%, while the daily

TABLE 10.1
RATED PSYCHIATRIC BED CAPACITY IN ALL INSTITUTIONS IN CANADA 1970 AND 1978-79, BY PROVINCE

	Rated Bed Capacity per 1,000 popn.	
	1970	1978-79
Newfoundland	1.7	0.9
Prince Edward Island	3.6	2.0
Nova Scotia	2.5	1.0
New Brunswick	3.0	1.5
Quebec	3.5	0.6
Ontario	2.8	1.0
Manitoba	3.0	1.1
Saskatchewan	3.0	0.7
Alberta	3.1	0.8
British Columbia	3.2	1.4
Canada	3.0	0.9

Source: *Mental Health Statistics, Vol. III*, Statistics Canada, 1978-79.

census in psychiatric units in general hospitals rose from 350 to 1500. In Ontario from 1965-1977, the number of psychiatric patients in homes for special care increased from 1,600 to 7,400. A significant part of the emptying of psychiatric hospitals was accomplished by merely moving the patients to other institutions.

Admission rates (first admissions and readmissions) in Canada are usually now in the range of 4 to 7 per 1000 (as compared to general hospital admission rates of 100-150 admissions per 1000 per year). Average length of stay for the psychiatric patients is several times that of physical health patients but the great majority of psychiatric admissions are now for less than one month. Admissions to psychiatric facilities are equal to only 2-5% of admissions to physical care facilities. Age patterns also differ. Ages 20-50 are the peak years for psychiatric admissions (at least partly because these are peak years for schizophrenia admissions). Rates for the elderly are 25-35% lower than the rates for younger adults. Costs of hospital treatment for mental illness in Canada are in the range of $2 to 3 billion per year, or about one tenth of the costs of the hospital care of physical ailments.

There are no nationally standardized approaches to the reporting of the utilization of community mental health services. Distress centers, for example, report the number of calls, which in Ottawa is about 40 calls per 1000 total population per year. Social centers usually report the number of visits; one large center in Ottawa with a low-income, isolated, unemployed and 90% male clientele reported 35,000 visits per year. This figure can be interpreted as 50 visits per 1000 per year (using the metropolitan population as a base), but it would also be reasonable, and at times much more useful, to report utilization as 100 visits per 1000 per year (using the City of Ottawa as the base), 350 visits per 1000 per year (using the metropolitan core of 100,000 as the base) or 3500 to 10,000 visits per 1000 per year if one relates utilization only to the 4 to 10% of the core population who are potential users of the center. Because many users come regularly, often daily, one can also conjecture a service base of 700 people if the average user comes 50 times per year or 100 people at 350 visits per year. With costs at $5 to $10 per visit, the possible costs per client per year can easily be estimated, but no matter how local reporting and analysis are done national comparisons will not be possible until data are standardized.

Many mental health programs and institutions, but especially the institutions, now have a Patients' Bill of Rights. Ontario psychiatric hospitals now have a formally trained patient advocate on staff whose role is to mediate institution-patient disputes and to assist patients in the protection of their rights.

Community based mental health services provide a broad range of advocacy, education, advice, protection and therapy. The networks tend to be dominated by a multiplicity of nonprofit, low-budget sources of care. Few agencies spend over $1 million a year. In 1985, over 300 community mental health programs in Ontario received, in total, less than $50 million of Ministry of Health funds.

Children's mental health services and facilities consist largely of quite expensive and usually residential treatment units, associated with psychiatric hospitals, children's hospitals or child protection agencies such as the Children's Aid Societies in Ontario.

Addicts are an important subgroup within the users of mental health services. They have a high rate of recidivism and often have little interest in treatment. Within this category, the alcoholics are almost surely the most numerous, expensive and socially disruptive group, with prescription drug abusers being their major competitor. Alcoholics and users of illicit drugs are often served through agencies or facilities that serve no other user groups; these include detoxification centers, half-way houses and Alcoholics Anonymous. Two to five percent of the adult population are alcohol dependent to the point of some interference with social and occupational life.

Detoxification centers provide short term care during recovery from bouts of intoxication. Most centers are of the nonmedical type with no medical staff and minimal nursing and counselling capability. Clients stay 3-5 days and are referred to treatment programs if that is their wish. Centers within the medical model are much more expensive and offer few if any proven advantages over the nonmedical model. In Ottawa-Carleton, there are 5-6 admissions per 1000 total population per year to detoxification centers — that is, 3000-3500 per year for 600,000 people.

Addiction recovery programs operate under many profit and nonprofit auspices. Intensive rehabilitation programs are in such short supply in Ontario that almost one third of those receiving such treatment go to programs in the New England states. The largest group of users of these non-Canadian programs are executives aged 35-64. A recent Ottawa-Carleton report (on a service area population of approximately 1 million people) proposed a need for 28 more in-patient alcoholic recovery beds and 120 day/evening spaces. One objective was to stop exporting approximately $300,000 a year for services that could just as adequately be provided within the region. Many less intensive alcohol and drug addiction recovery programs exist, often based in group homes or half-way houses. They have variable success rates, none of them very high, but they constitute a personalized and less expensive effort to deal with an endemic and serious disease. A few programs such as Alcoholics Anonymous operate successfully without public financial support.

The importance of community services for the chronically mentally ill is easily illustrated. Fifty percent of the patients admitted to the Queen Street Mental Health Centre in downtown Toronto have no fixed addresses. When discharged they will once again have no fixed addresses, and will have an increased likelihood of readmission, unless there is, within the community, an available network of residential, social and professional support. A 1982 study done in a Whitby, Ontario, psychiatric institution reported that 20% of patients were remaining in hospital because suitable community based support networks were not available.

Sheltered workshops may be described as a form of psychiatric facility. They allow individuals to work in a protective environment where stress is reduced, production standards are different and work can have a therapeutic component. They can be operated by many different sponsors and can serve the intellectually handicapped, the physically handicapped or the mentally/ emotionally handicapped.

Mental Health Manpower

British Columbia, in 1984, proposed that there should be one psychiatrist for every 11,000 people, a figure also proposed by the 1975 Report of the National Committee on Medical Manpower. The figure 11,000 appears to be largely chosen as something modestly below the available number of psychiatrists rather than on the basis of a more objective rationale. A 1983 Ontario Medical Association report predicted a 70% increase in demand for psychiatric services by 1991 if present trends continued. Ottawa has twice the provincial concentration of psychiatrists (1 per 3-5000) and they all are busy. There appears to be no visible ceiling to the capacity of psychiatrists to find patients and provide them with service. In Washington, DC, there is one psychiatrist for every 2000 persons and some parts of California are even better supplied.

If a person feels better (has a higher quality of life) when he or she spends an hour a week with a mental health worker and he or she is spending personal money then public policy is only marginally affected. In a publicly financed system, however, society is likely to eventually express an opinion regarding how frequently an hour of publicly financed therapy should be available (Table 10.2). Psychotherapy and counselling are definitely growth industries, but control should not be pursued unless there is equal attention given to the many types of physical health services that have also expanded, such as many types of surgery and infertility procedures.

TABLE 10.2
PSYCHOTHERAPY AND COUNSELLING BY FEE-FOR-SERVICE PHYSICIANS IN CANADA
1972-73 AND 1978-79 (000's)*

	1972-73	1978-79	% increase
by General Practitioners	848	1902	124%
by Psychiatrists	1454	2260	55%
Other	90	109	21%
	2392	4271	78%

Source: From *Mental Health Services in Canada*, 1982 Edition; data derived from Medical Care Data Bank of HWC.

ORGANIZATION AND ADMINISTRATION

Integrated, comprehensive networks of mental health services are more the exception than the rule although high quality exceptions exist. In most areas, mental health services are provided by an impressive list of uncoordinated and predominantly locally inspired programs. The yellow pages in the Ottawa-Carleton telephone directory list over 200 sources of mental health assistance including over 100 providing services exclusively for mental health needs. The Ontario Ministry of Health provides support to over 100 mental health services in the Ottawa-Carleton region. The historical centralization of mental health services in large rural hospitals has been replaced by a wide variety of agencies in which the components are varied and usually quite unplanned. The mix includes agencies specializing in providing health, social, vocational, recreational, housing, income support and educational services.

A few decades ago, most formal mental health (psychiatric) services were part of a psychiatric services branch of a provincial ministry of health. Today, the mental health services network is more complex and less predictable (Figure 10.1). Figure 10.1 is not an organization chart nor is it meant to describe any single province; it merely illustrates many of the components and relationships of mental health services in most provinces.

Institutions which provide only psychiatric services are usually operated by a ministry of health although some are operated by independent boards; examples include the Clarke Institute in Toronto and several institutions in Alberta. When institutions are operated by the ministry of health all personnel, including most psychiatrists, are provincial civil servants. Personnel policies and union affiliations are the same as for other civil servants. The physical plant and its maintenance or replacement may be the responsibility of a provincial department of public works or equivalent.

In Canadian general hospitals, a psychiatric unit (ward) together with its associated psychiatric outpatient services, make-up merely one part of the hospital. They are usually funded out of the hospital global budget and are operated in the same way as any other service unit. Physicians providing psychiatric services within the hospital are paid in the same way as other physicians — that is, as private practitioners on fee-for-service or within some negotiated university contract.

Psychiatric emergency patients benefit from specialized care. General hospitals whose emergency departments will receive psychiatric emergencies which cannot be immediately referred to an adjacent psychiatric emergency department should have appropriate support in the form of at least a psychiatrist and a psychiatric social worker or equivalent.

Community based mental health services are a mixed bag. Private psychiatrists often work alone and, at times, provide services largely to the type of clientele who do not need a multidisciplinary team. These patients might include the worried, the stressed and members of households in modest conflict. A variety of profit and nonprofit agencies provide personal or group

FIGURE 10.1
THE ROLE OF PROVINCIAL GOVERNMENTS IN MENTAL HEALTH SERVICES

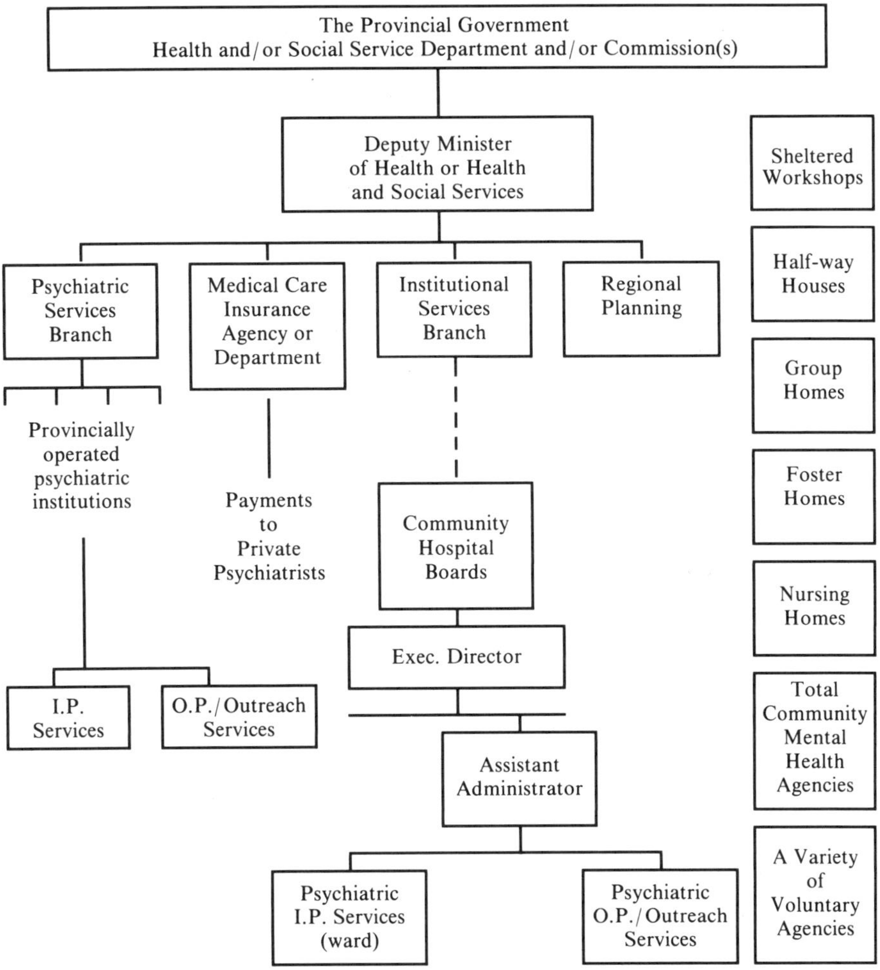

counselling, primarily through social workers or psychologists. Most of these cannot bill provincial medical care plans and income is, therefore, earned through private insurance, user-pay arrangements, charitable support or government grants. Other agencies, usually nonprofit, operate a variety of residential programs including group homes and half-way houses. Nursing homes and boarding homes, or homes for special care under a variety of names, are often an important part of the mental health services network because they house many individuals with mental disabilities, including many who have been discharged from psychiatric institutions. In this latter instance, public financing on a per diem basis has replaced public financing through an institutional budget.

Many institutional and noninstitutional mental health programs make regular use of case conferences in which 5-10 professionals and sometimes the patient and / or the patient's family discuss the diagnosis and develop a treatment plan. As with many committees, these case conferences have two sides; they are very useful when the complexities of the case require multidisciplinary comment and consensus, but they are expensive. Staff members can spend a good part of their day talking to each other, an activity which significantly reduces the time available to work with clients. One preferred alternative is to use some type of triage in which an intake worker makes a decision regarding the need for case conferencing. Although some patients would miss the benefit attributable to a conference, the patient contact hours per worker would be higher and outcomes perhaps better with a fixed amount of staff.

A few Canadian communities have, at various moments in the past, taken steps towards implementing an integrated, community-wide approach to mental health services. Over 25 years ago in Yorkton, Saskatchewan, it was shown that good, noninstitutional mental health services markedly altered the referral of patients to institutions. It was shown that long term care facilities which routinely referred disturbed, elderly patients to psychiatric facilities could deal quite adequately with these problems on their own if advice and support were available from mental health professionals. Saskatoon initiated a psychiatric home care program over two decades ago which showed how patients could be supported by a multifunctional, community based agency.

The biggest step forward was made in Vancouver in the mid 1970's with the establishment of a regional service, the Greater Vancouver Mental Health Service, serving several metropolitan municipalities with a combined population of about 500,000 people. This service was created by a special provincial statute and was operated by its own community board. It had close ties with the municipal public health authorities.

This regional service was designed to provide crisis intervention and continuing care for the chronically mentally ill. The short term ill were considered to be already reasonably adequately served by the private psychiatrists, the wards in general hospitals and a variety of community agencies, whereas the chronically ill who were repeatedly or permanently hospitalized had no one able to support and treat them in the community. In the Vancouver area, as elsewhere, there were large, isolated psychiatric institutions attempting to reduce census without the necessary coordinated community support in place.

This new service was multidisciplinary, was available 24 hours a day, seven days a week, had close liaison with the police, had good access to institutional care if needed, had temporary noninstitutional housing available and was willing to provide short term, high-intensity, around-the-clock support if needed. Service was provided by eight teams with special crisis intervention teams, based in the temporary housing. The general teams were led by social workers or psychiatric nurses; all teams included psychologists, psychiatric nurses and psychiatric social workers. Psychiatrists played a consulting role. Several research studies confirmed the benefits and adequacy of the Vancouver approach but despite international attention the model has not been duplicated in other Canadian cities.

Halifax-Dartmouth decided to take a completely different approach in its search for more rational and adequate community mental health services. The community had no overall plan until about ten years ago. There were many agencies but no way of reducing duplication and plugging gaps. It was decided that better inter-agency communication might be all that was needed; that is, everyone should be acquainted with what others were doing so that clients would be more appropriately referred and so that service adjustments would eliminate gaps.

The Minister of Health of Nova Scotia funded the Metropolitan Halifax-Dartmouth Mental Health Planning Board. There are a great many committees, and many person years have been spent in having professionals talk to each other, but this board has survived enough years for us to know that it has been successful.

Besides improving communications, the Halifax-Dartmouth board serves a planning function similar to that of DHCs in Ontario. Each year, the ministry of health invites the board to rank, in terms of need or importance, all of the proposals for new mental health programs in Halifax-Dartmouth. Recommendations are submitted to the ministry along with the rationale and criteria used, and these recommendations tend to be accepted by the ministry.

In Ontario, the District Health Councils have the task of developing plans for regional mental health networks and recommending steps to achieve them. In 1983 the Minister of Health in Ontario proposed that "designated general hospitals with psychiatric units be made the pivot for intramural and extramural community services" within a part of the catchment area of a larger provincial psychiatric hospital. Each community would be the direct responsibility of, and would receive inpatient and outpatient services from, a designated hospital. Services available from this hospital would include crisis intervention and back-up services for community based agencies. Implementation of the plan has, to date, been slow despite the appearance of a new psychiatric facility in the region of Grey Bruce with a broad range of community outreach.

In Québec, the CRSSSs have a broader mandate than DHCs in Ontario and can more easily honor their mandate because of the existence of a provincial network of CLSCs. Community mental health needs and services are among the responsibilities of the CLSCs.

When the Castonguay Commission was doing its work in Québec almost twenty years ago, it discovered that the major mental health facilities and programs in Montreal had no well defined community responsibilities. It was also discovered that most facilities chose not to identify with the 500,000 people in central Montreal. In response to this situation, each institution in the Montreal area was told that it was to be responsible for a portion of the total population. If a client showed up from a particular institution's geographic base, that institution had an obligation to provide care.

The failure to develop comprehensive, regional, mental health networks in much of Canada provides another illustration of the low status of mental health services. Ontario, in recent years, has introduced a provincial ground ambulance service, a number of central bed registries to assure optimum acceptance of non-psychiatric emergencies, a paramedic program to handle cardiac and other similar emergencies and a general hospital emergency room categorization scheme; yet it was only in 1984 that Toronto received its first community based psychiatric crisis service in the form of a house with 24-hour staff supported by a 10 bed, short-stay, stabilization unit.

Progress towards comprehensive mental health service networks is steady but painfully slow.

ISSUES AND PROBLEMS

1) Psychiatry is one of the few medical specialties in which a significant number of physicians providing patient care are on a salary. These psychiatrists are on salary as public servants in provincially operated psychiatric hospitals. They tend to want incomes comparable to psychiatrists on fee-for-service, for whom there are no income ceilings. This situation carries the seeds of continuing dispute.
2) The continued rapid growth of utilization of psychiatric and other mental health services may emerge as a real or perceived economic problem.
3) There is continuing difficulty with the concept of mental competence. This has historically been resolved by being arbitrary — the person in question was either fully competent or fully incompetent. The measures of competence tend to relate to socially acceptable conduct or opinion as well as to technical ability to understand or decide. Various provinces have, in recent years, increasingly sought compromises which preserve portions of personal autonomy while protecting clients or the public in areas of vulnerability.

   In the face of complete or partial mental incompetence, there is a need for the identification of someone else to act on behalf of the incompetent person, and this agent is commonly either a civil servant or a person to whom power of attorney has been given. Newer legislation, such as the 1978 *Alberta Dependent Adults Act*, provides for flexible arrangements for incomplete as well as complete transfers of powers.

   The transfer of authority usually creates a situation in which the new guardian can, if he or she wishes, act contrary to the previously expressed wishes of the person involved. This can be seen as ethically unacceptable, and in some provinces the guardian cannot reverse previously clearly stated intentions.

4) Deinstitutionalization is more a characteristic of the mental health world than of any other medical field.

There would probably be no argument with the proposition that some mentally ill individuals are best cared for in institutions. Disagreement, therefore, revolves around who should be cared for in this way, for how long and within what institutional environment.

In considering the extent to which noninstitutional care ought to be promoted, it is wise to assume that the environment within psychiatric facilities can be different from that which existed a few decades ago. The traditional psychiatric facility produced institutionalism, a condition characterized by submission, loss of initiative, reduced communication and personal deterioration. These inmate characteristics were the almost inevitable sequelae of loss of personal control, loss of privacy and dignity, loss of freedom, lack of social and intellectual opportunities and emotional if not physical brutality.

Institutions do not need to be dominated by the historical model and most are now significantly better; they show evidence of reduced congestion, more respect for the feelings and wishes of residents, a more personal approach to lifestyles and therapy and a search for resident improvement. In assisting individuals and families to choose between institutional and community based care, it is desirable that both of the options be recognized as having good, as well as less desirable features.

Institutions offer 24-hour support and protection. They can handle unpredictable changes in behavior and can offer a good range of social opportunities. They also tend to impose schedules, reduce privacy, disrupt households and alter lifestyles. Care in the community varies greatly in the extent to which it assures improved social opportunities and the opportunity for personal decision making. It is usually less able to handle crises. Whether institutional or community based care should be chosen by or encouraged for a given individual will depend as much on the characteristics of the institution and the community health services network as on the characteristics of the individual. Certainly institutionalized persons are still being released into communities without an adequate system of support services.

Deinstitutionalization has, at times, been promoted because institutions are considered to be all bad or because community care is thought to be cheaper. Neither reason is acceptable. Institutions are not all bad and community care may only be cheaper if the necessary community based, support services are not offered. It also may be more expensive. Deinstitutionalization does not occur at all when a patient is merely transferred from a psychiatric hospital to a large, highly structured and often socially unattractive residential facility or to a small room without a supporting social and professional network.

5) Global overcrowding, multinational famine, high levels of unemployment, the threat of nuclear annihilation and other global factors will increase the need for attention to the prediction, understanding and control of large-scale, irrational and emotional reactions; that is, the psychology of mass hysteria and of disaster response merits our attention.
6) Some psychiatrists and mental health workers work almost exclusively with the neurotics, acute psychotics or other patients with shorter term and more manageable problems. This pre-selection of patients could leave fewer and fewer workers to care for the difficult, more emotionally demanding and less emotionally rewarding patients.
7) It is difficult to obtain public and bureaucratic support for community mental health programming to a level approximating the degree of public support for physical health programs. As things which engage the public imagination, providing housing, income support, assistance with daily living and help in learning how to socialize are no match for test-tube babies and heart transplants.
8) Health care providers must consider what stresses people should be taught to adapt to, or be more accepting of, rather than be angry with. How should people be encouraged to respond to unemployment, demotion, divorce, single parenthood, criticism, poverty, discrimination, the possibility of unemployment, spending half of one's disposable income on housing, being unable to afford things, growing old, being disabled and being institutionalized or deinstitutionalized?
9) There will be continued conflict between the sanctity of personal (human) rights and the professional certainty that there are times when therapy must be initiated without the consent of the patient.

Those of us who believe that one's health is related more to one's state of mind than to anything else hope that society will enthusiastically support more rapid movement towards a stronger, more coordinated, better financed and fully client-oriented network of mental health services.

Suggested Reading

1. Heseltine, G.F., *Towards a Blueprint for Change: A Mental Health Policy and Program Perspective*. (A report produced for the Government of Ontario), 1983.

Chapter 11

PHYSICIANS

THE ROLE OF PHYSICIANS

Writers have long disagreed over whether physicians are the tail which wags the health services dog or whether they are the heart of the beast. There is no disagreement regarding the power inherent in their role, but there is disagreement with respect to the extent to which that role is played in the public interest. This chapter cannot resolve these disagreements nor will it try to. Physicians tend to be neither as public oriented or as valuable as they think they are, nor as despotic or machiavellian as they are sometimes said to be.

Most physicians are private practitioners, a term which is also applied to a number of other health care professionals including dentists, optometrists, chiropractors, denturists, herbalists, osteopaths, podiatrists, chiropodists, acupuncturists, clinical psychologists and a variety of other independent health care providers and counsellors. The term 'private practitioner' is not usually applied to those professionals who, by law, are limited to providing services only under the supervision of or on referral from others. This large group includes most nurses, physiotherapists, occupational therapists, speech pathologists and speech therapists, audiologists, laboratory technologists, radiology technicians, respiratory technicians, dieticians, nutritionists, health educators, health inspectors, midwives, nurse practitioners, clinical nurse specialists and dental hygenists. Although the term private practitioner can apply to many independent professionals, it will, for the remainder of this chapter, refer only to physicians.

Two features most strongly epitomize private medical practitioners. The first of these is their control of executive functions such as choice of location, hours of operation, hiring of support staff, choice of office procedures, selection of clients, keeping of records and distribution of revenue. Medical practitioners provide services to the population of their choice from the locations of their choice on the days and hours of their choice. They utilize facilities and auxiliary staff at least somewhat in the way they choose and limit services offered in whatever way they choose. In earlier times, they billed whom they chose on a fee-for-service basis in the amount that they chose.

The second major distinguishing feature is the use of fee-for-service as the dominant method of payment. A small number of private practitioners, such as those in Ontario who practice in a health service organization, receive income via capitation. Others receive major income through sessional payments (flat fee payment for half days or full days) or by salary (when hired by another doctor or by a health agency such as a health center, a hospital or a university), but fee-for-service dominates and is considered by some to be fundamental to the concept of private practice.

A third important feature of private practitioners (both those in health and elsewhere) is the probability that they evaluate themselves. Governments are increasingly expressing interest in the quality and cost of physicians' services but most fee-for-service professionals with executive control either are not evaluated or are evaluated primarily by their peers.

One product of the executive independence and the piece-work method of payment is the lack of opportunity or mechanisms for regional or community coordination of the activities of private practitioners with the many other sources of service. Coordination can be seen by private practitioners as an impediment to the entrepreneurial concept and an intrusion into areas of legitimate personal control, and certainly coordination is unlikely to occur unless incentives or disincentives promote it. Whatever else we may say about private practitioners, it is abundantly clear that regional planning and the rationalization of CHSs cannot be fully successful as long as one major and dominant component rejects coordination with the rest of the network.

The entrepreneurial features of private medical practice increase the difficulty of finding solutions to a number of health delivery problems including:

1. Poor geographic distribution of health professionals.
2. Inadequate availability of certain kinds of services (for example, counselling, house calls).
3. Inadequate availability of services at certain hours of the day, days of the week or seasons of the year.
4. Uncertainty with respect to quality of services rendered or the usefulness of the services rendered.
5. Incomplete regional planning and coordination.
6. Lack of consumer influence over the way in which an essential social service is organized and delivered.
7. The need for greater development of health care teams with greater use of other health professionals.

Physician spokesmen regularly contend that physicians are the group best qualified to design and evaluate health services networks. At the provincial and regional levels, this position is fairly universally rejected although physicians remain influential. At the institutional level, however, and especially in acute treatment hospitals, most priority setting decisions still tend to be made by the medical staff rather than the board or the administration.

There was a time when ministers of health were almost always physicians. Now it is unusual to have physicians in that role. Physicians do, however, continue to lead important commissions and boards of enquiry with a mandate to recommend changes in the health system. Recent examples include Dr. John Evans in Ontario in 1986, and Dr. Jean Rochon in Québec in 1985-86. Physician associations also continue to make submissions on most health policy issues and physician representatives are usually given special status in terms of access to ministries and ministers of health.

Usually between 2 and 5 of the deputy ministers of health in Canada are physicians. Physicians continue to fill most senior positions in provincial psychiatric services branches or divisions and frequently lead branches dealing with emergency services and public health.

Among decentralized nongovernmental sources of service such as hospitals, public health units, regional planning bodies and long term care facilities, only the public health units continue to prefer chief executive officers who are physicians.

In larger hospitals, the senior management team routinely includes a physician and the heads of clinical departments have important administrative as well as clinical duties. In recent years, the heads of clinical departments have, in some hospitals, acquired new budgetary and resource allocation roles.

Some authors refer to private practitioners as profit makers. In this text, they are thought of as workers who generate income through their personal effort and their income is, therefore, not considered to be profit. The concept of profit is reserved for income generated without work or through the work of others.

Physician Terminology

M.D. is the same as M.B. Neither is the same as D.Med. (Doctorate in Medicine), which is a second level medical degree, or D.Sc. which is a doctorate in health or medical science. (A D.Sc.Med. is a doctorate in mediaeval sciences.) A D.P.H. sometimes means Doctor of Public Health (Dr.P.H.) but, in Canada, usually means Diploma in Public Health (which is also written Dpl.P.H.). The Dr.P.H. has Ph.D. equivalency whereas the Dpl.P.H. is received after a one year academic program. C.M. can be an undergraduate award (usually made after the fourth of six years of medicine) granted by a small number of medical schools in much the same way as some other schools grant a B.Sc.; it can also indicate that the owner is a member of the Order of Canada. L.M.C.C. (Licentiate of the Medical Council of Canada) is a designation earned by all Canadian medical graduates at their time of obtaining an M.D.; passing these Medical Council exams makes them eligible for licensure in all Canadian provinces. Most foreign graduates must pass this exam on their way to being licenced in a province.

Specialist identification is somewhat confusing. FRCS(C) or FRCP(C), Fellow of the Royal College of Surgeons, or of Physicians, of Canada, or FACP or FACS (the American equivalents), always indicates successful completion of a period (usually five years) of organized, practical training (internship and residencies) plus exams. The setting of exams and the awarding of the specialist designation are functions of professional colleges and not of a university. Letters in brackets after FRCS or FRCP indicate where the designation was obtained. If obtained in Edinburgh, for instance, it would read FRCS (Ed.). Specialty designations won in Great Britain may represent academic success rather than a fixed amount of supervised clinical work. To know the level of clinical training of a physician with an FRCS, FRCP or FRCOG (Fellow of the Royal College of Obstetricians and Gynecologists) obtained in Great Britain, one must be aware of the amount of practical experience.

The basic fellowship awards merely designate whether the physician has a surgical or a nonsurgical specialty. In 1985, in Canada, there were, among the physicians with an FRCS and FRCP, 41 separate recognized specialties with others under active consideration. Critical care specialists may soon be number 42. In the United States, over 70 separate specialties are recognized.

Through the College of Family Physicians of Canada (CFPC) and the family practice training programs, family physicians (FP) have become recognized specialists. The CFPC, which was founded in the early 1960's, is fully separate from the Royal College of Physicians and Surgeons (RCPS), the agency which accredits medical specialists other than specialists in family medicine. The term 'family physician' has largely replaced the term 'general practitioner.'

In 1984, a CMA Task Force on the education of family physicians made a number of recommendations designed to resolve conflict over such things as whether FPs could or should be trained in hospital-based as well as office-based residency programs, whether the CFPC should be the only body involved in setting FP standards, and whether FP training should be more formally integrated with non FP, post-M.D., hospital-based training programs. There appears to be agreement that family physicians will be offered opportunities for special competence in selected clinical areas — that is, they will be mini-specialists — but conclusion of these discussions and the clarification of training processes and roles is still to come. Ongoing discussions may help reduce the historical split, often heated, between FPs (GPs) and specialists.

Today, all 16 Canadian medical schools have a department or division of family medicine and almost half of Canada's FPs (or GPs) are members of the CFPC. About two thirds of CFPC members have taken sufficient training to be certified by the college as specialists in family practice.

Osteopaths need a special comment because their status in Canada is so different from that of osteopaths practicing in the United States. In the United States, osteopathic schools of medicine are common and their graduates usually have the same opportunity for hospital privileges and entry to specialty training programs as do the graduates of schools of allopathic medicine. Canada, in contrast, has no osteopathic schools of medicine, despite the attractiveness of some of their basic concepts, and an American Doctor of Osteopathy (DO) coming to Canada cannot be licenced except as a drugless practitioner.

Canadian medical schools are all schools of allopathic medicine. The teaching in allopathic schools is based on a theory in which, for all diseases or body disorders, there is assumed to be an external neutralizer. These schools accept that something can be done from the outside to counteract the undesirable internal events. This external therapy model would appear inevitably to lead to major reliance on drugs and surgery and to be quite physical health oriented.

The theory of osteopathic medicine (osteopathy), holds that within the body, if it is operating well, there is the capacity to respond to many diseases and threats of disease. Osteopathy emphasizes strengthening the ability of the body to overcome disease through nutrition, exercise, manipulation and lifestyle although drugs and surgery are also regularly used.

Homeopathy is treatment or protection by use of minute doses of whatever makes you sick. Homeopathy is not usually thought of as consistent with modern scientific theory.

THE PROFESSIONAL ORGANIZATIONS OF PHYSICIANS

Most practitioner groups have provincial and national organizations. National organizations such as the Canadian Medical Association tend to have little power because health is a provincial matter and provincial governments tend to talk to their provincial counterparts.

In all provinces, physicians have a College of Physicians and Surgeons and a Medical Association or equivalent. The colleges carry out licencing and disciplinary functions in accordance with appropriate provincial legislation. The colleges in each province were created by provincial statute to protect the public. They investigate complaints, conduct peer evaluation programs and identify and work with physicians addicted to drugs or alcohol.

The provincial medical associations, syndicates or societies are fee setting/ collective bargaining/political organizations. They are the labor unions or quasi-labor unions of the medical profession. They exist to serve and protect their members, not society. They negotiate fees, lobby for legislative changes and may represent their members when in dispute with the licencing/ disciplining professional society. In a number of provinces there has been open conflict between the medical association and the college. Conflict usually centers around the vigor with which the college pursues its quality review functions.

In Québec, the trade union functions are performed by two syndicates, one for family physicians and one for specialists. The Québec Medical Association has tended to have questionable importance in the past but, in recent years, its membership has increased and its role may expand.

As physicians have increasingly come to think of their provincial associations as their collective bargaining instruments, they have begun to accept other labor union practices. In at least three provinces (Manitoba, Québec and Nova Scotia) physicians now have a closed shop; all licenced physicians must belong to both the College (the licencing body) and the provincial medical association (the trade union). In provinces without a closed shop, a physician must pay an annual fee only to the College and a significant minority of physicians, frequently one quarter or more, do not join the provincial medical association. The change to a closed shop significantly increases the funds available to the medical union.

Physician Incomes

Physicians, as a group, have always had high incomes. For decades, their average incomes before taxes but after expenses have been the highest among the professional groups. Despite this fact, they usually consider themselves underpaid. Physicians in Ontario a few years ago reported that they (on average) felt their personal incomes were $18,000 per year too low.

Frequent reference is made to the fact that physician incomes consumed a decreasing percentage of the total health dollar in the period 1973-1982. The early 1970's, however, were peak years which were the culmination of 15 years of steady improvement in doctor incomes. This 1956-1971 income trend was unlikely to continue; 1973-1980 was, therefore, merely a period of adjustment. The relationship between physician incomes and other professional incomes was, by 1978-1980, approximately the same as in 1956. Since the early 1980's, the relative income of physicians has risen steadily to the point where, in some provinces, the peak relative position of the early 1970's has been matched or exceeded.

Methods of Practitioner Payment

'Sessional' has been defined. Fee-for-service is piece work. The concept of salaries is understood. Capitation is payment or receipt of a fixed sum, usually to a single agency or group of providers, for a prescribed package of care or services to the extent they are needed in a prescribed period of time. It is the car insurance approach. It is the method of payment for general practitioner services in Britain and is the tool most heavily advocated in the United States as a means of bringing competition into the health care industry. It is used in Canada for physician services only in health service organizations and in one or two CHCs in Ontario.

THE DECREASING AUTONOMY OF PHYSICIANS

Autonomy is hardly ever absolute but physicians, in the past, came close to it. There were few if any limits on which diagnostic or therapeutic approaches were to be used, on where or how to practice, on which or how many patients to see or not to see, or on whom to charge or how much to charge.

Today, Canadian physicians have less autonomy than they previously had and the decrease applies to both individual physicians and to physicians as a group. In a relative sense, they remain quite independent but, to many physicians, the reduction in autonomy that has occurred is immense, unjustified, unacceptable, intolerable and abusive. These terms and the fervor with which they are used represent an overreaction which is intellectually inappropriate because the loss of physician autonomy in Canada has followed a predictable, understandable and defensible pattern and will probably continue to do so. Factors at work include technological developments, philosophical and political evolution, professional example, the appearance of new data and the increasing use of rationing.

Physicians, unfortunately, tend to pretend that the philosophical/political changes have not occurred and tend to have a less than adequate understanding of other factors. Physician spokesmen receive standing ovations for their attacks on 'pinkos' and 'weak-kneed politicians' but the loss of professional autonomy is occurring in all Canadian provinces and all developed countries regardless of the stature or stripe of the politicians.

Political/philosophical evolution has seen the emergence of consumerism and the acceptance of the idea that all Canadians should have access to publicly funded health care. Both of these events have made consumers or their representatives part of, and sometimes the most powerful members of, the decision making team.

Technological developments have created physicians who usually work in very narrow clinical areas. They no longer see a broad mix of patients and cannot be expected to retain a balanced view of the role or importance of their part of health care versus that of others. As physicians have become more and more diverse and dissimilar in their skills and interests, it has become more and more necessary that others be accepted as champions of the larger picture, and this role has been acquired by planners, administrators and other primarily nonmedical persons.

Professional examples, that is, examples set by physicians themselves, and the appearance of new data, are factors which have, in an unplanned way, contributed significantly to the alteration of the role and autonomy of physicians.

We do not know when information began to affect professional decision making but the Hippocratic Oath contains the words, "I will not cut persons laboring under the stone but will leave this to be done by men who are practitioners of this work". This edict, which prohibited surgery for the removal of kidney stones, was the first of many which impinged upon the freedom of individual physicians, and it was promulgated by the medical profession as a group.

By the middle and late 1800's — the age of Lister, Pasteur, Semmelweiss, Koch and others — information had definitely begun to affect physician choices. Semmelweiss, for instance, established that very modest levels of cleanliness sharply reduced maternal mortality. Numbers proved his point and physicians were frowned upon by their colleagues if they went from the autopsy room to the delivery room without washing their hands. Information had confirmed the need for altered physician practices although it would be many years before malpractice suits and the need for access to hospital privileges would make such alterations mandatory.

Seventy years ago, the intrusion into professional autonomy began to develop teeth. The Flexner Report had found that most physicians were poorly trained and most medical care badly documented, and shortly after World War I the American College of Surgeons founded the Joint Commission on Hospital Accreditation. This Commission and other professional bodies began to work with hospitals, universities and governments to upgrade the care of individual patients. These changes were a response to new information.

The second world war accelerated the evolution of medical specialists and the formalization of the process of appointing physicians to the medical staffs of hospitals. Studies increasingly confirmed the relationship between proper training and process on the one hand and good patient outcomes on the other.

Medical Audit Committees routinely used medical records to assess the appropriateness of medical care.

Tissue Committees in hospitals began to look for evidence of unnecessary surgery and the vermiform appendix became the first target. In very short order, at least in teaching hospitals with tissue committees, many fewer normal appendices were being removed. By the 1960's, the physician operated medical insurance plans had begun to study physician billing habits and, where these habits were found to be excessively deviant, payment was adjusted downwards. Policies created and applied by physician controlled bureaucracies were placing limits on the opportunities, choices and income of individual physicians and data were the origin of these limits.

Hospital medical staffs have, for decades, regularly rejected or recommended rejection of new medical staff applicants because there were said to be too few beds to go around; that is, the hospital already had enough doctors. Through this process, physicians denied other physicians the right to choose their places of practice and they denied patients the opportunity to be hospitalized by the physician of their choice. Physicians, sometimes for self-serving purposes, used bureaucratic methods to limit the freedom of location of other physicians long before the governments of British Columbia and Québec even discussed restricting physician access to medical insurance if they settled in communities with an oversupply of physicians.

Hospitals, many years ago, in an attempt to deal fairly with both patients and physicians, began to categorize patients waiting to be admitted to hospital. The categories of emergency, urgent and elective emerged with the involvement of or with leadership from the hospital medical staff. In the early years of implementation of this categorization, the process was primarily subjective and was much manipulated and abused but, soon, formal criteria were written, review procedures and committees were created, and data were collected. Rational people including physicians agreed that, in complex systems, fairness is unlikely if based only on collegial or professional statements of principle; the additional requirements are data and specific policy. Physicians did not forsee that, when policy and data replace professional judgment, physicians might no longer be the ones best equipped for decision making.

In the 1970's, Canadian governments began to seek ways to reduce the extent to which physician decisions threatened government spending limits, and in the United States exactly the same objective was sought by the large corporate employers. Evidence in Canada and elsewhere suggested, and some would say confirmed, that spending more on health care was a poor way to elevate the health status of the population. Data showed that spending money in a broad range of other social sectors would be more productive. Other information showed that the costs of caring for apparently similar patients varied a great deal from hospital to hospital, from doctor to doctor and between capitation and fee-for-service payment systems. When more than one clinical approach is professionally acceptable, and when outcome measurements are not available to indicate whether one clinical approach is better than another, it is financially prudent to promote the cheapest approach to care. Better data, in association with the acceptance of publicly financed and universally accessible health care, or, in the United States, the financial concerns of large corporate employers, allowed nonphysicians to know more about 'the big picture' than did physicians.

Physicians also led the march toward use of data in the evaluation of clinical care. More and more regulations and protocols obliged or coerced physicians to investigate, treat or refer within prescribed patterns. New medical audit programs appeared which used preset criteria to evaluate care of a large number of similar patients. Analysis of health records assessed the extent to which the habits of a physician met or failed to meet prescribed standards.

Prescribed policies have replaced individual professional opinion. Information systems analyze billing patterns, prescription patterns, surgical patterns, referral patterns, manpower distribution and physician incomes. Data are available to and, quite logically, are used by all interested parties. Physicians in groups have, for decades, reduced the autonomy of individual physicians; now consumer representatives or corporate representatives have been able to become parts of the controlling mechanisms because physicians laid the groundwork, and the clock cannot be turned back.

At various points in history, physicians as a group developed medical care standards and made them mandatory, controlled physician access to hospitals, used doctor profiles to alter physician habits and incomes, wrote policies governing the admission of patients to hospitals, described the training requirements for specialty status and, through their recommended fee schedules, estimated the relative value of various professional acts. In the evolution of policies in each of these areas, the decision making process moved from a reliance on opinion to a reliance on data. Physicians individually and collectively should not have been surprised when other interested parties also began to use these same data for the same reasons and purposes or for other purposes. When medical judgment was central to decision making, the physicians had cornered the market. Now, individuals with data analysis skills have become able to intelligently favor certain choices because data show that one option is better than the other options.

The question now is not whether physicians like the sequence of events; it is how will they choose to react. What role will they play, or be allowed to play, in the continuing evolution of rationing, resource allocation, manpower production, manpower distribution and the pricing of services? In the days before data were available, the system could not operate without professional opinion. Now it can. Decisions will not be as good as they should be if physicians are not participants in the decision making, but the decisions will be made whether or not physicians participate.

Physicians should not feel they are without power; they have a great deal of it. They need not feel they will be ignored but they should recognize that their advice will not be taken if it is inconsistent with the evidence or unacceptable to too many of the other major players. If they cry wolf, as is common, no one will listen because they are not truly in danger and are not likely to become so. Even if physicians live in the past the system will continue to examine the future and respond to new data (without physician input). If, however, physicians develop a cadre of informed and respected leaders and staff they will be able to significantly influence the rules and protocols that will continue to affect every physician.

On the surface, the choice looks easy. One option means decreasing influence over policy; the other means greater influence. Hence, many persons both within and outside the profession find it difficult to understand why medical leaders so often opt for uninformed bombast, the option which reduces their influence.

Technological evolution has made the potential cost of health care almost limitless. Political/philosophical evolution in Canada has made health care an area for public policy. Examples provided by physician organizations and leaders have demonstrated the desirability of many of the current public policies and programs which limit the options of individual physicians. It remains for physicians to decide whether they will be among the users of existing data and of the data of the future, and among the major participants in the writing of new policy, or whether they will remain aloof on the assumption that angry absence speaks more usefully than good argument.

External controls over physicians, both as individual caregivers and as a profession, will increase in the future. Society and policy makers cannot avoid limiting physician choices when certain of these choices are seen as threats to public budgets and public priorities. Physicians should, for their own sakes and for the sake of the system, continue to ask for and fill a seat at the negotiation table even though their power at that table is less than it formerly was.

FEE SETTING

Various physician organizations have disputed the constitutional and even the moral right of society to decide how much physicians must accept as payment in full for an insured service. The issue has been referred to the Supreme Court, but in the meantime, and probably for the forseeable future, physicians will be paid either what the government decides or what is negotiated.

In most provinces there are at least three fee schedules in use — the fee schedule set by the physicians, the fee schedule set by the government and used in its medical insurance program and, of lesser importance, the WCB fee schedule. Some provinces may also have fee schedules established by cancer foundations or other paying agencies. With the abolition of extra billing, which occurred in the three years following passage of the *Canada Health Act*, the medical association fee schedule has become of much less importance. Prior to the abolition of extra billing, the difference between the government fee and the medical association fee usually determined the amount of extra billing for that particular service.

Financial bargaining between physicians and government affects fees in two quite different ways. One set of decisions determines the percentage fee increase or the extent to which total physician payments will increase. The second type of decision deals with the relative worth of various physician services and increases or decreases some fees relative to other fees. Over the years, such adjustments have significantly decreased income disparities between specialties; the price of a surgical consultation, for example, is now approximately one half that of a consultation by an internist whereas many years ago they were the same. This second type of decision is, to varying degrees, assigned to the professional societies. Governments tend to dominate with respect to percentage increase of fees and in capping total payments to physicians.

There is increasing attention by government to the total increase in payments to physicians. Most provinces now do more than establish a percentage increase in fees; they establish a formula within which the fee increase will not be given if utilization changes or billing changes increase governmental costs to a level considered to be unreasonable. This interest in total payments to physicians rather than in individual fees is the product of experience.

Changes in Physician Billing Patterns

The fee-for-service method of payment allows practitioners to alter income by altering service volumes and/or billing patterns as well as through alterations in the fees themselves. In the period 1980-81 to 1983-84, the average annual increase in Ontario Health Insurance Plan payments to practitioners was 17.6%. The number of claims rose 5.7% per year. The average number of claims per resident rose 4.7% per year and the average cost per claim rose 11.2%.

The 1983 Report of the Federal-Provincial Advisory Committee on Health Manpower reported the same phenomenon.

> "On reviewing statistics on medical utilization in Canada (as measured by services provided by physicians under provincial medical care insurance plans) there were increases of per capita utilization of 3.3% per year from 1974/75 to 1982/83. Only about 0.5% could be explained by demographic changes."

Explanations given for the 85% that was not due to demographic changes were (a) changing consumer expectations or demand, (b) changing practitioner practice and billing patterns, at least partly due to increasing numbers and availability of physicians, (c) changing medical technology, which also will be altering practice patterns, and (d) availability of a wider range of diagnostic and therapeutic modalities, which may be part of (c). The report describes interprovincial per capita utilization differences which do not appear to have led to differences in health status. Physician over supply and the fee-for-service method of payment each present a major challenge to those trying to rationalize the system and control costs.

Does Method of Payment Affect the Quality of Care, the Doctor-Patient Relationship and Whether a Physician is Ethical?

The charge that physicians are unethical if they work for anyone but themselves or another doctor is not heard much now although it was a common bit of inaccurate rhetoric, especially in the United States, for three decades (1940-1970). It emerged briefly in Saskatchewan in 1962 when doctors on the staff of community clinics were denied hospital privileges because they were employed by community boards and, therefore, were considered to be unethical.

The proposition that fee-for-service is central to a good patient-doctor relationship and to an acceptable or high quality of care is nonsense. It is quite unfair to the large number of practicing physicians who work on salary in community health centers, with a university or elsewhere. Most workers, including most health workers, are not paid by fee-for-service, but there is no evidence that the way they are paid has reduced the quality of their services or the relationships they have with a variety of clients.

If method of payment can affect quality and the patient-doctor relationship, it is probable that fee-for-service is damaging to both. The physician gets paid the same amount whether a service is provided quickly or slowly, well or poorly. If one wishes a high income, one must perform many activities. A quickly done and perhaps less well done examination is worth the same as one done more thoroughly. Keeping good records and writing good referral letters are not income producing so there could be a tendency to omit them or do them poorly.

All methods of payment have advantages and disadvantages. When considering income and how to provide it, it may be desirable to note that income is not the same as worth and that both the amount and method of payment are set primarily by tradition and by market forces rather than by any predictable or fair evaluation or any rational process. Preferred method of payment tends to be related much more to tradition and to net income than to altruistic principles.

One of the unfortunate products of fee-for-service is that, in most cases, it definitely does not reward excellent physicians as well as it rewards some mediocre or poor ones. It definitely does increase the number of patients seen per hour and it increases hospital use and surgical volumes.

PHYSICIAN POWER OVER OTHER PROFESSIONS

In Canada, professionals operating within the medical model, a group which includes nurses, physiotherapists, speech therapists, radiology technicians and laboratory technologists, have few things they can legally do except when under the supervision of a physician. There is ongoing negotiation between nurses and physicians as to what procedures and duties can be appropriately and legally performed by nurses but the power remains with the physicians. It is they who are, in law, allowed to 'practice medicine'. Of the professionals within the medical model, it is the physicians who are legally entitled to diagnose and prescribe. Others carry out duties approved by physicians or make decisions delegated to them by physicians. This is legally the case, despite the fact that other health professionals have clearly described areas of expertise that are quite distinct from the expertise of physicians. Physiotherapists, nurses, speech pathologists and others routinely diagnose and develop treatment plans but all, in law, must act under the direction of a physician.

Some health professionals operate outside of the medical model. These include chiropractors, optometrists and osteopaths. These practitioners have usually, at some time, been in dispute with physicians, and sometimes the dispute continues. These health workers each have their own legislation and each can diagnose and treat within a prescribed spectrum. Physicians have no power over these professionals and play no direct role in determining what they can do.

Control Over Information

This is another area of interaction between government and physicians. In Québec, information belongs to the patient. The patient is entitled to read anything written down by the physician or other health worker. In most provinces, however, information is still perceived to be institutionally or professionally owned and patients have no guarantee of access.

Programs Which Influence Location of Practice

Independent (private) practitioners can still open an office wherever they wish (including in their homes in most municipalities) but governments are using an expanding array of incentives and disincentives to influence physicians and dentists in their selection of locations for their practices. These programs have the intent of increasing availability of practitioners in selected rural areas and/or of decreasing availability in selected urban areas.

Programs to improve the rural supply of physicians have been used by most provinces and have been directed towards both medical students and physicians licenced to practice. Incentives directed towards graduates have tended to be more successful than those directed towards students; half or more of the students buy their way out of their contracts after they graduate and few go on to provide long term service to rural areas. An Ontario program directed towards licenced physicians has led to 400-500 physician placements since 1979 plus 70-90 dentists. Of the physicians, about one fifth have been specialists. The incentive payment takes the form of a tax free grant over a four year period to a maximum (in 1985) of $10,000 per year. Québec has considered requiring agreement to provide a minimum of 1-2 years of rural service as a condition for acceptance into a Québec medical school.

Factors contributing to a disinclination for rural settlement include nonmonetary factors such as personal attachment to urban life, the lack of availability of medical colleagues and the lack of availability of educational opportunities for children. Financial incentives must offset these nonmonetary disincentives. Québec is experimenting with a twinning of rural and urban hospitals as a technique to reduce the isolation of rural practice.

Disincentives to locating in overserviced areas are usually monetary and range from reduced payments to exclusion from medicare. In Québec, physicians who settle in underserved areas are paid up to 120% of the regular fees. Settlement in overserviced areas is discouraged by payment at a rate as low as 70% of the regular fees for the first three years of practice. Preliminary assessment suggests that this plan has had little effect on physician location patterns although it may have saved the province a bit of money.

Refusal by the public insurance system to assign a billing number to physicians who settle where the supply is considered to be adequate is a more aggressive approach to the use of monetary disincentives. Without a billing number, no payments will be made directly to the physician by the insurance plan and no reimbursement will be made to patients receiving care. Québec considered this control of billing numbers several years ago but did not introduce the required legislation. British Columbia introduced the plan, had it struck down by the courts, and was accomplishing the same end through a second piece of legislation but that also is in legal trouble.

Only tradition can explain why it is acceptable for government to decide how many teachers or police officers should serve a particular community at public expense, but offensive when the same principle is applied to physicians.

Efforts to date to influence location have been limited to correction of rural-urban imbalances. Inappropriate intraurban distribution, especially the aggregation of specialists in medical towers either downtown or adjacent to teaching hospitals, has not been given attention. The recent rapid growth in doctor supply and the associated competition for patients have lead to a significant number of family physicians opening clinics in suburban areas. However, dispersion of specialists, including those, such as pediatricians and obstetricians who are practicing primary medicine, is still often narrower than is reasonable.

The Professional Functions

The most formal point of contact of physicians and governments is through those acts that govern the profession. These acts describe the functions that are delegated to the profession as well as its responsibilities and powers.

The question of who licences physicians is not as important as is usually thought. State licencing boards have, for decades, licenced physicians in the United States whereas, in Canada, physicians often believe self-licencing is a prerequisite to professional survival. In Canada, each province has delegated the licencing responsibility to a professionally controlled College.

Besides licencing, provincial laws make the profession responsible for the protection of the public against professional misconduct. This duty obligates the Colleges to evaluate physicians, a task done with varying vigor but done much better now than a decade ago.

Physicians are united in their objection to the direct intrusion of outside agencies, including government, into the way a physician deals with an individual patient. They have, historically, also been equally adamant about how physicians are evaluated. In both of these functional areas, physicians are usually aware of the extent to which their professional lives are becoming or have become bureaucratized by hospital limits on privileges, rules regarding referral, rules regarding billing and regulations pertaining to the care of specific types of patients. The wish of physicians and other professionals to have a major influence over how they carry out their work is legitimate and usually respected but physicians, in particular, tend to damage their credibility by being insensitive to the legitimate wishes of others who also wish to be involved. Questions of relative cost-effectiveness and of equity make external evaluation inescapable, and the availability of better data makes external evaluation possible.

For years, users have complained that the various professional committees set up to respond to public complaints and to evaluate professional conduct have not reasonably defended the public. In response to these concerns, most provinces now appoint nonphysician members to those quasi-judicial bodies that examine the conduct of physicians and investigate complaints from users.

The Bureaucratization of Medicine

Professionalism is, by definition, a decentralized and individualized concept with emphasis on personal responsibility and control. The term can also be used with reference to a self-governing profession in which there can be significant regulation and control of members by the profession itself. Having a professionally controlled bureaucracy which sets fees, controls professional training, determines specialty qualifications and designation, defines acceptable personal and professional conduct, sets penalties for misconduct and applies these penalties as it sees fit is, therefore, consistent with the concept of professionalism. In a pure sense, a professional reports either to no-one or to his or her peers, and a self-governing profession reports to no-one.

A bureaucracy is, by definition, centralized, systematized, regulated and supervised. Individuals within a hierarchical authority structure write rules and collect data to be certain the rules are obeyed. Individual decision-making takes place only within the constraints laid down by the system.

The fact that there is a professionally controlled bureaucracy affecting physicians is illustrated by such things as the existence of the medical association fee schedules, the peer review program operated by the Ontario College of Physicians and Surgeons, medical staff support for regulations governing mandatory referrals or protocols, professional discipline committees and procedures governing designation as a specialist. The presence of bureaucratization arising from external sources is illustrated by such things as the fee schedules of third party paying agencies (whether negotiated or arbitrarily applied), the banning of extra-billing, the mandatory reporting of certain diseases or events such as that required in suspected child abuse or in cases where pilots or automobile operators are thought to be unfit to drive, the application of income ceilings, the control by hospital boards of appointments to the medical staff, the mandatory provision of specified information to public insurance agencies and the production and use by government insurance bodies of doctor billing profiles.

The increase in external bureaucratic influence and control is usually associated with an increase in the use of objective data. This use brings with it a rigidity which can be seen as, and which certainly at times will be, a threat to the clinical decision-making freedom of a physician. There will be continuing tension associated with the need to prevent physician decision-making that is either clinically incorrect, culturally unacceptable or not cost-effective, on the one hand, and the need on the other hand to leave physicians with a reasonable degree of flexibility as they deal with the individual variations in patient need and response.

It is difficult to predict how fast the pendulum will swing or where it will pause, but the continuing reduction in physician control will be welcomed by the many health professionals who must regularly suffer the arrogance of physicians. In 1986, the Canadian Medical Association published a text called

Perspectives on Health Occupations. In a chapter titled "Occupations Concerned with Physical Medicine and Rehabilitation Services", there is the following statement: "Physicians who pass their responsibility for patient care to therapists are not safeguarding their patients and are forcing the therapists to take on a role for which they have not been prepared."

It must be frightening and annoying to competent and responsible professionals, each with his or her own unique diagnostic and therapeutic skills, to find such parochial attitudes and such arrogant self-aggrandizement in colleagues with great power. Certainly, the inability of physicians to appreciate their own limitations while overstating the limitations of others has been one factor contributing to the general erosion of physician power.

The next few decades will see increasing intervention by governments, boards, committees, administrators and courts into the professional lives of practitioners of many types. Keeping three thoughts in mind may allow health administrators to make these interventions more rationally and fairly.

1) Physicians are simply one group of workers. Whether one agrees with their positions or not, they should be dealt with in basically the same way as one deals with other classes of workers. At the individual level it is reasonable to remember that every human being can feel insecure, confused or threatened.
2) Physicians are powerful. When an administrator goes to war with them too aggressively, the administrator is likely to be the one that loses, especially in a hospital. If the administrator and the medical staff are permanently at odds, it is unlikely that the hospital board will keep the administrator and go out looking for another medical staff. Physicians are not famous for seeing the big picture, and they do tend to be arrogant, but their ability to close ranks when the herd is threatened should not be underestimated.
3) Policy creators and administrators should be frequently reminded of the fact that care providers constantly, and on short notice, make difficult decisions. Administrative decisions may also be difficult and may often be much more important to the community than the decisions of caregivers, but the decisions which physicians and other health professionals must make are highly personal, often made in an emotional atmosphere, often trivial to the point of annoyance, sometimes of great importance to somebody and often emotionally draining. Policies should not be designed with only physicians in mind, rather, effects on communities must come first, but in both policy selection and implementation administrators should be sensitive to the occupational pressures regularly faced by a number of health workers, including physicians.

Suggested Reading

York, Jeffrey, *The High Price of Health, a Patient's Guide to Medical Politics*, Lorimer, 1987.

Fulton, M.J., *The Regulation of Emerging Health Care Occupations*, Canadian Hospital Association, 1988.

Chapter 12

COMMUNITY HEALTH SERVICES

INTRODUCTION

The title of this chapter is more inclusive than its contents. Many community health services (CHS) are discussed elsewhere. Community mental health services have been covered in Chapter 10 and physicians' services in Chapter 11. Long term care is covered in chapter 14 and other chapters include discussion of specific elements of CHS. This chapter looks primarily at community health centers, care in the home and public health services. There is a discussion of the community development process because of its overlap with many of the current approaches to the planning and delivery of community health services.

Community health services are delivered from the broadest possible mix of nonhospital locations including homes, offices, clinics, the street, shopping centers, schools, work places, jails and recreation sites. CHS programs and workers deliver primary, secondary and tertiary care and prevention. They deal with personal and collective problems. They respond to every type of medical problem and most types of social problems, and use most types of technology.

CHSs are much more difficult to circumscribe than hospital services. Hospitals have a significant degree of control over the types of things they do; CHSs do almost anything. Hospitals are much more structured and are much more likely to admit and to discharge; these are neat ways to know whether one is responsible. In CHSs the users drop in and out at will.

Because community health services merge imperceptibly with a number of other social networks, it may help to identify some things that we will not be discussing, at least not in any great detail. We will give minimal attention to housing, employment, protective services, education, financial support, consumer protection, urban planning, recreation, transportation and services for the learning disabled. All of these are, at various times, crucial to persons in need, and health workers and programs must regularly consider these primarily nonhealth services if multiproblem individuals and families are to be reasonably supported and aided. These other networks operate alongside community health services and should not be forgotten just because this chapter will not give them much attention.

Although institutional services can be seen as different from CHSs, it is important to remember that the services provided in hospital outpatient clinics, as well as many services provided in the emergency department and in day programs, are very similar to those provided from various noninstitutional sources of care. In most communities, 5-10% of ambulatory care is provided by hospitals. The distinction being made in the various chapters is entirely for convenience, not because the different sources of care serve distinct clients or deal with completely different types of problems.

COMMUNITY HEALTH CENTERS (CHCs)

The term 'community health center' describes ambulatory care outlets which have a number of common features and which are quite different from traditional solo or group medical practice. They are reasonably recent developments that go back about 30 years in Canada and 50 years in the United States, although earlier precursors can be identified.

Community health centers are multidisciplinary and multifunctional, do not rely on fee-for-service payments as their primary source of income, are community-oriented, offer a broad range of services and are known by many names. Each of these features will be looked at in some detail. Despite their slow growth in Canada, CHCs continue to be seen as a desirable concept by a significant group of individuals and governments.

Methods of Financing

Fee-for-service billing is not the primary source of revenue although it tends to be used for certain clientele. Most income is received in the form of either capitation payments or a global budget. The global budget is the most common in Canada.

The absence of fee-for-service as a major method of producing income is seen by many as the most fundamental CHC feature. The use of both capitation and global budgets is compatible with the development of multidisciplinary teams, with an integrated, holistic and continuous rather than episodic approach to care, and with an emphasis on health promotion. All of these are central to the objectives of most CHCs. Capitation payments are made to the organization, not to individual providers of care. Physicians may be on salary or they may have a contract in which their income varies with the financial viability of the organization or with other factors.

The Multidisciplinary Team

Under fee-for-service the physician is the only major income producer; work done by others will usually not be paid for by the provincial insurance plan. CHCs, however, are able to distribute work to the most appropriate worker because their income does not come predominantly from fees. Even in small CHCs, the team is likely to consist of social workers, nurse practitioners, public health nurses and/or registered nurses as well as physicians. In larger CHCs the team can include dentists, optometrists, physiotherapists, community developers, mental health therapists and counsellors, health record analysts, dieticians, occupational therapists, pharmacists, psychologists, podiatrists or chiropodists, health educators and chiropractors. The range of physician specialists will also expand as the CHC enlarges. Different CHC models emphasize or exclude certain types of workers.

The integrated multidisciplinary approach allows all health care workers to utilize their special skills, to share in the planning and delivery of care and to share a common patient record. Patients can receive services from a variety of workers without changing location or being uncertain about their central place of care.

A reasonably comprehensive team cannot be developed until the CHC has a population base of at least 10-15,000 people, and 20-30,000 is a more commonly quoted range. A population of 20-30,000 people is an optimum size because, once a reasonably complete range of services is available, further enlargement may increase patient travel and decrease the personalization of care without increasing the advantages of economies of scale.

Multidisciplinary care is not easy to deliver. The idea of nonhierarchical teamwork (teams made up of equal members) is not part of the education of most professionals, especially physicians, and role models are scarce. Even the centralized multidisciplinary health record is not easy to introduce. The challenge is to encourage professionals such as psychologists, dentists and social workers, each with their own terminologies and forms, to both share a record and understand one another. This is a particularly difficult challenge if the semantic and technical communication problems are worsened by interprofessional rivalry or negative perceptions.

One Stop Shopping

Fragmented and dispersed ambulatory care and other social services are inconvenient and inappropriate for the multiproblem person or family. The CHC attempts to reduce client difficulties by putting the required health and social service professionals in one place and having one integrated record. In this respect, the CHC is like a hospital.

Community/User Control

There is no universal management arrangement but CHC boards usually represent communities or consumers rather than providers. Boards differ in the way they are chosen, the extent to which they are accountable and how they operate.

The terms 'membership' and 'roster' are sometimes used. Members tend to be those persons who wish to have a say in the management of the CHC, at least to the extent of voting at an annual meeting. They may or may not be users of the CHC. Roster is a financial term applying to Ontario Health Service Organizations (HSOs). The roster consists of those persons who have indicated that they consider the CHC to be their primary source of care. Monthly capitation payments are made to the HSO for all rostered patients who, in that month, did not obtain from an outside source a service which could have been provided by the HSO.

The Planning of Ambulatory Care Networks

It is, as was stated earlier, difficult to create coordinated and regional networks when the regional agency is unable to significantly control private practitioner planning or operations. CHCs are nonprofit and their trustees might be expected to have an interest in area-wide and integrated programs. CHCs tend to deal directly with a ministry with respect to such things as budgets, new services, productivity and reporting systems and, therefore, should have no difficulty co-operating with a ministry or regional agency on planning matters. CHCs are attractive to planners because they introduce an alternative to fee-for-service medicine. When one is seeking an efficient and responsive system and the one in use is uncertain on both counts, one ought to test alternative models; the CHC is such an alternative.

The Holistic Approach to Care

Many but not all CHCs put great emphasis on holistic, continuous and preventive medicine, including health promotion, rather than on the curative and episodic approach to care. This approach differs from that of many fee-for-service sources of care though, again, not all.

To consider CHCs to be the only place where one can receive holistic care, or the only place one can find health workers interested in it, is unfair to those fee-for-service physicians who work very hard at seeing the patient as a complete person in an interactive environment. These physicians routinely practice preventive medicine and contribute consciously to health promoting lifestyles. The appropriate position would seem to be to accept that physicians under all methods of payment can favor holistic and preventive care but that the environment in CHCs is much more conducive to these emphases than is an environment dependent on fees as the major source of income.

A few other less uniformly present characteristics have, on occasion, been made part of the description of CHCs. Ontario CHC guidelines, for example, ask that CHCs direct their services toward underserved or disadvantaged populations. This is an undesirable limitation because, although CHCs are especially well suited to meeting the needs of groups such as the adult mentally retarded or alcoholics, they are also fully appropriate for the entire population.

Cost, Quality and Benefit

There is no universal agreement as to the relative cost, quality and benefits of CHCs. After 30 years of valid and standardized data showing lower hospital use, lower surgical volumes, lower drug use and lower per capita costs, the organized medical community still rejects the proposition that the fee-for-service model is more expensive.

If one examines client satisfaction, the CHC and the private fee-for-service practitioner may look much the same. If one uses the traditional productivity measure of cost per visit the fee-for-service unit may look best. This traditional measure, however, ignores the availability of extra services in CHCs and the lower volume of visits per person per year. Comprehensive cost studies have not yet been conducted. If the total financial picture including direct and indirect costs and savings were considered, then documentation would include not only office costs and the costs of referrals, but also the extent to which CHCs and fee-for-service practices affect utilization of a broad range of community services including Children's Aid Societies, social service departments, emergency rooms and mental health services. To date, too many Canadian studies have used methodologies designed to fit the values or objectives of the researchers rather than to present a comprehensive picture.

Advantages of CHCs

For the consumer, a CHC provides one-stop shopping without fear of special charges. (CHCs never indulged in extra-billing.) Community and consumer control increases the likelihood of accountability to those who use the CHC. The average physician consultation is longer, meaning that there is more discussion and patient involvement.

To the government, CHCs bring financial predictability. There are fewer units to deal with, more opportunities for regional planning and no incentive to overutilization.

For the doctors on the staff of a CHC, there are the pleasures of holidays with pay, regular working hours, sick leave, opportunities for continuing education without loss of income and few administrative responsibilities. To other health professionals, CHCs offer the chance to make decisions and perform activities beyond the range of opportunities available in fee-for-service settings. To the advantage of all concerned there may, in the long term, be more desirable patterns of health service consumption.

Disadvantages of CHCs

To a physician culturally accustomed to provider control over executive decisions, the big disadvantage is loss of that control; a board makes the management decisions and the chief executive officer reports to that board. There are two ways this loss of executive control can be perceived:

a) loss of administrative control over such things as hours of work.

b) loss of control over the personal practice of medicine. Concern with respect to this second factor was fundamental to the 1962 doctor strike in Saskatchewan; doctors thought there was to be bureaucratic interference with their professional decisions.

Doctors object to nondoctors making decisions about how medicine will be practiced by physicians. Unfortunately, they do not always clearly distinguish between the concept of leaving a physician with considerable flexibility and discretion at the level of prescribing care for a specific patient and the concept of assuring political, board or executive influence over the method and amount of care that is provided by groups of caregivers to classes of patients. When care is being delivered to one patient at a point in time, physicians still have a high degree of professional freedom, but overall patterns of resource allocation belong in the public rather than the professional domain. Some physicians quite honestly confuse these two concepts and, therefore, administrators and policy makers must spend whatever time is necessary to separate the two. CHC or hospital boards and the makers of public policy can and should decide what activities to finance. Physicians should be, within the limitations imposed by many factors including policy, relatively free to treat patients in ways acceptable to the profession, to themselves and to their patients, and this desirable degree of freedom is the same in a CHC as in a fee-for-service office.

Besides physician loss of executive control, the CHC also asks for teamwork. Such co-operation may reduce physician control over how care is provided because there can be considerable negotiation in nonhierarchical teams. The potential for intrateam conflict can be seen as a disadvantage.

For the user, CHCs can be seen to carry the possibility of intentional underservicing. The provider no longer benefits when additional services are rendered and may gain if fewer services are rendered. There is no evidence that this practice is occurring in Canada but the potential is there, especially when payment is by capitation.

For governments, CHCs introduce the problem of evaluation. How does the bureaucracy decide the CHC is efficient and productive? Because a new method of delivery of care has been introduced with a new set of objectives and devices, new approaches to evaluation are needed. Unfortunately, there is a tendency to evaluate this new delivery model much more rigorously than the established fee-for-service model.

The increased delivery of health care by allied health professionals can also be seen by government as a disadvantage. Doctors in fee-for-service practice have considerable ability to control their incomes. Allied health professionals in CHCs may fully or partially provide services that would have been provided by the fee-for-service physicians if the CHC were not there. In this situation, the costs of the allied health professionals are add-on costs because the fee-for-service physician will find some other way to generate the expected income. Government may not wish to transfer physician functions to allied health professionals in CHCs or elsewhere unless it can control fee-for-service payments.

CHCs in Canada

Non fee-for-service ambulatory care alternatives have grown slowly except in Québec, and even in Québec, where there has been a rapid growth of CLSCs, over 95% of physicians are still on fee-for-service. Politicans have either been opposed to the new options, been favorably disposed to them but unprepared to aggressively promote them, or been seriously committed to the capitation or global budget options but unable to significantly reduce the number of physicians on fee-for-service. The private/public alliances that led to the rapid growth of health maintenance organizations in the United States are not present in Canada, and there does not appear to be much likelihood that CHCs will grow quickly here.

CHC Examples

For a small country, Canada has produced an impressive variety of community health center names and organizational arrangements. British

Columbia has Health and Human Resource Centers (HHRC). Saskatchewan has Community Clinics (CC). Ontario has two models, Community Health Centers (CHC) and Health Service Organizations (HSO). Most HSOs have two features which are unique in Canada;they are controlled by physicians rather than consumers and they are funded through capitation. In Québec, the CHC is called a Centre Locale des Services de Santé (CLSC) or Local Community Health Centre (LCHC).

The CLSC is the only Canadian model that operates within a provincially planned regional network and under a comprehensive provincial statute that determines services, board membership and relationships with other regional services. It is also the only CHC model that performs most of the functions performed in other provinces by public health units, and it is more closely related to a specific geographic area than most other examples.

Other Canadian names in use either now or in the past include Human Resource Centre, Group Health Foundation, Group Health Centre, Group Health Association and Street Clinics.

In 1985, HWC published a rather incomplete but still useful inventory of CHCs in Canada. Some agencies that definitely are CHCs are not included, for example, there is no listing of any centers in Saskatchewan. Some things that would definitely not usually be thought of as CHCs are listed, such as a 75-bed, long term care facility in Cumberland, British Columbia, called the Cumberland Health Centre. Many centers listed in the inventory appeared to offer no physician services and, therefore, were equivalent to the centers routinely staffed by public health units in many parts of Canada.

Of the listings that appear to fit the usual CHC criteria there were, in 1986, 10 in British Columbia, 2 in Alberta, 4 in Saskatchewan, 5 in Manitoba, more than 30 in Ontario, over 100 in Québec, 11 in New Brunswick, and one in Nova Scotia. The rate of establishment of CHCs tended to be greater in the 1970's, especially before 1977, than in the 1980's, although provinces differ significantly.

A few health centers have been resounding successes. In the Sault Ste. Marie Group Health Centre, 45-50 doctors and many other health professionals provide a broad range of general and special services to 45-50,000 people, about half of the local population. The Saskatoon Community Clinic is close to the size of the one in Sault Ste. Marie. Both operate a satellite unit as well as the original clinic. Several Québec CLSCs have received national attention, as has the Lac du Bonnet Centre in Manitoba and the James Bay Clinic in Victoria, B.C.

Perhaps the most puzzling aspect of CHCs is their failure to become more common. The answer lies in the lack of government support, the organized antagonism of the medical profession, the strong ties that tend to exist between the average Canadian and his or her physician(s) and the willingness of fee-for-service physicians to adapt when CHCs become a threat. When CLSCs, for example, offered easier access to evening and weekend care, the private practicing physicians in Québec responded with polyclinics offering more services over longer hours.

United States

Some mention of CHCs in the United States is desirable because of terminological confusion and because of the regularity with which reference is made to American experiences.

(1) Health Maintenance Organization (HMO). This rapidly growing model includes many famous early names that proved the worth of the CHC concept, such as the Kaiser networks, the Puget Sound Cooperative and the Health Insurance Plan of Greater New York (HIP). HMOs are all capitation based. They are owned and operated by a broad range of profit and nonprofit groups including labor unions, community groups, religious orders, universities, hospitals, physicians and insurance companies. A number of HMOs have enrollments of half a million people or more and HMOs provide care to close to 10% of Americans. More than one quarter of all American physicians now have some relationship with an HMO.

(2) Neighborhood Health Centers (NHC). These centers were a product of the race riots of the 1960's and are less emphasized now. Their establishment was an attempt to reduce the social alienation of an underserved, ignored and predominantly black population.

(3) Social and Health Maintenance Organizations (SHMOs). These organizations are an HMO variation in which the service spectrum is expanded to include social services.

(4) Group Practice. This term has a meaning in the United States that is quite different from its meaning in Canada. In Canada, it means merely a group of physicians (or other professionals) who co-operate or merge for mutual benefit. In the United States, it means prepaid, consumer-sponsored, non-fee-for-service, ambulatory care outlets and hospitals. The Kaiser-Permanente organizations were group practices before they became HMOs.

COMMUNITY DEVELOPMENT AND HEALTH SERVICES

Community Development (CD) is the process of working with communities to help them make decisions and be heard. It is a routine, essential, but seldom discussed part of CHSs. The CD process is inherent in all activities which promote community involvement in policy selection, planning or administration. It is a proactive process of consumer and community involvement for the purposes of consensus seeking, communication and conflict resolution. Patience, flexibility, the provision of reliable information and the creation of mutual trust are prerequisites to successful community development.

The centralized and paternalistic models of health care planning and the paternalistic/technocratic medical model of health care delivery have little need for community development skills, but our more modern democratic and participative models definitely do. Consumer and community opinions are now thought to be important and health planners and administrators who believe in the democratic model and in the idea of sensitive public institutions need to know how to work with communities and respond to them. The planners and administrators who do not like the social model also need to understand communities even if only to neutralize them.

In Québec, the functions of the CLSCs include working with the community to solve individual and general problems. Elements of community development are seen in most community needs studies, in many of the outreach programs of CHCs, in a minority of the outreach programs of hospitals, in many occupational health programs (especially when active health and safety committees exist), in the effort to transfer responsibility for health and social services to native groups, and in some health promotion activities directed to specific communities or specific local populations.

Consumer/community involvement in health services planning or delivery is supported by philosophical as well as practical arguments.

Political/Philosophical Reasons

The community development process strengthens the democratic process. An electorate that has a chance to be personally and regularly involved in policy selection, program development and executive decision-making at the community or institutional level can probably better identify indiginous leaders for larger electoral responsibilities and be better prepared for the casting of an informed ballot. Being involved should also reduce the sense of powerlessness and the associated cynicism toward governments.

The community development process makes it more likely that public policies and publicly funded programs will reflect the values and priorities of the community. In a society in which the consumer is said to be king, and in which it is said that he who pays the piper calls the tune, it is reasonable to develop mechanisms and skills that will allow the taxpayers and users to continuously exert influence.

Institutional/Agency Reasons

Decisions made with the participation of users and communities are not only likely to be more appropriate and more culturally sensitive, they may also be technically and administratively superior. There is a great deal of expertise and experience in the average community.

When an agency or institution must win arguments regarding budgets or a rezoning request, or wishes to raise funds or find volunteers, then expanded ties with communities are one possible route to success. The new associates act as advocates, a source of funds or a source of free labor.

Continuing agency/community interaction may also reduce the likelihood of future conflict. Through education or any form of cooptation, at least some parts of the community can be made into allies. These allies may bring the agency competitive advantage when seeking to establish satellite (outreach) operations or establish referral patterns.

The Community Development Process

There are a number of steps or perceptions that are prerequisites to any agency inviting users and communities to share in policy creation or the executive role. Failure to be aware of these prerequisites can lead to failure of the process.

1) Identify objectives and be honest. The community needs to know why its involvement is being sought.
2) Understand the CD techniques and options available. Learn how to prepare information for a nontechnocratic audience and learn how to generate feedback.
3) Clearly describe the extent to which decision-making or other responsibilities are to be assigned or shared. To be unclear can, at a later date, lead to feelings that the agency acted in bad faith.
4) Be prepared for limited understanding of the issues by consumers, for lack of early consensus and for frequent changes in consumer/community preferences.
5) Have a plan for dealing with feedback and for allowing people to act as they wish in areas in which they have been invited to make decisions.
6) Propose a schedule for completion of the process.
7) Use advisors if there is a shortage of internal experience regarding the CD process, schedule and expectations.

It is difficult to know whether consumer/community power will increase in the 1990's. Certainly its effectiveness has been increased by legislation enshrining consumer rights, and by experience with the process. Communities are also more effective if able to sustain efforts for prolonged periods, if they have financial resources and if they are able to find good leaders who will devote the required time. Many of these factors are most prevalent in the upper and middle socioeconomic groups. A better chance for success exists if there is assured public funding for community development activities, often to the extent of hiring full-time community organizers.

CARE IN THE HOME

We have come from a time when care at home was the normal thing, for all who had a home, through a period of emphasis on care in institutions. We are now in an era of humanization and cost control in which care at home is again of increasing interest. Care at home lost favour because the best care came to mean care in hospital. This trend toward institutional care was augmented when health insurance tended to cover the costs of institutional care or office care but not the costs of care at home, and when changes in the nature of and dispersion of the family unit made home care more difficult. Care at home is now regaining favor, first, because it is becoming increasingly recognized that care at home is best for some patients. Second, institutional costs have risen sharply and care at home is seen as cheaper. Third, services delivered to the home are becoming publicly financed, and, fourth, the concepts of patient control and protection of quality of life are most easily incorporated into care at home.

The Sources of Care in the Home

1) Public health programs. Public health nurses were early sources of care at home, and their visits remain important. These visits now, however, make up only part of a broad range of services which are sometimes delivered through a 'home care program.'
2) Mental health programs such as that in greater Vancouver.
3) Voluntary agencies such as the Victorian Order of Nurses (VON), The Arthritis Society, the Canadian Red Cross Society and visiting homemakers associations.
4) Home care programs. The organized home care program was created 40 years ago in the United States specifically to assist in the discharge of medically indigent patients who were tying up hospital beds. The basic function of these programs was to coordinate services from a number of community sources and provide care themselves only when it was not available from some other source. The model was obsolete in Canada before it was fully developed; Canadian home care programs quickly became major providers of care. Many provinces have made public health agencies responsible for home care. Manitoba has a provincial home care program which delivers home care to most of the province.
5) Community Health Centers. Québec, in the 1970's, largely eliminated the delivery of home care through separate home care organizations. Providing care in the home became part of the CLSC functions. Lately, however, home care is once again a separate program in some Québec communities.

The Types of Services Provided at Home or in Support of Care at Home:
(Based on a list prepared by the Manitoba Home Care Committee, 1974.)

1) Household maintenance services including shopping, cleaning, laundry, meal preparation, meal delivery, snow shovelling and heating (furnace) maintenance.
2) Personal hygiene and care services including assistance with bathing, grooming, dressing, walking, eating, oral medications, maintenance of dentures and glasses and care of feet and nails.
3) Health maintenance services including diet care, physiotherapy, occupational therapy, podiatry, health teaching and speech therapy.
4) Health treatment services including dressing wounds, drug care, catheterization and irrigation.
5) Individual and family social services including the provision of information, counselling and referral, and financial, employment and volunteer opportunity services.
6) Community liaison services including educational services, library services, visiting services, telephone assurance and telecheck services, child care, programs in seniors centers and recreational activities.
7) Facility care liaison services including adult day care, day hospital care and short term relief.

8) Support services including diagnostic services, transportation services, home equipment services, home improvement services, wheelchair and prosthetic appliance services, health education and health promotion services and nutritional counselling.

Factors Limiting Care in the Home.

Certain patients require services which cannot adequately be delivered in the home. These include major surgery, complex intensive care and recovery room services and the degree of supervision demanded by very aggressive behavior or severe dementia. The list of situations in which care at home cannot be adequate is not nearly as long as most people think. The suitability of home care may also be limited by patient unwillingness to accept care at home, the absence of responsible household members prepared to participate, the intelligence levels of the patient and family, the nature of the living accommodation and the range and volume of services offered by the home care program, although once again these factors tend to be used too often as a basis for excluding consideration of home care.

Home care may or may not be less expensive than institutional care. It may be a substitute for care in other locations or it may be an add-on cost. The degree to which home care is being utilized can be undesirably reduced by administrative inadequacies such as taking several days to admit a patient to the program.

Possible Determinants of Delivery of Publicly Financed Home Care

1) Client or agent willingness to receive care at home. If clients are to make informed choices among different types and volumes of support, they must understand the risks and benefits associated with the options.
2) Relative cost. Publicly financed programs might be expected to refuse to deliver care to the home, or to limit the amount and types of care, when it is feasible for that care to be obtained elsewhere at lower cost.
3) Relative need. When demand exceeds the volume of home care services that can be delivered, some patients will be offered less than optimal amounts of care and some will be offered none at all. The interpretation of need will vary with the values of society and of the technocrats.

It is sometimes said that community care is always preferable to institutional care. This is not true. Care at home at public expense ought to be seen as undesirable when a mentally competent client prefers institutional care and public costs for institutional care are not significantly greater than for care at home. For institutionalization to occur, the needs of the individual also ought to be greater than the needs of other persons on the institutional waiting list or already within the institution. Institutional care is, therefore, appropriate if it is consistent with client wish, taxpayer costs and resource allocation on the basis of need (a question of equity). Public safety is another factor which can make institutional care the preferred alternative. Care at home is less appropriate, although not ruled out, when the dependent person is not welcome at home. The preferences of professional caregivers should not dominate when deciding whether or not to provide care at home.

Whether a dependent person should remain in the community rather than be admitted to an institution is determined primarily by nonclinical factors. The nature of the dependency, especially among mentally competent persons, is not as important as the wishes of the client and other householders, the relative public cost, the willingness of other members of the household to provide care and whether there are any other household members. A study in Manitoba 10 years ago showed that, out of 1,000 persons over age 65 and living alone, 166 were admitted to home care over a one year period. Only 66 out of 1,000 persons living with a spouse were admitted. Whether there was standardization by age is unknown.

Assistance to Caregivers in the Home

As already stated, the presence, competence and willingness of household caregivers is usually more important in determining the viability of care at home than is the degree of dependency of the client. When planning to help these caregivers, one should consider financial assistance, respite care, personal and professional services delivered to the home, help with domestic chores, home maintenance and adaptation, transportation, assistance with trips out of the home, counselling for coping with stress, education and physician home visits.

Issues in Home Care

1) Objectives are often unclear. Earlier hospital discharge is often given as an objective but cannot be important when only 1 to 4% of discharged patients are transferred to home care. Delaying admission to hospital is often said to be an objective but if all institutions are full then the effects of the delay are rather invisible. Encouraging people to stay at home rather than to seek institutionalization is a commonly stated objective which is probably met, although institutional waiting lists still exist. Providing disabled individuals and their caregivers with a better quality of life is one objective that is almost surely routinely met. Other possible objectives include client safety or protection, the preservation of households, reducing the costs of health care by taking advantage of unpaid caregivers, reducing pressure on institutions, humanizing care, allowing individuals to be where they want to be or allowing them to spend disposable income as they wish, including for the purchase of additional care.
2) The financial implications of home care are poorly known. Studies examining the extent to which home care replaces institutional care tend to ignore the fact that institutions remain full whether or not home care is available. In this situation, home care is always an add-on cost, although its availability may reduce the demand for construction of new facilities. It also increases medical care costs by reducing hospital lengths of stay and allowing a greater number of surgical and other procedures to be done.

3) The total potential caseload is still unknown, but it appears that between 1 and 2% of the total population will, at any one time, be receiving services at home if there is a reasonable mix of services offered without direct cost to the recipient and without too many rules regarding admission.
4) There is no clearly preferred organizational approach, and no evidence as to whether home care is best delivered as a separate provincial program (Manitoba), as part of regional public health services (British Columbia and Ontario), as one of the services under the management of a multifunctional regional board (as in selected western Canadian communities), through a network of ambulatory care centres (Québec), by voluntary agencies (Ontario) or by hospitals (Ontario). Examination might find that organizational charts have little or no bearing on efficiency or anything else. In smaller, one-hospital communities, hospital based home care can work although probably no better than home care under other sponsorship. In multihospital urban centers, it is administratively more sensible to have a central administration than to have each hospital follow its own patients after discharge.
5) There is minimal understanding of the extent to which various types of patients benefit from home care. Receipt of care is, therefore, often on the basis of the perceived degree of crisis or on a first come-first served basis. The cost-effectiveness concept cannot be applied until more is known about the impact of home care on the health status of the clients and other household members.
6) There is some evidence that delayed termination of home care is common, and that it is most frequent when case managers have caseloads of 100 or more. Regular assessment of the satisfaction and needs of persons receiving home care may not be possible when case managers are responsible for more than 60 to 70 clients.
7) The New Brunswick extramural hospital program has been widely publicized but appears to offer no special advantages. All services provided in this program have been provided elsewhere. The most unusual feature of the New Brunswick program is the concept of a regular payment to a physician for each patient admitted by the physician to home care. No other province has found this practice to be necessary, but there appears to have been no study of the effects of this payment variation.

PUBLIC HEALTH SERVICES

Public health services became a local government responsibility in Britain with the passage of the Elizabethan Poor Laws in the seventeenth century. Concern with disposal of the dead and the operation of poor houses was followed by actions to dispose of sewage, assure clean water supplies, dispose of garbage and control vermin. By the 1900's, most provinces had modeled their public health legislation on the *English Public Health Act* of 1875. Earlier activities had been joined by immunization programs and the beginnings of public health nursing. Particular attention was given to the control of communicable diseases and to child and maternal health. The central themes throughout the first half of the twentieth century were public safety, health education and the use of regulation. The medical officer of health had almost unlimited powers of quarantine, isolation, entry and closure, powers that have persisted, although with modification.

In recent decades public health agencies have, in all provinces but Québec, expanded into many areas of counselling and personal care and their role in sanitation has decreased. Garbage disposal and water and sewage treatment are now municipal functions. Food inspection is, at least partly, taken care of by departments of agriculture or food.

In Québec, public health functions have been transferred to several agencies and departments. Community and personal care services are delivered mostly through CLSCs, the research and planning functions are mostly assigned to the departments of community health in regional hospitals or to the regional councils, and the environmental protection functions have been distributed to departments of labor, the environment and others.

The environmentally related functions that are the responsibility of public health departments are primarily performed by public health inspectors. Their responsibilities include the examination of selected aspects of air and water quality, the control of insects and animals, the testing of rural water and sewage systems, food testing, inspection of eating places and other food premises, inspection of a variety of public and residential buildings and spaces and responding to public complaints. There is considerable overlap between the duties of public health inspectors and the duties of municipal building inspectors and a broad range of environmental control officers.

Provinces also have quite different approaches to the use of public health personnel in such activities as immunization, family planning, home nursing, sex education, family-life education, prenatal classes and the provision of dental care.

For almost a decade, the Council on Community Health Accreditation in Ontario has been accrediting public health agencies. The accreditation process is, unfortunately, a copy of that applied to hospitals.The Council decided at its outset that management was the thing to examine. The examination of outcomes was avoided despite the long history in the public health field of relying heavily on outcome measures.

Many years ago, public health personnel discovered that if water was boiled people did not get cholera or typhoid; no one knew whether the pot was the right size or whether there was a committee to design it, and no one cared. They were pleased to have no cholera and typhoid. When polio vaccine prevented polio there were very few scholarly papers and no evaluation exercises that concentrated on how the immunization program was organized or whether the person giving the needle (or spoonful) was properly qualified; people were interested only in the effects of the program — the reduction in polio. When seat belt legislation and lower speed limits came into being, we looked for changes in highway accidents and deaths — and found them. There was no concern over which department wrote the legislation or the qualifications of those who enforced the laws. Dentists promote flossing and fluorine because of the effect of these things on dental caries; once again they look at the way the health of the population is affected. When personnel at poison information centers wonder if they are having an effect, they count reported poisonings and, similarly, people running anti-smoking campaigns count the number of smokers. The Ontario approach to the evaluation of public health units is an immense step backwards. It looks at the bureaucracy rather than the effects.

The exercise of counting visits, listing programs, reading minutes, evaluating the qualifications of staff and examining organization charts will merely delay the day when evaluators will have time to pay attention to whether priorities have been sensibly set, whether resources are being well used and whether public health activities are contributing as much as they can to the health status of the people of Ontario. Attention to qualifications, staffing and organization may lead to a search for more staff and the devising of new organizational structures just because administrative and professional personnel say that changes are in order. The public health industry should ask for more staff and more money only when it can prove that the need to be met or the hazard to be avoided is worth the money to be spent, and that spending more money will appropriately decrease the need or the hazard. Evaluation, therefore, must concentrate on outcomes.

Costs

Public health services cost in the range of $5 to $100 per capita, with the higher costs being associated with extensive personal care programs, especially home care. Most public health services are financed by the province although some municipally operated programs receive up to one half of their funds from the municipality.

Issues in Public Health Services

1) Medical officers of health are now primarily planners and administrators but most have little training in either planning or administration.
2) The historically established authoritarian approach is still sometimes seen. This concept is quite incompatible with the current role of public health personnel in lifestyle change, community development and the empowerment of individuals and groups.
3) Although the activities and responsibilities of public health personnel overlap and interact regularly with personnel in a variety of other health and social service programs, there is often limited coordination. Examples of integration or coordination include some community health centers, some multiagency centers (by various names) and the arrangements in Québec.

4) The degree of need for public health nurses in the schools as teachers or as caregivers is unclear. Provincial patterns vary considerably.
5) Should the historical organizational isolation of public health personnel and departments be continued? Québec has said it should not.

Summary

Only a few of the components of community health services have been discussed in this chapter. As already stated the omitted CHSs are covered in other chapters.

Community health services face one major obstacle, namely, the issue of financial support. Despite major percentage increases in isolated programs such as home care, there have been equivalent cutbacks in the funding of CHSs in several provinces. These cutbacks are even more common when one looks at social programs — the housing, income support, recreation, and other services that are crucial to the health of many Canadians. Perhaps the major national program titled 'Strengthening Community Health' and led by the Canadian Public Health Association will be able to reverse the trend.

Chapter 13

SHORT TERM ACUTE TREATMENT HOSPITALS

WHAT IS A HOSPITAL?

In addition to being a source of essential health care a hospital is also a legal entity, an employer, an educator, a laboratory for research, a neighbor, a competitor and a perceived panacea. It is, in our culture with its rejection of the concept of human mortality, a powerful political and emotional force whose worth is real but overestimated.

Hospitals as Determinants of Health Status of a Community

There is general agreement that the health status of a population is the product of many factors. The four main determinants of individual and collective health are often given as environment, lifestyle, health services and human biology. The World Health Organization has recently added public policy as a fifth major determinant although these policies can be seen as part of the environment. Environment includes the physical, emotional, social, political, economic, occupational and cultural environments. Lifestyle includes individual characteristics or habits over which the individual is considered to have at least a modest degree of control, such as alcohol use, expectations, exercise patterns, response to stress and diet. Health services include all those preventive, diagnostic, therapeutic and rehabilitative services delivered through health facilities and programs. Biological factors include those human frailties and strengths, primarily genetic, which determine our susceptibility to and response to illness and injury.

Of these four major determinants, the genetic factors are currently beyond both individual and collective control except in circumstances where prenatal screening is available. Some physical environmental factors are also unalterable. However, many of the environmental factors, most if not all of the lifestyle factors and all of the health services features are under human control.

Of the health status determinants that are under our control the environmental and lifestyle factors are either more important than health service factors or at least as important.Hospitals, therefore, are a major subheading under one of the three major areas over which we exercise control (Figure 13.1). Despite their psychological and financial importance it is obvious that hospitals cannot affect health status more than is compatible with being just one part of health services which are one part of the total network that affects our health.

In an age in which hospitals and their fund raising, their technical miracles and their requests for more money are in the media almost daily, it is difficult to keep the role of hospitals in perspective. Community health agencies and other services which are very important to health, for example social service agencies and employment programs, constantly struggle to be noticed in the face of the profile and clout of hospitals. Hospitals have most of the glamor, the greatest aggregation of clinical and administrative expertise and they have the eye of the public.

FIGURE 13.1
THE DETERMINANTS OF HEALTH STATUS

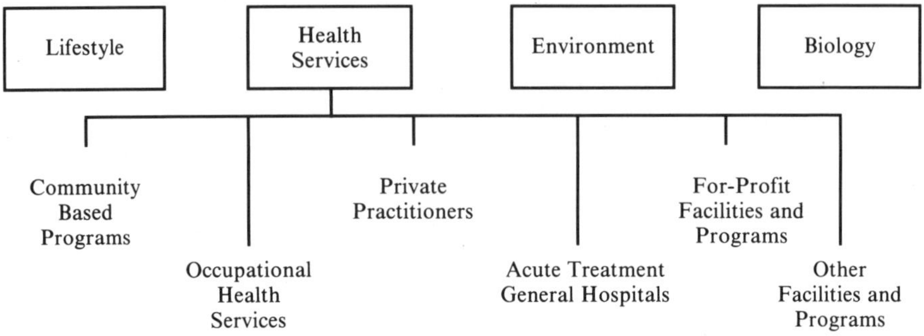

The political clout and the financial dominance of hospitals should not be allowed to overshadow the less dramatic and less expensive sources of health care or the other determinants of health. When evaluating the importance of hospitals we must look, not at cost or headlines, but, at effect on health status. No one knows to what extent hospitals contribute to the health status of a population, or how much influence is exerted by the total network of health services. Its seems unlikely that hospitals can be a major factor.

Hospitals should be of greater interest to treasury boards who must find money than to health planners who wish to improve community health status. There is crude evidence that if the supply of hospitals or physicians is expanded beyond a modest figure, there will be no further noticeable effect on the health status of the community or nation although the change in availability of hospitals will be of consequence to specific individuals.

HOSPITALS CLASSIFIED BY OWNERSHIP

Besides the hospitals owned and operated by community boards, there are also hospitals owned by churches, municipalities, provincial governments, the federal government and private-for-profit corporations.

Religious Hospitals

These hospitals may be individually incorporated or part of a multi-institutional corporation which may operate hospitals and other types of institutions.

Twenty or thirty years ago, organization charts of religious hospitals were very simple. A Sister Superior or equivalent in other religious denominations, who would now be called an Executive Director or President, would have executive authority but would report to a higher level of religious authority.

In the last 25 years many religious hospitals, especially Roman Catholic hospitals, have been transferred completely to community boards and therefore are no longer classed as religious institutions. Those that continue to exist as religious institutions are now often owned by the church but governed by a board whose members are selected largely or completely by the religious group. Prior to the appearance of an independent board with executive authority it was common to have an advisory board working with the chief executive officer.

Municipal Hospitals

Municipal hospitals, for example, the Hamilton Civic Hospitals, the Civic and Riverside Hospitals in Ottawa and the Union Hospitals in the prairie provinces, are owned by one or more municipalities but are not operated by them. Municipal operation of hospitals would be quite possible and reasonable (municipalities do operate LTC institutions) but is uncommon. The boards of these hospitals, which tend to be appointed by the municipality(ies), have full executive authority and do not report to the municipalities in any meaningful way. Since the introduction of universal hospital insurance, municipalities usually have accepted no responsibility for hospital deficits except when required to do so by the province, as has at times been the case in Alberta.

Some of the municipal hospital boards have been replaced by boards who are also responsible for a mix of public health, hospital, long term care (LTC) and occasionally other functions.

Provincial Hospitals

Most provincial hospitals are psychiatric institutions that are part of the physical inventory of the Department of Public Works (or equivalent) and are administered by the psychiatric services branch of the ministry of health. All staff are provincial civil servants.

A few of these provincially owned psychiatric hospitals are administered by community boards (as in Alberta). In New Brunswick some of the acute treatment hospitals are owned by the province but operated by community boards.

Federal Hospitals

The federal government operates military hospitals (Department of National Defense), hospitals for the native populations (Medical Services Branch, HWC), veterans' hospitals (although these are almost gone) and small specialty institutions including leprosariums and quarantine stations.

Proprietary (for-profit) Hospitals

Most provinces have a *Private Hospitals Act* or the equivalent. These Acts regulate institutions which are not governed by the *Public Hospitals Act*. These institutions tend to be fairly small and to provide specialized mental health or addiction-related services. They usually provide insured care to provincially insured persons but payment is on a fee-for-service or per diem basis rather than through a global budget.

Summary

There are significant variations in ownership and corporate structure of nonprofit hospitals but these differences have little impact on services. In every case the hospital serves basically the same functions, it has the same relationship to the minister of health, it has the same reliance on public funds and it fits well or poorly into a regional system. The options at the top of the hospital organization chart have been described because these affect the opportunities available to a citizen or a community for influence over an important community institution.

RELATIONSHIPS BETWEEN HOSPITALS AND MINISTRIES OF HEALTH

Ministries of Health or the Minister of Health (or equivalent) have, through their provincial hospital statutes, almost absolute legal power over hospitals. In dealing with ministries hospitals must, therefore, rely on tradition, public image, persuasion, and an awareness of the perceived importance of the services they provide. The hospitals definitely have the edge in tactical terms, but in those instances in which hospitals do not have public support or do not have a reasonable rationale for their demands the ministry can, if it chooses, flex its legal and financial muscle.

The Legal Relationships

Hospital-related statutes usually give the Minister final authority over whether a hospital exists (a list of approved hospitals is usually part of some Act), the range of services it provides, the wording of hospital by-laws, physical size and changes in size, capital and operating expenditures, the keeping and reporting of information, admission practices, volume of and price of preferred accommodation, medical staff appointment and appeal procedures, patient consent procedures, quality review processes and whatever other things the Minister chooses.

In recent years, ministers have expanded the *Public Hospitals Act* or equivalents to include procedures by which the power and function of hospital boards of trustees can be formally transferred to a ministry appointee when the Minister and/or cabinet considers this transfer appropriate. This unusual degree of intrusion by the ministry into trustee functioning, an intrusion that usually occurs as a series of steps with each additional step being more restrictive, has, to date, occurred in response to inadequate financial control, inadequate quality control or a combination of administrative and financial problems.

In Ontario, the confrontation between the ministry and hospitals and the subsequent amendments to the *Public Hospitals Act*, followed directly from a decision by a substantial number of large hospitals to refuse to operate within the funds allocated by the ministry. These hospitals set budgets that anticipated large deficits, some in the range of $15 to 20 million. The hospitals, in essence, dared the ministry not to provide the money. It was a situation in which the government either had to let the hospitals write the provincial budget or act quickly and firmly, and it chose to act. The hospitals then decided they would rather operate in a fashion acceptable to the ministry than be operated by someone named by the ministry. Hospitals have more or less accepted the fact that they, as well as schools and other kinds of public institutions, must operate within an assigned amount of public money.

Financial Relationships

Financial control of hospitals by the ministry is less complete than legal control, but is equally effective. For most public hospitals, 85-95% of operating funds come from their provincial ministries or from ministry financed hospital insurance commissions. Hospitals also receive operating income from preferred accommodation and from revenue producing activities such as TV rentals, and parking. Income is also generated from third-party payers such as WCB and from investments, donations, direct-pay patients and payment for out-of-province patients. Revenue from these last two sources can be substantial in hospitals on an interprovincial or international border or with a multiprovince function. Through the budget allocation process the Ministry can support or discourage the establishment or expansion of patient care or educational programs. The ministry can also determine the involvement of the hospital in regional or joint ventures.

The Business Oriented New Development (BOND) program in Ontario merits a comment. This program, which was introduced in response to the idea that hospitals should be more businesslike, invites hospitals to raise money through business ventures. Money raised is kept by the hospital. As part of the program, Ontario hospitals were allowed to keep all income from preferred accommodation (rather than only a portion of it as was previously the case) and to set their own rates for this accommodation. Rates for private and semiprivate rooms immediately rose by 30-100% producing a major financial windfall.

The BOND program was a mistake. Trustees and administrators became involved in a variety of profit making activities when they already lacked the time needed to do the priority setting and information production that is needed. There was hidden growth in total hospital expenditures that was not shown in ministry expenditures, with consumers providing most of the new money either by cash payments or through higher premiums for preferred accommodation.

A recent fleeting aberration in the hospital financing scene is a practice whereby hospitals sell assets to private corporations and then lease them back.

The hospitals get immediate capital above the amount which is reserved to pay all lease-back charges and the private investor gains tax write-off benefits. The net result is an increased cost of hospitals to taxpayers.

Other Areas of Ministry Impact on Hospitals

Ministries also affect hospitals by making available or failing to make available other health services such as long term care beds and home care programs and by making or allowing changes in health manpower. Decisions of the ministry regarding the presence and power of regional planning bodies affects hospitals because these regional bodies interfere with direct hospital-ministry discussions over planning options. In some provinces, collective bargaining with hospital-based unions is a ministry function.

HOSPITAL ORGANIZATION

Figure 13.2 illustrates one possible organizational skeleton of a teaching or nonteaching hospital. The organization chart would, in the corporate model, show a president and a number of vice-presidents. The more common organizational chart has the positions of executive director and a number of assistant executive directors. In the corporate model the president is a member of the board of trustees. The two models have no other significant differences.

Note that the medical staff has two quite distinct organizations with different functions and status. The chief of staff and the Medical Advisory Committee (MAC) are an integral part of the hospital organization whereas the organized medical staff with its president and other executives is very much a free standing organization.

The MAC is, in Ontario and some other provinces, given major statutory responsibilities. It must, in many situations, provide advice to the board, and the board is obligated to consult it. The *Ontario Public Hospitals Act* states: "The Committee shall advise and collaborate with the administration in all decisions affecting patient care including the allocation of space, the allocation of beds by department and the development of facilities," and the Committee shall "approve plans and priorities for the use of funds in all departments and divisions." MAC members in Ontario teaching hospitals are appointed by the board. In other hospitals, the MAC is elected. The MAC is composed of all chiefs of clinical departments and major sub-departments or divisions, which in a large teaching hospital results in a membership of 30 to 60 physicians. The MAC may also have nonvoting members from the administration, the board, the nursing department and occasionally from other departments. By law, in Ontario, the chief of staff is the chairman of the MAC. The chief of staff is usually appointed by the board and, therefore, is, in theory, its agent rather than being primarily a representative of the medical staff. MAC advice and decisions are received by the board via the presence of MAC minutes as part of the agenda of board meetings.

Figure 13.2
THE ORGANIZATION OF A TYPICAL ACUTE TREATMENT HOSPITAL

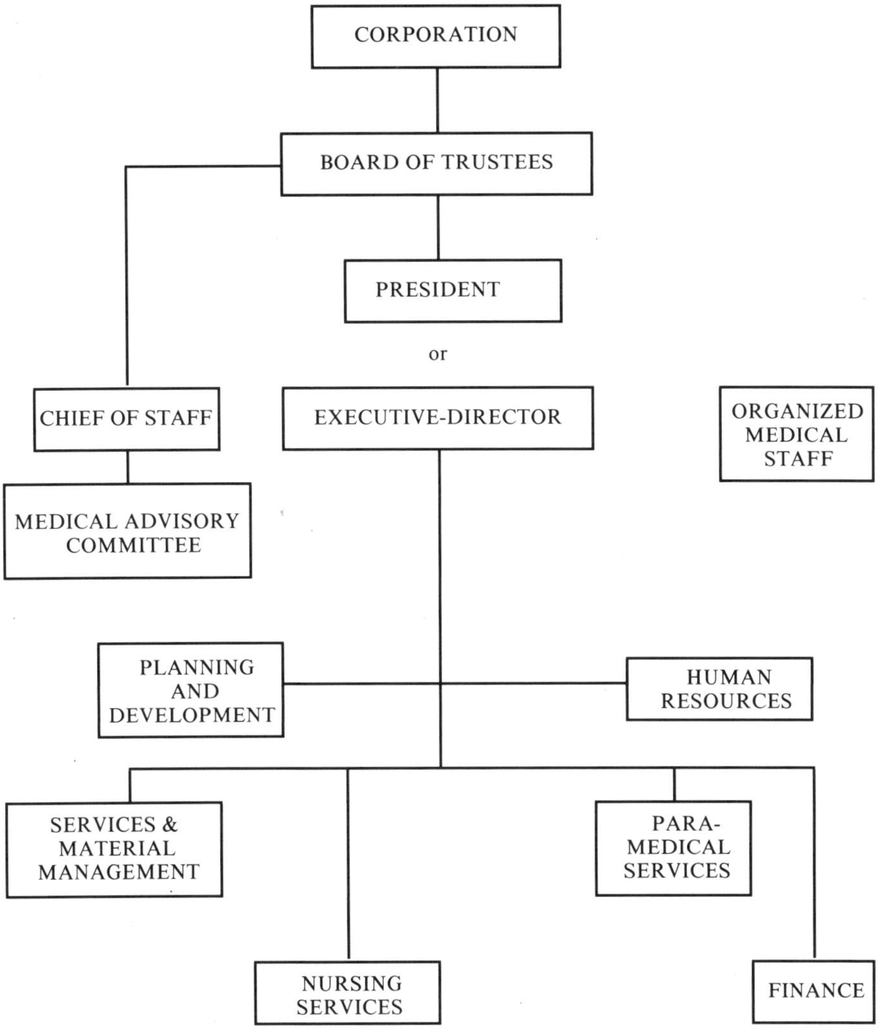

The medical staff, acting through its elected executive, may be active in institutional politics and in producing institutional policies or it can have primarily social/professional functions. Whereas the MAC represents the medical staff elite (the department heads plus chief of staff), the elected medical staff executive directly represents the entire active medical staff.

The medical staff consists of all physicians and dentists who have been approved by the board. The medical staff usually consists of active staff, (physicians and dentists whose primary affiliation is with this hospital), consulting and courtesy staff (physicians and dentists who usually have a closer affiliation with another hospital) and special categories of staff.

It must be emphasized that individual hospital organization charts may vary quite markedly from the brief description and the single diagram given. There are frequently, for example, multiple separate service units under one board of trustees and possibly one executive director. There can also be two or more separate corporations with very close operational ties, for example, the Ontario cancer clinics which are operated by a provincial board but whose day to day delivery of services is functionally very integrated into that of the hospital to which the clinic is attached.

Physicians in Management

The role of physicians in hospital management is unusual and as such has been the subject of study and comment by administrative theorists. Physician decisions are usually the primary determinants of resource consumption by patients but they are outside of the administrative line of command. This situation frequently leads to conflict regarding costs, use of staff, and allocation of resources. One of the devices commonly used to help resolve this type of conflict is the Joint Conference Committee (JCC). The JCC, which is not shown in Figure 13.2, is composed of equal numbers of representatives from the administrative staff and the medical staff, and reports to the board and to the medical staff. Its agenda consists of all issues of interest to both administration and the medical staff, and some authors believe it is essential to reasonably harmonious relations between the two camps.

The JCC may be more necessary in nonteaching hospitals where there is not a cadre of joint university/hospital appointees who, by virtue of their fixed incomes and their administrative as well as teaching and clinical functions, act as major points of contact between clinicians and the administrative staff. The JCC may be more necessary when there is a large nonteaching medical staff with a great deal of power and within which there is considerable competition for beds. These factors make it more likely that there will be major disagreement both within the medical staff and between it and the administration and/or board. However, the JCC is not in common use and other devices for conflict resolution appear to be preferred.

For several years there has been accelerating discussion of how, to what extent and with what payment medical staff should be involved in administrative decisions. In some budgetary experiments, clinical chiefs have been given a significant degree of actual control over the manner in which their departmental budgets are spent. In this model a number of cost centers have mini-global budgets. The institution, through an institution-wide priority setting exercise, determines the size of the departmental allocation, but priority setting within the department is, within institutional guidelines and controls, determined by the department.

The concept is, of course, not new. Departments such as dietary and admitting which are under the direction of department heads employed by the hospital, have always operated within an assigned budget. The new wrinkle is to give budgetary control to a clinician who is primarily a caregiver rather than an administrator. Both the old and new approach share one overwhelming problem; in the absence of an understanding of the cost-effectiveness of various activities, the choices between different expenditure patterns must continue to be intuitive.

Hospital Foundations

Although not shown in Figure 13.2, many hospitals have recently created foundations as legally separate but organizationally affiliated fund raising arms. Funds raised by the foundations are not hospital funds until transferred from the foundation, an arrangement which gives the hospital greater flexibility in the ways it can use the collected funds and greater assurance that these donated funds will not be seen as part of the basic operating or capital budget of the hospital.

Hospital By-Laws

As already described, the hospital's charter sets forth general institutional goals and characteristics. As a source of operational guidelines the charter is not very helpful and, therefore, the hospital needs a more detailed set of rules describing such things as the responsibilities and functions of the board and of senior staff, the composition of board committees and the schedule of board meetings, financial control procedures such as the use of closed tenders, conflict of interest guidelines, appointments to and review of medical staff membership, duties and constraints associated with medical staff membership, the major organizational divisions of the hospital and the medical staff, the major health care services of the hospital, the process of patient admission, and other similar matters. This detailed set of rules is known as the hospital by-laws. Hospital by-laws tend to be divided into two major parts, one part dealing with medical staff and the other part dealing with all other matters.

By-laws are in force when they have been ratified (approved) by a meeting of the corporation and approved by the minister. The required content of many parts of the by-laws is often quite specifically spelled out in governing legislation such as a *Public Hospitals Act*. Provincial hospital associations produce model by-laws meant to assist hospitals as they create or revise by-laws for review by the minister.

Medical Staff By-Laws

These by-laws describe the medical staff structure including titles of medical staff leaders, how these leaders are chosen, the standing committees that will exist, the role of the MAC or other components of medical staff organization in various decisions, the process of review of applications from physicians and dentists for the right to have privileges in the hospital, the categories of medical staff and their rights and responsibilities, procedures for appeal if an applicant is not happy with decisions affecting his or her opportunity to practice within the hospital, and educational and research responsibilities and vehicles. Central to many medical staff by-laws is the general principle that a public institution is expected to operate with rules that are clearly stated and are fair and non-discriminatory.

The functions of the medical staff fall almost entirely upon the active staff. In major urban centres it is now uncommon for a physician to have an active staff appointment in more than one hospital. Active staff members have voting rights, will be expected to participate in committee work and are usually required to attend the regularly held educational sessions (rounds) of the appropriate clinical group.

Medical Staff Committees

There is, once again, considerable variation among hospitals but common titles include the Admission and Discharge (A&D) Committee, the Utilization Committee, the Credentials Committee, the Infection Control Committee, the Quality Assurance (QA) Committee, the Medical (Health) Records and/or Audit Committee, the Central Committee for the Assessment of Medical Acts (Québec), the Tissue Committee, the Pharmacy and Therapeutics Committee, the Research Committee, the Therapeutic Abortion Committee, the Medical Education Committee, the Emergency Committee, and the Admissions and Length of Stay Committee (Québec). Not all of these committees will exist in any one hospital because the functions of some of them overlap, as is the case with the QA Committee and the Infection Control Committee, for example. The members of all medical staff committees tend to be named by the MAC.

The Process of Granting Medical Staff Privileges

Applications for medical staff membership or renewal are submitted to the hospital board. The application is referred to the MAC for assessment and the MAC makes a recommendation to the board. The recommendation is usually accepted but the final decision and the legal responsibility for that decision rests with the board. Physicians who do not agree with the decision of the board may initiate an appeal process which may end in review by a quasi-judicial body such as a provincial Hospital Appeals Board or in a provincial court.

Professional Staff Organization in Québec Hospitals

The medical, dental and other professionals in Québec hospitals are members of the Council of Physicians and Dentists (The Clinical Staff Advisory Committee). This Committee is quite analogous to the MAC but has a broader membership and shows some functional variations.

House Staff

The term 'house staff' refers to all medical interns and residents and does not include other professional trainees or medical students in the hospital. Dental trainees might be a rare exception. These interns and residents are employees of the hospital and are not part of the medical staff. The term intern is usually reserved for persons in their first year of training following graduation with an M.D.

Residents are enrolled in specialty training programs, including family practice residencies. Residents may be licenced to practice outside as well as inside the hospital. They tend to be paid $25,000 to $40,000 per year and often work very long hours, a fact which is due more to historical precedent than to necessity. House staff are found only in hospitals which have been approved by the Royal College of Physicians and Surgeons or the College of Family Physicians of Canada as locations for training.

House staff members examine patients on arrival, write their medical histories, and, to the extent that their rank and experience allow, write patient care orders. They also assist at surgery, perform many diagnostic and therapeutic procedures, see the patients as often as necessary during their hospital stays, perform obstetrical deliveries and accompany physicians on their rounds.

House staff members have been actively lobbying for a shorter work week. If their working hours are shortened (a very desirable event), other persons will be needed to perform some of the tasks which have less educational value. Nurses 15-20 years ago went through an educational change in which student nurses ceased to be seen as sources of cheap labor. In the process nurses became students and, therefore, lost their access to free room and board and began to pay tuition. They also graduated with too little clinical experience to be able to work alone in many situations. Interns and residents are both employees and trainees. There has been no clear understanding regarding the extent to which earning their pay takes precedence over, or is secondary to, their education. Policy in this area should assure a satisfactory educational experience, sensibly assign routine house staff functions to other personnel, and adjust rates of pay if necessary. However, there will probably be resistance to change.

Governments and hospitals see house staff as cheap labor. Medical staff want them to do work that they (the medical staff) would otherwise have to do. For hospitals and their medical staff, having such trainees is also a source of prestige and professional renewal.

The interest in having house staff is at times considerably greater than the interest in seeing them become practicing competitors. At various points in history, the failure rate among those writing exams for admission to specialty fields suffering from oversupply has been unreasonably high. Specialty exams can be written after five years of approved training with the exception of family physicians who write after three years.

Teaching Hospital/University Relationships

These relationships are made complex by legal, educational, quality of care and financial factors. They are, as a result, clearly set out in formal agreements.

Agreement is, in Canada, made more simple by the fact that most of the income of both institutions comes from government, but hospitals still may wish to limit the extent to which their global budget supports costs which they think universities ought to pick up. There is, therefore, a need for an understanding of the extent to which each party will finance lockers, parking, uniforms, liability insurance and supervision for educational programs.

Territorial disputes can also arise over appointments to the medical staff and the selection of clinical heads of departments. Mutually acceptable candidates are sought although the universities hold the strongest veto because, in a teaching hospital, it is essential that senior medical staff also hold a university appointment.

In the relationship between teaching hospitals and universities, the universities have become increasingly dominant through their control over department head appointments and their influence over development and staffing of residency programs. Clinical department heads in teaching hospitals usually have a university appointment as a geographic full time (GFT) professor and, therefore, university acceptance is a prerequisite to the hospital appointment.

MULTI-INSTITUTIONAL ARRANGEMENTS

The history of hospitals is replete with examples of multi-institutional arrangements. These include most psychiatric hospitals, some religious hospitals, Red Cross Hospitals (now all transferred to other operators), Grenfell Mission hospitals in Newfoundland and DVA hospitals (now mostly transferred to other management). These multi-institutional arrangements were a natural product of the nature and responsibilities of the owners. In the period since the 1950's, individual community (voluntary) hospitals have entered into collective solutions, either voluntarily or under direction from government, as a means of controlling costs and of improving the quality and/or the availability of services. In essence, these arrangements always implement some form of centralization.

There are three common and successful multi-institutional models which do not seriously threaten the autonomy of the participating hospitals.

Model #1 (Figure 13.3)

In this model one provider institution supplies a service to satellite user institutions. The provider hospital (or other institution, program or association) has by virtue of excess capacity, specialized skills, a central location or political or tactical skills, been chosen as the site of a central laundry, a computer center, a 24-hour pharmacy service, an inservice education program, a specialized maintenance staff or a specialized laboratory service, for example.

FIGURE 13.3
ONE MASTER PROVIDER AND SATELLITE USERS

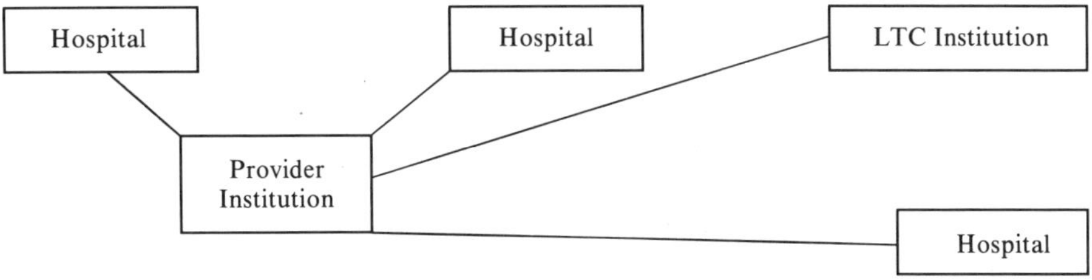

The centrally produced service may be purchased on a flat fee or fee-for-service basis or may be financed entirely within the global budget of the parent institution.

Model #2

A separate service center may be created (Figure 13.4). The center serves all member institutions but is not part of any of them. Examples include a data processing centre (Hospital Computer Services of Ontario), the Ottawa food commissariat and a separate regional laundry. All the users are equal in the sense that none of them perceives another institution to be in a position of excessive control or advantage.

When the new corporation or partnership is controlled by participating users, it is often referred to as a joint venture. The executive board may include community representatives and it may not include a representative of every user, but participation by all users is a popular model.

Provincial laboratories, or the federal virus laboratory, represent a variation in which the services of the laboratory are used by all who need them but none of the users has direct management influence over the service.

FIGURE 13.4
SHARED SERVICES VIA A NEW CORPORATE ENTITY

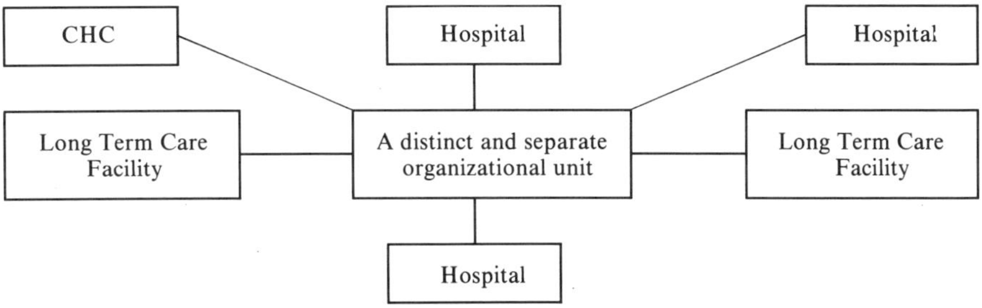

Model #3

In this model, which illustrates a co-operative and image preserving style, parts of a major function are assigned to more than one institution.

This selective distribution model is ideal when a number of institutions each wish to retain a piece of the action and the service involved can be provided from several different sites, as is the case, for instance, with surgical or pathology services. Dispersion of one part of the total range of services to each institution can preserve a role for everyone while concentrating a particular kind of equipment and expertise in one place. Figure 13.5 illustrates this approach to laboratory services.

Each hospital becomes a center of excellence, and each hospital must rely on all other hospitals. Operating agreements are needed to assure satisfactory service, rapid transfer of specimens and results when needed, and a method for resolving disputes.

The three models of multi-institutional services that have been described do not significantly reduce the autonomy of a hospital. Other models are more intrusive.

The most integrated model would be a regional hospital board as proposed in the Mustard Report in Ontario and as exists in Great Britain. There is no Canadian example of such a regional board but several provinces, especially British Columbia and Alberta, have in recent years shown increased interest in their creation.

FIGURE 13.5
CO-OPERATIVE DISPERSION

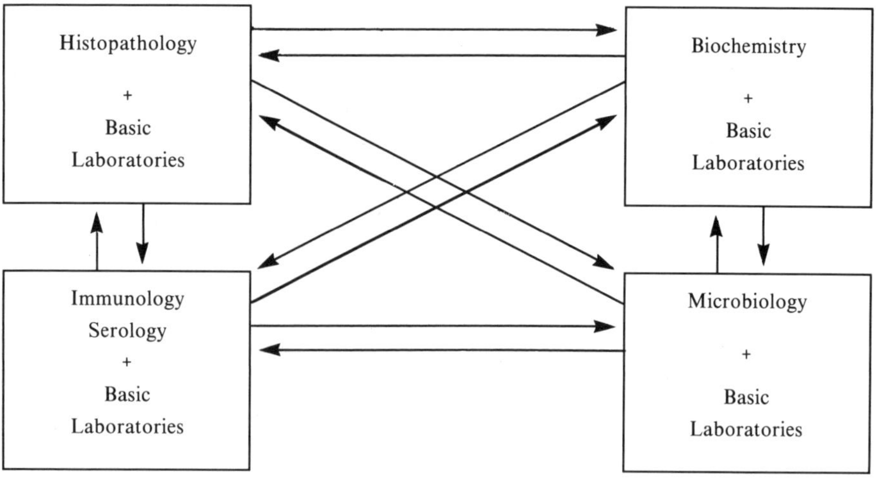

In British Columbia and Alberta a number of hospital boards have been eliminated as a direct result of ministry pressure and decisions, and hospitals built recently in these provinces have usually been placed under an existing hospital board. This centralization process is usually politically unattractive but appears to be proceeding without major confrontation.

Mergers

Mergers are sometimes seen as a cost reduction tool, but there is no evidence they save money. They may serve another major objective; they may make it easier to create a balanced and appropriately distributed network of regional resources operating in a coordinated and co-operative manner. The key to creating this network is a regional plan in which all major sources of health services, or, ideally, health and social services, are assigned an appropriate function and made to perform it. Having fewer hospital boards may not move us closer to a regional system and may not be necessary to achieve one, but one argument which suggests that multihospital boards might move us towards a balanced system is the possibility that hospitals, in total, have less influence when each does not have its own organizational identity.

Arguments in favor of each hospital having its own board are that there would be an increased number of community leaders who would participate and there would very likely be more charitable donations when institutions are clearly identified with their communities. The ideal situation would seem to be one in which at least community hospitals could continue to be specifically related to their communities, while at the same time hospital influence could be reduced to the point that ambulatory care, mental health services, long term care, health promotion, environmental hazards and occupational health could receive attention consistent with their importance.

Multi-Institutional Management

Specific mention of a few Canadian examples of multi-institutional management may illustrate some of the models presented.

Three Vancouver hospitals — the Shaughnessy, the Grace and the Children's (CGS) — merged a few years ago with each hospital keeping its own board and its own identity but with each operating under an umbrella agreement, a master board and a single senior executive body. The 'super' board is responsible for a fairly broad range of administrative and planning functions. There is only one staff, one set of collective bargaining agreements, and one set of personnel policies. Various major service functions such as radiology are concentrated in one place. The overall board acts as the policy and administrative controlling agency in all those areas where major conflict might occur or where the mass of all three hospitals is needed for reasonable efficiency and high quality of care.

This merger was expected by the government to save money, and it may have done so though no overall assessment has been made. In at least the radiology department, however, costs went up. A larger unit attracted specialists closer to the state of the art technology and more anxious to have it. The perception of adequate quality changed with the change from three 300 bed hospitals to a 700-800 bed complex.

In Kingston, a Joint Liaison Committee made up of representatives of Queen's University and four hospitals legally oversees the operation of the four hospitals. None can expand programs, alter functions or build additions without the agreement of the group. Each institution continues to exist but obviously not with the degree of independence it once had. This structure arose because, in the early 1970's when money started to become scarce, the Ontario government told a number of communities that, as soon as the community institutions got together and agreed on what actions were most collectively important to their community, the government would consider whether or not to fund them. The community institutions were obliged to agree upon local priorities and to co-operatively allocate many functions including paediatrics, obstetrics, types of surgery and emergency services.

The Vancouver and Kingston examples demonstrate that some of the advantages of multi-institutional boards can be achieved while at least partly preserving the images of the individual institutions.

Mergers are less common in the east, but have occurred in both smaller communities such as Smith Falls and larger urban areas such as Toronto where the Toronto General and Toronto Western hospitals were merged. The Montréal General and the Royal Victoria in Montréal were thought to be well on their way to a merger but discussions could not identify enough advantages.

HOSPITAL STATISTICS AND REPORTING

Number of Beds per 1000 Population.

The number of hospital beds is one of the major determinants of health services costs; the other is physician supply. Bed supply appears to be always slightly less than demand. Canadian centers have, or have had, a bed supply as high as 7-8 per 1000 and there were still calls for more. Ontario is now aiming for 3.5 beds per 1000 in urban centers and 4-4.5 in rural areas. Québec has similar objectives. A number of other provinces are still apparently committed to a more generous formula but the general trend during the last 10-15 years has been towards fewer beds per 1000 population. The national supply has fallen from 6 beds per 1000 to 5.

Health planning has often been dominated by questions concerning hospital bed supply. Unfortunately decisions have had to be arbitrary. There is no body of evidence that clearly describes the relationship between bed supply and community health. Figure 13.6 describes two relationships, either of which may exist.

FIGURE 13.6
THE RELATIONSHIP BETWEEN BED SUPPLY AND COMMUNITY HEALTH STATUS

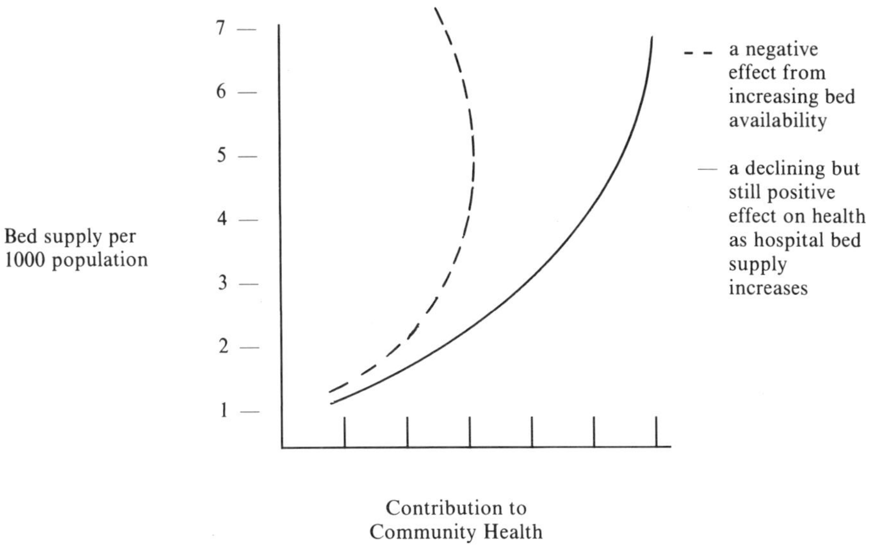

Figure 13.6 suggests that the first 2-3 hospital beds per 1000 population make a significant contribution to community health. The two curves vary in that one of them indicates that a bed supply in excess of 5 beds per 1000 has a negative effect on community health. This proposition can be defended on the basis of the undesirable trade offs that would have been made to finance the extra beds.

Number of Separations or Admissions per 1000 (per year)

This figure has fallen steadily as the number of acute treatment beds has declined and as more of the former short-stay patients are treated as outpatients or day surgical patients. Day surgery patients may or may not be counted as admissions, depending mostly on which is most financially advantageous to the hospital or what rules have been laid down by the ministry. Normal newborns are usually not counted as admissions but the mother is counted, just as bassinets in the newborn nursery are not counted as beds while beds on the maternity unit are counted. The national figure of annual admissions per 1,000 has fallen from 170-180 to 140-145.

Average Length of Stay (ALS)

In calculating ALS the day of admission is not counted and the day of discharge is counted. The ALS in teaching hospitals is usually 9-11 days with community hospitals ALS usually being 7-9 days. ALS has gone up slightly in the last decade.

Number of bed days per 1000 (total population per year)

This figure is obviously the product of ALS and the number of admissions per 1000. Provincial figures were, at one time, in the range of 1500-2000 but now they are more apt to be in the range of 1200-1600 bed days per 1000 total population per year.

Percentage Occupancy

Average daily census compared to a bed total gives an average occupancy. When working with this figure it is useful to know whether the bed total represents rated beds or beds set up.

The Reporting of Professional Productivity

The Canadian Hospital Association management information system under development will improve on current reporting. Earlier work, especially in diagnostic services, also contributed to better reporting. For example, laboratory tests have standard, although frequently unrepresentative, unit values. Automation and high volume so massively alter the production costs of individual lab tests that reasonable costs cannot be known merely by knowing unit volumes.

Annual Hospital Reporting

With the introduction of universal hospital insurance in 1958 under Bill 360, the *Hospital Insurance and Diagnostic Services Act* (HIDSA), it became necessary for the federal government to know exact hospital expenditures; consequently two national hospital reporting forms, Hospital Statistics 1 and 2 (HS1 and HS2) evolved. Although the HIDSA requirements no longer apply, these two forms continue to be used.

HS1 contains descriptive data including type of institution, nature of services provided, patients by classification, volume of diagnostic and hotel services, and paid hours of work and staff costs by activity center. HS2 reports audited financial data including expenditures by activity center, income by source and amount, assets and liabilities, and other information required to indicate the financial stability of the institution.

Provincial psychiatric hospitals do not complete HS1's or HS2's.

ISSUES AND QUESTIONS THAT FACE THE HOSPITAL INDUSTRY

This is a random list. In a general sense this list starts with issues related to overall institutional goals and missions and then moves to more limited issues such as those related to organization, money and quality. The items are not discussed in order of importance nor are they all very important. They are merely a series of issues that have already emerged or are likely to appear in the near future.

Responsibilities of Hospitals to Regional Planning or Service Bodies

Do hospital trustees and administrators, with their special skills and large budgets, have a responsibility to strengthen the total health care network? For example, should hospitals offer tangible and expert support to regional planning agencies, assist smaller agencies which lack educational or administrative expertise, and co-operatively accept decisions made at the regional or provincial level?

There is sometimes a tendency for hospitals, perhaps most marked in tertiary care hospitals, to wish to solve every community health related problem that appears. When a problem is identified the hospital may say "How can I (the hospital) respond?" instead of, "Who in the community is best suited to respond?" If the hospital takes the second approach then it may, by virtue of its highly developed capabilities and its capacity to find developmental funds, be the institution best suited to provide initiative and start up assistance for programs or functions that will become the responsibility of someone else. This second approach is the proper one and is more likely to lead to a balanced health services network with a full range of well developed sectors.

When the parochial approach is avoided, it becomes more likely that the larger institutions will be aware of how difficult it sometimes is for smaller institutions to offer reasonable continuing education opportunities or fringe benefit packages to their staff, or how difficult it is to create and maintain information systems, quality review mechanisms or a variety of special services. The larger hospital could, if it wished, and without absorbing or threatening the smaller institution, sponsor a variety of multi-institutional co-operative efforts in which the smaller institutions may be the only major beneficiaries.

If the hospital accepts a responsibility for the strength and adequacy of regional agencies, then the hospital will not use end-runs to the ministry when arguments are lost at the local level, and it will not actively seek to develop programs or levels of function that have been denied at the regional level.

Selection of Hospital Function

Should hospitals concentrate on, and limit themselves to, performing excellently in those functional areas which cannot be served by others, for example, major emergencies, major surgery, and all investigation and therapy requiring 24-hour supportive care? The alternative is to consider such things as home care, health promotion, long term care and satellite ambulatory care units as fields which are appropriate for hospital attention or which are, perhaps, even seen as most desirably delivered under the direction of hospitals.

Traditional inpatient services are an important and high volume part of the health services network. They require highly specialized clinical personnel and equipment as well as sophisticated management. They operate in a milieu dominated by high technology, high cost, high stress and rapid patient turnover. Personalization and client involvement must often be compromised in the interest of efficiency and high technical quality.

To deliver and administer high quality institutional priority setting and patient care is demanding, socially important and quite different from performing the same tasks in community based programs. These differences make it undesirable that hospitals become the managers of community based services. This limitation is both in the interest of optimal hospital performance and of community or long term care programs that should not be required to accept the in-hospital milieu and practices. It is preferable that the different parts of the health services network, for example ambulatory care, hospitals, long term care and health promotion, should each develop under their own set of specially trained and oriented workers and advocates. Coordination of the different sources of health related activities and services is the function of some regional umbrella organization that will not allow any particular service or need to be unreasonably dominant or unreasonably neglected.

Hospitals have a serious tactical problem regarding their chosen role. They have to decide whether to fight the trend toward noninstitutional care and be anachronistic or neanderthal, or to go with it and acknowledge that institutions have no reason to demand an increasing share of the health dollar. Either way hospitals lose — a rather natural consequence of having acquired a position of unreasonable preeminence.

The essence of these important resource allocation options is well illustrated by reference to a 1977 study done in Ottawa-Carleton by Dr. R. Robertson. This study identified the annual mortality rate from major trauma in this area as 21 persons per 100,000 population. It was estimated that if the region instituted a first class emergency health services response capability with better ambulances, better communications and greater population awareness, this mortality rate could be reduced from 21 to 18 per 100,000. On the benefit side we would save 18 lives per year if we assume a population of 600,000. New costs would arise from increased hospital response capabilities, from having paramedics in ambulances, and from a 911 emergency telephone system.

It is probably safe to assume that many of the fatal incidents were preventable, including car accidents (with other cars or with pedestrians or cyclists), falls, fires and cave-in's. Surely hospitals, which must receive the products of the carnage, should lead those who wish to know whether expenditures on prevention will save more lives than the same expenditures on better treatment.

Evaluation of Hospitals

Evaluation of hospitals and their activities is currently performed, either intentionally or unintentionally, by the Canadian Council on Health Facilities Accreditation (CCHFA), provincial governments, professional and academic bodies, auditors, researchers, hospital associations, the Professional Activities Study (PAS) and Hospital Medical Records Institute (HMRI), legal tribunals and users.

The evaluative role of each of these will be discussed in order.

1) The CCHFA accreditation surveys emphasize inputs (facilities, staff and their qualifications), process as documented in minutes of meetings and

on patient charts, and departmental (intermediate) outputs such as completed charts and autopsy rates. They have emphasized, and still overemphasize, the milieu (environment) in which care is delivered.

In recent years CCHFA clinical review procedures have been markedly improved by the introduction of the prospective medical audit. This mandatory audit applies pre-established criteria and standards to all cases of a particular type, which is a much more objective and inclusive approach than that followed by the former retrospective medical audit, in which a group of peers individually and subjectively reviewed randomly selected patient files. Nursing audits are also routinely expected.

2) Provincial ministries of health or some quasi-public body closely monitor approved budgets and monthly expenditure patterns. Through regular monitoring or through response to complaints, a variety of federal, provincial and municipal agencies or departments evaluate fire safety, the handling of noxious wastes, food handling procedures and personnel, exposure to radiation and the process of awarding hospital privileges to medical staff.

3) The College of Physicians and Surgeons of Ontario began, in about 1980, to sponsor peer review of private practices in which teams of physicians reviewed the facilities and medical records of physicians who agreed to the review. The program is now well established and successful and in 1984 by statute all physicians became subject to review. Although this peer review process looks only at physicians' offices and office records, the evaluation could comment on hospital care or follow up.

   The Royal College of Physicians and Surgeons and specialist organizations, such as the Canadian Association of Pathologists, regularly evaluate hospitals to determine whether or not medical internship or residency programs can be based there. Other professional associations, such as the Canadian Physiotherapy Association, evaluate the relevant departments of hospitals to determine whether internships should be approved in their field.

4) Auditors evaluate the acceptability of financial management and accounting practices, assure accuracy in reports and may comment on whether resources were used for purposes consistent with the mandate of the institution.

5) Researchers may evaluate individual institutions or the hospital industry. They analyze or report utilization patterns, production costs, service volumes, disease costs, and clinical outcomes. Either directly or indirectly, research findings may report the quality of the performance of institutions.

6) Evaluation of hospitals is not a primary hospital association function but these associations regularly collect information which allows institutional comparisons to be made — for example, on the incidence of accidents or the presence of deficits.

7) All or almost all Canadian hospitals send an abstract of every discharge to either PAS (Professional Activity Study), based in Ann Arbor, Michigan, or HMRI (Hospital Medical Records Institute) based in Toronto. These programs report the aggregated discharge data to each hospital in ways which allow comparisons with similar institutions or with established norms.
8) Coroners' inquests and malpractice suits often include an evaluation of hospital care, and other judicial activities can also alter hospital procedures.
9) Patient satisfaction surveys are routine in many hospitals. Although patients are usually unable to evaluate the quality of the technical care received they do provide valid evaluations of those aspects of hospital operations that are understandable or which pertain to values, courtesy, and caring.

Assessment of Hospital Evaluation Processes Currently in Use

Evaluation requires an appreciation of objectives. The objectives of a hospital should include all of the following:

1) To perform (offer) those services that will, in combination with other health and health related services in the community, and keeping in mind the role assigned to the hospital, best preserve or elevate the health status of the community. The hospital will set priorities that optimally reflect community needs or wants and the hospital's role in meeting those needs or wants.
2) To provide patient care at the highest quality compatible with (a) the resources available and (b) the concept of best use of resources. The quality of one type of care should be reduced when the savings will serve the community better by being spent elsewhere.
3) To distribute available resources within the general principle that some degree of avoidable risk will have to be accepted by most, if not all, patients. The degree of risk that will be tolerable will vary with the consequences inherent in the relevant hazard and the volume of resources needed to reduce the risk.
4) To co-operate with, and provide intellectual and tangible support to, the regional and/or provincial planning and evaluation process, and to operate in accordance with regional/provincial decisions reached regarding function and expenditures.
5) To use resources efficiently.
6) To operate in ways that reflect the culture, values and priorities of the community and to respect the individual values and culture of each user.
7) To contribute to research and education to whatever extent is compatible with the nature of the institution.
8) To be a good employer.
9) To be a good corporate citizen, including being a good neighbor.
10) To obey the law.

If these objectives are accepted (and they differ somewhat from those sometimes given), then evaluation of any hospital will need to report the extent to which each objective is being met. In examining the extent to which each objective is being met, it must be understood that various objectives may or will at times be in conflict, for example numbers 1 and 6, or 5 and 8. It must also be accepted that there may be major differences between wants (as expressed by clients) and needs (as expressed by professionals), and that deciding whether to respond to needs versus wants may be difficult.

A matching of the current hospital evaluation activities and the list of objectives shows that the hospital accreditation process looks (a) at patient care quality without giving much, if any, attention to the concept that quality should at times be consciously compromised in the interest of best use of resources, (b) at the question of patient risk without providing many, if any, formal guidelines which describe an acceptable level of avoidable risk, (c) at the extent of hospital sensitivity to patient values and priorities, and (d) at selected other elements of hospital performance. The activities of other sources of evaluation tend to relate to only one objective and seldom in a comprehensive way, although our rapidly improving production data does give us a preliminary feeling for efficiency.

It is clear that we do not know much, if anything, about the extent to which hospitals are meeting most of the objectives listed. We do not usually know whether they have an internal priority-setting process or, if they have one, how well it is working. No one regularly evaluates the extent to which a hospital supports or co-operates with regional agencies, nor do we know which hospitals have effectively coordinated their activities with other institutional and community based services, such as nursing homes or public health agencies, that are regularly used by the users of hospitals. Indicators, standards and a quality review process are equally lacking elsewhere.

There is need for refinement and expansion of what some authors have called the 'social responsibility index.' The terminology involved is not new (cost-effectiveness, outcome measures, community health status, quality of life, trade-offs, being responsive to consumers, conflicting objectives) but movement towards a comprehensive, coordinated approach which operationalizes our speeches and literature is painfully slow.

Can Improved Hospital Efficiency Solve our Financial Problems?

The answer is no. Our hospitals are already quite efficient. Much is written about how money can be saved (essentially how available money can be better spent) through such activities as group purchasing, preventive maintenance and increased production. Some people would put lower labor costs, primarily obtained through contracting out to avoid unionization, in this list of efficiency measures, but many hopefully would not. Eventually, one must accept that, regardless of how efficient the system becomes, it will still face a public and a professional demand that cannot be fully met with the dollars available.

When it is fully recognized that efficiency improvements will not allow demand to be met, the system will then turn its efforts towards determining which service cutbacks will be least threatening to the health status of the community. Other alternative approaches to cutting back are available but not so desirable. These include cutting services in ways that protect administration/medical staff relations or medical staff incomes more than community health, cutting back in ways that will make the most headlines so that government embarrassment or public pressure on government may lead to extra funding, or cutting back services to those populations with the least ability to fight back.

Physician Involvement in Decision-Making

There are frequently requests for greater involvement of the medical staff in hospital decision making and suggestions that there is greater need for physicians to recognize cost factors in their practice habits. These requests may not be realistic but they are regularly discussed and we must recognize why they are not being widely met. Some reasons are:

1) Physicians are not taught about budgets, costing or priority setting.
2) Physicians, when delivering care, should have first loyalty to their patient(s), not to the institution; they are patient advocates.
3) Physicians whose incomes are derived through fee-for-service only get paid when they are delivering care. They become charitable institutions when they sit on committees, evaluate each others' work, develop clinical protocols, prepare for accreditation, and carry out other similar activities. Teaching hospitals have a pool of salaried university-based physicians who can increase their involvement in management without loss of income, but most hospitals are not teaching hospitals.
4) Fee-for-service physicians may see the whole process of institutional rationalization as a threat to their incomes as well as their power (autonomy).

The Emotional Stress of Planned Inadequacy of Some Services with the Inevitable Bad Effects on Some Patients

The headlines will say "Lives Will be Lost", or "Patient Died because the Board decided to Skimp on Care." We may not be quite emotionally ready for decisions that knowingly place some persons at risk when they seek health services, despite the fact that we do the same thing quite casually and continuously when we are discussing unemployment, environmental damage or occupational risk.

Hospital administrators and trustees are already sometimes blamed for delays in admission of urgent (not emergency) patients including, for example, those with cancer. This is not a fair criticism. The order in which patients are admitted has, until now, been almost entirely the product of physician created priorities. If a patient waits, it is because other physicians have won the power struggles in the MAC. The number of urgent cases, especially those with proven cancer or a high degree of risk, is limited, and earlier admission of these patients would not seriously disturb the admission patterns of other patients. When physicians complain about their patients having to wait, it is fair to remind them that physicians, through their medical staff decisions, caused the delay.

The Presence of LTC Patients in Acute Treatment Beds

Are they a permanent feature? Probably. Should they be moved to LTC facilities? Probably not. Moving them would increase acute treatment hospital costs and related medicare costs, and moving them is not of as high a priority as strengthening community LTC services and supporting these services with access to LTC institutions when needed. Should hospitals develop special locations and programs for long stay patients? Yes on both counts. Since the situation is not likely to change the institution should adapt to it in whatever ways are reasonable.

The Use of and Cost of Preferred Accommodation

Preferred accomodation was described earlier as one source of income for hospitals. The current practices are, at times, coercive. One can in some hospitals be admitted earlier or more reliably on a particular day if one has insurance which covers preferred accommodation or will pay for a more expensive room. Charges for private and semi private rooms are a form of extra-billing which in Ontario has became an undesirable tool for hidden expansion of hospital income.

Should We Have A 'Two-Tier' System?

If one does not like the public school system one can, as a major personal add-on cost, use a private school. Taxes will still be paid to our good quality and universally available public education system, but there is an alternative. The private educational institutions are regularly monitored to be certain that quality is adequate.

Some argue that the same opportunities should exist in Canada for health care. The opportunities already exist if one chooses to go south to the Mayo Clinic or elsewhere; public subsidy will, in fact, be available to those who wish quicker or more luxurious care. The opportunity is also available for non-Canadians; they can enter a Canadian hospital and be direct-pay patients, a choice which, in Ontario, brings benefits only to the hospital (not to the Ontario taxpayer and certainly not to the Ontario resident who is waiting in the queue).

The private purchase of hospital care and other health services should be at least as legally possible in Canada by Canadians as by non-Canadians. Whether for-profit private hospitals and other institutions and programs would be built would depend on whether the private sector thought there was sufficient demand. It does seem preferable that these private services be available from hospitals or other facilities or programs that are separate from the public system, as is the case in the field of education.

The major argument against this two tier system is that health care is viewed as a right and that there should be equality of access for everyone. Other arguments favor the two-tiered system. Education at public expense is available to everyone but we accept the right of individuals to buy their education elsewhere if they wish, and education services are as important as health services. In many fields that are fundamental to health such as housing, recreation, occupational choice and transportation, there is no expectation of equality. In addition, there is already a two-tiered or multi-tiered system inherent in our ability to purchase home support services such as nursing at our own cost, in the benefits associated with access to preferred accommodation and in the ability to seek health care in the United States if we can afford it. The two-tiered system also exists in our varying ability to buy uninsured health care services such as dentistry or outpatient pharmaceuticals. As a final argument, the opportunity to spend one's disposable income on things that can be legally bought is a more fundamental and generic right than that of equal but limited access to health care services.

The Distribution of Beds Between Surgery, Medicine, Rehabilitation, Psychiatry, etc.

There has been a very rapid growth in the volume of surgical procedures. This growth is the product of (a) the performance in offices and day-surgery units of surgery previously performed on inpatients and (b) a shortened length of stay for patients who have their surgery performed in hospital. These improved bed utilization practices have, in practical terms, been the approximate equivalent of a doubling of surgical bed availability (with the effects upon different surgical specialties being quite different).

There should be a reassessment of the appropriateness of current bed distributions in light of the described changes. Increased productivity per bed may not be available in expanding specialties such as physical medicine (rehabilitation) and it might be fair to transfer some surgical beds to less well served patient groups.

The Incentive to Promote out of Province Income and Patients

When provinces allow hospitals to keep income from out of province patients the hospitals are in an undesirable conflict of interest situation. This income should be considered when setting and revising global budgets.

Funding for Life Support Programs and for New Programs

In Ontario there is special ministry funding for life support programs such as dialysis, total parenteral nutrition (TPN), or hemophiliac centers, as well as for certain new programs. This budgetary practice is undesirable.

The life support programs and the new programs are similar to other hospital programs. General surgery, cardiology and psychiatry are all life sustaining, and an ICU or CCU is certainly a life support unit. Every hospital program should be eligible for replacement or reduction (usually the latter) when other programs serve the community better, and ministries should assist hospitals in an improvement of their priority setting skills so that the zero based budgeting approach can be applied to all programs whether new or existing, expensive or inexpensive, life sustaining or life improving. The special budgets for existing life support services and for new services should, therefore, be rolled into the global budget. When they so wish, hospitals start new programs using funds within their global budget and this principle should be universally applied.

If existing programs were constantly reviewed, we might become more aware of the instances in which some need has been reduced or eliminated instead of hearing only of new pressures on hospitals and other services. It is difficult to recall ever hearing of a hospital that asked to have its global budget decreased because some need disappeared.

Hospitals as Entrepreneurs

The Ontario BOND program was discussed earlier. It invites the undesirable involvement of hospitals in a variety of business ventures, an involvement which is undesirable because such ventures are areas outside of the expertise of the board and the management staff and because they interfere with board and staff attention to the proper running of the hospital.

Some hospital products, however, are identical to products also sold by private businesses; laboratory services, prosthetic and orthotic devices, physiotherapy services and radiology services are examples. Governments which wish to assist hospitals might consider inviting them to compete, preferably on a tendering basis, in areas in which their excellence is established and in which they often have unused capacity. Opportunities exist in Ontario where $200-250 million are spent annually on services provided on a fee-for-service basis by private laboratories.

The New Hospital MIS being Developed by the CHA

This project is not in itself an issue but it is being oversold and the overselling is an issue. The new MIS will give us better cost data and better productivity data. It will tell us who is doing what to whom and at what cost per unit of service or episode of care. Instead of just knowing that cardiac surgery is expensive, we will know exactly how expensive it is and we will, if we wish, know the total cost of hospital care for any given patient. This information will allow hospitals to more validly examine their costs compared to other institutions, especially when combined with 'case mix' data.

The new MIS will not, however, tell a manager or board whether a particular expenditure is a good investment. It cannot do this because the effectiveness side of the cost-effectiveness equation will not be available.

The Training of Hospital Trustees

Action is needed to provide prospective trustees with an apprenticeship experience. At least two options exist:

1) Have some non-board members on all board committees where permitted. Opportunities for experience are greatest if there are trustee committees

which monitor ambulatory care, emergency care, patient relations, quality assurance and regional co-operation.

2) Conduct institutionally (or otherwise) financed trustee training programs. Such a program would be a minor burden if hospitals, DHCs, LTC institutions and CHCs were to work together.

The Granting of or Continuance of Hospital Privileges

The Medical Advisory Committee through the Credentials Committee provides recommendations to the board regarding new additions to the medical staff. When the MAC feels that the hospital has enough psychiatrists, orthopedic surgeons, etc. it sends negative recommendations.

Boards and medical staffs have to date usually successfully refused privileges on no grounds other than their wish for no more doctors of a particular type. It seems likely that in the future courts and hospital appeal boards will ask the hospital for ratios or other evidence in support of their concern with oversupply.

As doctor supply increases and bed supply does not there will be greater competition for beds and an increasing likelihood that new applicants will be rejected, or will be accepted, for discriminatory reasons. At some point in time, the community and/or its agents will demand rejection or acceptance on the basis of previously established and known criteria which are fairly applied to all applicants. This practice will increase the likelihood that qualified physicians whose clinical field requires hospital access will not be excluded from hospital use by colleagues defending their established positions or favoring their friends.

The elimination of a mandatory retirement age may either worsen or relieve the situation. If physicians work longer the competition for medical staff membership will increase. The loss of a mandatory retirement age could, however, lead to the evolution of evaluation processes that, when applied to all ages, would result in an even earlier average retirement age.

As age becomes less and less a factor in a variety of administrative decisions, and this trend is inevitable and desirable, hospitals will hopefully become more precise, objective and skillful in identifying the medical staff role most appropriate for all physicians, regardless of age.

A Reduction in the Number of 24 Hour Emergency Departments

The community hospitals in large urban centers are resisting closure of their emergency departments at night, even though this closure is desirable.Good evidence supports any decision to operate only one major 24 hour emergency service for each 500,000 people or more. Such a center can offer immediate availability of high quality life support teams of all kinds and can also handle the semi or nonemergency walk-in patients between 11 P.M. and 7 A.M..

Objections come primarily from physicians who derive a significant part of their practice from the major emergencies which will seldom come to their hospital when the emergency service is down graded. Institutional pride may also be a source of objections.

Changes in Birthing

The future of midwives is unclear but hopefully traditional obstetricians will not be able to indefinitely prevent the creation of obstetrical units that will, for those who prefer it, combine the full safety of hospital back-up services with a personalized, family-based and less technical experience. Users and their supporters should not allow hospitals or physicians to inappropriately make it seem that the only choices are either home births or case room stirrups; there is a practical and attainable middle ground.

The Role of Family Physicians (FP)

In major urban hospitals this role is small and rapidly shrinking. The urban family physician without a hospital affiliation, a common but unhappy feature of the Toronto scene for many decades, has become more common and is now acceptable. Hospital surgery is done only by specialists; obstetrics, pediatrics and emergency medicine are rapidly following suit.

In rural or smaller urban communities the change is less marked although in rural Manitoba in the years from 1973 to 1978 the percentage of hysterectomies done in rural hospitals by general practitioners fell from 85% to 50%. This also is a desirable trend.

The exodus (or the banishment) of the FP from large urban hospitals is not alarming but hospitals and medical schools should give thought to how physicians who have no hospital affiliation can be attracted to relevant continuing education programs. Attendance of medical staff at hospital rounds is compulsory in the better hospitals but no penalties can be applied to someone not on staff. Medical leaders can help by refuting a 1983 quote from the Chairman of the FP section of the OMA, who described hospital activities as the "elements of medicine that have made medical practice exciting." Office practice can be both exciting and rewarding.

Issues that Appear to be Fading;

1) The question of how to operate a hospital when major staff components go on strike.
2) The contracting out of hospital management (without major financial dependency). This practice will soon be seen to be analogous to the contracting out of any other function.
3) The malpractice insurance scare. This subject will be both understood and resolved in the near future.

Summary

Hospitals have been described as the cathedrals of modern society; they are institutions of awesome power in that they are seen to be the route to eternal replacement and renewal. To be unable to enter one when the need for one is perceived to be present (by doctor, family or patient) sometimes carries the anxiety producing capability of excommunication in the middle ages. On the other hand, hospitals are also described as technocratic monsters, money consuming preservers of the medical model, and the place where one leaves one's individuality at the door and becomes a test tube with a number on it.

We hope you will subscribe to neither of these extremes. Hospitals provide important services but there are many other kinds of equally health-preserving services. There is no doubt that hospitals definitely have an insatiable appetite for resources, they are very powerful, and that they may, therefore, obtain more resources than can be justified. Limits on hospitals must be successful if resources are to be available for other activities that will produce greater social benefits per dollar. In applying restraints, however, society must remember, firstly, that hospital physicians, managers and other staff are doing only what others with power usually do -- they take all they can get. Secondly, society must realize that as restraints continue to be applied hospitals will require a great deal of help with the problems that those restraints will bring.

Chapter 14

LONG TERM CARE

INTRODUCTION

'Long term care' (LTC) and 'chronic care' cannot be precisely defined. Most people would agree that facilities such as nursing homes and chronic hospitals provide LTC, and that persons in these facilities are receiving LTC, but agreement then begins to weaken.

A person with a long term illness such as asthma, psoriasis, hypertension or diabetes, who is receiving regular and multidisciplinary services but is leading an active and normal life, is not considered to be receiving LTC. Similarly, a person with a chronic disability such as an amputated finger or foot, a moderate hearing loss, a speech impediment or absence of vision in one eye is not considered to be someone who needs LTC. Continuing care in psychiatric facilities is also not considered to be part of long term care. If, however, psychiatric patients are cared for in a nursing home, then the patients will by virtue of their location be categorized as LTC patients even if not physically disabled or dependent. It is clear that, through custom and evolution, we consider the term long term care to have a strong institutional connotation although it can be delivered in the community, and that a person is considered to be a candidate for LTC only if quite physically dependent with little or no possibility of future physical independence.

Distinctions between psychiatric and nonpsychiatric patients are unclear and changing although institutional classifications remain relatively unchanged. Persons with long term brain dysfunction arising from physical disease or injury, whether accidents, Alzheimers, or toxic agents, are increasingly likely to be cared for in LTC facilities and programs. At one time, these persons were admitted to psychiatric facilities. Persons with quite similar handicaps arising from psychiatric disorders are more likely to be cared for in the mental health services network (unless there is also major physical disability, in which case care may come from outside of the psychiatric network). Terminology has become convenient for statisticians, institutional operators and those who pay bills but is often of minimal use to planners and makes little sense to users.

It is useful to distinguish between disability and handicap while recognizing that some people use them synonymously. An amputated hand or emotional instability is a disability. A handicap is the effect of a disability, for example, handicaps associated with the loss of a hand include inability to play most musical instruments, to open a door or to be a laborer, while those associated with emotional instability restrict one's employment opportunities and endanger personal relationships. Disabilities and handicaps can be minor or major, temporary or permanent. Many disabilities, even quite severe ones, produce few if any handicaps, and sometimes the biggest handicaps flow not from the disability but from the way others see it. A paraplegic or a blind person, for instance, may not be thought to be capable of managing a job. In some instances there are major handicaps and no disability, as when a stabilized epileptic is refused employment.

Two final definitional comments may add clarity. Firstly, 'senior citizens' and 'long term care' are not synonymous. The majority of the persons receiving LTC are elderly, but the great majority of the elderly are not in LTC. The LTC network responds to dependency (handicap), usually a physical dependency, in persons of all ages. Secondly, geriatrics is that branch of medicine which treats problems peculiar to old age; gerontology is the clinical, biological, sociological and historical study of aging. Neither term will be used much in this chapter.

The Evolution of LTC in Canada

Much of the evolution of LTC merely reflects the larger events in society. Elitism, for example, has given ground to universality, and human worth now has dimensions other than productivity. Three evolutionary phases are easily described.

The first phase was characterized by social disinterest. Families cared for their disabled members as well as they could. Public assistance for the indigent portion of this unproductive population was limited to isolated and low-cost institutional warehousing. Charitable (usually religious) institutions were the only other option. In phase one the objectives of government, to the extent that it was involved through funding or by means of legislation, were to keep costs down and keep the disabled and the indigent elderly out of sight. The institutionalized persons were treated as inmates and frequently referred to as inmates.

The second phase was firmly in place by the 1960's. It brought benevolent paternalism characterized by family, professional and societal protection and dominance of 'the less fortunate.' Patronizing institutions and professionals using the medical model became surrogate parents, regardless of the mental competence of the dependent persons. The concept of second childhood became enshrined in our processes of assessment, placement and care. Professionals evaluated the patient, decided the appropriate location for care and then planned its delivery; the role of the user in decision making was minimal.

In the early stages of this period of benevolent paternalism the LTC institutions copied the hospital model through the use of regular schedules, professional control, uniformed staff, prohibition of alcohol and limited visiting. As phase 2 has matured, serious efforts have been made to make institutions more stimulating, flexible, personal and pleasant — that is, more home-like — and to recognize client individuality. Many institutional professionals and administrators and many families, however, still believe that institutionalized adults, regardless of their mental competence, need someone to make sure that they do nothing foolish. The LTC client who was earlier treated as if he or she were in kindergarten is now treated like an adolescent.

The objectives of phase 2, at least the latter part of it, could be described as: a) to protect life by providing a safe physical environment and regular (or at least available) medical supervision, by paying attention to nutrition, by encouraging exercise if possible, and by demanding compliance with professional decisions when thought necessary, and b) to improve quality of life by humanizing institutions and by offering greater opportunity for resident decision making. When the two major objectives come into conflict, the policy makers, administrators and care givers, unfortunately, still often opt for protection of life over protection of quality of life, although the trend is towards client choice.

Paternalistic phase 2 is steadily and peacefully merging into phase 3. In the third phase of LTC evolution, the dependent adult is treated as an adult rather than a child. This phase is dominated by the idea that adult status is not compromised by physical dependency. The extent to which this latest phase has arrived, how its full arrival can be hastened, and the implications of its arrival, are questions open for discussion. This chapter may, on occasion, read as if phase 3 has fully arrived, but that is just wishful thinking.

All contemporary LTC has one or more of the following goals or objectives, but never all of them:

— to prolong life and maintain health
— to improve the quality of life of the LTC recipient
— to support household care givers and protect their quality of life
— to reduce agency or program cost
— to reduce total system cost
— to reduce departmental cost
— to reduce user and household cost
— to protect acute treatment hospital beds from 'bed-blockers'
— to make a profit
— to be cost-effective compared to other sources of similar care.

Factors Affecting the Size of the LTC System

The size of the LTC system is a product of the number of people receiving care and the volume of care delivered per person.

The number of persons receiving care in the total network, or any part of it, is controlled by the same general categories of determinants that apply to all health services, that is, (a) by factors which lead the user and the system to feel that entry (admission) is appropriate, (b) by factors which determine the volume of care to be delivered and (c) by factors which affect how long the user remains in the system. Some interpretations and considerations, however, are quite specific to LTC.

As stated earlier, many of the people in LTC, especially in LTC institutions, are there for life. (Until a few years ago discharge for other than acute illness or injury was rare; now it is either common or at least not rare.) For those institutionalized persons who will not be discharged into the community, length of institutionalization is determined entirely by how long they live.

The duration of the final admission should, if admission criteria have remained constant, be lengthening, because both the physical care and the quality of life of LTC clients are improving. Because quality of life is a major determinant of length of life, the humanizing of our LTC institutions may not only be improving the quality of life of residents, it may also be decreasing the number of new admissions by lengthening the life of residents.

The entry of an individual into LTC, and the mix of services delivered, is determined (a) partly by type and degree of measurable disability/ dependency, (b) partly by societal perceptions of dependency and (c) partly by the volume of LTC resources available for purchase with private or public money. Diagnoses are almost completely irrelevant and age is of only slightly more significance. Inability to walk, feed oneself or think clearly requires approximately the same group of services whether the person in need is 25, 45, 65 or 85 years of age. Some changes in need arise from different interests in such things as education, employment, sex, marriage and children, but many needs are the same regardless of age.

PRINCIPLES THAT SHOULD GOVERN THE ORGANIZATION AND DELIVERY OF LTC

Attention to the following thirteen principles might assure the presence of a LTC network where caregivers and others truly believe that an elderly or disabled person in need should be dealt with according to the same rules as any other person with needs:

1) The place where a person gets his or her mail and is enumerated to vote should be considered his or her home; therefore, LTC services are always delivered at home.
2) The mentally competent but significantly physically dependent population has the same rights, privileges and responsibilities as the less dependent population, including the right to make decisions and choices. For example:
    a) This population should be able to use disposable income to increase the levels of or quantities of care received, to improve the nature of their accommodation, or to be catered to in whatever ways they can afford. This is already the case with respect to paying for private or semi-private institutional accommodation but the choices should and can be much broader.
    b) They should personally choose those with whom they share private living space. No person should, for prolonged periods, be forced to share his or her home or bedroom with one or more strangers whom he or she did not choose. (This practice is not considered to be desirable even in a jail.)
    c) They should be as free to opt for risk, security, comfort or sin as are the rest of us. Dependent adults should be as much in charge of their lives and lifestyle choices as the rest of us can be given our respective dependencies. Personal preferences should be honored to roughly the same extent that the rest of us have the opportunity to have our

personal preferences honored. Choice should be possible with respect to sexual activity or orientation, private consumption of alcohol, use of addicting substances, refusal to comply with professional advice, privacy, social contact, employment, travel, and how and where to spend leisure time.

In any population the extent to which personal control is possible or desired varies a great deal according to wealth, culture and experience. For some people control over only a few small items is all they expect (or want); they may be quite content with a selective menu, choosing the number of visitors they will have or the opportunity to care for a plant. This small amount of independence may fully preserve self-image. Other persons will wish for, and expect, control over finances, the nature and scheduling of services being received or other major decisions.

d) They have the same responsibility as do the rest of us to be considerate, thoughtful, respectful and positive, and to refrain from demanding or expecting more care or attention than is appropriate.

e) They have the right to a reasonable level of health care, usually without reduction in quality or quantity merely because they are elderly or disabled.

3) All adults have the right to be considered mentally competent until proven otherwise, and the determination of mental competence should rely on legal criteria, process and decisions rather than on medical ones. LTC practices and personnel frequently appear to assume mental incompetence in the elderly or the disabled when there is no evidence for the assumption; families and friends do the same. Younger or less disabled persons with no greater level of mental competence are assumed to be capable of handling more responsibility and are much more apt to be invited to make decisions.

4) Partial loss of or limited development of mental competence should not prevent client choice and control in areas in which adequate competence exists. A person may be unable to find his or her way home from shopping but may, at the same time, recognize surroundings, have a good recollection of the past and remember the financial details of his or her life.

5) Persons with even very limited cognition (perceiving, thinking, remembering) should be given adequate and respectful care. (The question of how much care to provide to persons with permanent absence of cognitive skills is an ethical issue on which current consensus is unlikely. It needs active discussion.)

6) Family and social networks represent more than a vital part of the psychosocial environment of the disabled; they are major sources of care. Preserving households and outside social contacts reduces the loss associated with disability and reduces the need for and cost of outside care.

7) Because we wish to give the disabled choices with respect to where they live, who they live with and what risks they take, it is incumbent on planners and policy makers to be certain that these choices exist if they can be made available at reasonable cost.
8) Image is important and self-image reflects social image. If society sees dependency as synonymous with inferiority, then dependent persons will see themselves as inferior. Society must, therefore, promote and support the concept of equality.
9) When the primary objective is the protection of and elevation of quality of life, an institution or care provider must allocate available resources in such a way that highest priority is given to meeting the needs (providing the services) that are seen by the consumer as most important. The number/amount of total resources assigned may not increase but the way they are assigned, or the mix that is assigned, should represent consumer rather than provider or institutional priorities.
10) Prevention is relevant to all age groups.
11) New LTC accommodation should be designed and operated as adapted housing and not as modified hospitals. Efforts should be directed towards the delivery of institutional services to special housing rather than towards the conversion of institutional rooms (or parts of rooms) into homes.
12) Society has the right to decide what volume of resources will be made available at public expense to a particular group of persons or to any one person. Being physically dependent should not markedly reduce one's mental independence but it also should not allow the user to demand residential or other options that are deemed by society to be unnecessary or overly extravagant.

    In long term care, as in all other fields of social expenditure, society will not necessarily decide that all needs or wants or demands should or can be met. Social decisions can quite legitimately be based on consideration of cost as well as matters of ethics, culture or perceived relative need.
13) Persons requiring long term support should be able to exercise significant control over how they choose to use whatever resources society chooses to assign to them. This is the principle within which some other social support programs now operate, to at least some extent; our financial support systems, our ambulatory health system and our educational systems are examples.

Besides the above principles that should govern the planning and delivery of care, there are at least two different perceptions within which we can plan and provide LTC. One of these leads to the proposition that regardless of the extent to which noninstitutional options are improved, there will always be a large number of persons, including many mentally competent persons, who must be housed in institutions. This assumption underlies our continued construction of LTC facilities. Another concept, significantly different from the first, proposes that LTC services of virtually any degree of complexity and volume can be delivered to people living in personal rather than institutional accommodation. The only significant proviso associated with the second concept is that, for some clientele, this personal accommodation may need to be specially constructed if adequate service is to be provided at acceptable cost.

Deciding which concept is correct is fortunately quite simple. Endless experiences and examples have shown that the immobile, the incontinent, the visually impaired, those who need respiratory assistance, those who cannot feed or dress themselves, and those who are frail, medically unstable or in need of regular injections or dressings or other procedures, can all be cared for either in institutions or outside of them. The assumption that institutionalization is the only credible option in the face of major physical dependency is, therefore, invalid.

Not all persons seeking to help the elderly have put forward principles similar to those just proposed. A White House Conference on Aging in the early 1980's, for example, adopted the following set of rights for the elderly:

"To have self-esteem in an agist and sexist society.

To have adequate economic support to cover needs for food, shelter, clothes and health care.

To have adequate health care and to be treated with respect, as an individual whose life is valuable, by sensitive health care providers.

To have access to honest legal and financial advice and consumer protection.

To have a positive representation in the media.

To be free from fear of crime, isolation, poverty and abandonment.

To be seen as a unique individual who is productive, attractive, intelligent and interesting.

To express sexuality in whatever manner is preferred.

To be free from society's stigma of incompleteness which is applied to a woman who is alone.

To have employment opportunities when work is wanted, and to receive fair wages.

To have worthwhile volunteer opportunities available.

To choose alternate life styles and living arrangements.

To maintain optimum control over one's life and possessions.

To be given the opportunity to continue to grow intellectually, spiritually and socially.

To avoid dependence on others, to speak for oneself, and to learn to serve oneself."

The principles in this list are of importance to all persons, not just the elderly or the disabled. To write rules such as these merely strengthens the incorrect supposition that the rights and responsibilities of the elderly (and the disabled) are fundamentally different from those of the rest of the population. The acceptance of the elderly as a 'normal' part of the population is best accomplished by acceptance of the general proposal that the disabled have the same rights and responsibilities as the less disabled and that age does not alter those rights and responsibilities.

THE ELDERLY AND THE FUTURE ELDERLY

Because most dependent persons are elderly, and because planners and society are inordinately preoccupied with the aging of the population, the elderly will be looked at as a population before looking at the dependent population of all ages.

In 1986, approximately 11% of Canadians (2.7 million) were 65 years of age or older. If projected life expectancies, fertility rates and immigration volumes materialize this percentage will increase over the next 40-50 years to 22-25%. Our population is aging partly because people are living longer but mostly because our fertility and birth rates since about 1970 have been low and our immigration volumes also low, whereas in 1950-70 both our birth rate and immigration rates were quite high. Beyond 2035-2040, the elderly as a percentage of the total population will, unless predictions are in error, fall to current European levels of 15-19%.

Until 1972 or 1973 there had always been more males than females in the total Canadian population but long before then females had dominated the older age groups (see Table 14.1). Projections suggest that in 35-40 years there will be 3 females for every male among 80 year olds.

Life expectancy at birth is now about 72 years for males and 78 years for females. The gap between the sexes steadily widened after female life expectancy passed that of males early in the twentieth century but in 1984 and 1985 the gap remained relatively constant. Perhaps changes in female lifestyles (using tobacco more, taking on male occupations) or an improvement in male lifestyles (less smoking) are at work.

The fact that females live longer than males partly explains why there are more widows than widowers (part of the explanation also lies in the fact that husbands tend to be older than wives) but does not directly or fully explain why there are more females in LTC. The major cause of this is the fact that females not only live longer but they also have, on average, twice as many years of major dependency, a difference that is apparently more sex related than age related.

Table 14.1
Number of Females per 100 Males by Age Group 1971 and 1981

	80 & over	65-79	50-64	all ages
1971	143	118	103	99
1981	185	124	106	102

Source: Derived from data from Statistics Canada, Census data 1971 and 1981

One very impressive feature of our elderly population is not that 4% (at age 65) or 35% (at age 85) are in institutions, but that 96% (at age 65) and 65% (at age 85) are not. Aging does not lead to automatic dependency, as is sometimes portrayed. It is, however, commonly associated with certain changes:

a) Senses deteriorate (sight, smell, touch, adaptation to dark).
b) Reflexes are slower.
c) Vital organ functions become less adequate.
d) Recovery time is slower.
e) Height goes down, posture changes, joints deteriorate.
f) Wrinkles and grey hair appear and there is less subcutaneous fat.

There are a number of other perceptions of aging that are, however, myth rather than fact:

a) That old age is a disease.
b) That all elderly people suffer the 'regular' bad effects of aging.
c) That the elderly cannot be creative or innovative.
d) That sexual interests disappear.
e) That memory and other mental abilities become automatically poorer.
f) That the elderly cannot do a day's work.
g) That the elderly cannot learn new skills or change their values.
h) That old age brings tranquility.
i) That there is usually fear of death.

Various authors have shown that judgement, vocabulary, comprehension, problem solving skills and concentration can increase up to a very advanced age.

Will Our Aging Population Overwhelm Us?

Many experts speak of a crisis, of national bankruptcy, of pension plan bankruptcy, of no institutional space for acute care, of thousands of LTC beds needed, and of doddering elderly everywhere with no one to care for them. These predictions are so widespread and so often overstated that the assumptions on which they are founded need to be examined.

Certainly the population is aging. Barring some major global catastrophe, a surge in birth rates, or massive immigration, the number of older people in Canada will almost certainly increase in both an absolute and a relative sense until 45-60 years from now, at which point both absolute and relative numbers are likely to fall. What will be the effects of this steady increase in the number of elderly over the next 3-5 decades, and how should we prepare for those effects?

Dependency ratios are a common basis for propositions that we will be short of caregivers and unable to afford the burden of an enlarged elderly population. The most commonly used dependency ratio refers to the ratio of workers (20-64 or 18-64) to nonworkers (0-19 or 0-17 plus those 65 years and older).

In 1901 there were 99 dependent children (0-19) and older persons (65 and over) for every 100 persons in the working ages (20-64) in Canada. Ten of the 99 were older persons and 89 were 0-19 years of age. By 1981 these figures were 16 and 56 respectively for a total of 72, and in 2031, the year with the highest projected dependent population, the estimate is that the figures will be 33 elderly and 47 children for a total of 80. Dependency ratios, if they mean anything of consequence (and they do not) do not present a frightening picture. As currently calculated, they should be ignored. They understate the size of the dependent population by ignoring (a) the 1-2% of those 18-65 who are permanently incapacitated and dependent, (b) the 1-2% of those 18-65 who are in school, (c) the 8-12% of the workforce (6-8% of those 18-65) who are unemployed and (d) others such as single parents who are on welfare or other social assistance. The dependent population is overstated primarily by assuming that all those 65 and over are dependent. Five to ten percent of this population are working and many others are living primarily on savings and pensions accumulated during their working years. In addition, many of those over 65 who are not working are fully able to work. If Canada reaches the point where workers are needed and/or we merely want to make the dependency ratio look better we can gradually change the entry age of the 'elderly.' In association with a change in the age at which one becomes elderly, we could change the point of onset of the automatic old age pension; there could be a phased extension to age 70, and we could encourage the 65-69 age group to remain at work if workers are needed.

More sophisticated calculations incorporating all or various dependent and independent populations could be made to allow us to more rationally discuss dependency ratios of the future. Unfortunately, two other factors make such calculations rather academic. We do not fully understand the probable impact of technological change, but it will surely eliminate many jobs, which may worsen the dependency ratios more rapidly than the aging population, and we do not know how much will be spent on war or on preparation for it.

Conclusion #1: Dependency ratios as presently calculated are of no value.

Will our pension plans and the national economy be able to tolerate the costs of an aging population? This question is more difficult to dispose of, but it is worth noting that other countries have coped with high numbers of the elderly for many years.

England and Wales	15.1% (1980)
France	13.5% (1982)
Sweden	16.3% (1980)
United States	11.3% (1980)
All developed countries	11.1% (1980)
The world	5.8% (1980)

Many industrialized countries have successfully sustained old age income maintenance programs while remaining competitive, and many countries have much higher payroll deductions for pensions than we have.

Conclusion #2: We should be able to meet manpower needs arising from the incapacities of an aging population without great difficulty.

Conclusion #3: We can still adequately fund our future income supplement programs if we increase our Canada and Québec Pension Plan deductions, but the rate of increase must be greater than the miniscule changes put in place in 1986.

What about the proposals that we will need to build hundreds of LTC beds per year for the next 50 years, or that the onslaught of the elderly will completely fill our acute care beds? The former contention is easier to deal with than the latter. Our predicted LTC institutional needs become unreasonable when we note that Britain, Denmark and others have only 50-70% as many LTC beds per 1000 people over 65 as we have, that a variety of Canadian governments and regional planning agencies are committed to controlling institutionalization, and that there are excellent alternatives to institutions that are cheaper and more suited to the LTC objectives and philosophies of today.

Conclusion #4. If we used LTC institutions as sparingly as other countries, our current supply could be adequate until our elderly population reached 15-18% of the total population, around the year 2010. If we keep building at our present rate we may, by the year 2000, have enough LTC beds to last until 2035, after which we may have empty beds as the percentage of elderly falls.

The question of the impact of the elderly on acute care facilities is one on which this chapter has elected to reach no conclusions. The impact will vary immensely with our expectations and our ethics as well as with more objectively measurable factors.

USERS OF LTC WHO ARE PHYSICALLY DEPENDENT BUT MENTALLY COMPETENT

The prevalence of major physical dependency increases with age but there is a physically dependent population in all age groups. Physically dependent persons who are mentally competent are, in many respects, similar to the remainder of the population, that is:

1) They have varied lifestyles, personalities, expectations, likes, dislikes and prejudices. They are not homogeneous. Systems designed to serve them, therefore, need to be pluralistic rather than monolithic, and within the limitations of practical constraints each person in need should be able to have his or her needs met in a way that is consistent with his/her values and preferences.

   Elderly or disabled persons are likely to be fundamentally the same as before they were elderly or disabled. They are not apt to be fundamentally different in terms of emotional independence, emotional stability, intelligence, interests, vigor (laziness), reliability, work habits, life styles, values or personality.
2) The majority of them are living at home.
3) Maslow's hierarchy of needs is valid. Some attention must be given to food, shelter and safety before giving attention to such things as the need for affection, self-esteem, human contact and peer approval.
4) All people need emotional support; without it we all, sooner or later, feel alone, depressed and forgotten. We all have our own special fears, our own special interests and our own special memories, and we all need the feeling that there are a few special activities or things that are just for us.

The dependent are the same as the rest of us in this respect, and, therefore, if their quality of life is to be reasonably good we must acknowledge their wishes for their own life styles, their own rules, their own worlds.

5) The health and social needs of women differ from those of men.
6) There are varying degrees of need and want for emotional support, social contact, privacy and the opportunity to be productive or useful.
7) Different people have quite different perceptions of what is most important for a good quality of life.
8) They exhibit the same mix of medical problems although in the dependent population there are more diagnoses per patient. The need for LTC is based, however, in the number of services needed, not in the number of diagnoses that can be listed.
9) Almost everyone has an address and, therefore, a home.
10) Almost everyone has his or her own relatively unique network of family, friends, confidantes and advisors.

However, this physically dependent but mentally competent population is, in other ways, quite different from the less physically dependent population:

1) They are more dependent, a self evident but fundamental point. They need more support and help; they never had, or have lost, the degree of independence that most of us have and they need services that the rest of the population does not need.
2) Because they are more dependent, they are more vulnerable. They are easier to coerce, constrain, exploit or abuse. They know that as problems increase in size and complexity there will be increasing need for assistance with such things as income, housing and transportation. In such a situation of need it is difficult to resist advice or instruction from family, friends or professionals even when one does not like it. All who are in a position to give such advice or instruction should be aware of the need to encourage the disabled to make their own decisions if they wish to.
3) They are older (covered earlier).
4) They respond differently to illness and injury:
   a) Recovery time is much longer. The termination of an acute illness is often not followed quickly by a return to the former level of activity or capability. Even short periods of inactivity can produce long term sequelae.
   b) Acute illness or new disability is frequently masked by the chronic disabilities or illness.
   c) They are frequently slow to report illness or change in status. Regular screening or continued surveillance of high-risk populations can, therefore, be of great importance.
5) The disabled, especially the elderly disabled, sometimes adapt poorly to new environments and may be confused by them. Relocation, or major changes in the living environment, should therefore be accompanied by appropriate resident involvement, information and comment where appropriate. Handled correctly, the change may become a positive event.

6) They tend to have multiple diagnoses and disabilities; assessments must, therefore, be thorough.
7) Social and economic services are increasingly important to independence; in a relative sense health services, therefore, become less important.

The Effects of Dependency

A chapter on LTC is basically a discussion of social response to physical deterioration with or without associated reduction in mental competence. To improve the LTC service network, one must understand the effects of dependency.

Dependency is a very relative thing. All of us have many disabilities and handicaps but, because they are the norm, we adapt ourselves and our environment and do not notice our dependency. For example, we heat our homes and use rear view mirrors. In LTC, we are concerned with those individuals who have a disability that requires special kinds of personal or environmental adaptation and who require special types of external support. We are not concerned with that large group of people who have chronic illnesses or disabilities that are not seriously interfering with one of the basic areas of activity such as work, school or the activities of daily living.

These persons with dependencies greater than usual have no common characteristics except their dependence on us. They are a mix of all ages, sexes, religions and cultures, they have all levels of intelligence and education and they come from all socioeconomic classes and all occupations. They have adapted to their disabilities with varying success, and they get their support through a variety of organizations and ministries. Some are moribund and/or terminally ill while some go to work every day and will for years.

In general terms, one can divide the LTC clients into the physically handicapped, the socially/emotionally handicapped and the developmentally handicapped. This chapter gives special attention to the physically disabled because the socially/emotionally disabled are given special attention in the chapter on mental health services and the developmentally handicapped are not primarily clients of the health system.

Within the physically dependent population, there are those who require agents (children and the mentally incompetent adults) and those who can be their own agents (the mentally competent). Between these two groups, and very differently identified by different people, are the large group of semicompetent persons whose need for agents may vary from situation to situation. The physically dependent can also be categorized by whether their functional loss interferes with mobility, vision, hearing, feeding, dressing, toiletting and/or balance, by their diagnosis (multiple sclerosis, muscular dystrophy, cerebral palsy, cancer, trauma, Alzheimers disease, alcoholic neuropathy) and by demographic characteristics such as age and sex.

Loss of independence deprives the involved person of opportunities the rest of us take for granted. Loss of independence is, in itself, a stressful event, and all who deal with dependent persons and their families should be careful not to add to the stress. There should usually be special tolerance of actions triggered by frustration and disappointment.

Chronic severe dependency introduces a new way of life. It dictates new life styles. It means regular, often unsatisfying, involvement with a mix of health workers and programs. It requires new behaviors, new attitudes and new expectations. It may mean partial or complete loss of the people, activities and personal capabilities most highly prized. Consider the tragedy of being cut off from family and friends, many of whom have died, and having few conversations with those who share your memories; being surrounded by strangers; having poor hearing and/or eyesight and, therefore, not being able to fully enjoy the radio, TV, books and newspapers; not being able to do the little things you loved such as bird watching, playing with children, being sexy, cooking, gardening; having people lose interest in you; having to put up with things you detest; giving up your personal belongings and your privacy; being treated like a 6 year old when your brain is still working well.

In the face of the limitations imposed on the dependent person three things determine how well the individual will adapt or survive; these are his or her inherent ego strength, the severity and duration of the stress and the support system available. The LTC services network can do almost nothing regarding the first, can affect the second, and is largely responsible for the third.

Long term dependency by definition means a loss of some independence; it means loss of control over some parts of one's life. Paternalism by definition places limits on the range of decision making of the child or anyone treated like a child. When paternalistic attitudes and practices are imposed on physically or psychiatrically disabled and dependent persons who have a significant degree of mental competence, these persons are forced to deal with a double threat to their sense of control.

Power and Quality of Life

Power is vital to all people. Everyone wishes to control something. How much control is expected, and over how many things, varies immensely from person to person. The required sense of power/control can, for some people, be centered in what appears to others to be quite trivial events, opportunities or objects. Words such as status, prestige, and self-image are central to the concept of power and how each person preserves his or her self-image or status is usually fully known only to him or her.

Prolonged loss of power, especially if the loss is seen by the client as permanent, produces anxieties, insecurity and depression, which, if sustained, will lead to confusion and serious mental deterioration. LTC administrators and caregivers must, if they value the quality of life of their clients, develop attitudes, skills and practices which decrease the client's sense of powerlessness, in particular the feelings of powerlessness arising from:

1) Loss of control over self or environment.

2) Lack of understanding of what is happening and of the future.
3) Loss of abilities and income.
4) Loss of social contacts.
5) Controls and barriers set up by administration such as imposed schedules and routines which cannot be overcome.

When assertiveness fails and optimism goes, the next state is apt to be aggressiveness and depression. Restoration of control can be in the intellectual, emotional or physical domain. Several strategies are available:

a) Involve the user in decision making and respect her or his choices whenever the making of those choices is consistent with individual rights.
b) Provide information. Knowledge is more likely to increase than decrease security.
c) Create trust that preferences and choices will be accepted without retaliation or ostracism. Remember that the dependent are vulnerable and are not likely to exercise control if they sense that the family or caregiver also wants control.
d) Help families and staff to acquire the skills and attitudes that will allow the dependent person to have control.
e) Modify the environment. Remove physical barriers and provide devices to allow performance of tasks without outside help.
f) Help the individual to set attainable goals.

In offering people the opportunity to exercise control, that is, to have power, it must be remembered that how much control a person chooses to exercise is for him/her to decide, and some people do not wish to make many decisions. New opportunities for control may also, at times, lead to behavior which is considered unacceptable or undesirable. This result is most likely to occur when control has been absent for a long time (as is the case after long term institutionalization) or is thought not to be sincerely offered (when the user may be testing the system).

THE MENTALLY INCOMPETENT USERS OF LTC

Earlier in this chapter institutional care has been described as an unnecessary and undesirable interference with the rights and life of mentally competent but physically dependent adults unless being institutionalized is their preference. There are unfortunately a growing number of adults who are permanently unable to exercise choice.

Classification of this mentally incompetent population is hazardous but it can be described as a mix of the severely brain damaged, the severely mentally retarded, the severely psychiatrically disabled and those with advanced dementia. The brain damaged include accident victims (mostly injured in motor vehicle accidents), victims of prolonged anoxia (as after cardiac arrest), some post-stroke patients and severe organic brain syndrome patients (often the sequelae of chronic alcoholism).

The moderately or severely demented are mostly persons with Alzheimers disease. In early decades many were housed in chronic psychiatric facilities but most are now either in LTC facilities or being cared for at home. There is considerable disagreement regarding the extent to which home care, day care and other services can allow this severely cognitively impaired population to stay at home. The wishes, capabilities and emotional survival of the family caregivers deserve major consideration when creating care plans. Caring for a severely brain damaged individual has been described as a living funeral. The caregivers often receive no emotional rewards for their emotionally exhausting services.

Many LTC facilities do not accept demented individuals, especially if the dementia is accompanied by aggression, noise or other unacceptable intrusion into the lives of other residents. Segregation of the seriously disruptive is recommended, although there is disagreement with regard to the degree of disorientation and disruption that merits segregation.

Staff who care for the severely cognitively impaired are subject to burnout with associated insensitivity, depression, absenteeism and transfer. They need access to counselling, education and periods of relief. They benefit from knowledgeable and interested senior administrators, and criticism should be tempered with appreciation and by awareness of the difficulty of their jobs. It is difficult to be eternally patient, kind and loving to individuals who either do not respond or who respond with anger or abuse.

There is much written about the benefits to the demented of freedom to move about and to be outside in pleasant surroundings. Reality therapy or other behavior modification therapies can be helpful and there is a need for humane and rehabilitative surroundings. All of these are desirable but all are sharply limited in their effects. This population must be worked with to be understood. Cost-effectiveness questions will be difficult to answer.

The mobile brain damaged may progress to immobility and vegetation. In an age of scarce resources, society needs to seriously and calmly search for a definition of life as well as death. How many unresponsive adults should be diapered, tube fed, regularly turned and routinely medically treated, and for how many months or years should such treatment be offered?

LONG TERM CARE SERVICES

We have discussed the philosophy within which LTC should be delivered and the characteristics of those who will be served. This section will look at the services that are usually offered in Canada and some of the options that are available.

LTC services and their delivery are fundamentally different from acute care. Acute (short term) care can usually concentrate on diagnosis, therapy and rehabilitation while chronic care should always give major attention to long term preservation of the quality of life of the individual. Chronic care is always delivered in a person's home, even when that person is living in one of the beds in a public ward in a LTC institution. Chronic care can be immensely supported by and delivered by friends, family and strangers, and most neighborhoods have these sources of care. Bureaucratic and professionally dominated systems should seek to use and sustain, rather than exclude, this massive potential source of help and human warmth which is of much less importance during episodes of acute care.

LTC is obviously more sustained than acute (short term) care. Everyone would agree that a few weeks of illness or of recovery from injury usually would be and should be cared for within the acute care system. There would also be agreement that multidisciplinary care over a number of years to a permanently, significantly, physically dependent person is LTC; but the grey area between these two examples is large. It is, of course, common for patients to intermittently receive care in the acute care facilities and programs while more permanently receiving LTC.

Society appears to have responded to the needs of the dependent of all ages through a cycle in which economic assistance was provided first, health care and housing were offered next and individualized quality of care items such as recreation, independence (autonomy) and leisure-time opportunities were made available last. This sequence exemplifies the breadth of the network that serves our dependent friends.

Income Maintenance

There is minimal direct financial assistance routinely available to families caring for children requiring LTC, but low-income, permanently dependent adults qualify for disability-based support payments usually financed and administered by a provincial government. Special groups such as pensioned war veterans or persons injured at work have other income. Elderly persons, including the disabled (dependent) elderly, have a number of potential federal, provincial and private sources of income. Private pension payments are available primarily to persons who had stable employment with an employer who had an associated private pension plan. A variety of devices are also available to the elderly to protect their incomes including reduced travel fares, extra income tax deductions, reduced recreation and entertainment admission fees, special shopping discounts, reduced tuition fees, municipal tax exemptions and home maintenance or renovation assistance.

Many of the elderly are poor, but because of the increasing availability of CPP or QPP and private pension incomes the percentage of the elderly who qualify for the means-tested pension supplements has fallen from 55% in 1976 to 50% in 1983. This fall is a direct effect of the appearance in the last 30 years of both governmental and private (usually employment related) pension plans.

Although age 65 should be of no importance in itself, it has acquired significance by virtue of its selection as the age at which retirement occurs and private and public pension payments usually begin. Its relevance here is that income maintenance has an important bearing on the need for LTC.

Transportation

Most larger urban communities and some individual facilities and programs now have special buses or bus systems to respond to the local transportation needs of the transportation handicapped. Costs per passenger are 4-10 times those of regular transit systems and service is usually less developed.

Recreation and Social Activities

Most of these services are offered by churches and other private nonprofit agencies but municipalities increasingly offer special recreation programs through public facilities. Unfortunately, many private facilities, including churches, are not very accessible to the mobility impaired. Recreation and social functions are also within the scope of day care centers, day hospitals and senior citizen centers.

Residential Options

Only major categories are listed. Terminology is a problem. All types of LTC institutions are considered to be residential options.

LTC institutions include chronic hospitals (which include auxiliary hospitals, chronic care units in acute treatment hospitals, and palliative care units), and intermediate care facilities such as nursing homes and homes for special care, homes for the aged, hospices and geriatric assessment units. Other residential (domiciliary) options include boarding homes, hostels, half-way houses, group homes, foster homes and sheltered housing.

Long term care institutions are not usually thought of as residences but they should be. The *Ontario Nursing Homes Act* contains the phrase,". . . a nursing home is primarily the home of its residents. . ." Despite this acknowledgement, the resident is admitted (as to a hospital), is obliged to ask others for permission to go out for an evening or weekend (as in a jail), may be charged exorbitant fees for a private room (without the protection of rent control), may live in a multibed room with strangers (as in the army), has no lock on the door and no right to restrict staff entry (as in a hospital), and cannot usually be in charge of his or her own medication regardless of mental competency. There are usually few things that will remind the resident that he or she is 'at home.'

The *Ontario Nursing Homes Act* also states that residents must be consulted on and involved in the planning of any program affecting their lifestyles, a strange burden for the nursing home administration to bear considering that the *Act* itself demands regular and continuous actions that affect lifestyle but over which neither the resident nor the nursing homes have any control. The *Act* even has the gall to include a patients' Bill of Rights dealing with such things as privacy and freedom to associate, things that the institutional environment and the operating regulations have already almost destroyed.

Community LTC services can be categorized in many ways. Our choice is arbitrary:

1) Services delivered to an individual at home. These may be provided by agencies able to deliver a broad spectrum of multidisciplinary services or by agencies which specialize in only one type of assistance such as homemaking, public health nursing, meals on wheels, telephone

monitoring or emergency reporting systems. Agencies may deliver care to many types of users or may be user-specific as with palliative care.

2) Services outside the home. These include legal aid, wheels to meals, social centers, respite (vacation) care, sheltered workshops, day care and day hospitals.

Among the community LTC services, only day care, day hospitals, palliative care and placement coordination services have been selected for specific comment.

Day Care and Day Hospitals (Geriatric Day Care and Geriatric Day Hospitals)

These two programs are discussed together because their separation may be more clear in theory than practice. Both programs receive clients 1-5 days a week (usually 2-3 days a week) for 5-6 hours a day. The day hospitals offer a more extensive range of professional services (physicians, nurses, PT, OT, SW and perhaps others), give greater emphasis to rehabilitation and are twice as expensive per day ($60-80 vs $30-40). All usually provide a noon meal; they may or may not provide transportation.

The line between clients who significantly benefit from regular professional evaluation and therapy and those who require only social and recreational services and/or nonprofessional supervision is unclear. It seems likely that day hospitals regularly provide more expensive care than is appropriate.

Palliative Care (PC)

PC is more an attitude and a philosophy than a single program or institution. PC programs arose because of the inability or unwillingness of caregivers and health care institutions to respond appropriately to the needs of the terminally ill.

The ideal palliative care program is both community based and institutionally based. The institutions may be part of the acute care or LTC network or they may be special purpose free-standing palliative care institutions usually called hospices, but whatever the form of the institution, the PC team should be able to follow the patient into the community as well as be involved in institutional care.

PC in hospitals is sometimes delivered by teams who go to the patients on any ward and is sometimes delivered on wards used only for the terminally ill. Some PC programs use the same personnel to provide support at home and in hospital, an attractive arrangement. Most programs deal primarily with persons dying with cancer and a few deal exclusively with cancer patients. Most PC patients are persons whose death will be painful and/or whose death is considered untimely. The PC services respond to the stress suffered by the family as well as by the patient and some programs stay in touch with families during the period after their family loss.

PC is not cheap and is not promoted as being a means of reducing cost. Investigative, surgical and therapeutic costs tend to be significantly lower, as is hospital use, but total nursing and social service costs rise. The objective is to replace technological and cure oriented personnel with a calm, caring and supportive team who help the patient and family to deal with death and its associated stress.

The palliative care and modern hospice concepts are usually credited to Dr. Cecily Saunders in England who was a pioneer in the field. In the past decade the movement has expanded quickly in Canada. In 1987, the Palliative Care Foundation of Canada, (established in 1981), reported that about 300 PC programs were operating across the country; 42% were entirely hospital based, 24% were operating only in the community and 34% operated both in the hospital and in the community.

Despite the increase in the number of programs, they serve less than 5% of all dying patients and perhaps 10% of patients dying with cancer.

Assessment and Placement Services

The use of regionally or provincially standardized assessment practices is necessary if selection of the volume and the types of care that should be delivered to each LTC patient at public expense is to be equitable. Common assessment forms and personnel reduce the likelihood of institutional or practitioner manipulation of who is eligible for various levels of publicly financed services. They also reduce the ability of institutions to manipulate in the interest of getting long stay patients out of acute care beds.

Central control, or at least influence, over placement (a term which smacks of veterinary medicine rather than a patient-centered process) is crucial if the needs of patients, as seen by them, are to be reasonably matched with the capabilities of various programs and institutions and if individuals in the community and in acute care hospitals are to have relatively equal access to all LTC spaces. It reduces the likelihood that there will be informal arrangements between LTC and acute care facilities, arrangements designed to serve the institutions rather than the individuals involved. Central assessment and placement can also assure consideration of utilization of noninstitutional options when possible, although many regional agencies have been undesirably institutionally oriented. Standardized procedures should be designed to provide ample opportunity for users to examine placement and treatment options and decide which they prefer.

The Role of Acute Treatment Hospitals in LTC

Acute treatment hospitals will continue to have a major role in the provision of LTC. A number of years ago, Québec hospitals were told to designate 10% of acute beds as chronic beds and to make the necessary program adaptations. In Ontario, available LTC beds in chronic hospitals, NHs and homes for the aged are given first to qualified applicants living in the community. Those receiving care in another institution are admitted next. This policy assures people at home that they will be admitted reasonably quickly if conditions worsen; it is hoped that this assurance will encourage dependent persons to stay in the community as long as possible. Acute treatment hospitals should accept their responsibility for the care of many LTC patients and should develop special programs for them.

Foster Homes, Home Sharing and Granny Flats

These are not designed for persons with significant degrees of dependency. Each is attractive to some persons and households.

Foster homes usually offer room and board and minimal if any personal care or supervision. It is quite reasonable, however, for foster homes to care for individuals with more severe dependency. Payment should vary with the level of care required.

Home sharing matches the homeless with persons who have extra space. It can offer advantages to both parties in the form of income, social contact or assistance of many kinds.

Granny flats, small mobile residences in the yards of family caregivers, have a new name but are not new in concept. The older generation in rural societies has, for years, shared a yard with younger generations. The biggest hazards to this program are bureaucrats who write unreasonably complex rules and who demand unreasonable standards, and neighborhoods which are more concerned about property values or street esthetics than about helping families support and be close to elderly or dependent members who wish a home of their own.

Sheltered Housing

This term refers to a variety of architectural and service arrangements in which a number of domiciliary units are supported by on-site staff. The support staff can be limited to a live-in 'warden' (the British term) offering only basic assistance, or it can consist of three shifts of full-time workers able to offer levels of care comparable to those available in LTC facilities. As many as 5% of the elderly in the United Kingdom live in sheltered housing.

In Canada, this arrangement is routinely available only for the young physically disabled. Quadriplegics in special housing may require up to six hours of personal care a day. This care may include being turned through the night, being helped in and out of bed, being dressed for school or work, being fed and the equivalent. This need for a large volume of care does not prevent the disabled from being tenants in the fullest sense rather than institutional residents. The care is delivered as home care rather than as institutional care and costs compare favorably. This model merits major consideration as another residential option for the disabled elderly.

Services with the Primary Objectives of Prolonging Life and Maintaining Physical Health

Prolonging life has often been considered the prime objective of LTC. Compassion and client involvement in decision making become expendable in the face of the fear that clients might, for example, fall and be hurt.

Most LTC services at least indirectly protect life or maintain physical health, but a few of these services have no other primary objective. Some disabled, for example, now carry devices through which they can call for assistance if it is needed. Others live in apartments with communication or alarm mechanisms that will, in an emergency, alert neighbours or staff who will then visit. Programs such as Postal Alert or those offering a daily telephone call are designed to prevent prolonged failure to get help. The telephone monitoring services are usually conducted by the elderly themselves, sometimes by residents in LTC institutions.

Services with the Primary Objective of Protection and Elevation of Quality of Life

Having a decent home and enough money to remain there comfortably and safely are probably more important to most people than a comprehensive network of community-based health and social services, but as dependency increases the latter eventually are needed. One cannot predict which programs and services will protect or elevate quality of life for a specific person, but this objective is usually thought to be served by those things that allow people to stay in their own homes if they wish, that help to preserve households, and that encourage user decision making with respect to such things as accommodation, privacy and social activities.

The protection of quality of life is not assured by the mere availability of a full range of services. It also requires planners who vigorously seek to provide viable choices (without viable choices no one has any significant degree of control), and caregivers and advisors (professionals, family members and friends) who will sincerely support whatever option the client chooses. The concept of viable options can refer to levels of privacy, volumes of social contact or physical activity, types of recreation or entertainment, degrees of decision making or degrees of risk or safety, among other things.

Services which can make it Possible for a User to Remain at Home

These services fall into four main categories.

1) Services which make the physical environment more tolerable or manageable:
   a) Home maintenance activities such as the removal and installation of storm windows.
   b) Home adaptations such as the installation of ramps, grab bars in the bathroom or better lighting.
   c) Improved security and emergency alarm systems. These were listed earlier as services that protect life but for that part of the population for whom a feeling of security/safety is essential to peace of mind, these services also improve quality of life and eliminate one of the reasons for leaving one's own home.
2) Services which provide basic householder functions:
   a) Meals on wheels. These services, most of which are run by voluntary organizations, usually pick up meals from a hospital or LTC facility and sell them at cost to persons unable to prepare meals. There is

usually one delivery per day, five days a week, of a hot lunch and cold supper. Drivers are often volunteers.

b) Wheels to meals. Drivers, once again usually volunteers, deliver isolated individuals to central dining locations. This service provides social opportunities as well as nutritional support.

c) Homemaker services. This service provides assistance with cooking, cleaning, laundry, and perhaps some counselling and socializing. Homemakers are available with or without public subsidy and subsidy, when available, may be with or without means testing. The homemakers may have almost no training or be graduates from 3-6 month homemaking courses. The services are available from profit and nonprofit agencies although the great majority are provided by staff of nonprofit agencies.

3) Services which deliver personal care such as assistance with bathing, toiletting or transferring. These services are usually delivered by semiskilled personnel.

4) Professional services. These services are offered through several administrative arrangements and several kinds of personnel:

a) Nurse visits to the home. Most programs limit attendance to 1-2 visits per day maximum and 1-3 visits per week as an average, although for palliative care or short term problems more frequent visits may be available.

b) Home visits by physicians, physiotherapists, speech therapists, nutritionists, clinical nurse specialists, and other professionals. Physicians' home visits appear to be more appreciated than needed. Their availability, or lack of availability, does not appear to be a factor in whether or not patients stay in their own homes versus being admitted to an institution. Physician visits are most likely to be needed for prescribing medication, giving advice, assessing the patient, carrying out procedures or doing counselling.

c) In some provinces, certain senior citizen buildings have an in-house medical office with regular attendance of a variety of health care professionals but with the P.H.N. being the central caregiver. Office and apartment visits are available during normal working hours.

d) 24 hour staff adjacent to disabled persons in private residential units. This variation on home care is not called home care. It is provided through several different noninstitutional models in which the residents are tenants rather than 'admitted' patients. The apartments and group homes may be owned and operated for profit or they may be nonprofit. There may or may not be a central dining room. They may or may not accept disabled persons with families. The staff may be all nonprofessional or a mix of professional and nonprofessional. Costs vary with the extent to which services are provided. When the residents pay all costs the rent and services may cost $2000 per month or more for a very modest level of assistance.

Services which Preserve Households

When a household requires levels or types of care that cannot be delivered through existing programs or by other members of the household the person in need will either not get the care or will lose the pleasures of staying with friends and/or family. Of the service arrangements listed earlier, only the option of 24 hour immediate availability of adequate volumes and types of care, delivered to residential units of the needed size, can preserve households in the face of almost all situations of dependency. Other arrangements can meet intermediate levels of dependency.

In speaking of the preservation of households one must remember that the dependent person is only one of the individuals to be considered. Other household members also face financial, career and personal challenges and the LTC network must consciously identify and work to meet these challenges if the household is to be preserved and the quality of life of all household members protected. Additional stress may be placed on women (as traditional caregivers) if they also work outside the home.

Stress to the household caregiver(s) arises from the dependent person's wandering, aggression and incontinence, from the additional expense, from the destruction of the quality of the caregiver's personal life, from the inability to obtain short term relief and from fear of injury or illness. Supporting the household caregivers would seem to be logical both to reduce these stresses and in the interest of cost control through continued involvement of no-cost providers. Unfortunately the system has, in the past, often failed to welcome or to support family caregivers. Fifteen years ago in Ontario, a family with a developmentally handicapped or autistic child, for example, either provided care without system support or admitted the child to an institution. The caregivers were isolated and exploited. In recent years several devices have been used to support household caregivers:

1) Financial aid.
   a) In British Columbia, funds are provided by government to families who care for their severely retarded children at home. The amount to be paid is determined by a voluntary agency (The Living Society) acting as an assessor, counsellor and quality control vehicle (within Ministry guidelines). Financial aid can be used to hire help, to enable the family caregiver to stay at home or to meet various direct and indirect costs such as drugs, equipment and laundry.
   b) A number of states in the United States provide tax incentives. These are not very effective at best and are of no value to households that pay no tax.
   c) When the dependent person is mentally competent, the required extra money can be given to him/her to purchase required services. This practice is followed in some European countries.
2) Legislated or voluntary sabbaticals from work without penalty and with job protection.
3) Training and education regarding caregiving skills, understanding the situation and coping with stress.

4) Respite care (vacation care) programs which provide household caregivers with relief for a few hours, days or weeks; the need may be scheduled, so as to allow vacations, or unexpected, as when the caregiver becomes ill. Relief may be obtained by bringing another person into the home or by taking the dependent person to another location (which could be an institution or another home). Generally speaking, the terms respite care or vacation care are not meant to include short term relief such as that provided by a homemaker or a day care or day hospital unit, although the benefits are similar to those associated with longer term separation of regular caregiver and care recipient.

Respite care arrangements are currently not adequate. Most accommodation is in the form of one bed in a home for the aged or nursing home. It may not always be available and it usually is poorly publicized. There are too often rules that limit access to not less than one week or not more then 2-4 weeks per year. There is minimal if any availability of regular weekend relief.

Administrators do not tend to welcome personalized arrangements. Just as there is little if any effort to help institutionalized persons to regularly spend time with family on weekends or for longer periods (whatever the household and dependent person wish), there is not much imagination applied to the question of how to help dependent persons stay at home for 50, 48, 40 or 30 weeks of the year, or for 4, 5 or 6 days a week. The household is routinely expected to adapt to bureaucratic rigidities instead of the system adapting to household problems and constraints. The same attitudes are seen in day care programs that serve a major relief function but are useful only to those caregivers who can adapt to 9:30 to 3:30 service.

For selected persons, in particular those who are confused or acutely distressed by new caregivers and surroundings, consideration should be given to respite care in which the alternate caregivers are persons who are known and who will provide care in familiar surroundings.

In summary, the services that most directly preserve households include all those which either protect the household caregivers from financial, emotional and/or physical burnout or which provide care at home of a type that cannot be provided by the household caregiver.

Services Which Promote User Control

Any service or adaptation which allows anyone to be independent in any respect, obviously increases that individual's opportunities for control. Examples of such services or adaptations might be a seeing eye dog, a ramp, a telephone adaptation for the hearing impaired, an electric wheel chair or additional disposable income. Conversely, anything which prevents a person from exercising independence reduces that individual's opportunity for control; such barriers to independence include institutional regulations regarding pets, plants, visitors, outside visiting or how one may spend available wealth.

In general, it is assumed that all of those services which allow a person to stay out of an institution also increase the opportunity for user control. This assumption, however, is not always correct; the private living arrangements of many dependent persons may be isolated, not physically adapted and generally more restrictive than the environment of an institution committed to resident decision making.

The Financing of LTC

Acute care in Canada is almost routinely financed through global budgets or fee-for-service. The financing of LTC, however, has no standard pattern.

Some degree of care at home, at least to the level of public health nursing, is publicly funded in all provinces. Beyond this level of service there is a mixture of public/private financing in the Atlantic provinces with those who request additional services usually being means tested. In six provinces, additional levels of care at home are universal and are publicly funded.

Long term care institutions are partly or entirely publicly funded through either a global budget, a per diem rate, or, as with municipally owned Homes for the Aged in Ontario, an initial budget plus assured coverage of operating deficits. Institutions such as chronic hospitals in Ontario or extended care level institutions in British Columbia, which care for the most severely disabled, are, in Ontario, funded through a global budget in exactly the same way as an acute care hospital, whereas in some other provinces payment is via a fixed and standardized per diem rate. Alberta and British Columbia have led the way in establishing standard assessment procedures and standard payments for persons at a particular level of care. Payments do not vary on the basis of the ownership of the institutions; rates are the same for profit and nonprofit institutions.

In all provinces, most clients/residents pay $300-600 per month towards the cost of care in a public ward. The payment is usually set so that it can be met by the OAS-GIS while leaving a $50-100 per month comfort allowance. Residents also pay for semiprivate and private accommodation in most institutions. A private room in Ontario in a chronic hospital can cost over $600 a month; this outrageous fee for the privilege of being alone in a small room represents the only residential rental payment in Ontario to which rent control does not apply. (Several years ago the Ontario government removed the ceiling from preferred accommodation rates and gave 100% of that revenue to the institutions. Many hospitals, both acute and chronic, immediately sharply increased their rates.)

LTC can also be financed by making funds available to the users or their guardians or agents. (See earlier comments about the program in British Columbia).

Summary

Many questions have been raised. Should we consider the elderly to be the same as the rest of us but older? The answer is, very definitely, yes. Do we believe the disabled population should have the same opportunities as the rest of us to the extent feasible? Once again, the answer is definitely yes, and this answer rules out all paternalistic, professional control that reduces the opportunity for a disabled person to make decisions.

Existing LTC institutions and some of the legislation which governs them are incompatible with the principles enshrined in the literature, the political speeches and the mission statements of the institutions themselves. Social intent is good but adaptation of professionals and institutions is slow to the point of being a barrier to progress. Never have such a large group of users been so in need of advocates.

Suggested Reading

1) Metropolitan Toronto District Health Council, *Housing and the Health of the Elderly*, March 1988.
2) McDaniel, Susan A. *Canada's Aging Population*, Butterworth, 1986.
3) Kane, L. and Kane, R., *A Will and a Way — What the United States Can Learn from Canada about Caring for the Elderly*, 1984.

Chapter 15

TRUSTEES

Trustees are unpaid, often unprepared and often unsung, but they have an immensely important task. They manage large sums of money that the government raises and distributes, and they manage most of the health services that Canadians use.

Many of these trustees manage hospitals, and this chapter will almost exclusively discuss the hospital trustee, but other trustees manage community health centers, public health units, voluntary agencies, research foundations, half-way houses, sheltered workshops, group homes, mental health programs, hostels, etc. The discussion of the hospital trustee will be of varying relevance to other trustees. Certainly many of the challenges facing hospital trustees are on the agenda of the trustees of many other health programs and facilities.

THE EVOLUTIONARY ERAS

Four time periods will be referred to in illustrating the changes in hospitals and in the functions of their trustees. These comments will usually not apply to the roles and environments of senior executives in provincial psychiatric hospitals, and they will only partially pertain to chronic (LTC) hospitals.

Time Period #1 — Before World War II

Hospitals in this era were almost always individualistic free standing corporate entities unless they were part of a religious network. Almost all were, as now, either lay, religious or municipal and, therefore, nonprofit.

There was very little government regulation. Patient care quality was predominantly left to the judgment of the medical staff. There was no formal,and very little informal, regional planning. Hospitals provided whatever range of services they chose to provide and often were highly parochial and competitive.

Trustees were responsible for capital and operating decisions. They made do with whatever capital and operational financing they could find.Trustees decided whether or not they could afford new equipment, space, or programs, and these choices were dominated by the need to satisfy a medical staff who tended to have hospital privileges in more than one hospital. Hospital revenue varied with the extent to which the hospital could attract paying patients and the attraction of paying patients was more likely if you could please prestigious physicians. Deficits were an institutional problem unless the hospital was affiliated with a municipality.

Relationships with universities were rather informal but physicians with university appointments had the ability to bring paying patients and unpaid house staff into the hospital. Teaching, especially in the university affiliated hospitals of central Canada, was carried out in 'public' wards, or in outpatient clinics, on 'public' patients who could not pay their medical or hospital bills. Public wards were often large (20-40 beds to a room) and, in some hospitals, had significantly less nursing service than was available for the private (paying) patients in smaller rooms. Public patients had no choice of physician. Private patients did not attend hospital outpatient clinics. Medical staff were expected to work regularly and without pay in the hospital outpatient clinics and the public wards, and to supervise the work of house staff on these clinics and wards.

In some provinces, provincial grants were routinely available to hospitals although not in any guaranteed pattern, for example in Ontario in the early part of this century, the province paid a per bed grant to its hospitals. Because municipalities were responsible for indigents, including some minimum level of medical care, the municipal hospitals tended to have an above average population of public patients and, as a result, usually had major teaching programs. Municipal grants, or assistance with deficits, were available either in return for the care of indigents and/or as an expression of the interest of the municipality in preserving the hospital as an essential local source of health care for all residents.

In this era, the role of the hospital board was primarily to keep the hospital financially viable through fund raising and management control. Board members were interested in their medical staff primarily because the image of the medical staff was important to the solvency, the reputation, and, where applicable, to the teaching program of the hospital. Accreditation was available but not nearly so universally sought as it is today, and accreditation reviews dealt primarily with basic features of physical plant and medical records.

As this period came to an end, the hospital was becoming increasingly seen as a place where scientific and successful care could be given. The image of the hospital as a place to die, especially if you were poor, was not fully gone but was rapidly changing.

Full-time or part-time physician superintendents were the administrators in larger hospitals, with smaller hospitals usually being under the direction of a matron who was almost always a nurse.

Time Period #2 — From World War II to Universal Hospital Insurance

In the 1940's, the winds of change began, in irreversible ways, to alter the financial, scientific and social milieu of hospitals. The number and degree of sophistication of technical procedures grew rapidly as physicians either returned from the war with new skills or received government support to obtain them. As specialization and technological complexity increased, it became more difficult for all hospitals to be all things to all people. It also became more and more essential for doctors to have hospital privileges. Medical staff organization became more like the models we now have.

As health care became more of a right than a privilege, governments began to write hospital standards and courts began, in very tentative ways, to find hospitals responsible for the quality of patient care. More of the population began to be covered by private hospital and medical insurance and the hospital financial picture became more stable. The second 'era' was very short in Saskatchewan and British Columbia because hospital care became a universally available publicly financed social service in the late 1940's, but in other provinces this interval of private insurance lasted until 1958-60.

These years saw the emergence of the professional hospital administrator — whether a physician or otherwise. The Diploma in Hospital Administration was awarded to the first class of graduates by the University of Toronto in the mid 1940's.

Hospitals continued to be extremely autonomous. There was little or no compulsory regional planning although many voluntary area wide planning bodies were created. These bodies tended to work poorly when faced with decisions that were markedly unfavorable to any of their members but they did initiate many multiinstitutional co-operative ventures and they evaluated capital projects so that donors, in particular large corporate donors, would be more aware of which projects were most worthy of support.

Time Period #3 — The Period of Open Ended Hospital Spending

This interval extended from the introduction of universal hospital insurance to the beginning of serious provincial and federal concern over the increases in hospital costs.

Before universal hospital insurance, hospital trustees and administrators were constantly sensitive to the hazards of a deficit. They had to be very conscious of bad debts arising from nonpaying patients. After the arrival of universal insurance there were almost none of these patients and, to make things even more financially secure, there was agreement by government that justifiable deficits would be covered. The responsibility for institutional solvency fell much more on the ministries of health, or on quasi-public commissions in some provinces, than on the trustees and administrators. The hospital leaders became bargainers whose function was to obtain as much money as possible from another set of decision makers.

In the early years of hospital insurance, the cards were stacked very much in favor of the institutions. Most political and nonpolitical planners were committed to the principle of providing medically necessary care to all people, and most leaders believed that when the backlog of unmet need had been taken care of there would be a levelling off of hospital costs. In this situation the rapid growth of hospital costs was alarming but tolerable. In addition, hospitals were very much better prepared for financial negotiations than were the paying agencies; most of the experienced staff were on the hospital side of the bargaining table.

In these years governments financed hospitals through detailed line by line budgets. Hospital funds were bargained for at the departmental level; trustees and senior managers usually could not transfer funds from one department to another. Trustees frequently felt very unimportant because their former functions were predominantly financial and now financial decisions were almost entirely the product of negotiations between hospital staff and government or paying agency staff. The trustees now were able to worry a great deal less about the financial stability of their hospitals but, in return, they lost financial control.

Prior to universal government sponsored insurance, third-party payers had very little negotiating clout. The major hospital sponsored nonprofit hospital insurance plans (such as Blue Cross) had little incentive to limit payments to their member hospitals, and other paying agencies were too small, too divided or too uninterested to be able to exercise control. With the appearance of government as the paying agency, however, there was only one major banker. This new financial actor initially offered a great deal of money but rapidly began to wish to have a major say in how that money was spent.

In the interval between the introduction of universal hospital insurance and the introduction of universal medical insurance (a period of 10-15 years), there was a gradual disappearance of the indigent 'public' patient. Not only did almost everyone have hospital insurance, but an increasing percentage of patients also had private (profit or nonprofit) medical care insurance.

There was a greatly exaggerated fear that medical teaching could not succeed in the absence of public patients. Who, it was asked, would let an intern operate on him or her when the government would pay for a specialist to do it. This fear was short-lived; it was learned that you could teach using nonindigent patients. Canadian physicians-in-training do not now have the same volume of unsupervised experience that they would get in some American hospitals, but no one has suggested they are inappropriately prepared because of the higher level of supervision.

With stable government financing of hospitals, there was rapid unionization of personnel. Hospital staff had, historically, been poorly paid and the catch up was badly needed. By the 1970's the health industry had adapted to, or was adapting to, the idea of even professional staff being unionized and being prepared to strike. Nurses were the last large group of hospital workers to organize but they achieved rapid and stunning success when they did. New contracts with income increases of 40-60% were signed. Before the era of serious financial restraint arrived, hospital workers had achieved parity or better than parity with workers in other sectors.

The 1960's and 1970's saw growth in the competence and influence of regional and provincial planning personnel. There was immense improvement in the quality and quantity of information, especially with respect to utilization and hospital costs. The new competence and data allowed planning decisions to be more rational although the power of the hospitals was difficult to control.

By the end of the 1960's hospital autonomy had reached its lowest point. Line-by-line budget review was in place and hospitals were increasingly described as unreasonably expensive.

Time Period #4 — The Era of Hospital Constraint

The energy crunch of the early 1970's coincided with an accelerating concern over hospital and medical care costs. The line-by-line budget had been found to be incompatible with good management and with cost control and was therefore replaced by the global budget concept. The global budget allowed financial flexibility within a relatively fixed and provincially determined total allocation to the hospital. Boards of trustees once again had the opportunity to make resource allocation decisions, an opportunity still waiting to be seized. The global budget has allowed boards, if they wish (within general limits regarding essential programs), to alter the emphasis given to various clients, services and departments, and deficits are once again (to at least some degree) their responsibility.

With operating income relatively assured but fixed, and with planning decisions occurring primarily at the regional and provincial levels, boards are now free to give major attention to internal priority setting. Hospitals often, if not always, will want to spend much more than they can get, and in the face of this real or perceived shortage of money, boards and their senior administrators can either expend their energies on constant battles with regional and provincial personnel or they can assign the same energy to the intrainstitutional priority setting that is their responsibility.

Unfortunately senior administrative staff do not know how to support their boards in this priority setting task and some of them do not want to. Hospitals have, historically, not put resources into examining the relative social return from spending money on one group of patients or services as opposed to another, and even boards that seriously wish to tackle this new responsibility are having trouble getting started. A large industry with many product lines spends a great deal of money being certain that the things being produced are the ones that produce the most profit. In health care, which also is a multiproduct industry, we spend very little money trying to learn which products contribute most (per dollar spent) towards a longer or a better life.

Boards must now look at departmental and institutional outcomes. There has been no other time in history during which boards have been asked to consciously and continually compare the effect on the community of different service delivery patterns. Medical staff have, historically, decided what services would be delivered, and the minutes of Medical Advisory Committees, or equivalent committees by other names, show that they are still performing this function; however boards must now decide whether these resource consuming decisions that affect communities should be made by community representatives or by one group of providers of care.

The evolution of board responsibility for priority setting has, in many institutions, not begun at all. The hospital industry is rapidly learning the cost of various services and patient types but an understanding of the impact of various levels of expenditure on outcomes is barely on the horizon. This next step requires measurement of the extent to which outcomes change as resource consumption (cost) patterns change.

In seeking to identify the relationship between resource use and outcomes, there will be a need for indicators of quality as well as quantity of life; devising these indicators will be another challenge for administrators and boards already overwhelmed with this new area of responsibility.

Where will boards find the time to learn about priority setting and then implement their new skills? First, they should look for duties that do not need board input and leave these largely to administrative staff; an example might be dealing with financial matters. Provincial departments now ask for monthly financial reports. If expenditures are out of line with the expected budget, provincial authorities come to see why. When money is needed for a new program administrators do not negotiate for it with their trustees; they go to the regional council and/or the government. Financial matters are adequately handled by civil servants, administrators and auditors adhering to rigid reporting patterns. Trustees should consciously delegate operating financial decisions to staff and civil servants and leave fund raising to foundations.

Objectives or mission statements of hospitals frequently indicate an intention to be aware of, or measure, the needs of the community and, where the hospital is the appropriate source of care, respond to them. This is a new and natural trustee responsibility because trustees represent the community and have been chosen, at least partly, because they understand the local population, politics and culture. Priority setting based on community needs has been decentralized, or has remained decentralized, because trustees are thought to be better able to decide what the priorities ought to be for that community.

Because hospitals and trustees are now part of a larger network, it seems appropriate that one of their responsibilities is the support of regional planning and the appropriate integration of their institutions into health services throughout the region. Hospitals tend to have the largest single pool of well trained administrative staff, they tend to have the greatest capacity for data collection and handling and they tend to have budgets large enough to allow some funds to be spent on the development of briefs and the creation of proposals. These unique skills and abilities can be used in a parochial way as tools to manipulate or interfere with the regional planning process or they can be used to increase the likelihood that the regional decisions will emphasize community needs first and institutional growth second.

Hospital boards in recent years have also increasingly had to decide on ethical issues such as whether or not their hospital would do abortions, whether there should be an applied patients bill of rights, whether to ban smoking, whether to have open or closed board meetings, whether to promote participative or top down management, whether or not to discipline workers who take part in illegal walkouts, whom to exclude from membership on the board, how to deal with questions of safety in the workplace and whether or not to try to operate within the budget allotted to them by government. In some provinces, boards have, unfortunately, been invited to become involved in business ventures as sources of revenue (for example, The Business Oriented New Development program in Ontario).

Trustees have more responsibilities now than they have ever had because the agenda has changed. Trustees must now accomplish the new tasks of contributing positively to regional decision making including measurement of community need, making sound resource allocation/priority setting decisions within their institutions, and responding to a new administrative and social milieu.

We passed through a time when trustees and management were seen as the persons who allowed doctors to perform well. Now these trustees and administrators have the function of assuring a proper relationship between the activities of their institution and the elevation or protection of the community health status. This last function requires the proper distribution of resources among clinical areas and this responsibility may bring the board and the administration into major conflict with doctors.

Unfortunately, neither the managers nor the trustees are ready for this new role; they need help which can probably be made available only through ministry action. Ministries must consciously and tangibly assist those institutions that wish to improve internal resource allocation, just as ministries have financed regional priority setting processes.

A trend over the decades towards increasing hospital responsibility for all aspects of patient care has now culminated in a situation in which the hospital is likely to be among those sued when the quality of physician performance is in doubt.

THE EVOLUTION OF SPECIFIC BOARD FUNCTIONS

The changes in hospital board functions over time can also be described in terms of functions.

Capital Financing

Fund raising for capital purposes was an early function of all boards although, from early times, municipal and other governments have, when they wished, given construction grants to general hospitals. In 1948 the federal government guaranteed matching money to a maximum of $2,000 a bed, a program now terminated. From 1966-76 projects financed under the Health Resources Fund received 100% federal funding. Provincial government money has been and is routinely available for approved capital projects with the support being 100% of project costs in some provinces such as Alberta. In the 1980's boards have, once again, become major fund raisers as government contributions to capital costs have become both smaller in percentage terms and less likely to be immediately available.

Operational Financing

Trustees have moved from a time when balancing the books at year's end was a dominant function to a time when ministries and institutional personnel are dominant in financial planning. Trustees are now likely to play a major role only when administrative staff ask for support, or direction, so that expenditures can be reduced. The global budget tends to be set without much trustee input.

Involvement in Internal Operations of the Hospital

As the competence of senior administrators increased, as the complexity of the institution increased, and as new trustee functions have appeared, the trustees have been less and less involved in day-to-day or even overall operating decisions. These changes have largely eliminated the need for the historical tendency to try to have, within the board membership, a mix of practical skills. Thirty years ago a typical board might have included a lawyer, an accountant, a construction expert, a pharmacist, a nurse and an investment expert.

Quality of Patient Care

Trustees, at one time, accepted minimal if any responsibility for the care provided to private patients and only limited responsibility for the care provided to public patients. This distinction is now gone. Trustees who once assumed almost no responsibility for physician conduct now have a responsibility for all patient care activities in the hospital.

Responsibility to the Community and to the Network of Services Used by that Community

Trustees who once operated a free standing, uncoordinated institution now usually must adapt to a reasonably well organized regional network. In addition they have, at least in theory, a responsibility to relate their services to community need.

Trustees who once made decisions in isolation and privacy are now often reminded that they and their administrations operate in an age of consumerism, advocacy and the extraparliamentary processes. Trustee practices now include communication via the media, adherence to an open door policy and the adoption of a variety of techniques to respond to community complaints and concerns.

Summary of Changes in Hospital Trustee Functions in the Last Half Century

1) Trustee functions and roles that have remained intact:
   a) Selection and ongoing evaluation of senior staff, and by virtue of this selection and evaluation, the choice of an institutional management style.
   b) Acceptance of legal responsibility for the actions of nonmedical staff.
   c) Deciding on public fund raising campaigns.
2) Trustee functions and authority that have either disappeared or been significantly decreased:
   a) Collective bargaining at the level of the individual institution, largely gone in the last 10 years.
   b) Approval of major capital projects.

c) Beginning or discontinuing major programs.
d) Final approval of an operating budget, including whether or not to budget for a substantial deficit.
e) Selection of the manner in which data is collected and reported.
f) Control over size and number of teaching programs and medical school/hospital relationships.

3) New trustee functions:
a) Interaction with regional planning bodies.
b) Priority setting within a global budget (this is the most important responsibility at this time).
c) Accepting increased responsibility for the performance of physicians.
d) Being sensitive to neighbors, especially when the hospital is in a residential neighborhood.
e) Responding to new ethical-moral-legal questions such as those related to human and animal experimentation, resuscitation, release of information, patients' rights and obtaining organs for transplant.

Trustees have too many tasks for the time available. The average part-time and unpaid trustee probably spends one night a week at his/her job, or 10-20 hours per month. In 8-10 years, the trustee works the equivalent of one year as a full time worker. How can even an experienced trustee with 2-3 years on the board review budgets, oversee capital projects, examine patient care quality, set priorities and do all the rest of the things that trustees do?

It is clear there is both a shortage of trustee time and of trustee expertise. In the face of these handicaps it is important that trustees are careful to spend time only on those things that are important and which are unlikely to be done by someone else.

HOW SHOULD TRUSTEES SPEND THEIR TIME

Trustee time is a scarce and precious resource. Which of the following activities should be allowed to take up some of that time? Which could quite safely be delegated to a board committee or someone not on the board? Which are already getting adequate attention from other persons or agencies? What will happen if the board ignores a particular function?

These items are not in any special order. Each deserves review by every board of trustees to see whether it is being given a reasonable degree of attention, but many that are of interest should be largely ignored so that other, higher priority items get the attention needed.

1) *Review of operating financial performance.* This review may examine monthly financial statements including bad debt and outstanding accounts ratios. These are also routinely examined by ministries of health which, along with institutional staff, constantly watch for and respond to areas of budgetary over-run. Boards should do no more than ask for an oral and/or written comment in the regular CEO reports.

2) *Setting and approving budgets.* Trustees should merely want assurance that their policies regarding deficits and program priorities are honored in

budget setting and expenditure patterns. Next year's budget should only be on the agenda of the full board once a year; a finance committee could give it more attention but, even here, trustee involvement can be minimal. Trustees need not be involved in negotiations with regional or provincial representatives for either money or equipment.

3) *Technical aspects of capital projects.* Reviewing plans, admiring models, approving specifications, opening bids, helping to get a building permit and touring the construction site are a waste of trustee time. Administrators, planners, architects, lawyers and government representatives ought to be fully responsible for implementing the objectives and priorities identified by the board.

4) *Hiring and evaluating senior staff.* Choosing a new CEO is an uncommon event but is the most important single decision that a board will make. Evaluation of the incumbent CEO is also important, but a decision to replace is seldom made and, therefore, the decision to hire is more crucial. Whether a board should play a role in the selection of the assistant CEOs (the V.P.s) is debatable but these advisors and members of the senior management team can legitimately be seen as too important to be chosen and evaluated only by the CEO.

5) *Trustee education.* This function must obviously use up some trustee time, but the content of the learning should not be selected until duties have been chosen.

6) *Negotiating the regional hospital role.* Trustees, if properly prepared, can represent the community in discussions about the role of the hospital within the regional health services network. The discussions could be with regional or provincial representatives or with representatives of other hospitals and other health agencies. Parochial advocacy should be secondary to creation of a balanced and accessible health care network.

7) *Working with other sources of health care.* Boards should establish objectives that cover external relationships and should ask for proof that these relationships are operating in accordance with the objectives, but direct trustee involvement in the external interaction should not be necessary.

8) *Writing hospital mission statements.* Strategic planning, which includes drawing up mission statements and their associated goals and objectives, is definitely a trustee function. There is no one else with a mandate to do it, and it is a prerequisite to resource allocation and other priority setting activities.

9) *Priority Setting within the global budget.* Priority setting identifies the amount of emphasis that is to be given to various activities. It includes the approval of new programs or the discontinuance or merging of outdated programs. The priority assigned should be based on the relative cost-effectiveness of various activities. Assigning these priorities requires an understanding of costs and of benefits, and of the relationship of each activity to the mission and goals of the hospital. These exercises will be expensive and difficult but research and development expenditures are a necessary part of any enterprise.

Resource allocation, including the allocation of space, staff and equipment to various programs and activities, follows naturally from the priority setting exercise. Trustees should be certain that resource allocation reflects the priorities set, but they may not need to be, or have time to be, directly involved in the allocation of resources. This is a legitimate administrator function.

The priority assigned to different activities will vary with the mission statement. A mission to optimally improve the health status of the community will produce quite different priorities than a mission to make the hospital a world class institution that is locally dominant.

10) *Medical staff appointments.* Trustees should decide which types of medical staff will serve the institutional mission. To the extent legally possible the mechanics of appointing individual physicians should be ignored or transferred to a committee of the board. Procedural safeguards should be in place to reduce the likelihood of bias for or against particular candidates.

11) *Public relations.* Leave this to the staff. Only be sure that PR serves the mission of the hospital and not the agenda of hospital staff or other vested interests.

12) *Teaching programs and applications.* Delegate responsibility for these programs. The board needs merely to be informed and to be assured that the programs reflect the mission statement.

13) *Institutionally based research.* The board could usefully encourage and seek outside help with the cost-effectiveness and priority setting research that is urgently needed. The board should be informed of other research efforts only to the extent necessary to be certain that research emphases support the hospital mission.

14) *Being a good corporate neighbor.* Hospitals, especially when they are situated in a residential neighborhood, should be sensitive to neighborhood concerns regarding traffic, parking, institutional odors, ambulance noise, the disposal of toxic wastes, incinerator pollution or other intrusions into the life of the community. This function requires board attention only to the extent of a statement of philosophy or objectives regarding corporate neighborliness.

15) *Being a good employer.* Hospitals have responsibilities to their staff as well as to their patients and their community. Boards should declare in writing their perceptions of this role, for example, will the hospital be paternalistic, participative, defensive, supportive, combative, collegial and willing to share information. Senior executives and unionized staff are entitled to know the philosophy within which the board expects the hospital to operate.

16) *Creating and operating hospital owned profit-making activities.* Taking profit from a variety of businesses, such as newsstands, florists, foodstores, pharmacies and dry cleaning, is an increasing trend. These money-making ventures merely make an unnecessary additional demand upon scarce trustee time. Trustees already have more tasks, and more important tasks, than they can handle and profit-making diversions should get no time at all.

17) *Ethical issues.* These topics cannot be avoided. They can be dealt with

proactively or reactively. Either way boards should use committees or other devices to keep the demands on the total board to a minimum.

18) *Assuring that the hospital is obeying all laws.* This responsibility should be delegated, although it cannot be avoided.

19) *Preparing for accreditation.* Trustees have no related role not covered under other headings.

20) *The organization of the board.* Reorganization of committees, for example, should receive only infrequent and scanty attention. The quality of the trustees and the appropriateness of agendas are more important.

21) *Quality assurance.* This activity is, at the moment, too undefined to know the role of the trustee in it. Generally speaking, trustees should be certain that the quality of many aspects of hospital life, including patient care, is being regularly monitored. Trustees can improve the monitoring process by being certain that the health status of the community is reflected in the indicators chosen, and that indicators reflect mental as well as physical health.

Each of the 21 agenda items can be seen as worthy of trustee attention, but hiring senior staff, approving mission statements, priority setting within the global budget, and deciding on ethical questions are the most important. Each of these must be the specific responsibility of the board. Other items, such as making medical staff appointments, must, by law, receive some trustee time. Several items require board attention only at times of preparation or revision of the mission statement including accepting corporate responsibility for patient care and being a good employer. Others merit attention but not with the degree of urgency associated with those listed above.

Many board members will have difficulty abandoning or sharply reducing attention to long-standing trustee agenda items such as reviewing financial performance but these must be given very little attention if the board is to play a role in the much more difficult but much more important priority setting/resource allocation decisions that are central to providing optimal service to the community.

HOSPITALS AS CORPORATIONS

Some of these comments are also made in Chapter 13. Hospital rooms, corridors and patient care are the tangible products of some corporate entity. A hospital could not do the organizational and operational things it does such as pay bills, enter into contracts, borrow money, hire staff and own property, without being individually incorporated or being within some larger corporation. The larger organization can be a multi-institutional corporation (religious or otherwise) or some level of government.

A hospital corporation is formed when a legislature or the appropriate government department approves a statute, a charter or some other legal vehicle in response to an application from some organization or group of individuals. The charter or statute sets out the general purposes and organization of the corporation. Most hospitals are incorporated under a provincial statute (such as a *Corporations Act* or a *Charities Act*) although it seems reasonable that multi-institutional systems including some religious networks and profit chains might operate under a federally granted charter. Some old hospitals such as the Ottawa Civic, and some not so old, such as the University Hospital in Saskatoon, have their origins in a separate bill.

The inanimate and ethereal, but very legal, hospital corporation is controlled by members who are the equivalent of the shareholders who control commercial corporations. In nonprofit corporations, however, it is customary for each member to have only one vote. The number and characteristics of persons who may be members of a corporation or an association may be spelled out in a charter or in by-laws or may be controlled by a provincial statute. The fee for membership, if any, is likely to be described in corporate by-laws.

Corporate or association membership may be closed or open. Open memberships are unlimited in number although other constraints such as age, place of residence, fees or agency affiliations still apply. At least in Ontario, membership is also unavailable without hospital board support. The hospital board have, in the *Public Hospitals Act of Ontario*, the right to refuse to accept applications for membership in the association. The group already elected can refuse to franchise persons who appear entitled to vote.

This power of the board to reject selected applicants has been granted on the belief that it is desirable to exclude from the association persons who wish to join for a specific reason rather than because of a general interest in the hospital. Rejected persons tend to be those who represent a single interest that is unattractive to existing board membership, for example they might be persons representing antiabortion groups or labor unions.

There is, however, another side to this coin. The concept of democracy does not give any government or bureaucrat the right to disenfranchise voters with whom they already know they disagree. The arrangement described is undemocratic and anachronistic. Block voting by a special interest group may be a short term threat to one's perception of the way a hospital should be managed but tampering with democratic principles is a bigger threat.

Other hospital associations that are ostensibly and legally open may, in reality, be quite closed because the membership fee is significant or the availability of membership is a well kept secret. The Ottawa General Hospital (OGH), for example, had a $15 annual membership fee (which was waived for at least some board members), and its meetings were closed to the press and public; these produced what was in effect a closed association.

Most boards represent some mix of appointed members and members elected at an annual meeting of the association, and the percentage of members who are elected rather than appointed varies greatly. The appointed members may be there because of the specific position they hold. They may, for example, be executive members of the medical staff or they may be on the board because they have been named by some municipality, religious order, institution, agency or labor union that is, by law or charter, guaranteed representation on the board.

In some provinces certain persons cannot be members of the board. In Saskatchewan, for example, practicing physicians were excluded.

Corporate or association members tend to meet only once a year for the purpose of electing a board. The board will, within the limitations imposed by provincial statutes, the charter, the by-laws and (uncommonly) the general membership of the corporation, manage the hospital. The board has full executive and legal authority between meetings of the corporation and within the constraints listed.

The board, within the limits of provincial legislation and regulations (in Ontario, primarily the *Public Hospitals Act and Regulations* although dozens of other statutes affect hospitals), writes the rules that govern the hospital. Within constraints, the board provides the policy; the hospital administration implements the policy.

Being a board member, especially being chairman, is demanding. In a big hospital the board chairman is at the hospital several times a week for meetings, the signing of documents, publicity or staff events or discussions with administration. Other board members will, if they are reasonably responsible members, spend at least one evening a week on hospital business.

In Québec the hospital board membership is spelled out in detail in the governing statute. The boards are made up of representatives of the professional staff, other staff, municipalities, post secondary educational institutions, other facilities in the region and the community. The community representatives, who usually make up less than one-quarter of the total board, are elected at an annual meeting. Other members are named by the appropriate group, agency or government.

There is considerable dispute about who are the best board members and about how they should be chosen. When it was the function of the board members to provide technical advice with respect to fund raising, construction, budgetary control and legal matters then board members were chosen because they had these competencies. Now that the function of the board is, first of all, to reflect community needs and values a democratic process is best. This process has hazards. Board members may be incompetent or disinterested, they may represent only one minority point of view or be controlled by some minority constituency, but if one believes in democracy then it should be encouraged, supported and tolerated in small social institutions as well as in our more formally identified governments. Hospital boards are governments just as much as school boards, library boards or municipal councils, all of which write or implement public policy and spend public funds.

Hospital trustees, as with the trustees of all other nonprofit organizations, manage within a changing and critical environment. Failure to respond to the changes described in this chapter will sharply reduce the service that the community will receive from the agencies and institutions involved.

Chapter 16

OTHER HEALTH SERVICES

RESPONSE TO PHYSICAL EMERGENCIES

Medical emergencies can require either physical health services or mental health services, but mental health emergencies were discussed in Chapter 10 and, therefore, this section will discuss only emergencies associated with physical injury, physical illness or obstetrical crisis.

Physical emergencies occur everywhere — at home, at work, at play, at school and in the hospital. Major components of the emergency response system, the emergency services network, include a communications network, case finding mechanisms, on-site first aid, on-site professional care, transportation arrangements, care in hospital emergency departments (ED) or rooms (ER) and disaster planning.

Many minor physical emergencies including minor injuries and illnesses are routinely adequately handled at home, at work, in physician's offices or in school health offices. These sites, which are outside of or peripheral to the emergency services network, have been discussed elsewhere. As we discuss the ambulances and hospital emergency departments, it is useful to remember that many other sources of health care also look after emergencies.

The Area Wide Approach to Emergency Care

There was a time when every hospital had an emergency department and serious emergency cases were spread among them all. Specialization and referrals were uncommon. Evidence is now conclusive that high quality emergency care requires a different model. In Russia, some hospitals are dedicated fully to trauma care. British experts believe that a population of approximately one million is the proper base for one highly sophisticated trauma centre with a full range of specialized services available 24 hours a day seven days a week. The armies of the world are masters of triage (the categorization of cases so they may be sent to the most appropriate place), and triage plus a hierarchical and integrated network of care centers has immensely improved recovery rates.

Emergency services are a stand-by network. They never know when difficult obstetrical, cardiac, dental, infectious, traumatic or hypothermic cases may arrive. They must be ready for head injuries, eye injuries, chest injuries, burns, respiratory difficulties and severe blood loss, and each of these requires its own mix of specialized services. It is economically unreasonable to maintain the highest level of stand-by capability in any institution at which very few complex cases arrive per month or per year. It is also impossible to maintain the clinical skills of the medical, nursing and other staff unless there is a reasonably steady arrival of cases requiring those special skills.

Canada has been very slow to rationalize its emergency care although some progress has been made. In many smaller urban centers, for example, only one of the two or three hospitals is now operating an emergency room, and global planning in large metropolitan centers is beginning.

In the early 1980's, Ontario proposed that all hospital emergency departments be placed in one of four categories — comprehensive, (of which the most sophisticated would be called a trauma centre), major, general and basic. Staffing, budgeting and hours of operation would correspond to the category assigned. This categorization, which is still in its earliest stages of implementation, will help clients and ambulance personnel know where to go and it will provide better care at less cost. In time, if the categorization is implemented, only a few urban hospitals will operate a 24-hour emergency service, with most other hospitals and some free standing health care units operating a less comprehensive service for 10-18 hours a day. The volume of minor emergencies during the night hours is low enough to be handled by the stand-by staff in the higher level emergency centers.

Sudbury, Ontario is an example of a city with fully integrated hospital emergency care. Sudbury General has 24-hour emergency coverage, Sudbury Memorial closes its emergency at midnight and Sudbury Laurentian has no emergency department at all. In Toronto three hospitals have been designated as trauma centers — Sunnybrook, St. Michaels and The Hospital for Sick Children. Wellesley Hospital has the only burn center in Toronto.

The major fear of the population when a reduction in the number of 24-hour emergency departments is suggested is that people will suffer or die because of the additional travelling time. There is no doubt that occasional headlines will arise when someone dies en route to an urban emergency department that could have been closer, but there will be many more people who will be saved because they arrive at a better equipped and better staffed emergency department. The number who are harmed by a few more minutes of travel will be even less if patients are transported in well equipped and well staffed ambulances, and the quality of these vehicles and staff is constantly improving. The person who dies while travelling a bit farther will usually be someone who would have died anyway. The principle of centralization of 24-hour emergency services is much less applicable to rural areas but even here patients would often be better served by travelling farther in a good ambulance to a better equipped and better staffed emergency department.

Reducing the functions of emergency departments will be most firmly resisted by medical staff. Many medical practitioners expect some of their patients to be admitted through the emergency department, and rerouting of emergency patients to another hospital will transfer those patients to the caseloads of physicians who are on staff at the other hospital. The clinical realignments will be quite major in some communities. For example, in Ottawa-Hull, with less than a million people, there are 9 emergency units staffed 24-hours a day, and many other cities show the same oversupply.

Hospital emergency departments designed to handle major emergencies should expect to have periods without much to do. At other times there will be too much to do. The more one tries to make sure the staff are always busy the less prepared the department will be for new major emergencies (see Figure 16.1).

If staffing is maintained at level A for all shifts no-one will have to wait for service. At staffing level D people will wait routinely during the day shift and occasionally at night. Queuing theory, an operations research technique, will, at various levels of staffing predict the likelihood of idle time and of people waiting. Use of this type of data, plus the use of triage, can bring reasonable assurance that those in greatest need will be served first and that there will almost always be enough staff to give immediate and adequate care to the serious emergencies.

Central Monitoring

When several or many emergency departments are operating, as is the case in all major urban centers, there is no good way of predicting which departments will be under excessive pressure at any given hour. The unexpected arrival of an unmanageable volume of patients, or a back up in the ER of patients waiting for transfer to wards with no empty beds has, in the past, led to some hospitals declaring their emergency departments temporarily closed. This closure has, at times, occurred without knowledge of whether other hospitals were any better able to handle the emergencies being turned away.

Several major centers (Hamilton, Toronto) now have or will soon have a centralized monitoring service constantly aware of the availability of beds in all hospitals and of the volume of patients awaiting care in all emergency departments. This central office can advise ambulances, and others, of the best pace to go, and it can determine whether or not it is reasonable for a particular

FIGURE 16.1
THE STAFFING DILEMMA IN
HOSPITAL EMERGENCY DEPARTMENTS

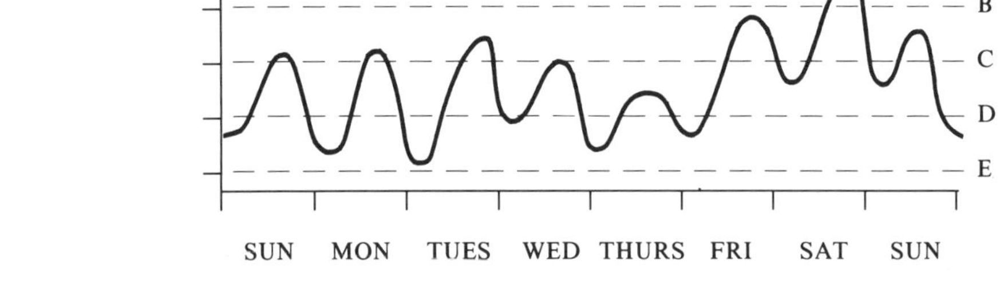

emergency department to be temporarily closed. The central monitoring (often referred to as a central bed registry), plus ER classification, will allow ERs to act more like a coordinated network.

Emergency departments with over 30-40,000 visits per year should have a permanent formal referral arrangement through which selected patients can be referred to an ambulatory care unit during high volume hours. Toronto General Hospital has made such referrals since 1986. Many patients who come to ERs are better cared for in a normal office setting, where routine examinations and counselling are the service best delivered, than in an ER where heroic measures and early referral are the norm. Referral can, after triage, transfer many patients to a hospital outpatient department, a community health center or some other site of office based care. These offices are much more appropriate for the immediate care and the follow-up of the kinds of emotional, social and medical problems that are common among ER patients.

ER's and Routine Ambulatory Care

Seventy-five to ninety percent of patients who come to emergency departments have problems (a) that are not life threatening, (b) which can be dealt with in a relatively ordinary office, treatment room or minor surgery, and (c) whose treatment can be safely deferred for a few minutes or hours. A small percentage of patients have a major illness or injury which, after examination and minimal stabilization, leads to rapid transfer to an intensive care unit, a coronary care unit or an inpatient ward (assuming that a bed is available). A very small group require major, immediate, and sometimes quite sustained, multidisciplinary attention in the emergency room.

The volume of patients in the first group (the 75-90%) is on the basis of previous experience fairly predictable for any good-sized emergency department. Volumes vary with time of day, day of week, season of year and specific local events or conditions. The second two categories of patients arrive quite randomly although higher volumes can be expected on selected evenings such as Saturdays, in certain weather conditions, or on selected long weekends. These seriously ill or injured persons are the ones who require the major stand-by capability that characterizes a high quality trauma centre.

ERs are a major source of routine medical care, receiving 0.5 to 1 visit per person per year. There is considerable disagreement over whether or not most of these users are receiving care in the right place. Certainly many could be cared for at home (though few doctors make house calls), or in an office (though offices are more often closed than open), but do these facts mean that the visit is inappropriate? Providers of care are often critical of persons who come to the ER with a rash, a headache, or a sore back, especially when the problem has been present for some time or appears to be minor. These persons are often referred to as abusers of the system; that is, they are thought of as persons who are taking advantage of the service and should somehow be discouraged.

Patients who are seen as abusers of emergency services also include the inebriated, the neurotic, the terminally ill, the chronically ill, the socially detached or maladjusted, and those who drop in on the way home from a party for advice about a chronic complaint because they do not want to take time off from work. All but the last group are persons to whom emergency services should be offered without complaint. Emergency assistance should be available through social work staff, mental health staff and formal referral arrangements. To be hungry, cold, confused or drunk can be as hazardous as having pneumonia or a protruded intervertebral disc.

The terminally ill are especially stressful for caregivers as well as family. The family is frightened and may become angry when hospital admission is refused. The family is emotionally unsupported in the face of an impending family death and they quite rightly would like some help. Emergency physicians, on the other hand, may quite rightly feel that acute treatment hospital services are not needed and may not be appropriate. Referral to a palliative care team should be routine, but palliative care back up is not always available.

The chronically ill can be equally difficult. These include patients with panic syndrome, chronic asthma, muscular dystrophy or chronic obstructive lung disease (emphysema). Good links with social work staff and home support systems will reduce the user/institutional conflict arising from unwillingness to admit.

It is easy to be quite critical of 'callous' emergency room staff but, in the face of quite precise and necessary criteria for hospital admission, these caregivers must regularly play the role of gatekeepers. Their decisions cannot always be acceptable to everyone nor will they always be right, but most of them do as well as the rest of us would.

The discussion of when individuals are abusing emergency departments is not worth much effort since no good devices have been found to keep patients away. Long waiting times aggravate everyone and bring unreasonable inconvenience, discomfort and sometimes hazard. User fees will deter a few of the working poor but have no effect on patients exempted from the fee or on those who will not be deterred by it. It is far more sensible to expect current utilization patterns to continue and to plan to efficiently and safely deal with them. Triage and the use of an affiliated ambulatory care unit can improve efficiency and quality and can protect the stand-by capability needed in major ERs.

Primary routine care provided in an ER may or may not be more expensive than the same care provided in an ambulatory care center. Findings depend primarily on how, and how much, physicians are paid, and on whether or not ER stand-by costs are allocated to the walk-in patients requiring routine office care.

Special Communication Problems

All medical care, including emergency care, must be delivered to the deaf, the aphasic, the mentally retarded, the emotionally disturbed and those who speak languages other than that or those most commonly in use. Some hospitals, such as The Hospital for Sick Children in Toronto, have a vast army of volunteer interpreters. All major emergency departments should be prepared for patients speaking any of the languages used fairly commonly in their community, and all should have personnel trained in the handling of persons with other communication problems.

Disaster Response

The emergency department in even a sophisticated trauma center is hard pressed to handle 5-10 serious injuries that arrive simultaneously. Occasionally, however, a community is faced with hundreds of casualties or with the need to evacuate hospitals and/or communities; how does it cope? It usually copes best if it has a carefully described disaster plan that has been regularly tested.

The basic components of a disaster plan are:

(1) A pre-established authority structure which disregards existing physician and administrator prerogatives. Someone must be in overall command and specified persons must be in charge of specific tasks such as triage, identifying hospital patients who are to go home or be moved to other facilities, arranging patient transfer, providing information and traffic control, and calling in off-duty staff. The most senior administrative personnel should operate from a central command post well away from the disaster and the ER.

(2) A pre-established role for, and co-operation among, the police, the fire department, the ambulance system, the ham radio operators and other adjacent institutions, and possibly the armed forces, the Red Cross and other such groups, all of whom may be essential in various situations.

(3) A central casualty distribution plan to ensure that those in need when picked up from their place of injury are delivered to the place most able to care for them in terms of special competence and/or available space. Without this despatch arrangement, all casualties may show up in one place. Minor emergencies should go to some established first-aid post quite geographically separate from the hospital(s) so that hospitals can receive only the seriously injured or ill.

(4) A communications network to handle outside enquiries (families, friends, the press) and ensure the continued availability of contact between all participants in the disaster response.

(5) A pre-established plan for each of the functions listed.

The effects of smaller disasters can be handled within the region; examples might be a fire requiring evacuation of one institution, or a structural collapse or other event whose casualties require less than 15-25% of locally available beds. In other situations, all local institutions may be out of action, as in Mississauga in 1979 when 3 hospitals, six nursing homes and a quarter of a million people were evacuated because of an overturned railroad car leaking chlorine. One thousand hospital patients were transferred either home (42%) or to one of over a dozen hospitals outside Mississauga. Only 2-3% of the LTC patients were able to go home; the remainder went to outside LTC institutions or to emergency accommodation. The move involved 160 ambulances and other vehicles and took 19 hours, and there had been no disaster.

A tornado in Barrie, Ontario, in May 1985 demonstrated the chaos that accompanies a disaster with 8 killed, 160 injured, hundreds of homes and other buildings destroyed and major disruption of communication, transportation and electrical systems. Emergency housing, the allocation, feeding and sheltering of hundreds of emergency workers, the unmanageable volume of enquiries and the documentation of the dead, injured and displaced were only reasonably well done. Follow-up counselling, especially of children, was needed for many months to overcome feelings of panic whenever high winds or similar sounds brought back memories of the tornado. Another and less expected need in the recovery period was protection of the victims from unscrupulous builders and a wide range of exploitive prices.

On July 31, 1987 the Edmonton area was hit with lightning storms and a series of tornados. Lightning knocked out the ambulance dispatch tower, the telephone answering service (controlling all physician pagers) and many of the city's telephones. The tornado produced over 25 deaths and many hospital admissions. The vulnerability of a disaster plan to the loss of communication networks was vividly illustrated. No one knew what was going on.

When analyzing the Mississauga, Edmonton and Barrie experiences one must remember how modest these challenges were compared to the Halifax explosion of World War I or the more recent disasters at Bhopal, India or Chernobyl in the Soviet Union. Planning for the chaos that would follow nuclear war (the home defence placebo) is a waste of time (one cannot effectively plan for the end of the majority of the human race), but we can benefit from planning for those large scale disasters that are more common than we think.

Mobilizing the System for the Usual Small Scale Emergency

The first step in the emergency care sequence is knowing that an emergency exists. In most cases this need for emergency care is immediately reported by the victim, co-workers, family members, bystanders, or others. The report is made to the police, fire department, ambulance system or health care worker or facility. In a small minority of cases, however, factors will interfere with the call for help. Occasionally the person in need, or someone who is aware of the need, will not be able to contact help. What can be done to reduce communication breakdown?

A special, easily remembered and toll free telephone number, usually 911, providing direct contact with the emergency network can help. Not only is the call simpler to make but the message is received by a center, usually the police, the fire department or an ambulance dispatch office, that can respond immediately and that is in radio contact with all resources.

Sometimes the call for help is more automatic. High-risk patients may carry monitoring devices that will call for help when it is needed. The postmen play a role through their Postal Alert program (in which the postman alerts authorities when mail has not been picked up), as do the many programs in which a high-risk person is phoned daily at a prearranged time. If there is no answer an investigation begins. Some of these programs are staffed by residents of LTC institutions. The signalling device which transmits after a plane crash is another example.

Ambulance Services

Uncoordinated, user pay and privately operated ambulance services are now uncommon in Canada. They had the disadvantages of being financially hazardous to the operators (many clients were uninsured and did not pay), very duplicative (people in need often called several ambulances and only the first one there had a fare), somewhat unreliable (all companies might decide this was a good call to ignore), and of variable quality.

These unsatisfactory features have been steadily reduced or eliminated by regional or provincial organization, regional dispatch systems and co-insurance plus provincial financing. Central dispatch systems for ambulances arrived about 20 years after they were firmly established in the taxi industry but technology is slowly being effectively used to ensure high quality contact between ambulances, the police, the fire department and the major hospitals.

Ambulance utilization is in the range of 50-150 trips per 1000 population per year, of which up to 30% may be for scheduled services such as interhospital transport or taking patients home for the weekend. These trips may appear to be the inappropriate use of expensive staff and equipment but they are an economical use if the expensive stand-by team would otherwise be idle. Besides the usual, well-equipped ambulances there are now a few $80,000 superambulances able to provide sophisticated life support during transportation.

For a number of years ambulance costs in Canada rose rapidly, but as of about 1982, as ambulance systems in a number of provinces matured, costs have stabilized.

In Ontario the total emergency services network cost $165-170 million in 1987-88, or about $20 per capita. These costs cover air transport, 640 ambulances (1:13,000 population) a small number of special support units and of critical care transport units (for interinstitutional transfer of stabilized patients), over 200 first response/administrative vehicles, regional dispatch centers and central administration. In 1987-88, about one million ambulance calls were made, or 120 calls per 1000 population.

All Ontario ambulance services operate under the *Ambulance Act*, and all are fully or primarily financed provincially. Nine area ambulance services are administered directly under the Ministry of Health, five (including that of Metro Toronto) are municipally managed, 66 are hospital operated, primarily in smaller communities with one hospital, 65 are privately owned and operated and 32 remote areas are served by volunteer services. Metro Toronto is unique in that Metro is reimbursed by the Ministry of Health for only about 65% of its costs and the system is operated by the regional government.

Ambulance services have no national pattern. The degree of public financing and of provincial organization is extremely varied.

The characteristics of a good emergency transportation system include providing prompt response and having competent staff, modern equipment, good communication with physicians in hospitals and a knowledge of the best destination for a particular patient. Improvements have, in the past decade, occurred in all respects, primarily because of increased public planning and financing.

Field health care personnel in the armies of the world have always been well trained, but the calibre of staff in Canadian ambulances has only recently begun to reflect the best features of military experience. Most provinces now use ambulance personnel with community college or university training; in Ontario, for example, they have at least one year of training. Basic ambulance attendant training may be followed by trauma training and by training in advanced cardio-pulmonary life support skills.

In 1984, Ontario began training paramedics who must take a one year course on top of lower level attendant training. As these graduates become available they are joining the ambulance network. They are trained in advanced life support (ALS) including the use of laryngoscopes, intubation, defibrillation, physical assessment, cardiac monitoring and use of drugs. One area under constant review is the range of judgments that can be made and acted upon without referral to a hospital. In light of the amount of training and the regular field experience of these personnel, it will be in everyone's interest if they are left to exercise considerable judgment as to when to contact a physician for advice or authorization.

The upgrading of emergency care personnel has occurred in hospital emergency departments as well as in ambulances. The practice of rotating a large number of physicians through the emergency department of the hospital has now been discontinued in most larger cities although it is still common in smaller centers. Emergency departments are now staffed primarily by full time physicians, sometimes with special training in emergency medicine. (The staff may also be hospital residents in training or physicians earning extra money while they develop a practice.)

In most provinces the physicians who work in hospital emergency departments are paid by fee-for-service although use of this method of payment has made the low volume night shift unpopular. In some provinces such as Manitoba,the physicians in at least some emergency departments are salaried. In 1987,the Manitoba salaries of $50-60,000 could not compete with incomes offered elsewhere, including those available to emergency physicians on fee-for-service in the same province. Some emergency departments were temporarily closed for lack of medical staff.

Walk-in clinics, an exploding phenomenon in several western cities, are a new competitor for hospital emergency departments. There were, in mid-1987, an estimated 35-40 of these clinics in Winnipeg and a smaller number in Calgary.

Both the Alberta and Manitoba governments have expressed concern over the lack of continuity of care, the possible encouragement of unnecessary utilization and the impact of these clinics on the per unit costs of hospital emergency departments where stand-by capability must be maintained. The walk-in clinics are usually in shopping centers and operate during shopping center hours.

A new type of 'hospital without beds' is also being added to the emergency care spectrum. These facilities offer diagnostic services, usually integrate health and social services, may offer day care or other quasi-institutional services, may offer general medical care, may offer outpatient surgical services, usually offer 15-18 hours a day of minor emergency care, and may have a 1-2 bed holding unit for emergency stabilization before transfer. The first of these in Ontario is to be at Stony Creek outside Hamilton and will cost $12-15 million dollars. Two others are being planned for suburban communities immediately to the east and west of Ottawa.

A province-wide, provincially operated and financed air ambulance service was started in Saskatchewan almost 40 years ago and most provinces offer some air evacuation assistance.

Emergency services staff may have legal as well as clinical responsibilities. For example, failure to report suspected child abuse is an offence in Ontario and British Columbia. Studies have shown that wife battering is regularly missed, (perhaps to a level of 90-95%) and, although reporting of this abuse is not legally mandatory, there is certainly some moral obligation.

The role of the public in emergency care is long established through such organizations as St. John Ambulance. The role of the public in cardiopulmonary resuscitation (CPR) is more controversial. In Seattle, one in five adults has CPR training, compared to one in eighty in Toronto.

Some information services are important to emergency care. Poison information centers tell mothers and other caregivers what to do. Telecommunication networks advise caregivers in isolated communities as to the most appropriate treatment and/or referral of patients, sometimes after transmittal of x-rays or other images for review by the central specialists. Patient registries and computerized patient medical histories will increasingly be valuable to a physician or other caregiver faced with a seriously injured person.

A 1986 survey of the Ontario public showed that only 59% rated emergency hospital care as 'good' or 'excellent', far below the 82% accorded hospital services overall. Waiting times, waiting areas and staff attitudes are cited as unacceptable. Administrators and planners will need an open mind as they seek new processes to improve both the care and the image of emergency care, especially hospital emergency departments.

Emergency services are not part of our current push for prevention, but they can, at any moment, be important to any of us.

DENTAL SERVICES

Providers of dental care still look after teeth but dental occupations and patterns of morbidity, financing and organization have, in the past 20 years, undergone significant change.

Manpower

The dental model, in which the dentist is the only one who can prescribe, has been modified. It is now common for a denturologist (Québec), a denture therapist, a denturist or a similar dental worker by some other name to legally fit, produce and sell a denture or partial denture, or to repair a denture, with little or no contact with a dentist. In Saskatchewan for almost 15 years, dental therapists (originally called dental nurses) filled, extracted and capped the teeth of children without on-site supervision by a dentist.

The range of dental specialization has increased and now includes orthodontics, dental (oral and maxillofacial) surgery, public health dentistry, paedodontics (children), periodontics (care of gums), endodontics (care of roots of teeth), prosthodontics (the production and use of prostheses) and oral pathology. Orthodontists are the largest specialty group followed by dental surgeons.

In addition to increasing specialization by dentists, but moving in the opposite direction, there has been aggressive entry of many unspecialized general dentists into some of the specialty fields. Whether all specialties, especially pediatric dentistry and endodontics, can survive in the face of this trend remains to be seen.

Dental hygienists, whose role is primarily patient education and the cleaning and assessing of teeth, continue to work under the immediate direction of dentists. Dental assistants, who may or may not have formal training, provide chairside assistance to dentists. Canada has one dentist per 2000-2200 population with regional variations of from 1 per 1500 (British Columbia) to 1 per 4400 (Newfoundland).

After peaking in 1983 dental school enrollment in Canada has been steady at about 450 entering students per year, but reductions are expected in the near future. Dental school enrollment in the United States fell 23% from 1978 to 1985 and the trend is likely to occur in Canada. The supply of dental assistants and dental hygienists continues to increase. They work primarily in dentists' offices on salary and are sources of assistance and additional income for the dentist.

There is general acceptance that both Canada and the United States have a current oversupply of dentists. Whether a condition of oversupply continues will depend on such diverse factors as (a) whether the current middle-aged population, who use dental care quite regularly, will continue to do so when they are elderly, (b) whether the capitation approach to financing increases with its associated need for fewer dentists, (c) whether the use of auxiliaries, whose adequacy was confirmed in the Saskatchewan dental program, will be controlled or allowed to grow and (d) whether or not research, by virologists or immunologists for example, will develop vaccines or new therapies to control periodontal disease.

The greatest growth in dentistry has been in the field of esthetics. Orthodontists were, at one time, interested in a good bite, that is, in a good fit of upper and lower teeth. Now both they and their patients wish a perfect appearancc as well as a perfect bite. Braces are now chic and crooked or darkened teeth are passé. There has also been a marked increase in dental involvement in therapy of the temporomandibular joint.

There is now also an increasing sense that teeth are to be saved at all costs. A lost tooth or a removable denture represent dental failure. Root canals and implants have increased. One area of probable growth in dental services is in long term care institutions, many of which now operate with minimal consideration of the dental needs of residents.

The Saskatchewan Children's Dental Program

No discussion of Canadian dental care would be complete without a reasonably detailed description of the creation and partial destruction of the children's dental care plan in Saskatchewan.

In 1968, with federal assistance, a three-year pilot program of dental care for children 3-12 years of age was put in place in the town of Oxbow, Saskatchewan. Teams of 1 dentist, 2 dental nurses and 3 dental assistants provided the care with the nurses extracting deciduous (baby) teeth and placing fillings in deciduous and permanent teeth. On the strength of the success of this trial, which drew extensively on the dental nurse program in New Zealand, plans were made to introduce a province-wide children's dental program.

Training of the necessary staff was provided through a specially created community college program. The *Saskatchewan Dental Nurses Act* was passed (1973) authorizing the dental nurses to do selected dental work, and in 1974, with the graduation of the first class of the new dental workers, the program was begun. In 1974 services were offered only to children born in 1968. The program was expanded at a rate consistent with the expanding supply of dental nurses until all children over the age of 3 were enrolled. Over 400 permanent clinics were established in schools throughout the province. Enrollment was voluntary but over 85% of eligible non-native children were enrolled. Less than half of eligible native children enrolled.

In 1976, three outside dental specialists evaluated more than 2000 fillings and 97 steel crowns in 410 children. They did not know whether the work had been done by dentists or by dental nurses and work was classified as unacceptable, adequate or superior (see Table 16.1). The work of the nurses was considerably better than that of the dentists.

TABLE 16.1
QUALITY OF DENTAL WORK IN 410 SASKATCHEWAN CHILDREN BY TYPE OF PROVIDER — 1976

	Dentist	Dental Nurse
Superior	16.5	47.4
Adequate	62.4	48.6
Unacceptable	21.1	3.7

Source: Annual Reports, Saskatchewan Health Dental Plan.

Costs per child fell steadily for the first 6-8 years and then climbed in keeping with inflation. The condition of the teeth of the children improved markedly, at least partly because of the large educational component of the program.

The initial dental team in the Oxbow trial had one dentist and 5 auxiliary workers. By the early 1980's the team ratio had become 1 dentist and approximately 20 auxiliaries. In 1978 there were 14 dentists, 137 dental nurses, 148 dental assistants, 2 hygenists and 7 dental technicians. (In usual dental practice the team is 1 dentist to two or three auxiliary workers.)

This program is one of the truly excellent cases of how new health programs should be introduced. The new program was tested and shown to be feasible, a program was created to train necessary staff, the necessary legislation was written to allow the new staff to provide dental care and there was preservation of a consultative role for dentists but a steady trend toward transfer of work to less expensive personnel. The services emphasized prevention as well as treatment. The program was expanded at a rate consistent with the production of new personnel so that jobs were available for the new graduates and so that those promised services were able to get them. Moreover, the quality of the dental work was evaluated by outside, extremely credible dentist evaluators (members of dental school faculty). There was a regular and startling (sometimes 50%) annual reduction in the dental pathology in the children seen and costs per child fell steadily throughout all of the early years of the program.

The unique features of the Saskatchewan dental plan are now largely dismantled. The dental nurses (who were officially renamed dental therapists) are largely unemployed and dental care has been returned to dentists on a fee-for-service basis with limited provincial financial responsibility. Political debts and orientations, plus the wish to reduce public expenditures even when private costs for the same or fewer benefits would be higher, have eliminated an administrative and service model that should have swept the country.

The Dental Health of Canadians

In Ontario between 1972 and 1986, there was a 51% reduction in caries in 5 year olds and a 53% reduction in 13 year olds. The percentage of these children with no caries rose from 42 to 66% for 5 year olds and from 8% to 31% for 13 year olds. The decline has been greatest in communities with fluoridated water but has occurred everywhere. Other factors at work include fluoride toothpaste, fluoride mouth rinses, the addition of vitamin D and other nutritional requirements to milk and other products, and better oral hygiene. Preventive activities in dental offices, including cleaning and use of topical fluorides and of sealants, also contribute, as does a higher level of treatment of existing caries. There is a possibility that the widespread use of antibiotics may also be a factor. Improvement does not appear to be due to changes in dietary habits, in particular in our consumption of sugar.

Despite these improvements, there are still great inequities in accessibility and utilization of dental services. Eighty percent of the caries that are identified exist in 20% of the children. Improvements in the dental health of children will be reflected in the health of future adults.

Dental Care Costs, Payment and Financing

The use of salaried personnel in the Saskatchewan children's dental program has already been discussed.

Dentist earnings have, for a number of years, stayed close to 5.5% of each dollar spent on Canadian health care. Dental care by other than dentists would add very little to this figure.

Although almost all dentists are paid on a fee-for-service basis there has, in recent years, been an increase in the number of prepaid dental insurance programs in which dentist payment is by patient year or family year, that is, by capitation. The plans are often operated by insurance companies which wish to have more predictable costs. They are attractive to dentists because there is an assured supply of patients and a guaranteed income in a highly competitive market. Dental associations are vigorously opposed to these new plans on the grounds that patients will be underserviced. There has not been equal concern about the probability that fee-for-service is associated with the provision of unnecessary care. The capitation approach has been shown to cut costs per patient per year by approximately 40%.

Provincial (public) dental insurance plans have varied over time. In 1974, Alberta introduced a dental program for the elderly, and in the same year Quebec introduced a program for children. Both Alberta and Quebec use the fee-for-service approach. In 1982, Quebec moved away from its original universal approach.

Employer/employee sponsored dental plans have grown rapidly since the early 1970's with about one third of the Canadian population now enrolled. Coverage is highest in Ontario.

PHARMACEUTICALS

The use of medication is as old as man. The apothecary and his pestle and mortar were early symbols of health care. The pestle and mortar are largely museum pieces, the apothecary is now a pharmacist, and the pharmacopia has changed, but the 'magic' of medication is unchanged. Tincture of belladonna, mustard plasters and spirits of camphor have been replaced by tagamet, valium, hydrocortisone and tens of thousands of other names. Arsenic and opium stayed in vogue for hundreds, if not thousands of years whereas the average medication brought into the market now is barely into the literature before it is obsolete.

Medication in ancient times could usually offer little except psychological benefit and it was often very hazardous. Today the odds are better. Most medication does more good than harm, especially when used wisely, but the volume of inappropriate or questionable drug use in which patient hazard exceeds patient benefit is still high.

Costs

Drugs, not including drugs used during institutional care, represent about one-tenth of our health care costs. This portion of our health dollar is divided fairly evenly between prescription and nonprescription purchases. Pharmacy services in hospitals, including the cost of the drugs and the operations of the pharmacy department, represent 2 to 4% of a hospital's budget and therefore 1 to 2% of the national health dollar. In 1985, prescription drugs in Canada cost approximately $2.3 billion, of which 80-90% was spent in drugstores and the remainder in hospitals.

The cost of prescription drugs was held down for over a decade through increased access of generic drug manufacturers to the market. Companies could produce and market a copy of someone else's drug after 3 years of patent protection and on payment of a royalty to the patent holder. In the last year or two, drug costs have been rising quickly and the increases will likely continue as a result of the new 1987 legislation which reduced generic competition through amended patent regulation. This new legislation was vigorously opposed by Canadian hospitals and consumers. Various reports in the 1968-87 period have documented the lowering of prices that occurred due to patent law changes almost 20 years ago, savings being estimated at over $200 million per annum.

In 1984 Saskatchewan and Manitoba had universal drug insurance. All provinces but Prince Edward Island had drug insurance plans for persons 65 or over, and all provinces provided drug benefits to persons on social assistance. Only Alberta, Québec, Prince Edward Island and Newfoundland did not provide drugs to persons in nursing homes.

Total drug expenditures per capita in 1982 varied from $60 in the Northwest Territories and $98 in Manitoba to $179 in Newfoundland and Nova Scotia. Prescribed drug expenditures per capita varied (1982) from $93 in New Brunswick and $90 in Newfoundland to $42 in the Territories and $45 in Manitoba. Per capita costs in the Atlantic provinces were 56% above those in Ontario and Québec and 90% above Manitoba. Prescription to nonprescription drug expenditures varied markedly from a ratio of 92 to 58 in New Brunswick to 71 to 85 in Saskatchewan.

In 1987, Saskatchewan introduced a more complicated system of patient charges into its prescription drug program. This introduction occurred in association with a prescription fee increase from $3.95 to $5.95. Each patient now pays a variable annual deductible fee. Most families and singles must pay 100% for the first $125 and a portion of drug costs after that.

The effect of universal public drug insurance on prescription drug costs is unclear as is the effect of population aging. Effects of public programs are masked by the widespread coverage of private drug insurance. Costs also vary significantly with the extent to which nonprescription items (bandages and aspirin) are covered as long as they are prescribed.

Provinces use three basic methods to control their expenditures on prescription drugs: these are limitations on the population who will be given free drugs, limiting the list of drugs and supplies that can be obtained through the drug insurance plans, and controlling druggist prices. The drug store costs are controlled through mandated prescription fees and/or requirements regarding substitution. In 1984, five provinces had legislation assuring use of low cost suppliers when more than one company supplied the same drug. Substitution was automatic unless the physician specifically ordered, on the prescription, that there should be no substitution.

In the period from 1971-82, the number of new prescriptions written each year increased an average of 3.2%. The number of prescriptions per year per person covered by PARCOST, the Ontario plan for the elderly and those on public assistance, was eleven per person in 1977 and has risen since then.

Provincial formularies list the drugs that will be paid for under provincial drug insurance plans. These formularies can, if wisely and courageously used, both reduce costs and improve patient care. Formularies can identify interchangeable drugs and can set prices for these drugs.

Advertising

Drug advertising is ostensibly governed by the 'Code of Advertising Acceptance of the Pharmaceutical Advertising Advisory Board,' but ads routinely offend clauses governing risk, efficacy, support for therapeutic claims and description of negative features of drugs. Drug companies and drug salesmen (detail men) use an endless supply of gloss, patience, samples and free dinners to aid in the delivery of their messages.

HWC is in the process of requiring more detailed reporting of the ingredients in nonprescription drugs, including herbal and other natural medications.

The widespread problem of drug abuse associated with double-doctoring (or even more than two) may be reduced by 1986 changes to the *Food and Drug Act*. These changes make it an offence not to inform a physician that you have also received narcotics or other controlled drugs from another physician in the preceding 30 days.

The control of drug consumption may lie in new patterns of practice. Studies at the Sault Ste. Marie Group Health Centre showed that the use of mood altering drugs could be cut in half by adequate counselling done by a nurse or social worker.

Suggested Reading

Pre Hospital Emergency Care Services; Report of the Subcommittee on Special Services in Hospitals, Health Services and Promotion Branch, HWC, 1983.

Directions for the Development of Emergency Health Services in Ontario, Ontario Ministry of Health, 1986.

Lexchin, Joel, MD, *The Real Pushers — A Critical Analysis of the Canadian Drug Industry*, New Star Books Ltd., Vancouver, 1984, p. 270.

Comments on Proposed Amendments to the Patient Act, Consumer & Corporate Affairs Canada, October, 1986.

Henderson, Brian J. *The Future of Dentistry in Canada*, A paper presented in the Health Care Lecture Series, Health Administration Program, University of Ottawa, March 1987.

Chapter 17

EPILOGUE

This is a difficult book to end. There is so much that has not been said. Chapters on ethics, cost control, priority setting, the future and factors shaping our health services network would have contributed significantly. Important topics, such as occupational health, communication, services for the blind and the deaf, the role of information and new roles for consumers have been hardly touched. There has been only cursory comment about such immense issues as the inevitable, continuing conflict between care providers, who must be agents of individuals, and planners and administrators who must aim for equity within and among groups.

We particularly regret not having completed the two chapters that would have been titled 'Ethics in Health Care' and 'The Future'. It would have been fun to struggle with advice to the federal government on what it should do to follow up the leadership shown in 1958 and 1968. There would certainly have been a proposal to slowly reduce federal financial support for curative health care so that the money could be offered to the provinces for the support of other, more health maintaining activities. And there could have been proposals regarding how to prepare Canadians for the epidemic of fear that may snowball as the 60,000 American deaths from AIDS moves on to 600,000. In offering advice to provincial governments we would have expanded on the proposition that efforts to control health care costs will fail unless the supply of physicians is controlled. In the ethics chapter we would have defended our thesis that one's opinion regarding abortion is a matter of definition, not of ethics, and that the dominant ethical issue related to abortion is the question of how civilized people react to those with different opinions. These kinds of propositions will certainly be part of our second edition, which will appear, we believe, in 1991.

We apologize once again for the overemphasis on Ontario. In the second edition the innovations and failures of all provinces will be more fairly presented.

This book has been an attempt to describe a fascinating system in which cost control may be a prerequisite to optimal national health status. The lack of understanding of the relative benefits of various health services has been frequently stressed; unfortunately, there has been little discussion of the policies and actions needed if resource allocation is to become based on factors other than intuition, precedent and power. The problems of unnecessary surgery, overmedication, overinvestigation, dehumanization, inappropriate institutionalization and heroic surgery have received inadequate attention.

Canadian reticence to finance many effective preventive activities while being generous with sickness services has been identified but not explored. Perhaps Canada is not paying enough attention to trends in other countries. In Finland, the life expectancy of a middle-aged male is less now than 10 years ago despite the availability of sophisticated, expensive, hospital centered health care. In Hungary, the life expectancy of a male is 2.5 years less than it was 20 years ago despite regular advances in health care sophistication, and females aged 45-54 are also now at higher risk of dying than they were in previous years. In Hungary, the use of both tobacco and alcohol has increased 50-100% in the last 25 years and suicide rates have increased markedly. We can learn from these countries, especially from Finland.

This book has described a battleground. Hospitals, for example, are given limited budgets to provide services to an unpredictable number of people for whom physicians will prescribe an unpredictable volume of investigations and therapies. The power, responsibility and obligations of physicians logically come into conflict with the financial constraints placed upon hospitals. Similarly, the ability and willingness of both the hospital and the physician to consume resources inevitably leads to conflict with taxpayers, especially when benefits received are not commensurate with financial demands. These conflicts will worsen as society and its leaders struggle to identify the point at which additional spending on a broad range of community based and institutional sickness services becomes a poor investment.

Considerable, but we believe not excessive attention has been given to what Canadians can do to counteract our technological obsessions, modern epidemics and overemphasis on physical health. A number of propositions that have been made are worth restating.

First, we should raise our awareness of the massive epidemics and pandemics that face us which are not particularly amenable to technological control. These include depression, anxiety, stress, loneliness and insecurity. Every time a person becomes aware of how much the quality of his or her day, or the quality of someone else's day, is related to the emotional rather than the technological side of life, then that is a day when the relative importance of cardio-pulmonary-resuscitation or heart-lung transplants may be brought into proper perspective. Every time society comes closer to accepting the inevitability of death, and to recognizing the paramount importance of a good life, we move a step closer to being certain that resources will be as generously assigned to quality of life activities as they are to those activities which may cause at least one of us to live a bit longer.

Second, we urgently need evidence showing which services bring enough social benefits to warrant the related expenditures. Will new high technology institutions bring as much social good as a program to avoid some of the 3000-4000 highway deaths annually, or the almost 1000 drownings, or the 700-800 deaths in fires, or the 300 plus teenage suicides, or the isolation and depression of the elderly? If we even crudely quantify risk before allocating resources, we will spend one thousand times as much on research into schizophrenia or Alzheimers disease as we do on retinal detachment or a safer anesthetic. We will pour resources into the study of autistic, emotionally disturbed and learning disabled children and become disinterested in test tube babies. We will be more concerned about relieving the depression of literally millions of people than anticipating an outbreak of Lassa fever or improving performance in situations where performance is already almost perfect. We will routinely opt for resources for prevention rather than treatment when prevention has been shown to be more cost-effective than treatment.

Third, in our search for ways to overcome our technological domination, we must make full use of excellent evidence which says that quality of life is a significant determinant of length of life, especially when one is speaking of the elderly or the chronically disabled. Often the best way to prolong life is to make it a life worth living. Involvement, independence, confidence, usefulness and fun can be more health creating than microsurgery or chemotherapy and, therefore, are worth our attention and our resources.

Fourth, society should consistently complain to government when technologically complex health institutions, primarily acute treatment hospitals, drastically over-spend. Hospital representatives and some of the public may believe that the social benefits derived from hospital care are so great that governments should divert funds to hospitals from schools, housing programs, environmental protection, income support programs and every other publicly supported program, but to believe this is to be wrong. A dollar spent in other areas often contributes more to the quality of life and frequently contributes more to the maintenance of life than does a dollar spent in hospitals. Lobbying in favor of preventive and multisectoral actions is necessary if the technological lobby is not to further distort social priorities.

Fifth, for the benefit of all, society must accelerate the recent trend towards developing a more human health system. This acceleration should not be a passive event; it cannot be passive because the life sustaining and technologically based health service system is not passive. It is voracious; it consumes resources endlessly and there is no point within its total spectum where it cannot double its resource consumption at a moment's notice. There is also a limitless ability in many technocrats, and not all of them are in hospitals, to produce dramatic headlines and these, in turn, can increase the public tendency to wish for another technical expansion to feed the mirage of personal protection through technological growth. If we oppose this trend we must consciously, repeatedly and sincerely, and with full awareness of the visciousness with which the technocrats can attack those who oppose technocratic perfection, advise governments and the public that the greatest social returns lie not in surrendering to machines but in demanding that they serve only when their value has been proven.

Sixth, health planning in the past emphasized institutional quantity and sophistication and manpower production. It now must emphasize outcomes in terms of the health status of communities and nations. When outcomes become dominant, health planning will be redirected to consumer centered and community based services and to initiatives throughout the full public policy spectrum.

We hope you will participate in the second edition of *Health Care in Canada* by giving us your opinions and sharing your knowledge about the health services which serve Canadians.

INDEX

- D -

- E -

- F -

- M -

- N -

- Q -

- R -